READINGS IN MORAL THEOLOGY

No. 6:

Dissent in the Church

Edited by
Charles E. Curran
and
Richard A. McCormick, S.J.

PAULIST PRESS
New York/Mahwah

Library of Congress Cataloging-in-Publication Data

Dissent in the church.

    (Readings in moral theology ; no. 6)
    Includes bibliographies.
    1. Catholic Church—Teaching office. 2. Dissenters, Religious. 3. Curran, Charles E. 4. Academic freedom—United States. 5. Catholic Church—United States. 6. Christian ethics—Study and teaching. I. Curran, Charles E. II. McCormick, Richard A., 1922— . III. Series.
BX1746.D52   1988   262'.8   87-32757
ISBN 0-8091-2930-2 (pbk.)

Published by Paulist Press
997 Macarthur Boulevard
Mahwah, New Jersey 07430

Printed and bound in the
United States of America

Contents

STATEMENTS OF BISHOPS ON DISSENT

PART TWO:
CANONICAL ASPECTS

PART THREE:
ACADEMIC ASPECTS

PART FOUR:
MORAL THEOLOGY IN PARTICULAR

PART FIVE:
THE CURRAN CASE AND ITS AFTERMATH

Acknowledgements

The articles reprinted in Moral Theology No 6. first appeared in the following publications and are reprinted with permission: "Theology and Magisterium: Self-Appraisals" from *Theology Digest* 29 (1981): 257–261 by Karl Rahner; "Authority and Conscience" in *Church* (Fall 1986): 8–15 by Avery Dulles; "Dissent in the Church" in *Catholicism in Crisis* 4 (January 1986): 8–13 by Michael Novak; "Dissent and the Catholic Religion Teacher" by William J. Levada. S.T.D. in *Origins* 16 (1986): 195–200; "Dissent in the Church" in *Origins* 16 (1986): 175–178 by Daniel Pilarczyk, D.D.; "The Magisterium and Theological Dissent" by Roger Mahony, D.D. in *Origins* 16 (1986) pp. 372–375; "Thought on Freedom, Conscience and Obedience" by Michael Pfeifer, O.M.I. in *Origins* 16 (1986): 391–392; "Teaching Authority in the 1983 Code" in Jurist 45 (1985): 136–170 by John P. Boyle; "Reflections on the Text of a Canon" by Ladislas Orsy in *America* 154 (1986): 396–399; "Theological Pluralism and Canonical Mandate" in *Jurist* 42 (1982): 524–532 by John Strynkowski; "The Catholic College vs. Academic Freedom" by Edward J. Berbusse in *Homiletic and Pastoral Review* 86 (Aug–Sept 1986): 11–20; "On Defending Catholic Higher Education in America" in *Communio* 13 (Fall 1986) pp. 257–267 by Mark Jordan; "The Drama of Morality and Remarks on Dissent" by Joseph Ratzinger from *The Ratzinger Report*, printed by permission of Ignatius Press. "On the Other Hand. . ." by John Mahoney in *New Blackfriars* 66 (June 1985): 288–298; "Teaching Morality: The Tension Between Bishops and Theologians within the Church" by Joseph Fuchs in *Christian Ethics in a Secular Arena*, pp. 131–153; "Public Dissent in the Church" by Charles Curran in *Origins* 16 (1986): 178–184; "L'Affair Curran" by Richard McCormick in *America*, April 5, 1986; "The Search for Truth in the Catholic Context" in *America*, November 8, 1986 by Richard McCormick; "How to Deal with Dissent" in *Homiletic and Pastoral Review*, November and December 1986 by Germain Grisez; "Comments on the Curran Case" by Kevin Kelly in *Tablet*, June 14 and June 21, 1986, pp. 619–620 and 647–649; "Comments on the Curran Case" by Christine Gudorf in *Christianity and Crisis*, May 5, 1986, pp. 151–154; "Comments on Curran Case" by Hitchcock, Melady, Wolfe in *Catholicism in Crisis*, May 1986; "Ecumenical Dimensions of the Curran Case" by John C. Bennett and Roger Shinn in *Christianity and Crisis*, October 6, 1986, pp. 331–332, 336–337; "Ecumenical Impact of Curran Case" by J. Philip Wogaman in *Christian Century*, December 10, 1986, pp. 1108–1109; "Dissent in Moral Theology and Its Implications" by Richard A. McCormick in *Theological Studies*, March 1987.

Foreword

We have chosen "Dissent in the Church" as the topic around which to organize this sixth volume in our *Readings in Moral Theology*. There are many reasons for this choice. The issue of dissent has touched the Catholic University, American Catholic theology and the American church in a very concrete way in the person of one of the co-editors of this series. Decisions that impact this broadly and deeply invite careful study. Second, the issue of dissent is inseparable from very important theological concerns and problems: the nature of the church; the proper concept and functioning of authority in the church; the development of doctrine; the understanding of the guidance of the Holy Spirit to the magisterium; the nature of theology; the relation of the academy and academic freedom to the authority of the church; the proper understanding of *obsequium religiosum,* etc.

This dissent inevitably raises the question of the relation of the local church to the pope and Roman curia. For instance, why should doctrinal oversight be handled at the Roman level at all? Cardinal Franz König has raised this question and suggested that it need not be. Fourth, there will undoubtedly be an ecumenical dimension to the direction this discussion and discipline takes. It is for these and other reasons that we believe the subject of dissent to be timely and deserving of careful theological scrutiny.

As in the previous volumes in this series, we have endeavored to include all points of view, not because we agree with them, but because they do exist and undoubtedly represent greater or lesser segments of Catholic thought and practice. As such they deserve attention even if the form that attention takes is criticism and rejection.

It is our own conviction, as is obvious from our own contributions to this volume, that loyalty can coexist with dissent, indeed that there are times when loyalty inspires and demands the type of distancing and correction known as dissent. Some share this view;

some do not. Whatever one's personal perspectives and conclusions, if greater clarity is achieved—whether in the process of ratification, modification, or transformation—the purpose of this volume will have been served.

Charles E. Curran
Richard A. McCormick, S.J.

Part One

THEOLOGICAL DISSENT IN GENERAL

The Rights and Responsibilities of Theologians: A Theological Perspective

Jon Nilson

This article originally appeared in *Cooperation Between Theologians and the Ecclesiastical Magisterium,* a Report of the Joint Committee of the Canon Law Society of America and the Catholic Theology Society of America, 1982.

I.
INTRODUCTION[1]

There is no single normative paradigm governing the relationship between theologians and the teaching authority of the church vested in the hierarchy. Instead, historical studies have shown that a great variety of forms of this relationship have existed across time.[2] The same studies show that the particular form which the relationship takes in a given era is determined in great part by that era's dominant theology of revelation, church, faith, and teaching authority.

So it is not surprising that we are now compelled to reconsider this relationship. In the era marked by the hegemony of neo-scholasticism (roughly 1850–1962), it seemed as if this issue had been settled for good. The precision of its terminology, the rigor of its logic, and its status as the quasi-official theology of Roman Catholicism lent neo-scholasticism a prestige unequalled by any other theology in the history of the church. Its clarity, its relentlessly systematic character, and its repeated approbations by the popes strongly suggested that the positions of Roman Catholicism were definite, permanent, and unambiguous on all the fundamental issues and most of the secondary issues of Christian faith.

The era of the neo-scholastic hegemony is now over, a fact well recognized by theologians and the hierarchical teaching authority alike. Moreover, no similar uniform, unifying, and purportedly universal theology is emerging to replace it. Today there is no single Roman Catholic theology. Rather, within the Roman Catholic Church, there are a number of theologies with different methodologies and approaches to the fundamental doctrines of our faith. Thus we are compelled to reconsider the rights and responsibilities of theologians in a spirit of fidelity to our Roman Catholic tradition but without the guidance of a single, commanding theological perspective. Nonetheless, the task is rich in possiblity for the renewal of both theology and the office of authoritative teaching in the church.

At the present time, the relationship between the episcopal and the theological communities in North America can be fairly described as cordial and mutually appreciative. Unfortunately, this fact often goes unnoticed when attention is focused upon the relatively few cases of conflict and confrontation.[3] As a result, it is easy to get the impression that contention and mutual suspicion are the dominant tones of the relationship. Theologians themselves are not immune to the effects of this distorted view.

Theologians are also aware that, despite the public statements of gratitude and appreciation for the work of theologians made by Popes John XXIII, Paul VI, and John Paul II, the ecclesiastical magisterium has taken on a very active role in theology for well over a century. That role has largely been one of intervention, judgment, warning, and condemnation. History plus some recent actions of Roman Congregations lead theologians sometimes to regard the magisterium with a certain apprehensiveness and mistrust.

Structures and procedures by which these attitudes might be changed do not yet exist. In general, theologians in North America today receive their terminal degrees from civilly chartered universities, not from ecclesiastical faculties. Their teaching appointments are not made by a bishop but by their academic peers. While they may hold themselves responsible theologically to the Church, they also hold themselves responsible to the canons of inquiry prevailing in the academy. This latter responsibility is inculcated by and realized through a number of effective procedures and structures:

initially, graduate education itself; later, professional meetings, colloquia, refereed publications, book reviews, and the like. At the same time, there are as yet no structures and procedures by which theologians' awareness of their theological responsibility to the church might be fostered and deepened and a spirit of mutual trust and cooperation with the magisterium might be engendered and developed.[4]

Among the more promising indications that this lack may soon be remedied is the 1980 statement of the bishops of the United States on higher education:

> Conscious of our different roles in the church, and also of our mutual responsibilities, we seek a fruitful cooperation with theologians. Together we must work to build up the body of Christ and to bring the truth and power of the gospel to our society and culture with due respect for the legitimate autonomy of culture and the sciences.

> We encourage the universities to develop ways which will bring bishops and theologians together with other members of the church and the academy to examine theological issues with wisdom and learning, with faith, and with mutual charity and esteem. We shall all need to recall and to work for "that delicate balance . . . between the autonomy of a Catholic university and the responsibilities of the hierarchy." There need be no conflict between the two.[5]

II.
HISTORICAL BACKGROUND: VATICAN I TO VATICAN II

From 1870 to 1962, the Constitutions *Dei Filius* and *Pastor Aeternus* of Vatican I largely determined the specific form of the relationship between theologians and the teaching authority vested in the hierarchy.[6]

While revelation is first described in *Dei Filius* as God's supernatural way of disclosing God's own self and the eternal decrees of God's will (DS 3004), revelation is considered as a body of truths throughout the rest of the document. It is contained in written books and unwritten traditions received by the apostles from the mouth of Christ himself (DS 3006). Faith is the supernatural capacity by which we believe the truths revealed by God (DS 3008). While reason illumined by faith can acquire a very fruitful understanding of the revealed mysteries (DS 3016), it remains that the church is always the divinely appointed guardian and teacher of the revealed word (DS 3012). Hence, that sense of the sacred dogmas which the church once declared is to be kept perpetually and never departed from (DS 3020).

While *Dei Filius* did not specify the persons or groups in the church who were to guard, teach, and authoritatively interpret the revealed truths, *Pastor Aeternus* did. Despite the important nuances and the official explanations of *Pastor Aeternus,* the premature end of Vatican I left the pope perceived as the sole and supreme governor and authoritative teacher in the church. Thus *Pastor Aeternus* was the climax of a trend begun in the early nineteenth century to concentrate ecclesiastical jurisdiction and teaching authority in the papacy and to minimize the roles of other sources of jurisdiction and teaching. Seen as a response to attempts to curtail the independence of the church and to make her subservient to the purposes of civil powers or nationalism, this trend is quite understandable. Nonetheless, one of its effects was to establish a single paradigm as normative for the relationship between theologians and the hierarchical teaching authority, although the Roman Catholic tradition had embraced many different paradigms through the centuries. The single paradigm it did establish can be imagined as a pyramid in which all teaching descends vertically from the apex and in which it is difficult to legitimate a lateral, much less upward, movement of authentic teaching.

The other important factor in this period was the adoption of neo-scholasticism as the semi-official theology of the church.[7] While the Fathers of Vatican I surely did not intend to make neo-scholasticism an official theology, in fact neo-scholastic modes of thought dominate its constitutions. Leo XIII's *Aeterni Patris* (1879) was interpreted as an official ratification of neo-scholasticism, as was Pius X's *Pascendi Dominici Gregis* (1907) and *Sacrorum Antistites* (1910), the oath against modernism.

So neo-scholasticism was, in effect, supported by the authority of the divinely constituted guardian and interpreter of revelation, such that opposition to neo-scholasticism could be (and was) construed as opposition to that authority itself. Concessions as to the legitimacy of other forms of theology were few, so that there was no way to gain a sincere hearing for anything other than a neo-scholastic theology which was proving itself to be increasingly inadequate to the twentieth century's issues and questions. Neo-scholasticism was, ironically, unable to fulfill Leo XIII's mandate, "vetera novis augere et perficere," precisely due to its inability to recognize the existence of genuine *nova* and their potential value as means of expressing the Christian faith.

The clearest expression and development of the paradigm which was implicit in Vatican I and dominated Roman Catholicism till Vatican II can be found in Pius XII's *Humani Generis* (1950). Pius affirms that the role of guarding, explaining, and interpreting the divinely revealed truths which constitute the deposit of faith belongs solely to the teaching authority of the church.[8] That authority elucidates and explains what is contained in the deposit only obscurely or implicitly.[9] Consequently, the role of theology is to show how a doctrine of the church is contained in the sources of revelation in that sense in which it has been defined by the magisterium.[10] For the office of teacher in faith and morals is the proximate and universal criterion of truth for all theologians.[11]

Therefore, theologians cooperate with the magisterium by explaining and defending what the magisterium has taught. It is their responsibility to defend natural and supernatural truth and to instill it in the hearts of people[12] by beginning with the clarity of magisterial statements and using them to explain what is obscure in the sources of revelation.[13] Theologians have the right and the responsibility to study erroneous theories in order to grasp the partial truth in them, to render philosophical and theological discussion more precise, and to diagnose them more effectively.[14] They also have the right to investigate matters under dispute until the pope in an official document passes judgment on such matters.[15]

It is relatively easy to understand why this view of the relationship between theologians and the magisterium came to dominate the pre-Vatican II era. First, the ecclesiology of the time presented the church in largely juridical and hierarchical terms. Everything which was essential to the life of the church was seen to descend vertically down the pyramid. Second, the a-historical character of neo-scholastic philosophy and theology yielded a diminished awareness of the many different forms which the relationship between theologians and the magisterium had taken over time. As a result, there was little data available to legitimize theological positions at variance with neo-scholasticism or with magisterial statements, few ways to ground these positions as differently but undeniably Catholic. Third, the same lack of historical consciousness produced a diminished awareness of the difficult but real distinction between the substance of revelation and the language used to express it. Neo-scholastic language and methods were regarded as perennially valid, so that any departure from them would weaken both dogma and speculative theology.[16] Fourth, the theologians' responsibility to the teaching authority of the church was grounded not only theologically but also juridically, since most theologians were also clerics and carried on their theological activity in seminaries. As theologians, therefore, they were both juridically and theologically subject to the magisterium, and so their rights and responsibilities were understood in exclusively intramural terms. This tended to diminish theologians' sense of responsibility to the canons and methods of secular scientific inquiry. Fifth, and finally, excepting the theologies of the Eastern rites, there were no indigenous theologies developed in non-European countries. Roman Catholic theology in the non-European world was exported from Europe. This insured that everywhere not only theology but praxis as well would conform to European models.

III.
Historical Background: Vatican II

The discussions and debates at Vatican II revealed a consensus among the Fathers that the self-understanding of the pre-conciliar church and its supporting theology were simply inadequate to the tasks of contemporary evangelization and effective nurture of the faith of Catholic Christians. The desirability of change was evident. The possibility and the legitimacy of change were supported by the historical investigations precipitated by *Aeterni Patris* and *Pascendi*. Both in its explicit statements and in its manner of operation, Vatican II decisively ended the era of neo-scholastic dominance of Roman Catholic thought. Let me review some of the major accomplishments of Vatican II which have made it imperative to reconsider the relationship between theologians and the magisterium.

The Council envisioned the church as a community marked by a "feeling of deep solidarity with the human race and its history" (GS 1). ". . . The church . . . travels the same journey as all mankind and shares the same earthly lot with the world. . . ." (GS 40). While the church seeks to aid the human family, it knows ". . . how much it has profited from the history and development of humanity" (GS 44).

The achievements of human culture have helped the church to fulfill more adequately her mission of bringing the message of Christ to mankind. The Council even identifies these achievements as rich and important resources for theology. Thus it affirmed that one task of theologians is ". . . to listen to and distinguish the many voices of our times and to interpret them in light of the divine word, in order that the revealed truth may be more deeply penetrated, better understood, and more suitably presented" (GS 44).

Not only are theologians charged to heed the voices of our times but also the voices and witness of non-Catholic Christians. For ". . . anything wrought by the grace of the Holy Spirit in the hearts of our separated brethren can contribute to our own edification . . . it can always bring a more perfect realization of the very mystery of Christ and the Church" (UR 4). Since this is so, the Council urged that "sacred theology and other branches of knowledge . . . must be taught with due regard for the ecumenical point of view, so that they may correspond as exactly as possible with the facts" (UR 10). The Council Fathers considered it important that future bishops and priests master a theology developed ecumenically, not polemically (UR 10).

Consequently, a theology developed from explicitly Roman Catholic resources alone can only be regarded as impoverished and short-sighted. In the Council's view, Roman Catholic theology is to become more truly catholic. Yet this mandate vastly complicates the theological enterprise. How should theology now enter into a mutually enriching dialogue with the world, avoiding the Scylla of assimilating its content and criteria to those of secular culture and the Charybdis of keeping itself "unsullied" but also unchallenged and untransformed by the real questions culture poses? What now constitutes the essential uniqueness of Roman Catholic theology which employs ecumenical resources and is presented from an ecumenical point of view?

When the Council thus vastly extended the boundaries of the traditional *loci theologici,* it left to theologians the daunting task of determining and distinguishing the meanings expressed therein. Discerning the sum and substance of the apostolic faith in the many possibilities of its expression and evaluating their adequacy have thus become paramount among the theological tasks of our time. In response to the Council's mandate, theologians today must ask questions that go to the heart of the Catholic Christian faith. It is no wonder that such inquiries are sometimes perceived as dangerous.

Vatican II also reinvigorated a cooperative, relational understanding of the church. In the Council documents, this understanding balances and nuances the juridical, hierarchical emphasis characteristic of pre-conciliar ecclesiology. Thus, according to Vatican II, the unity which the church enjoys is not produced solely "from above" nor is it purely doctrinal. The church's unity is basically one of fellowship and service (LG 4) in which the gifts of the Holy Spirit are given to each member of the church for the renewal and building up of the church as a whole (LG 13).

Though the Council stressed that the task of authoritatively interpreting the word of God, whether written or handed on, belongs exclusively to the church's teaching authority,[17] it also affirmed that the Holy Spirit effects

> . . .a growth in insight into the realities and words that are being passed on. This comes about in various ways . . . through the contemplation and study of believers . . . from the intimate sense of spiritual realities which they

experience . . . from the preaching of those who have received, along with their right of succession in the episcopate, the sure charism of truth (DV 8).

Here, as elsewhere in the documents, cooperation between all
believers, theologians, and bishops is seen as essential. The Council does not repeat Pius XII's view of the magisterium as the proximate rule of faith. All are bound to listen to the bishops. Yet the
bishops who serve the word of God must also heed those in whom
the Holy Spirit has produced an experience and understanding of
the faith, although it remains the bishops' role to judge and to
make use of that understanding (LG 12).

In their own practice, the Fathers of Vatican II gave the
church a remarkable example of cooperation between themselves
and the theologians or *periti*. They fulfilled their own mandate to
listen, judge, and make use of whatever the Holy Spirit and long,
patient study had effected in the theologians. They made their
renewed understanding of the importance of cooperation in the
church prove its worth and validity in the concrete.

The Council also emphasized the essentially missionary character of the church. Throughout, the documents echo, stress, and
repeat in various contexts the idea that the church "receives the
mission of proclaiming and establishing among all peoples the Kingdom of Christ and God. . ." (LG 5). Consequently, the church has
tried ". . . to adapt the gospel to the understanding of all and the
requirements of the learned, insofar as this could be done" (GS
44).[18] "Indeed," say the Fathers, "this kind of adaptation and
preaching of the revealed Word must ever be the law of all evangelization" (GS 44). To proclaim the message in this way, the church
has to call ". . . upon the help of people who are living in the
world . . ." (GS 44). While this help is sought from the whole
people of God, the Council singles out bishops and theologians as
having an especially important role in the effort whose goal is
". . . that the revealed truth may be more deeply penetrated, better understood, and more suitably presented" (GS 44).

While the Council seems not to underestimate the difficulties
of evangelization today, it regards these difficulties more as opportunities than threats to the integrity of the faith:

These difficulties do not necessarily harm the life of faith, but can rather stimulate a more precise and deeper understanding of that faith. In fact, recent research and discoveries in the sciences, in history and philosophy bring up new problems which have an important bearing on life itself and demand new scrutiny by theologians. Furthermore, theologians are now being asked, within the methods and limits of the science of theology, to seek out more efficient ways—provided the meaning and understanding of them is safeguarded—of presenting their teaching to modern men and women: for the deposit and the truths of faith are one thing, the manner of expressing them is quite another (GS 62).

Since the church is divinely commissioned to preach the gospel and since this preaching must be adapted to the needs of all and theology has an important role to play here, the Council has clearly recognized and legitimated a necessary and authentic pluralism of theologies within the one church past and present, each of which can disclose the saving power of the gospel. Yet theological pluralism in practice is bound to produce misunderstanding and even tension. Fidelity to the Council's vision, however, requires that means be sought not to eliminate theological pluralism but to insure that it serves the missionary function of the church.

Vatican II develops the implications of the missionary nature of the church for every one of its members. It affirms that ". . . the Christian vocation is, of its nature, a vocation to the apostolate as well" (AA 2). "On all Christians, accordingly, rests the noble obligation of working to bring all people throughout the whole world to hear and accept the divine message of salvation" (AA 3).[19] Commission to the apostolate comes through baptism and confirmation. Sustenance for the apostolate comes through the reception of the other sacraments. Yet the Council also recognizes that the Holy Spirit distributes special gifts or charisms to everyone as the Spirit wills (AA 3). A charism is given to individuals not for their own benefit but for the good of the world and the church (AA 3; LG 4, 7, 12). Further, these charisms, which are given directly by the Holy Spirit and are not mediated through the church's hierarchical structure, give rise to the right and duty to exercise them in the freedom of the Holy Spirit, but also ". . . in communion with . . . brothers in Christ, and with . . . pastors especially. It is for the pastors to pass judgment on the authenticity and good use of these gifts . . ." (AA 3). This right and duty, stemming from the Christian vocation and charisms, are not to be exercised only under the direction and the specific discretion of the hierarchy. Rather, again the Council envisions a cooperative relationship between the bishops and all believers.

Given the importance and prevalence of charisms in the life of the church and their role in the apostolate, and given the importance of theology in the fulfillment of the church's mission, could one conclude to the existence of a charism of the theologian such that one could specify certain rights and duties of the theologian which would be typically exercised in a cooperative, not a derivative, relationship to the hierarchy? The theology of charism appears to be too underdeveloped at this time to make such a conclusion certain.[20] Nonetheless, it appears that the Council has strongly implied that there exists a theological charism which gives rise to rights and duties. In the conciliar vision, the burden of proof would be on anyone who denied the existence of such a charism. Thus, in the practical order, occasions of theological conflict and tension ought to be handled by all in the spirit of the Gamaliel principle: "If their purpose or activity is human in its origins, it will destroy itself. If, on the other hand, it comes from God, you will not be able to destroy them without fighting God himself" (Acts 5:38b–39).

Finally, Vatican II promoted change in Roman Catholic theology by urging that ". . . more of the laity . . . receive adequate theological formation and that some among them will dedicate themselves professionally to these studies and contribute to their advancement" (GS 62).[21] The Council implicitly affirmed that certain persons possess an inalienable right to advanced theological study, since all have a right to an education suitable to their particular destinies and adapted to their abilities (GE 1). Seeming to envision the prospect of change and tension in the church as a result, the Council said that ". . . for the proper exercise of this role, the faithful, both clerical and lay, should be accorded a lawful freedom of inquiry, of thought, and of expression, tempered by humility and courage in whatever branch of study they have specialized" (GS 62).

Yet the Council's view of the role of theology in the church has raised more questions than it answered. Among the most important are: the specific role theology ought to play in the church; theology's relationship to the world outside the church; and theology's own self-understanding.

Affirming that theology has a necessary role to play in the church leads to asking what particular structures and procedures must be developed to allow theologians to render their services to the fullest extent possible. And if the task of the magisterium is to judge and to make use of the work of the theologians, how is that task to be implemented concretely?

IV.
THE PROBLEM OF PRESUPPOSITIONS

Is it possible to set forth a list of theologians' rights and responsibilities specific enough to be practically useful and general enough to command a broad consensus? The theological diversity in the North American church today makes this a genuine and pressing question. For particular specifications of theologians' rights and responsibilities clearly depend on the way certain fundamental realities of faith, such as revelation, church, Scripture and dogma are conceived.[22] Yet the varying methodologies and approaches operative in Catholic theology today yield varying conceptualizations of these fundamental realities. Nor does it seem likely that any single theology will emerge in the near future to play the role of neo-scholasticism in the pre-Vatican II era. Yet the fundamental elements cannot be simply overlooked. If they were, then any specification of theologians' rights and responsibilities would be vulnerable to charges of being motivated by a deracinated pragmatism, opportunism, or authoritarianism.

In the effort to determine the rights and responsibilities of theologians, fundamental elements of our faith can be adequately taken into account by having recourse to a thematization of the faith-formed standpoint we share as Catholic Christians. Such a thematization would be helpful if it substantially crystalized our experience and focused attention upon that common ground beneath the pluralistic theological level at which we can and do differ. Of course, it would not be helpful if mutually inconsistent specifications of those rights and responsibilities could be derived from it.

Given the present diversity in our church, it is most unlikely that any individual or group could compose such a thematization. Nonetheless, texts already exist which express our common standpoint as Catholic Christians. They are not nor can they be specific enough to serve as proof texts. Yet they are valuable in this context insofar as they remind us of who we are and how we live our common life in the church. So they can give reliable direction to thought when the question of theologians' rights and responsibilities is taken up.

Expressions of our common standpoint as Catholic Christians can be found in our liturgy. In its words, we find a way of speaking and celebrating what unites us all as Roman Catholics.

The Roman Canon (Eucharistic Prayer I) is particularly useful as an expression of our common standpoint. Its words are the words which Catholics have used for centuries when they remember, celebrate, and recommit themselves to the mystery of salvation which has conferred their specific identity upon them. They are the words in which all believers have discovered and expressed the Catholic unity which exists beneath and in spite of all the differentiating factors of culture, historical epoch, and theology. The Roman Canon, substantially completed by the time of Gregory the Great, was used almost universally and exclusively in the Western Church from the twelfth century to Vatican II. Granted its drawbacks as a liturgical prayer which have been perceived in our own time,[23] its long usage and contemporary retention argue well for its ability to express the faith which unites us all as Catholic Christians.

The Canon is not the product of a single individual but is the work of the Western Church in its composition and reception. It is a text which draws its material from both Scripture and tradition. Praying in these words, we acknowledge our roots in the Scripture and in our ancient tradition. For we draw upon these to say who we are and what we believe in the act wherein we are most authentically ourselves as Catholic Christians. At the same time, the prayer shows us that our roots in the past nourish us to meet the new challenges of the present and the future. The Latin style of the text (still discernible in the official English translation) testifies to the desirability and the necessity of expressing the faith in the language and thought-forms of the age. The Canon declares the content of the faith to which we are committed; it shows how God's saving act in Christ and our experience of his salvation in the present yields a confession which is clearly reflective of the time yet has roots beyond time and looks forward to the end of time.

"We come to you, Father, with praise and thanksgiving, through Jesus Christ your Son." In this first sentence of the prayer, we acknowledge our identity as Christians. We are the community which approaches God with praise and thanksgiving through Christ. If we approach with genuine praise and thanksgiving, we can do so only because we are aware of what God has done, is doing, and will be doing for us through Christ. Lacking this awareness as a base, our acknowledgement would be false and inauthentic. Yet the awareness which calls forth our praise and thanks can, indeed should, change over time, rendering our approach to the Father more whole-hearted. We pray for this change in ourselves implicitly when we ask later on in the Canon that ". . . as we receive . . . the sacred body and blood of your Son, let us be filled with every grace and blessing." We pray for this again and again throughout our lives. The church as a whole prays for it over and over across the centuries. Our prayer is a confession that we ourselves and the church to which we belong are still incomplete in our awareness of the salvation wrought by God in Christ, that we are still being perfected in our approach to God.

Theology understood simply as "faith seeking understanding" has always played a very important role in this continual and communal process of discovery ingredient to Catholic Christian identity. Our church has always needed and been nourished by the labors of men and women who sought and found greater understanding of what they believed. This point is made more explicitly in the next part of the Canon.

The first intercession is for the church, that God watch over it, guide it, and grant it peace and unity throughout the world. Then we pray for those through whom God does this: the pope, the bishops, and "all who hold and teach the Catholic faith that comes to us from the apostles." The specific mention of pope and bishop indicates that they have an important role exclusive to them alone in the task of watching over, guiding, and leading the church to peace and unity. Yet in this task there is also a role belonging to all those who hold and teach the faith.[24] All who do this also help to watch over, guide, and lead the church to peace and unity. The Canon suggests that there are distinct and complementary roles belonging to the church's bishops and teachers and, further, that there must be cooperation between them. Neither group bears exclusive responsibility for watching over, guiding, and leading the church to peace and unity. The distinct but related responsibilities imply that each group possesses those rights necessary to fulfill their responsibilities.

The faith that comes to us from the apostles is described more fully in the words over the cup. The new and everlasting covenant established by Christ is the mystery of faith. As mystery, the new covenant can never be fully comprehended. Yet the church can and does grow in its understanding, as the next section of the Canon suggests.

Here are named some through whom the faith has come to us: Peter, Paul, Andrew, James, John; and later Stephen, Matthias, Barnabas, Ignatius, Felicity, Perpetua, Agatha, Lucy, Agnes, Cecilia, and Anastasia.[25] We acknowledge our union with them in the faith as well as continual dependence on their witness. Yet as we name them, we are reminded that the unity of our Catholic faith is not to be equated with uniformity of teaching. For Peter, Paul, James, and John, to name just some, did not teach in the same way, using the same words, operating within the same intellectual horizon. It was precisely their teaching in all its enriching diversity that built up the one Catholic faith. Indeed, the list of names even suggests that the authentic unity of faith sometimes emerges only by way of disagreement and conflict, trial and error. Without the conflict between Paul and the Jerusalem Church and the open-minded, open-hearted way in which it was finally resolved (Acts 15, Gal 2), the fuller range, depth, and power of the new covenant might not have come to light nor would the church have discovered so soon that the unity of faith can subsist in variant theological positions. To have insisted on uniformity in theology and Christian practice at that point would have stifled the gospel.

V.
Who Is a Roman Catholic Theologian?

The Roman Canon as a thematization of our common standpoint as Catholics suggests an answer to the question: who is a Roman Catholic theologian, i.e., who is justifiably numbered among those who hold and teach the faith that comes to us from the apostles and therefore bears certain responsibilities and enjoys certain rights in exercising that function?

A purely formal or juridical determination of this issue is obviously inadequate. While nowadays competence recognized in the form of a terminal degree in Catholic theology from an accredited faculty is important, it is not a necessary or sufficient condition. Again, while an individual may receive a clearly specified mission to teach theology, say, in a seminary, or an individual may be a cleric or a religious who teaches with the permission and encouragement of an ecclesiastical superior, this too is not a necessary or sufficient condition. If it were, lay persons recognizably competent in theology and teaching in religiously affiliated or secular colleges and universities could not be called Roman Catholic theologians.

The Roman Canon suggests criteria, besides the obvious one of full incorporation into the church (LG 14), for determining who is and who is not a Roman Catholic theologian. The following criteria are suggested by the association the Canon establishes between teaching the faith and watching over, guiding, and leading the church to peace and unity.

A. *A Roman Catholic theologian is one whose theological activity is focused upon the apostolic faith and serves to promote the church's understanding of its faith and its proclamation of the gospel in the world.*

Thus, Catholics who were otherwise well-qualified in theology but whose work showed little concern for the life of the church would not be called Roman Catholic theologians in the sense that they would bear certain responsibilities and enjoy certain rights in the Catholic community. Such individuals should be more accurately regarded as scholars of religion.

The setting or environment in which the theological activity is carried out does not determine the identity of the Roman Catholic theologian. It is the focus and outcome of the activity, not its place, that is decisive. It makes no difference whether or not the theologian works in a Catholic organization, institution, or circumstances.

As is the case with all research and its dissemination, the specific nature and quality of service rendered by theologians' work cannot be measured by the immediacy or the popularity of its appeal nor by its relevance to what may generally be perceived to be the most pressing issues in the Church.

B. *A Roman Catholic theologian is one whose theological service to the church is publicly recognized as creditable and valuable.*

This criterion serves to distinguish the theologian from others in the church who also hold and teach the faith in ordained and non-ordained ministries. In North America today, the ways by which the quality of one's theological service becomes evident typically include the following:

— adequate preparation for theological service by means of post-graduate theological education;
— formal recognition of the adequacy of this preparation by means of a terminal degree in theology awarded by an accredited faculty;
— recognition of one's competence by professional peers;
— active membership in a Roman Catholic professional theological society;
— continuation of one's studies by research;
— disseminating the results of one's studies by teaching, writing, delivering lectures and scholarly papers, etc.;
— recognition of one's competence as a Roman Catholic theo-

logian in various ways by one's fellow Catholics, laity, clergy, and hierarchy, although this recognition need not be made formally.

Note that these are not criteria but ways by which the quality of theological service typically becomes evident. They are not all equally necessary and important for every Roman Catholic theologian all the time. For instance, recognition of one's competence by professional peers could well compensate for the lack of terminal degree or an outstanding publication record could compensate for lack of active membership in a professional society.

C. *A Roman Catholic theologian is one who is willing both to give and to receive constructive commentary and criticism concerning theological work.*

This criterion is demanded by the communal character of the church's life and teaching function. As was seen above, this communal character is recognized in the Roman Canon. It is also demanded by the communal character of theology as an academic discipline today. Like the other disciplines, theology too has developed certain structures to engender dialogue for the purpose of mutual instruction.

What constitutes "constructive commentary and criticism" in specific situations? This is finally decided by a prudential judgment. In general, however, constructive commentary and criticism can be rendered only by those who understand the issues adequately and whose concern is to promote a more accurate grasp of the truth in the issues at hand. Commentary and criticism are constructive when offered on the appropriate occasions by the appropriate means.

D. *A Roman Catholic theologian is one who understands the importance and necessity of the role of the hierarchical teaching authority in the church and, consequently, respects that authority according to the conditions, circumstances, and variety of its proper exercise.*

This criterion is demanded by the special role which the Roman Canon ascribes to the pope and bishops in watching over, guiding, and leading the church to peace and unity. Yet the manner of its implementation in concrete cases is a very difficult question. LG 25 describes the way in which authoritative teaching is to be received. As helpful as this description is, it still remains vague. Nor does it take sufficient account of the instances of authoritative teaching which clearly do not obligate the faithful to complete assent. In fact, the theory and practice of authoritative teaching is still too undifferentiated. Lack of sufficient precision not only makes this criterion difficult to apply but it is also a cause of real and potential conflict between theologians and bishops.[26]

Obviously, these criteria cannot and should not be translated into certain minimal or maximal standards to be applied within the church in a hard, fast, and heedless way. For they reflect (or perhaps better, seek to reflect) the character of our church's life. As the Roman Canon indicates, the Catholic Christian community is still incomplete in understanding and living the mystery to which it is committed. Consequently, the forms and requirements of theological service to this church cannot be frozen into painstakingly exact and pre-set standards and rules.

VI.
THE RIGHTS AND RESPONSIBILITIES OF THEOLOGIANS

With the preceding two sections as groundwork, it can now be shown that a Roman Catholic theologian as such bears certain responsibilities and enjoys certain rights in the church. The term "responsibility" here means an obligation incumbent upon theologians in virtue of their identity as Roman Catholic theologians. While the terms "duty" and "obligation" might also serve, "responsibility" is preferable because it connotes the intrinsically relational character of the theologian's obligations. The term "right" here means a power, privilege, or immunity vested in persons in virtue of their identity as Roman Catholic theologians and necessary to enable them to discharge the responsibilities to the fullest extent of their capabilities.

A. The Responsibilities of Theologians

1. Roman Catholic theologians have the responsibility to be critically faithful to the "catholic faith that comes to us from the apostles."

According to the Canon, our identity is grounded in the "new and everlasting covenant" established by Christ which is the mystery of faith and comes to us from the apostles. Without fidelity to that faith, an individual, no matter how well qualified, has no legitimate claim to the title Roman Catholic theologian. The Canon indicates and Vatican II makes explicit that the contents of the catholic faith remain utterly essential as a foundation, guide and goal of theological inquiry.

As noted above, however, Vatican II itself made it more difficult to discern precisely the contours of our catholic faith today, more difficult to determine whether or not a theological position is congruent with the faith. Our times are such that, while it is not *a priori* impossible to render this responsibility of fidelity into specific and universally binding obligations, it is at least extraordinarily difficult and probably premature to do so.

Theological fidelity to the faith must be critical. In recalling the names of our forebears in faith, the apostles and teachers, the Canon reminds us of the pluralism of ways in which the apostolic faith can be held, taught, and expressed. It reveals that even if the content of faith could be determined with precision, it would still not serve as a fund of ready-made answers and formulae just waiting to be fitted to contemporary theological problems. We must struggle to let it speak and let it be "good news" for our times and situations.

Vatican II makes this clear when it affirms that ". . . the deposit and the truths of faith are one thing, the manner of expressing them is quite another" (GS 62) and sees the goal of the theologians' work as the deeper penetration, better understanding, and more suitable presentation of the revealed truth (GS 44).

Progress towards this goal is effectively promoted by theologians' adherence to the standards of scholarship that govern teaching and research in the academic disciplines. The norms generally accepted in North America for scholarly investigation and communication seek to insure genuine discovery and progress in research and teaching. Thus theologians who hold themselves accountable to these standards enact that critical fidelity necessary for the church's growth in understanding.[27] They also further the process of enculturation, which is the adaptation of ". . . the gospel to the understanding of all people and the requirements of the learned . . ." (GS 44).

2. *Roman Catholic theologians have the responsibility to use their talents, gifts, and expertise in ways that promote the growth of genuine faith, unity, and peace in the church.*

This responsibility is indicated in the Roman Canon when it speaks of all those who hold and teach the apostolic faith as helping to watch over and guide the church and lead it to peace and unity. It is stated more explicitly in GS 44 and 62. If it could be shown that the theologian enjoys a specific charism, a number of other texts from Vatican II could be cited to establish this responsibility even more firmly.[28]

Awareness of this responsibility ought to develop a willingness in theologians to assist the church when called upon to do so, e.g., by accepting invitations to speak to non-academic audiences, by participating in religious formation projects, by agreeing to serve as consultants, even when such activities do not advance their academic careers.

It should also lead theologians to consider writing occasionally for nonacademic readers and offering their services to non-theological groups in the church.

Since theologians as such hold no canonically established position in the church but generally do hold official positions in the academy, most of their work will necessarily be carried on in an academic context and performed in the accepted academic styles, e.g., teaching in a seminary, college, or university; publishing in scholarly journals; or in other forms of service. However, there is no essential conflict between academic theological work and service to the church. Theologians should be aware of the mediate and long-term ways in which their academic work can and does serve the church.

To meet this responsibility, the theologian's work ought to be marked by charity and humility. At times, the union of intellectual agreement may be broken. The bond of faith and the unity of love should not be broken by theologians, even when they feel sorely tried by misunderstanding, unfair treatment, and even slander.

This responsibility also entails prudence and discretion in the theologian's choice of ways to serve the church. Theologians must try to minimize the possibility that their thought will be used against the church or used by one group in the church against another. They must also try to reduce any harm to the unsophisticated which might result from premature or inappropriate dissemination of their thought.

Roman Catholic theologians have the responsibility to be critically faithful to the disciplinary norms which the church adopts to enable it to fulfill its mission more effectively.

3. *The Roman Catholic theologian has the responsibility of respecting the hierarchical teaching authority in the church according to the conditions, circumstances, and variety of its proper exercise.*

The Canon indicates this responsibility when it prays especially for the pope and bishop among those who hold and teach the faith. Vatican II, again, makes this responsibility explicit when it affirms that ". . . the task of giving an authoritative interpretation of the word of God, whether in its written form or in the form of tradition, has been entrusted to the living teaching office of the church alone. Its authority in this matter is exercised in the name of Jesus Christ" (DV 10).

4. *Roman Catholic theologians have the responsibility to object publicly to church policies and practices and to dissent publicly from church teachings when:* (a) *all the possibilities for resolving*

the issues privately have been exhausted; and (b) *they are convinced, as a result of careful consideration, that they must speak out for the good of the church and in critical fidelity to the catholic, apostolic faith.*

As the Canon indicates by its list of apostles and teachers, authentic church unity cannot be simply equated with uniformity of teaching and practice. No teaching, not even authoritative teaching, can perfectly express the mystery of which it speaks. No policy, practice, or teaching is *a priori* immune from the obscuring effects of sinfulness.[29] Thus there are occasions (e.g., Paul's conflict with the Jerusalem church) when open disagreement and dissent are necessary to expose a truth which otherwise would be understood only partially by one or both sides. If theologians keep silence when they are convinced that an authoritative teaching or practice is at substantial variance with the faith, they fail to meet their responsibility to the faith and to the church.

Vatican II affirms this responsibility: "By reason of the knowledge, competence or pre-eminence which they have, the laity are empowered—indeed sometimes obliged—to manifest their opinion on those things which pertain to the good of the Church" (LG 37). A clerical theologian who by virtue of ordination and mission ". . . (is) given a share in his (Christ's) ministry, through which the Church here on earth is being ceaselessly built up . ." (PO 1) could hardly have less of the same responsibility.

The duty of theologians to maintain a "silentium obsequiosum" in case of dissent is appropriate within the context of a pre-Vatican II ecclesiology in which the magisterium is the locus of all authority in the church. The documents of Vatican II, however, expand and differentiate the bearers, kinds, and forms of exercise of authority in the church. Exercise of church authority can no longer be regarded as the service of one particular person or group. Consequently, to submit theological dissent to the judgment of authority in the church today may well require in certain circumstances the use of a public forum.

5. *Roman Catholic theologians have the responsibility not only to give but also to accept constructive criticism of their work ren-*

*dered by their peers, by brothers and sisters in the faith, and by
the office of authoritative teaching in the church.*

As the Canon indicates, teaching is a communal and cooperative function in the church. Thus theologians who were unrecep-
tive to constructive criticism would not fulfill a necessary condition
for the proper and beneficial exercise of their role in the church.

The documents of Vatican II are replete with references to the
church as a community, a unity of fellowship and service, of mutual dependence and cooperation. Theologians in this church,
therefore, have the responsibility of incarnating this ideal in the
ways in which they perform their particular service to the church.

B. THE RIGHTS OF THEOLOGIANS

If Roman Catholic theologians bear certain responsibilities in
the church, it follows that they must also enjoy certain rights without which the fulfillment of the responsibilities would be impossible or at least diminished. Relating rights and responsibilities underlines again the fact that the role of the theologian is to serve the
church in its proclamation of the gospel to the world.

1. Related to the responsibility for being critically faithful to the
   catholic, apostolic faith is *the theologian's right publicly to explore and to articulate new ways of understanding that faith.*

The Roman Canon's implicit acceptance and affirmation of
theological diversity, as well as Vatican II's recognition of the
importance of the role of the theologian in developing an effective
evangelization (GS 44) both undergird this right.[30]

The church cannot arrest or direct changes in the meanings of
language which accompany historical and cultural shifts. Such
changes in meaning can make church teaching appear unintelligible and even erroneous to contemporary ears.[31] When this occurs,
the gospel message will not be heard as good news unless new ways
of understanding and articulating it are found—and a great portion
of this task falls to theologians.

Consequently, recognition of this right demands that others in the church, including the hierarchical teaching authority, refrain from approaching a theologian's work with the *a priori* presupposition that traditional theological terminology and methods are the best and only way of expressing the faith of the Church.

Today the mass media inadvertently complicate theologians' exercise of this right. Conclusions theologians submit to the judgment of their peers can be (and often are) exposed to an audience which has neither the expertise needed to understand and properly assess the conclusions nor familiarity with the ways and means of theological discussion and progress. When this happens, the audience may see a theologian as a subverter of the church's faith and call for disciplinary action by the bishops. While theologians themselves must seek to insure that their views are not disseminated by inappropriate means, church leaders too must educate the faithful to the necessity of care and patience in approaching theological work.

2. Related to the responsibility for using their talents, gifts, and expertise in the service of the church is *the theologians' right to the exercise of those freedoms which they must enjoy if they are to meet their responsibilities adequately.*

Thus Vatican II calls for a "lawful freedom of inquiry, of thought, and of expression" (GS 62). It is necessary that others in the church recognize these freedoms and do not try to inhibit or prevent them from being exercised by the use of coercive methods (DH 10, 14). The effect of this right is not to deny to others their right to criticize the work of theologians in a careful and constructive manner; indeed, this can only be helpful to theologians and serve to increase the quality of their service to the church. Rather, recognition of this right would, among other results, render the theologian immune from having to spend time and energy defending the right to discharge a responsibility.

This right includes the theologians' immunity from comprehensive prohibitions to publish, commands to keep silence, and removal from their teaching positions. This right would not be abridged if the proper authority, on the basis of the kind of inquiry proposed in No. 4 below, declared a particular opinion of a theologian to be at substantial variance with the apostolic faith as received and taught by the church and ordered the theologian not to speak, publish, or teach on that issue. But sweeping condemnations and prohibitions would make it impossible for the theologian's talents, gifts, and expertise to be used in other areas. Recognition of this right demands that the hierarchical teaching authority be discriminating.

Theologians also have the right of access to the resources necessary to conduct their theological inquiry. E.g., a competent theologian has the right of access to archival resources when such access does not injure the rights of others.

3. Related to the responsibility to respect the office of authoritative teaching according to the conditions, circumstances, and variety of its proper exercise is *the right of theologians to the apostolic witness and cooperation of the hierarchical teaching authority in the church.*

Both the Roman Canon and Vatican II show the communal, cooperative character of teaching in the church. The Council in many places specifies the duties of bishops. But "among the most important duties of bishops that of preaching the Gospel has pride of place" (LG 25).[32] As society grows more complex, however, and the church develops structures to meet society's needs, there is a danger that bishops may become merely program administrators. In the press of their many obligations, they may neglect one of their chief duties, preaching the gospel. Then they not only fail the faithful entrusted to their care. They also fail the theologians by withholding that indispensable contribution to the dialogue which promotes the church's growth in faith.

Given the communal, cooperative character of teaching in the church, theologians have a right to the bishops' participation, if not initiative, in the task of developing structures to maximize the range and effectiveness of theological service to the church. Not only would these structures help the bishops to ". . . present Christian doctrine in a manner adapted to the needs of the times" (CD 13), but they would also function as means whereby theologians' loyalty to the church would be strengthened and their service more fully rendered. Such structures would also establish a setting of mutual respect and trust wherein real or potential conflicts might more likely help rather than hinder the church in its mission.

4. Related to the responsibilities of theologians given above is *the right of theologians to the benefits of the exercise of the office of official teaching authority.*

The Roman Canon indicates and Vatican II clearly affirms the existence and role of a doctrinal teaching authority vested in the pope and the bishops (DV 10; LG 21, 25, and elsewhere). Theologians, therefore, have a right to this service when there exists demonstrably a grave threat to the integrity of the apostolic faith. The same responsibility of the pope and the bishops, considered in light of the "hierarchy of truths" (UR 11), would demand that their particular manner of service be congruent with the proximity of the issue to the heart of the faith.

Should there be good grounds for the hypothesis that the work of a theologian calls for intervention by doctrinal teaching authority, the theologian has the right to be heard openly in a constructive atmosphere by those who are able to understand adequately the work of that theologian. If formal procedures are required to enable all parties to discharge their responsibilities in a particular case, these procedures must safeguard the rights of all the parties.[33] All parties to such procedures should act ". . . with love, prudence and patience. . ." (DH 14).

VII.
CONCLUSION

As the Introduction noted, there are a number of well established ways by which theologians' loyalties to the academy are inculcated and their service to the academy is enacted. Yet, despite the fact that "theology has always had and continues to have great importance for the church, the people of God, to be able to share creatively and fruitfully in Christ's mission as prophet,"[34] the picture in the North American church is quite different. Too few ways are available to strengthen theologians' loyalties to the church.

Too few opportunities exist for their important services to be utilized.

During his visit to the Catholic University of America, Pope John Paul II declared: "The church needs her theologians, particularly in this time and age so profoundly marked by deep changes in all areas of life and society." A church which needs her theologians and still neglects to develop structures to meet that need is a church which impoverishes herself. It is a church which hampers its growth in faith and its proclamation of the message of salvation to a world which hungers for it.

Notes

1. Sources I found particularly helpful in developing this paper include:

Yves Congar, "Pour une histoire sémantique du terme 'magisterium,' " *RSPT* 60 (1976), 85–98.

————, "Bref historique des formes du 'magistère' et de ses relations avec les docteurs," ibid., 99–112.

Joseph Komonchak, "Magisterium and Theology," Position paper prepared for the NCCB Committee on Doctrine, January, 1978.

————, "*Humanae Vitae* and Its Reception: Ecclesiological Reflections," *TS* 39 (1978) 221–57.

Karl Rahner, "Theologie und Lehramt," *Stimmen der Zeit* 198 (1980) 363–75.

"The Magisterium, the Theologian, and the Educator," a special issue of *Chicago Studies* 17 (Summer, 1978). Henceforth cited *CS*.

2. See the studies listed in note 1.

3. See Raymond E. Brown, "The Dilemma of the Magisterium Versus the Theologians," *CS* 17 (1978) 290–307.

4. I am grateful to my friend and colleague, Thomas H. Tobin, S.J., for this analysis.

5. "Catholic higher education and the Church's pastoral mission," *Origins* 10 (1980) 381.

6. In the studies listed in n. 1, see especially T. Howland Sanks, "Co-

operation, Co-optation, Condemnation: Theologians and the Magisterium 1870–1978," *CS* 17 (1978) 242–63.

7. See Gerald A. McCool, *Catholic Theology in the Nineteenth Century: The Quest for a Unitary Method* (New York: Seabury, 1977).

8. AAS 42 (1950) 567.

9. Ibid., 568.

10. Ibid.

11. ". . . hoc sacrum Magisterium, in rebus fidei et morum, cuilibet theologo proxima et universalies veritatis norma esse debet. . ." Ibid., 567.

12. Ibid., 563.

13. Ibid., 568.

14. Ibid., 563–64.

15. Ibid., 568.

16. Ibid., 567.

17. On the reasons for translating *authentice* as *authoritatively*, see Komonchak's "*Humanae Vitae*" and Avery Dulles, "The Two Magisteria: An Interim Reflection," *PCTSA* 35 (1980) 156.

18. Translation amended slightly.

19. Translation amended slightly.

20. *Pace* Myles M. Bourke ("Collegial Decision-Making in the New Testament," *The Jurist* 31 [1971] 13): "If there is any group in the church which has the right to be heard when the church makes decisions it is that composed of those to whom the charism of teaching has been given, the *didaskoloi*, who, in the list of 1 Cor 12:28 rank third after the apostles and prophets. If this charism now exists in the church apart from the hierarchy—and to deny that it does is utterly arbitrary—it is surely possessed by the theologians." I am grateful to Patrick Granfield for calling this reference to my attention.

21. See also LG 35; AA 29, 32; GE 10.

22. "CTSA Committee Report on Cooperation Between Theologians and the Church's Teaching Authority," *PCTSA* 35 (1980) 327.

23. Bishops' Committee on the Liturgy, *The New Eucharistic Prayers and Prefaces* (Washington: National Conference of Catholic Bishops, 1968) 13–15.

24. For a detailed discussion of this interpretation of the prayer, see Joseph A. Jungmann, *The Mass of the Roman Rite: Its Origins and Development (Missarum Sollemnia)*, v. 2, Francis A. Brunner, trans., (New York: Benzinger, 1955) 156–57.

25. On martyrs as witnesses and so as "teachers," see Karl Rahner, "Martyrdom," *Encyclopedia of Theology*, Karl Rahner, ed. (New York: Seabury, 1975), 937–39.

26. See Rahner, "Theologie und Lehramt."

27. See the "Report on Inclusion of Provisions Regarding *Missio Canonica* and *Nihil Obstat* in Statutes of Weston School of Theology," Spring, 1980 (privately printed and circulated).

28. E.g., AA 3 and LG 12.

29. See Karl Rahner, "What is a Dogmatic Statement?" *Theological Investigations* 5 (Baltimore: Helicon, 1966), pp. 42–66.

30. See also GS 62 and UR 4: "While preserving unity in essentials, let everyone in the church, according to the office entrusted to him, preserve a proper freedom . . . even in the theological elaborations of revealed truth."

31. See, for example, Karl Rahner's discussion *The Trinity,* Joseph Donceel, trans. (New York: Seabury, 1974), pp. 103–14.

32. See also LG 21, 24, 27; DV 25; GS 43; AG 38; CD 2, 13, 16.

33. See the accompanying paper of Patrick Granfield, "Theological Evaluation of Current Procedures."

34. John Paul II, "Redemptor Hominis," *Origins* 8 (1979) 639.

Theology and Magisterium: Self-Appraisals

Karl Rahner

This article originally appeared in *Theology Digest* in 1981.

The Roman magisterium assumes that given knowledge and good will, its statements and their import need no clarification and hence that it should have the last word, the theologian humbly respecting the (relatively) binding character of that word. The theologian's task becomes that of defending and explaining such pronouncements.

Theologians, on the other hand, remark the historically conditioned nature of the human author who draws up the pronouncement: the statement may not be as "clear" as assumed in the author's unconscious horizon of understanding. Theology, moreover, does not begin and end with magisterial declarations; the theologian must take up many matters—of great import for Christian faith and life—that escape such declarations. This means an inquiry that is free from outside control, that cannot be realized if the risk of error is the primary and constant concern, if one demands theological conformity and so suppresses a legitimate pluralism as dangerous or unacceptable.

The two sets of claims need not be contradictory. The trouble is that each side sees the other's position in dependence on its own and acts in practice as if only its maxims mattered. In what follows, let me set forth what each side must be willing to grant, in theory and practice, to the other.

MAGISTERIUM'S SELF-APPRAISAL

Those who exercise magisterium must aver in word and deed:

"We too are human; apart from infallible papal and conciliar definitions, we can be and, in fact, often have been wrong. This is a self-assessment, a risk that we must live with if we are to fulfill our task—a physician can't wait until he has an absolutely sure diagnosis! But you theologians have no right to brand such decisions false merely because they go against what many of you previously maintained.

"Conversely, we have a duty (largely shirked) of noting the non-binding quality of non-binding statements. But theologians must avoid the impression that unless authentic declarations are infallibly defined, they have in effect no worthwhile meaning. We must both cooperate to produce a climate where non-binding, authentic declarations have genuine meaning for the church.

"This raises a host of questions: When should the theologian resort to open protest? When is it part of his calling to support Rome's pronouncements? When is 'respectful silence' not out of order? When should he probe and evaluate a statement and so register correctives (differing interpretations) that we in Rome had not foreseen? When should he set the thematic of a declaration within a wider horizon so that we in Rome can learn that the essential meaning stands though the wording is not adhered to?

"We realize that a period of *silentium obsequiosum* shouldn't last too long. (The present pope spoke publicly of 'the Yahwist'; and 70 years ago we didn't deal too kindly with the Catholic exegete who used the same expression!) There are as yet no case-by-case rules for determining when a theologian's reaction shows due respect; in such areas of value-judgment we must reckon with the fact that we can both be wrong. However, we must not use this request for your patience and understanding as a license for presumption, but as a reminder of the difficulties of our task—a task that must be shouldered in a spirit of self-criticism.

"We must accept the practical need for the church on earth not to rest content with a vague 'permanence in truth' but to define its faith in infallibly binding (though human) propositions. Obviously, the magisterium cannot tolerate a theologian who mounts a frontal attack on these truths of Catholic belief and publicly rejects them.

"But what about the case where the theologian contends that the incompatibility of his position with the church dogma is a claim made by the magisterium? In asking him to 'retract' the matter becomes more complex than we once realized. Does 'retraction' mean the theologian now recognizes that his position is in fact contrary to the dogma—a point he previously denied? How long must he have to come to this realization? By what right do we require such clarification when our assertion of incompatibility may be wrong? Must we be content with the theologian's profession that [a] he accepts the dogma, the legitimacy of its formulation, and the normativity of its language, but [b] stands by the freedom to express his opinion in the matter though Rome may not see eye-to-eye?

"We in Rome must realize that already defined dogmas cannot be some locus where the theologian's work begins or ends, but that these dogmas themselves must be thoroughly 're-questioned': their bearing, their distinction from co-transmitted interpretations, their assessment relative to the whole of faith and to the spirit of a new age—all these questions must be carefully investigated if the Good News is to be proclaimed effectively. Living in a clerical milieu, we in Rome can forget this need for on-going interpretations of defined dogmas.

"If basic Christian dogmas are to be proclaimed in a non-traditional milieu, then widespread, intensive efforts must be made to search out fresh interpretations. I'm afraid that the average Christian's picture of three Persons in God is heretical! Since dogma has an on-going history, we may not assume that the traditional formulations of classical christology remain up to date and that their meaning can find no better expression.

"The theologian's challenges are many: an evolving worldview, a conception of salvation history as all-inclusive, the positive meaning for salvation of non-Christian religions, a more positive reading of Christianity's divisions, today's secularized world, a 'continentally' pluralist theology—Africa, Latin America, East Asia. We should all be disturbed when dogma is seen as a sacrosanct untouchable and not as a living force.

"The history of truth does not end in a definition. The pope should no longer compose his encyclicals as though they were 'private' documents. Why does the International Theological Commission lead such a stunted existence, the head of the Congregation for the Doctrine of the Faith refusing even to consult it? The CDF's theologians should have international standing."

—Of course, all particulars of the process must be disclosed to the theologian who is cited by the CDF. A few years ago a book-long dossier—containing written denunciations—was withheld from the theologian indicted therein. For too long he was not permitted to know the name of the man deputed to defend him. Such secretiveness is absurd. The Roman curia violates those very human rights that the church professes to stand for.

The CDF's procedure—the final decision resting with ten cardinals—is outmoded and bizarre. True, the magisterium's authority does not ultimately rest on the weight of theological argumentation (though it has the duty of zealously availing itself of such means). But this is a far cry from these cardinals—who (*salva omni reverentia*) know for the most part nothing of theology beyond trite seminary tags—alone deliberating and deciding. What harm would be done if theologians were first to sit down with a few competent cardinals? Further, it is unreasonable for the theologian to have to wait with apprehension for a year or more while the Roman bureaucracy makes up its mind. And the international curia of a world church can surely see to it that the colloquium between the theologian and the Roman administration be conducted in the public forum of world-wide dialog.

Theologian's Self-Appraisal

Theologians should be ready to subscribe to the following:
"We are no Mafia: we make no claim that we alone can speak for theology, nor do we feel that we must blast away for truth and

freedom whenever a theologian is in conflict with Rome. If Rome's decision is correct, it is our right and duty to say so. Does a theologian have nothing to contribute if he supports a decision from Rome?

"Rome must take joint declarations by theologians seriously. The legal fact that there is no appeal from this 'highest See' does not mean that dialog with theologians runs counter to the magisterium's essence. Such joint declarations, however, are a dubious venture—mere modernity is not sufficient justification. And calls for greater freedom are particularly suspicious and ineffectual unless they spell out exactly what this does and does not mean.

"We theologians must accept our obligations to the magisterium. True, we do have our own function and pastoral responsibility—we are not mere jobbers for church authorities. But we must view our task within the hierarchical Roman Catholic Church. That task goes beyond mere apologetics, for the magisterium alone is not equipped to guide the church's evolving awareness of its faith. And yet this task can be pursued only in solid agreement with the magisterium.

"We theologians must not rush out and flood the world with declarations that seek to exempt our freedom from the magisterium. The magisterium need not be presumptuous in censuring us, nor need such intervention threaten freedom of theological inquiry. Great as is the distance between faith and scientific theology, a theology that bears no relation to the church's proclamation of that faith is not a Christian theology. On the other hand, the scope and methods of scientific theology itself lie totally outside magisterial competence. Nevertheless, if theology is not to degenerate into mere religious science but live and think within a believing church, then even professional theological publications may not lie outside the magisterium's control.

"We theologians must indeed respect the magisterium, but it is not clear, concretely, what that means. There are varying degrees of binding character and normativity—hence our response should vary accordingly. But in the effort to concretize this gradation the magisterium leaves us with norms that, in their vagueness, are either false or unhelpful.

"*Lumen Gentium* (n. 25) calls for 'religious submission of mind and will.' If this is valid without further qualification, then moral theologians' worldwide dissent to *Humanae vitae* would be a massive attack on magisterial authority. The magisterium's toleration of such dissent shows that *Lumen Gentium* does not provide a sufficiently precise norm for working out, in practice, the relation between magisterium and theologians. How ought, e.g., moral theologians react to Rome's recent declarations on sexual morality—declarations they find too imprecise?

"There are times when we must have the courage to risk losing our posts or being censured by Rome. But though such censure be received docilely, the matter is not thereby settled. It's not certain that the theology (interpretation) Rome takes as traditional is identical with a dogma. In such a case the magisterium's formal authority is not irreformable and has often, as history shows, been mistaken. But suppose further that the theologian remains sincerely unconvinced by the magisterium's arguments and that, the matter being important, he feels the duty to intervene further on behalf of the truth.

"In such a case, can a 'respectful silence' be enough? May, must the theologian announce his opposition? How, then, is the magisterium to know that beneath his opposition on this particular point there lies a genuine, inner respect? Those who say the theologian should simply keep quiet ignore the important question as to how the church's life and faith is to move forward. If, for example, all theologians had maintained an obedient silence toward Pius X's biblical decrees, then the present pope could not, today, refer to the Yahwist nor could a New Testament introduction state that Luke's Gospel was written after the fall of Jerusalem.

"In sum: the theologian, after mature reflection, has the right and, at times, the duty to speak out against a magisterial declaration. The magisterium can certainly try to win the theologian over to its side. But when the question is where truth resides, the issue should be left to the future.

"The magisterium's needful right to settle a theological controversy does not mean that it must always do so, nor that a non-defined decision should end further discussion. In individual cases, the magisterium's administrative measures can constitute an unjust and biased infringement on legitimate freedom. Such cases have existed and continue to exist. Tolerance of opposition to non-binding magisterial statements has grown in Rome's recent practice. Does this *de facto* tolerance result from a backlog of cases or—hopefully—from the realization that such tolerance is inherently justified?

"A goal being praiseworthy does not mean that any and all means may be used to reach it—e.g. denying the freedom so necessary to the theologian. True theological freedom does not come about by facilely made declarations, but by allowing opinions that one doesn't agree with, though having the power to prevent them.

"Theologians should not, as recently happened, react with supercilious barbs that are also quite 'un-Jesus-like.' But man's sinfulness and vulnerability to temptation permit us to lay the burden of proof not at theology's doorstep, but at the doorstep of those who want to restrict freedom.—Why doesn't someone in Rome say so? Is it fear? Why isn't it clear that stating such principles would augment, not diminish, magisterial authority?"

The Authority of the Magisterium on Questions of Natural Moral Law

Francis A. Sullivan, S.J.

This article originally appeared in *Magisterium: Teaching Authority in the Catholic Church*, 1983.

Vatican II deals with this question in two places. In *Gaudium et Spes*, apropos of the judgments which parents have to make about bringing more children into the world, the Council says:

> The parents themselves should ultimately make this judgment, in the sight of God. But in their manner of acting, spouses should be aware they cannot proceed arbitrarily. They must always be governed according to a conscience dutifully conformed to the divine law itself, and should be submissive toward the Church's teaching office, which authentically interprets the law in the light of the gospel.

There is every reason to believe that when the Council speaks of the 'divine law' in this context, it means the natural law, which of course is divine in its origin.

The other text of Vatican II on this issue is found in the Declaration on Religious Freedom, *Dignitatis Humanae:*

> In the formation of their consciences, the Christian faithful ought carefully to attend to the sacred and certain doctrine of the Church. The Church is, by the will of Christ, the teacher of the truth. It is her duty to give utterance to, and authoritatively to teach, that Truth which is Christ Himself, and also to declare and confirm

by her authority those principles of the moral order which have their origin in human nature itself.

In view of this clear teaching of Vatican II, it does not seem necessary to multiply citations from the many papal encyclicals which have affirmed and exercised such teaching authority on concrete moral issues. One brief citation, however, will be given which suggests the reasoning on which the claim to teaching authority in these matters is based. It is a statement of Pope Pius XII:

> The power of the Church is not bound by the limits of 'matters strictly religious,' as they say, but the whole matter of the natural law, its foundation, its interpretation, its application, so far as their moral aspect extends, are within the Church's power. For the keeping of the natural law, by God's appointment, has reference to the road by which man has to approach his supernatural end. But on this road the Church is man's guide and guardian in what concerns his supreme end. The apostles observed this in times past, and afterward from the earliest centuries the Church has kept to this manner of acting, and keeps to it today, not indeed like some private guide or adviser, but by virtue of the Lord's command and authority.

I realise that this claim of the magisterium to teach with authority on questions of the natural moral law raises a number of questions, concerning, for instance, the obligation on the part of the faithful to form their consciences in conformity with such teaching, and the possibility, conditions and consequences of legitimate dissent from such teaching. I intend to consider such questions in a later chapter. For now it suffices to know that most Catholic theologians agree that the magisterium does have the right to speak with authority on such issues. They differ on whether one can rightly argue from its authority to its authority on this kind of question. Let us now look at the reasons given by those who argue for infallibility.

Arguments for the Infallibility of the Magisterium on Questions of Natural Law

I shall begin with an argument that is rather simplistic, but is still sometimes heard: namely, that the magisterium is infallible in matters of faith and morals: but particular norms of the natural law are matters of morals; therefore the magisterium can speak infallibly about them.

The weakness of this argument is that it ignores the difference between what is revealed and what is not revealed with regard to morals. It presumes that the term 'matters of faith and morals' is rightly understood to include all moral issues, regardless of their relationship to the deposit of revelation. But this is certainly not the case. An illuminating proof of this is found in a response made by Bishop Gasser, the spokesman for the *Deputatio de Fide* of Vatican I, to a proposal to substitute the term 'principles of morals' for the more usual term: *res morum.* One of the reasons this proposal was rejected was given by Gasser as follows: 'Insuper principia morum possunt esse alia mere philosophica naturalis honestatis, quae non sub omni respectu pertinent ad depositum fidei.' I translate: 'Moreover, principles of morals can be other merely philosophical principles of natural morality, which do not in every respect pertain to the deposit of faith.' This is striking evidence that the term *res fidei et morum* was not understood at Vatican I to embrace all possible questions of natural morality.

The second argument I shall consider is taken from the draft of the Constitution on the Church which was drawn up by the Preparatory Theological Commission and submitted to the first session of Vatican II in 1962. As is well known, this *schema* was found so unsatisfactory that it was withdrawn without ever being put to a vote. In Chapter 7, n. 29, this *schema* contained the following statement:

> Cum vero idem magisterium sit ministerium salutis, quo homines docentur quam viam sequi debeant ut ad aeternam vitam valeant pervenire, ideo munus et ius illi competunt non modo revelatam sed et naturalem legem interpretandi et infallibiliter declarandi, et de obiectiva conformitate omnium actionum humanarum cum evangel-

ica doctrina et divina lege iudicandi. (I translate): Since this same magisterium is the ministry of salvation by which men are taught the way they must follow in order to be able to attain to eternal life, it therefore has the office and the right of interpreting and of infallibly declaring not only the revealed law but also the natural law, and of making judgments about the objective conformity of all human actions with the teaching of the Gospel and the divine law.

There is no officially promulgated document of the magisterium which makes such an explicit claim to infallibility in interpreting the natural law. It must surely be seen as significant that this claim was not retained in the new draft of the Constitution on the Church which was substituted for that of the Preparatory Commission, nor was any such claim subsequently introduced in any document of Vatican II.

What is the force of the argument offered for this claim in the statement we have quoted? It seems to suppose that the magisterium could not fulfil its ministry of teaching men the way to salvation unless it could interpret and declare the requirements of the natural law not only with pastoral authority but also with infallibility. But this is what needs to be proven. The omission of this claim to infallibility regarding the natural law, in the treatment of the magisterium in *Lumen gentium,* suggests that the bishops were not convinced of this argument.

The third argument for infallibility is the one suggested in the report of the minority of the commission of experts appointed by Pope Paul VI to study the question of birth control, prior to the encyclical *Humanae vitae.* The argument is based on the grave consequences of erroneous moral teaching by the Church. Speaking of the Church's teaching on the sinfulness of contraception, this report declares:

. . . there is no possibility that the teaching itself is other than substantially true. It is true because the Catholic Church, instituted by Christ to show men the sure road to eternal life, could not err so atrociously through all the centuries of its history. The Church cannot substantially err in teaching a very serious doctrine of faith or morals through all the centuries—even through one century—a doctrine constantly and insistently proposed as one necessarily to be followed in order to attain eternal salvation. The Church could not substantially err through so many centuries—even through one century—in imposing very heavy burdens under grave obligation in the name of Jesus Christ as it would have erred if Jesus Christ does not in fact impose these burdens. The Catholic Church could not in the name of Jesus Christ offer to the vast multitude of the faithful, everywhere in the world, for so many centuries an occasion of formal sin and spiritual ruin on account of a false doctrine promulgated in the name of Jesus Christ.

What is to be said of such an argument? It draws its conclusion, that the Church cannot err in its moral teaching, from two assertions: 1) that error in the Church's moral teaching would be the occasion of formal sin and spiritual ruin of the faithful; and 2) that it is impossible that the Church should be the cause or occasion of such harmful consequences.

One problem with this argument is that if it were valid, and its conclusion were true, it would also have to be true that the Church has never erred when it has taught something to be gravely sinful. The argument would have to be able to stand up to the test of history. As I am not a historian of moral theology, I leave this question to those who are competent in the field.

Another problem is that this argument seems to suppose that we know how much spiritual harm God is prepared to allow the leaders of the Church to be the occasion of. How can it be shown that erroneous moral teaching would cause more spiritual harm than has been caused by the scandalous conduct of which Church leaders have certainly been guilty? If God has permitted the latter, why could He not permit the former as well?

Now we come to the arguments which John C. Ford and Germain Grisez have proposed in a recent article, the whole burden of which is to prove that all the conditions required for the infallibility of the ordinary universal magisterium have been fulfilled in the case of the Church's teaching on the sinfulness of contraception. Essentially, what they wish to prove is that this moral norm falls within at least the secondary object of infallibility, and that it has actually been infallibly taught, because it has been taught for a long time by the whole Catholic episcopate as a norm definitely to be held.

The Arguments of Ford and Grisez for the Infallibility of the Church's Teaching on Contraception

My purpose in this discussion, as I have said at the beginning of this chapter, is to illustrate the ecclesiological principles regarding the infallibility of the ordinary universal magisterium by applying them to the controverted question whether the sinfulness of contraception has been infallibly taught. Hence I shall be looking especially at the premises on which Ford and Grisez have based their arguments.

Let us look first at the premises on which they base their contention that the morality of contraception falls within at least the secondary object of infallible teaching. They present their position as follows:

> We do not assert that the norm is divinely revealed. This question is one from which we have prescinded. Our position rather is this: if the norm is not contained in revelation, it is at least connected with it as a truth required to guard the deposit as inviolable and to expound it with fidelity. . . . Admittedly, it does not seem there is any way to establish *conclusively* that this teaching either pertains to revelation or is connected with it apart from the fact that the ordinary magisterium has proposed the teaching in the manner in which it has, and the faithful as a whole until recently have accepted the norm as binding. But a similar state of affairs has been used as a basis for solemnly defining at least one dogma: that of the Assumption of the Blessed Virgin Mary.

Let us now analyse this statement. The clause that begins 'apart from' clearly implies that there is one way to establish conclusively that the morality of contraception falls within at least the secondary object of infallibility: namely from the way the magisterium has proposed this teaching, and the way the faithful have accepted it. If I understand this correctly, what it means is that we can know for certain that this is a proper object for infallible teaching from the fact that the magisterium has taught it infallibly. And, as we shall see, the fact that the magisterium has taught it infallibly is seen in the fact that the magisterium has consistently taught it as an obligatory norm, binding under grave sin, and that the faithful have accepted it as such.

In support of this argument, Ford and Grisez appeal to what they see as a parallel, in the case of the definition of the dogma of the Assumption. In a footnote they point out where they see the analogy: 'In defining the dogma of the Assumption, Pius XII argues . . . from the universality of the acceptance of the doctrine as a matter of faith to its objective status as a truth pertaining to divine revelation.'

Now it seems to me that the differences between these two issues are so great as to rule out the conclusion that Ford and Grisez wish to draw from the analogy between them. What justified the conclusion that the doctrine of the Assumption must be a revealed truth was the fact that for centuries it had been a matter of universal Christian *faith*. The major premise there was the infallibility of the whole People of God in its faith.

On the other hand, the fact that the faithful accepted the Church's teaching on contraception as binding does not prove that they accepted it as revealed or even as necessarily connected with revealed truth. Indeed, it seems likely that many of them accepted it simply as a binding law of the Church, which they had to observe whether they were convinced of its truth or not. So I do not see the parallel with the dogma of the Assumption as convincing.

My major difficulty with the argument that Ford and Grisez have proposed as the one that in their opinion would conclusively establish their case, is that it would eliminate the possibility of challenging any magisterial act that was claimed to be infallible by questioning whether the subject-matter of that act fell within the limits of the proper object of infallibility. In other words, the supposition of their argument seems to be: if the magisterium speaks in a definitive way about something, it must necessarily be the case that what they speak about is a proper object of infallible teaching. The question of the object would no longer be an independent criterion by which it could conceivably be judged that the magisterium had not really spoken infallibly, on the ground that the matter on which it spoke was not a proper object of infallible teaching.

Against such a view I would argue that if it were true, there would be no point at all in the insistence of Vatican I and Vatican II that the magisterium can speak infallibly only on matters of faith and morals. It would have been necessary to say only this: whenever the magisterium speaks in a definitive way it must be speaking infallibly, because the very fact that it speaks in a definitive way would guarantee that what it speaks about would be a proper matter for infallible teaching. What then would have been the point of mentioning the limits of the matter about which the Church can teach infallibly? It seems to me that the supposition underlying the argument of Ford and Grisez would open the door to absolutism in the exercise of magisterium.

With regard to the other arguments which they offer in support of their view that the question of the morality of contraception falls within at least the secondary object of infallibility, I will say only that I believe that at most they would suffice to show that this moral teaching is connected with revelation; however, I do not think they show that it is so necessarily connected with revelation that the magisterium could not safeguard and expound revelation if it could not teach this particular norm with infallibility.

As we have just seen, the only argument which Ford and Grisez think would conclusively prove that the morality of contraception is a proper matter for infallible teaching is based on their contention that it has actually been infallibly taught. And their case that it has been infallibly taught is based on their contention that for many centuries it was taught by the universal Catholic episcopate as a moral norm *to be held definitively*. This brings us to the crucial question: how do they understand what it means to teach something as to be held definitively?

Before discussing the answer which Ford and Grisez give to this question, I remind the reader that I have already treated it earlier in this chapter, where I expressed my agreement with the view of Salaverri and Rahner that to propose a teaching to be held definitively means to oblige the faithful to give it their irrevocable assent. This is quite different from the way that Ford and Grisez explain what it means to teach something as to be held definitively. They say:

> A point of teaching surely is proposed as one to be held definitively if a bishop proposes it in the following way: not at his option but as part of his duty to hand on the teaching he has received; not as doubtful or even as very probable but as certainly true; and not as one which the faithful are free to accept or to reject but as one which every Catholic must accept.

Now it seems to me that there is a very real difference between authoritative teaching which calls upon the faithful to give their assent to it as certainly true, and the kind of teaching which proposes a doctrine as irreformably true and calls for an irrevocable assent.

The question, then, is: which of these is the correct interpretation of what it means to teach something as definitively to be held? Is this the same thing as to teach something as certainly true? I find the following remarks of John Reed helpful in answering this question:

> Besides infallible teachings of the magisterium, however, whether in solemn definition or in constant and universal ordinary teaching, there is that exercise of its authority which, while not infallible, is still authentic and binding. This is perhaps even more important in matters of natural law than in other areas of Catholic doctrine. In this connection it is important to distinguish the notions of infallibility and certainty. In matters of conduct, a doctrine which is not taught with the plenitude of infallibility may still be taught with certainty, in the sense of moral, practical, certitude, so as to exclude any solidly probable opin-

ion to the contrary here and now, i.e. with the effect that at a given time a particular mode of conduct is certainly licit or certainly illicit, without the abstract question of its relation to right order being definitively closed. Infallibility excludes the absolute possibility of error. Certitude, in the sense of moral, or practical, certitude, excludes the prudent, proximate fear of error. While such a teaching does not altogether close the question from a speculative point of view, it does normally preclude the possibility of acting in contradiction of the doctrine, relying on the principle of probabilism.

This explanation by Reed of how a mode of conduct can be taught as certainly illicit without the question of its relation to right order being definitively closed also brings out the weakness of the principal argument which Ford and Grisez have advanced to show that the sinfulness of contraception was being taught as a moral doctrine to be held definitively. They base this claim primarily on the fact that the magisterium condemned contraceptive behaviour as gravely sinful. And, in their view, 'to propose a norm excluding some kind of act as mortally sinful is to propose a teaching to be held definitively.' Now, when Reed speaks of teaching that an act is 'certainly illicit', I think it safe to assume that he would include 'gravely illicit'. And yet he insists that such teaching does not necessarily mean that the speculative question is definitively closed.

Karl Rahner takes the same position in his reply to Hans Küng, who argued, as Ford and Grisez do, from the fact that the bishops taught that contraception was gravely sinful, to the conclusion that they must have been teaching this as a doctrine to be held definitively. Rahner replied:

> The only question is whether the teaching of Pius XI and *Humanae vitae* is proclaimed as a teaching that must be 'definitively' affirmed . . . Küng has not at all proven that such an absolute assent was demanded—which is something completely different from a very urgent claim on an assent which is not qualified as absolutely definitive (even over a long period of time and under the appeal to

Church teaching authority.) It is also something completely different from the assertion that such a theoretical
teaching implies a serious moral obligation before God.

In other words, it is one thing to teach that something involves
a serious moral obligation; it is quite another to claim that this
teaching is now absolutely definitive, and demands an irrevocable
assent. But if the argument proposed by Ford, Grisez and Küng
were valid, it would mean that the Church could not declare any
mode of conduct gravely wrong unless it were prepared to make an
irreversible judgment on the matter. This would practically rule
out any ordinary, noninfallible exercise of the Church's teaching
authority on moral issues.

The other argument which Ford and Grisez use to show that
the doctrine on contraception was being taught as to be held definitively is that it was often proposed as a divinely revealed moral
norm. They argue from this in the following way:

The teaching on the morality of contraception often was
proposed as a moral norm divinely revealed. Since it was
proposed as revealed, a fortiori it was proposed as a teaching *to be held definitively.* We prescind from the question
whether the evidence alleged to show that the condemnation of contraception is divinely revealed does or does not
show this. The point we wish to make is simply this: when
one who is proposing a teaching appeals to divine revelation to confirm the truth of what he proposes, he implicitly calls for an assent of divine faith, and thus proposes
the teaching as one to be held definitively. . . . If one
considers the explicit appeals made to Gen 38:9–10 together with the implicit appeals made to the same passage, to Rom 1:26–27, and to the Ten Commandments,
one realizes that most who handed on the Catholic teaching on contraception claimed the authority of Scripture,
which they believed to be the authority of divine revelation, in support of this teaching. Whether one thinks this
claim was valid or not—a question we are not considering
here—no one can deny that those who made it proposed

the teaching on behalf of which they made it as a moral norm *to be held definitively*.

Now it seems to me that if this argument were valid, it would eliminate practically all ordinary, non-definitive teaching by the magisterium. For, whenever any appeal was made to Scripture in support of what was being taught, this would automatically become definitive teaching. Are we to conclude that the popes, who regularly appeal to Scripture in their encyclicals, have in all such cases been proposing their doctrine as definitively to be held?

The More Common Opinion: Particular Norms of Natural Law Are Not Object of Infallible Teaching

Having spent perhaps too much time examining the arguments of those who claim that the magisterium can infallibly determine the concrete norms of the natural moral law, I shall conclude this chapter with a brief consideration of the views of those who reject this claim.

First a word about the opinion of the Catholic moralist, Daniel Maguire, who seems to rule out the possibility that the magisterium could speak with infallibility on any moral issue whatever, when he says flatly that the term 'infallible' does not in fact aptly describe the nature or function of the moral magisterium. However, it seems that what he has in mind as the 'function of the moral magisterium' is 'to apply the moral vision of the Gospel to complex natural law questions such as are presented by medical ethics, genetics, business ethics, international law, social reconstruction, and war and peace.' In this case, his position, while more radically stated, would not differ substantially from the more common view, which distinguishes between the moral general principles of the natural law, and the determination of the requirements of the natural law when it is applied to the concrete moral problems that face people in the modern world.

I believe that the majority of Catholic moral theologians today would subscribe to the following propositions concerning the 'moral magisterium'.

1. At least some of the basic principles of the natural law are also formally revealed, and as such, belong to the primary object

of infallible magisterium. It does not seem that any such moral principle has ever been solemnly defined, but since Vatican I declared that the pope has the same infallibility which the Church has in defining 'doctrine of faith and morals', it seems necessary to conclude that at least some doctrines regarding morals could be infallibly defined. Catholic moralists generally agree that those basic norms of the natural law which have also been revealed to us 'for the sake of our salvation' could be infallibly taught, either by solemn definition or by the universal ordinary magisterium.

2. The magisterium is competent to exercise its ordinary teaching authority by applying the natural law, in the light of the Gospel, to the particular and concrete moral issues facing individuals and society today. It is true that at least one Catholic moralist, Jakob David, invokes a distinction between 'magisterial' and 'pastoral' authority, and denies that the competence of the hierarchy regarding concrete issues of natural law can be called 'magisterial' authority. But it seems to me that he is identifying magisterial authority with the capacity to teach infallibly. He explains 'pastoral authority' regarding the natural law as the competence of the bishops and pope to guide the faithful in the formation of their consciences. Following St. Thomas, who speaks of the *magisterium cathedrae pastoralis* of the bishops, I see no reason not to speak of the teaching function of the bishops, especially in its ordinary exercise, as 'pastoral magisterium'. It is this magisterium which they exercise when they help the faithful to form their consciences on concrete problems of the natural law.

3. The concrete determinations of the natural law with regard to the complex problems facing people today are neither formally nor virtually revealed. That is to say, they are not among the truths which God has revealed to us for the sake of our salvation, nor can they be strictly deduced from any such truths. It is now generally agreed that the process by which we arrive at the knowledge of the concrete norms of the natural law is through shared reflection on human experience; it is rather an inductive process than a deductive one. Christians seek the answers to concrete moral problems in the light of the Gospel, but these answers are not conclusions that follow with metaphysical certitude from revealed premises.

4. Nor can it be shown that the magisterium would not be able to defend and explain the moral principles and values of the Gospel unless it could infallibly determine the correct application of the natural law to the concrete and complex problems of modern man. No doubt these are moral issues, and they are connected with the moral values of Christian revelation. But, as we have seen, in order for something which is neither formally nor virtually revealed to fall within the 'secondary object' of infallibility, it has to be so necessarily connected with revealed truth that the magisterium would be unable to defend or explain revelation itself if it could not speak infallibly about this also. Since 'nothing is to be considered infallibly defined or declared unless this is manifestly the case', the burden of proof is on those who would claim that the magisterium could not defend or explain some revealed truth unless it could infallibly determine some particular application of the natural law.

5. Finally, to say that a proposition has been infallibly taught is to say that it must be irreversibly true. From this it follows that for a moral norm to be the proper object of infallible teaching, it must be a norm which, at some point in history, can be so irreversibly determined that no future development could possibly call for the substantial revision of this determination of what the natural law requires. It is the more common opinion of Catholic moralists today that the concrete norms of the natural law simply do not admit of such irreversible determination.

This judgment is based on an understanding of the very process by which we arrive at our knowledge of the natural law as it applies to concrete moral issues. This understanding involves the following elements: (a) the moral problems facing mankind today tend to be particularly complex; (b) while the Gospel sheds light on these problems, it does not provide their solution; (c) an indispensable role in the process of finding answers to concrete moral problems is played by human intelligence, reflecting on human experience; (d) Christians share this arduous search along with all other men of good will.

Several passages of *Gaudium et Spes* suggest that this was the approach of Vatican II to this issue. For instance:

Through loyalty to conscience Christians are joined to other men in the search for truth and for the right solution to so many moral problems which arise both in the life of individuals and from social relationships (GS 16). The Church is guardian of the heritage of the divine Word and draws religious and moral principles from it, but she does not always have a ready answer to every question. Still, she is eager to associate the light of revelation with the experience of mankind in trying to clarify the course upon which mankind has just entered (GS 33). Having set forth the dignity of the human person and his individual and social role in the universe, the Council now draws the attention of men to the consideration, in the light of the Gospel and of human experience, of some more urgent problems deeply affecting the human race at the present day (GS 46).

Now if the process by which we have to arrive at our knowledge of the concrete norms of the natural law is by the exercise of human intelligence, reflecting on human experience, it must be admitted that there are elements in this process which militate against the possibility of reaching an absolutely irreversible determination of a concrete norm of the natural law. One is the fact that human experience is an on-going, open-ended reality. We can never exclude the possibility that future experience, hitherto unimagined, might put a moral problem into a new frame of reference which would call for a revision of a norm that, when formulated, could not have taken such new experience into account.

Another factor is that human nature itself is not a static, closed reality, but a dynamic, evolving one. As Karl Rahner explains it, the immediate norm of natural morality is man himself in his concrete nature. But this concrete nature of man in all its dimensions (biological, social, etc.) is itself precisely subject to a most far-reaching process of change. While some universal moral norms may be said to flow from the metaphysical nature of man, the particular norms are based on human nature as it exists in history, as subject to change. Such norms cannot lay claim to any absolute or permanent validity.

It is the consideration of such factors as these in the process by which we come to know the particular norms of the natural law, which has led most of the Catholic theologians who have written on this question in recent years, to the conclusion that such norms are not proper matter for irreformable teaching. This judgment rules out not only the possibility of the infallible definition of such a norm, but also the claim that such a norm has ever been, or could be, infallibly taught by the ordinary universal magisterium.

However, this judgment would not at all rule out the exercise of that ordinary, non-infallible magisterium by which the pastors of the Church offer their authoritative guidance to the faithful for the formation of their conscience on complex moral issues. It is to this ordinary magisterium that we must now turn our attention.

Infallibility and Specific
Moral Norms: A Review Discussion[1]

Germain Grisez

This article originally appeared in *The Thomist*.

Francis A. Sullivan, S.J., who for many years has been professor of ecclesiology at the Gregorian University in Rome, has written an important book on the magisterium. In it he explains and defends the teaching of Vatican I and Vatican II on apostolicity, infallibility, and unalterable dogmatic truths. Because Sullivan engages in authentic Catholic theological reflection, his work must be taken seriously. I wish to make it clear that I agree with much of Sullivan's theology of magisterium and admire his fidelity to the Catholic theologian's vocation. Here, however, I must take issue with certain aspects of his argument in chapter six: "The Infallibility of the Ordinary Universal Magisterium and the Limits of the Object of Infallibility."

Sullivan criticizes a position John C. Ford, S.J., and I defended: that the received Catholic teaching on contraception (and, by implication, on many other questions about sex, marriage, and innocent life) has been taught infallibly by the ordinary magisterium. Sullivan maintains that no specific moral norm can be taught infallibly. In what follows, I try to show that he has neither refuted our position nor established his.

I

During the controversy following *Humanae vitae*, it was widely assumed that since the encyclical contains no solemn definition, the teaching it reaffirms is not proposed infallibly and could be mistaken. That assumption simply ignored the entire category of teachings infallibly proposed by the ordinary magisterium.[2] However, in *Dei filius,* Vatican I definitively teaches that there is such a category: "Further, all those things are to be believed with divine and Catholic faith which are contained in the word of God, written or handed down, and which the Church either by a solemn judgment or by her ordinary and universal magisterium proposes for belief as divinely revealed."[3] Because *Dei filius* concerns revelation, its teaching is limited to revealed truths. Still, it shows the unsoundness of the assumption that only what is defined is infallibly taught.

Vatican II articulates criteria for the infallibility of the ordinary magisterium: "Although the bishops individually do not enjoy the prerogative of infallibility, they nevertheless proclaim the teaching of Christ infallibly, even when they are dispersed throughout the world, provided that they remain in communion with each other and with the successor of Peter and that in authoritatively teaching on a matter of faith and morals they agree in one judgment as that to be held definitively."[4] Vatican II's formulation is not limited to revealed truths. It allows for a secondary object of infallibility: truths required for revelation's safeguarding and development.[5]

Reflecting on Vatican II's formulation, Ford and I became convinced that the received teaching on contraception meets the criteria. In an article, we clarified the conditions for the infallible exercise of the ordinary magisterium by tracing the development of Vatican II's text in the conciliar proceedings. We then argued that the facts show that the received Catholic teaching on contraception has met these conditions.[6]

In making our case, we did not try to show that the norm concerning contraception pertains to revelation, because Vatican II does not include that among the criteria by which infallible teachings of the ordinary magisterium are to be recognized. However, in specifying the limits of infallibility in defining, the Council states: "Now this infallibility, with which the divine Redeemer willed his Church to be endowed in defining a doctrine of faith or morals, extends as far as extends the deposit of divine revelation, which must be guarded as inviolable and expounded with fidelity."[7] This statement of the limits of infallibility makes it clear that if anything is taught infallibly, it must pertain to revelation, at least by being a truth required to safeguard and develop revelation itself.

The connection is essential. But it does not follow that no teaching can be recognized as infallible without first being recognized as pertaining to revelation. Essential conditions for a reality need not be conditions for recognizing instances of that kind of reality. For instance, water is H_2O, but one can recognize instances of water without first knowing them to be H_2O. Similarly, the fact that a moral teaching within the infallible competence of the magisterium must either be revealed or closely connected with revelation need not prevent one from first recognizing instances of such points of morals and only thereby coming to know that they *somehow* pertain to revelation.

Therefore, Ford and I proceeded on the assumption that if a teaching meets the conditions articulated by Vatican II, it can be recognized as infallibly proposed, and from the fact that it has been infallibly proposed, it can be known to pertain to revelation. The question how it pertains is secondary. Still, since the connection between infallibility and revelation is essential, if the norm concerning contraception has been proposed infallibly, this secondary question is important. Thus we treated it first in a series of subordinate questions and objections.

In beginning our account of the way in which the norm concerning contraception pertains to revelation, we expected the objection: Your argument is going in the wrong direction; you ought first to have shown how this teaching pertains to revelation, and then how the Church has taught it. That objection would have been based on the supposition: Nothing can be recognized as pertaining to revelation from the manner in which the Church holds and hands it on. A single counterexample falsifies a general thesis, so we offered one counterexample: the dogma of the Assumption and the argument Pius XII offered for its being revealed when he defined it.[8]

II

Instead of beginning his criticism of Ford's and my position by examining our basic argument, Sullivan starts with our treatment of the subordinate question: How does the teaching pertain to revelation? Omitting our introduction to the question, which makes clear the status we allow it, Sullivan says: 'Let us look first at the premises on which they base their contention that the morality of contraception falls within at least the secondary object of infallible teaching.'[9] He then quotes the first paragraph of our three and one-half page answer to the question, and in doing so omits a sentence which calls attention to the fact that this paragraph is not a complete argument:

> We do not assert that the norm is divinely revealed. This question is one from which we have prescinded. Our position rather is this: if the norm is not contained in revelation, it is at least connected with it as a truth required to guard the deposit as inviolable and to expound it with fidelity. [The following sentence is omitted by Sullivan.] In support of this position, we first point out that no one has seriously tried to show that anything in revelation is *incompatible* with the Church's teaching on the morality of contraception. Admittedly, it does not seem there is any way to establish *conclusively* that this teaching either pertains to revelation or is connected with it apart from the fact that the ordinary magisterium has proposed the teaching in the manner in which it has, and the faithful as a whole until recently have accepted the norm as binding. But a similar state of affairs has been used as a basis for solemnly defining at least one dogma: that of the Assumption of the Blessed Virgin Mary.[10]

A careless reader might be misled into thinking that Sullivan is about to criticize the premises of Ford's and my main argument.[11]

Sullivan says that when Ford and I refer to the doctrine of the Assumption, we are trying to prove by analogy that the morality of contraception is a proper object for the infallible magisterium.[12] Therefore, he begins his criticism by pointing out disanalogies. The Assumption had for centuries "been a matter of universal Christian *faith*." But the fact that the faithful accepted the "teaching on contraception as binding does not prove that they accepted it as revealed or even as necessarily connected with revealed truth.

Indeed, it seems likely that many of them accepted it simply as a binding law of the Church, which they had to observe whether they were convinced of its truth or not."[13]

Even if Ford and I were arguing by analogy, Sullivan's criticism would not be decisive. Of course, the norm concerning contraception was not accepted as a matter of faith, for it is a matter of morals. Sullivan may well be right in doubting that the faithful accepted the teaching on contraception as revealed or even as closely connected with revelation. But he offers no evidence that the faithful assented to the Assumption under such theological formalities. Moreover, it is mere speculation to say that it seems likely the teaching on contraception was accepted only as a binding law of the Church. Admittedly, widespread legalism led people to confuse moral norms with laws. But instructed Catholics always knew the difference between laws of the Church and laws of God, between eating meat on Friday and contraception.

Actually, however, a counterexample is not an argument by analogy, so the disanalogies, even if they were as great as Sullivan thinks, would not tell against Ford's and my point: One can legitimately argue from the way the Church holds and teaches something to its pertaining to revelation; one need not show that something pertains to revelation, or how it pertains, to recognize it as an integral part of the Church's teaching.

Sullivan reformulates what he takes to be the supposition of our argument: "If the magisterium speaks in a definitive way about something, it must necessarily be the case that what they speak about is a proper object of infallible teaching."[14] He says this supposition "would eliminate the possibility of challenging any magisterial act that was claimed to be infallible by questioning whether the subject-matter of that act fell within the limits of the proper object of infallibility."[15] Sullivan then states his major difficulty with what he thinks is Ford's and my view:

> Against such a view I would argue that if it were true, there would be no point at all in the insistence of Vatican I and Vatican II that the magisterium can speak infallibly only on matters of faith and morals. It would have been necessary to say only this: whenever the magisterium

speaks in a definitive way it must be speaking infallibly, because the very fact that it speaks in a definitive way would guarantee that what it speaks about would be a proper matter for infallible teaching. What then would have been the point of mentioning the limits of the matter about which the Church can teach infallibly?[16]

And Sullivan concludes that our view would open the door to "absolutism" in the exercise of the magisterium.

Sullivan claims that Ford and I are arguing that we can only know for certain that the morality of contraception is a *proper object* for infallible teaching from the fact that the magisterium has taught it infallibly. I distinguish: We do say that the only way to prove conclusively that this teaching either pertains to revelation or is closely connected with it—and in *this* sense is a proper object of infallible teaching—is the fact that the magisterium has proposed it infallibly. But we do not say that the only way to recognize the teaching as a matter of "faith or morals"—and in *this* sense as falling within the magisterium's competence as a *potential* object of an infallible teaching—is the fact that the magisterium has proposed it infallibly.

Sullivan equivocates; his argument succeeds only on the assumption that "faith and morals" in *Lumen gentium, 25,* really means "a point of faith or morals *known* to pertain to revelation." This assumption of Sullivan's is the general thesis Ford and I showed to be false by the example of the doctrine of the Assumption. And there are other ways of seeing that Sullivan's assumption is mistaken.

If Sullivan were right in assuming that "faith and morals" can refer only to those matters already *known* to pertain to revelation, Vatican II's articulation of conditions for the infallibility of the ordinary magisterium would be useless. Christians who ponder revelation can come to see truths not yet widely grasped in the Church; when they do so, they can believe such truths, although the magisterium never has proposed them for belief. If Sullivan were right, nothing could ever be found to meet the conditions for infallible teaching by the ordinary magisterium without first being grasped by such independent Christian insight as divinely revealed or closely connected with revelation. But whatever was so recognized independently of the magisterium's proposal of it would not require the seal of magisterial authority.

Moreover, Christians always have believed that the apostles and their successors bonded together in communion enjoy an unfailing charism of truth. That is why, when disputes arose concerning what really is revealed truth, appeals were made to what had been held and handed down in all the churches. The force of that appeal never depended on an independent showing that the truth in question was revealed. That condition, which Sullivan wishes to impose, would have blocked the attempt to proceed from the way truths are held and handed on to their status as pertaining to revelation.

As for the "absolutism in the exercise of the magisterium" which Sullivan fears, that seems a threat only because of his oversimplification of our position when he says: "It would have been necessary to say only this: whenever the magisterium speaks in a definitive way it must be speaking infallibly."[17] This reformulation might lead one to imagine that Ford and I suppose that if one's bishop were to tell one definitively what cold remedy to use, his judgment would be infallible. For Sullivan omits the other conditions for infallible teaching: that the bishops agree in one judgment on a matter within the magisterium's competence—faith and morals. But Ford and I include these conditions. We simply do not grant Sullivan's assumptions that one cannot recognize what falls under "faith and morals" without knowing beforehand that and how it pertains to revelation.

III

Having disposed of what he mistakes for Ford's and my "principal argument," Sullivan devotes one more paragraph to the three pages in which we articulate the explanation on whose introductory paragraph he focuses his attack. These pages contain our reasons for thinking that the norm excluding contraception either is included in revelation or was a legitimate development of revelation's shaping of Christian life.[18] In line with his misreading of the introductory paragraph of our argument, Sullivan considers these pages not as an explanation of *how* but as "other arguments" *that* the question of the morality of contraception is at least within the secondary object of infallibility. Without summarizing our explanation and without offering ground for his verdict, Sullivan says these "other arguments" would at most "suffice to show that this moral teaching is connected with revelation; however, I do not think they show that it is so necessarily connected with revelation that the magisterium could not safeguard and expound revelation if it could not teach this particular norm with infallibility."[19]

The key to Sullivan's summary judgment is his phrase, "so necessarily connected." To understand the issue here, one must bear in mind that according to Vatican II infallibility extends not only to revelation itself but also to truths closely connected with revelation. Sullivan commendably defends this "secondary object of infallible magisterium," signified by Vatican II's phrase, "which must be religiously guarded and faithfully expounded."[20] He also rightly rejects the view which would include in this secondary object everything connected with revelation, no matter how loosely. For Vatican II's formula limits the magisterium to truths it is required to teach if it is to fulfill its ministry.

However, Sullivan needs more than "required"; his criticism turns on "so necessarily connected." Moreover, as we shall see, one of Sullivan's key arguments to exclude specific moral norms from the object of the infallible magisterium is that they cannot be derived with logical *necessity* from revealed principles.

Where does Sullivan get "necessarily" as a qualification of the connection? Not from Vatican II, for the Council does not use the word and the official clarification of the phrase, "divine revelation, which must be guarded as inviolable and expounded with fidelity," simply is: "all those things and only those things which either directly belong to the very revealed deposit, or which are required to guard as inviolable and expound with fidelity this same deposit."[21]

To obtain "necessarily," Sullivan invokes a never completed project of Vatican I, which is not mentioned in this context by Vatican II, and so has little or no theological weight: "The commission which drew up the draft of the Constitution on the Church at

Vatican I chose a much more restrictive term to describe the secondary object: 'veritates quae necessario requiruntur, ut revelationis depositum integrum custodiatur' (truths which are necessarily required, in order that the deposit of revelation may be preserved intact)."[22] Having thus introduced "necessarily," Sullivan reads it into *Mysterium ecclesiae,* a 1973 declaration of the Doctrinal Congregation, which says that the competence of the magisterium extends "to those things, without which this deposit cannot be properly safeguarded and explained."[23]

There are two reasons for rejecting Sullivan's reading of "without which cannot properly" as "necessarily required." First, it is reasonable to understand Church teaching since Vatican II in accord with that Council's completed work, not in accord with an unfinished project of Vatican I. Second, Vatican I's schema was concerned only with truths necessarily required in order that the deposit of revelation may be *preserved intact,* while Vatican II's teaching refers not only to truths required in order that the deposit may be religiously safeguarded (preserved intact) but also to those required for it to be *faithfully expounded.* This last phrase points to a different requirement—the need for development not only of theology but of doctrine.[24]

The distinction is important, because what is required to unfold revelation as the basis of God's ongoing relationship with his people might not be *necessarily* required to preserve intact the already given deposit of revelation. Furthermore, as soon as one attends to the fact that Vatican II's formula leaves room for authentic doctrinal development, one sees the untenability of any attempt to restrict the secondary object of infallibility to what can be derived with formal, logical necessity—that is, to what can be deduced.

For although many theologians once defended a deductivist model of doctrinal development, since Newman it has become recognized that such a model cannot accommodate the facts.[25] Indeed, Sullivan himself, explaining the development of Marian doctrine earlier in his book, says: "Admittedly, these conclusions do not follow with metaphysical necessity from what Scripture tells us about Mary. They are seen to be contained in the total mystery of Christ, by a kind of intuition, rather than by a process of logical deduction."[26]

In sum, if the development of the Church's teaching on contraception involved a dialectic which cannot be reduced to deductive form, that does not put the teaching outside the scope of the infallible magisterium. If the norm is not revealed—and it might be—it can be required to guard the deposit as inviolable or *expound it with fidelity*, as Ford and I show, without meeting Sullivan's demand that it be logically deducible from explicitly revealed truths or "so necessarily connected with revelation that the magisterium could not safeguard and expound revelation if it could not teach this norm with infallibility."

IV

Ford and I offered an argument that the norm concerning contraception is a matter of morals: "Vatican II itself, in *Gaudium et spes*, 51, at least affirmed the competency of the magisterium in this very matter when it stated: 'Relying on these principles, it is not allowed that children of the Church in regulating procreation should use methods which are disapproved of by the magisterium in its explaining of the divine law.' "[27] We thought that "in its explaining of the divine law" shows that the morality of contraception falls under "faith or morals."

Sullivan himself grants that the magisterium can speak authoritatively on particular moral issues. To show this, he quotes a few texts, including Vatican II's statement that in the matter of birth regulation parents "must always be governed according to a conscience dutifully conformed to the divine law itself, and should be submissive toward the Church's teaching office, which authentically interprets that law in the light of the gospel."[28] Sullivan asserts that "there is every reason to believe that, when the Council speaks of the 'divine law' in this context, it means the natural law, which of course is divine in its origin."[29] Thus, Sullivan admits that the Church can teach authoritatively—although he denies she can teach infallibly—specific norms of natural law, including that concerning contraception.

Before examining Sullivan's position on this issue, it is worth noticing that there are good reasons to think he moves too quickly when he reads "divine law" as meaning no more than "natural law, which of course is divine in its origin." "Divine law" and "natural law" often refer to the same reality, but do not have exactly the same sense, as can be seen in other statements of Vatican II, such as: "In pursuit of her divine mission, the Church preaches the gospel to all men and dispenses the treasures of grace. Thus, by imparting knowledge of the divine and natural law. . . ."[30] The Church is concerned with the natural law of the handing on of life insofar as it is divine law to be interpreted "in the light of the gospel" and belongs to the plan of "God, the Lord of Life."[31] Moreover, the footnote, immediately after "in its explaining of the divine law," first refers to *Casti connubii,* where contraception is condemned as against the "law of God and of nature," after nature and the revealed will of God have been treated separately and *seriatim* as sources of the condemnation.[32] Thus, in speaking of "divine law" in reference to contraception, Vatican II means more than natural law, divine in its origin.

No one doubts that the magisterium sometimes teaches authoritatively without teaching infallibly. That clearly is so where new and complex issues must be faced, and a pope or other bishop—or a group of bishops—finds it necessary to provide guidance, yet cannot at once tell whether the judgment proposed will be accepted eventually by the entire magisterium or precisely how it is related to revealed truth.

But it is a different matter to suppose that the magisterium cannot teach infallibly on a specific moral question even when all the bishops in communion with the pope hold the same position and propose it to the faithful throughout the world as an obligatory norm to be held definitively. Sullivan's position is that even if (as he admits) the morality of contraception is within the magisterium's competence, and if (which he does not deny) the magisterium has agreed in the same judgment about it, and if (which he denies) the judgment has been proposed to be held definitively, still the teaching *could not possibly be infallible.* For he thinks that no specific moral norm can be taught infallibly.[35]

That opinion emerged only since Vatican II. Sullivan himself implies as much, for when he first raises the question, "How much of the natural law is also revealed?" he proposes the view which excludes specific moral norms as "the strong trend in current moral thinking."[34] He concludes the chapter by treating with approval the opinion, which he thinks is that of the majority of Catholic moral theologians today, that "particular norms of natural law are not objects of infallible teaching."[35] At the end he summarizes the point he wishes to make:

> It is the consideration of such factors as these in the pro-
> cess by which we come to know the particular norms of
> the natural law, which has led most of the Catholic theolo-
> gians who have written on this question in recent years, to
> the conclusion that such norms are not proper matter for
> irreformable teaching. [Note omitted.] This judgment
> rules out not only the possibility of the infallible defini-
> tion of such a norm, but also the claim that such a norm
> has ever been, or could be, infallibly taught by the ordi-
> nary universal magisterium.[36]

Both Sullivan's own formulation of this opinion and the stated positions of some of the authors he cites in his note to support it make it clear that by "particular norms of the natural law" he means all specific moral norms.

In section VII, I will examine Sullivan's use of current theo-logical opinion and criticize the arguments he draws from it. Here I wish to stress the position's novelty.

The view common among Catholic theologians before Vatican II was articulated forcefully by Karl Rahner, S.J., in an essay on conscience, which he published in the late 1950s. Rahner says that Christians must accept binding norms:

> Furthermore, the Church teaches these commandments
> with divine authority exactly as she teaches the other
> "truths of the Faith," either through her "ordinary" magi-
> sterium or through an act of her "extraordinary" magister-
> ium in *ex cathedra* definitions of the Pope or a general
> council. But also through her *ordinary* magisterium, that
> is in the normal teaching of the Faith to the faithful in
> schools, sermons and all the other kinds of instruction. In

the nature of the case this will be the normal way in which moral norms are taught, and definitions by Pope or general council the exception; but it is binding on the faithful in conscience just as the teaching through the extraordinary magisterium is.

It is therefore quite untrue that only those moral norms for which there is a solemn definition (and these are criticized from all sides in the "world") are binding in faith on the Christian as revealed by God, and must be accepted by him as the rule for his own behaviour; and of course it is equally untrue—and this is often unadmittedly expected— that the moral law preached by the Church must necessarily receive the assent (even if it is only theoretical) of the non-Christian world. When the whole Church in her everyday teaching does in fact teach a moral rule everywhere in the world *as* a commandment of God, she is preserved from error by the assistance of the Holy Ghost, and this rule is therefore really the will of God and is binding on the faithful in conscience, even before it has been expressly confirmed by a solemn definition.[37]

One can see why Catholics at that time believed that the Church's teaching on contraception could never change.

But the current opinion Sullivan embraces denies the possibility of moral absolutes as such, not merely the moral norm concerning contraception. The challenge extends to other questions about sex, marriage, and innocent life.[38] On the new theory, "Thou shalt not commit adultery," is always a correct norm of Christian life only if "adultery" is understood to mean *wrongful* extramarital intercourse. The theory is that no "material" norm—that is, no norm without a built-in moral characterization of the act it concerns—can possibly hold always and everywhere.[39] From this it would follow, of course, that no such norm can be an unchanging truth, and so no such norm can be proposed infallibly.

It is significant that many apologists for contraception in the mid-1960s said it was an isolated issue, but today almost all who approve contraception defend exceptions to other received moral absolutes. This development is evidence that one cannot abandon the Church's teaching on contraception without threatening her entire view of sex, marriage, and innocent life. It seems to me that this close connection provides further evidence that the norm concerning contraception pertains at least to the secondary object of the infallible magisterium. Of course, this argument will not impress those who hold that revelation includes no specific moral norms at all.

V

Since it was commonly supposed until after Vatican II that revelation does include specific moral norms, it is reasonable to take "faith and morals" in the Council's documents as including reference to such norms. To take the conditions which Vatican II articulated for the infallible exercise of the ordinary magisterium as if they included the restriction Sullivan tries to impose is to replace the view the Council Fathers took for granted with a different view which they had never thought of. I do not say that such a replacement would *contradict* the Council's formal teaching. But one cannot simply read it into the Council's formulation. Sullivan needs some cogent theological grounds for setting this limit to "morals." He tries to find such support in certain documents of Trent, Vatican I, and Vatican II.

Sullivan points out that Trent is a primary source for the specification of the magisterium's field of competence by the phrase *res fidei et morum*. He says that in Trent's language, *mores* includes more than what we would call "morals" and suggest the translation: "matters pertaining to Christian faith and practice." Trent also teaches that the gospel—that is, Christian revelation—is the source of everything essential to Christian life. Sullivan concludes, "the bishops and the pope cannot claim to speak authoritatively, much less infallibly, unless the matter about which they speak pertains to Christian belief or the practice of the Christian way of life. In some real way, the *doctrina de fide vel moribus* has to go back to the Gospel as its source."[40]

I agree with that conclusion. The question is whether specific moral norms, such as that concerning contraception, can go back to the gospel as their source. Nothing Sullivan finds in Trent shows that they cannot, and he himself agrees that the Church can speak *authoritatively* on such matters. Some claim that "morals" in Trent does not refer to specific moral norms; perhaps Sullivan accepts that view. However, substantial studies of Trent's documents in their historical context show that "morals' in Trent should be taken to refer to specific moral norms along with much else.[41] In any case, Vatican I and Vatican II could add to Trent's teaching without contradicting it. So what the later councils mean by "morals" is more relevant than what Trent meant.

As an argument for the view that the Church can infallibly propose specific moral norms, Sullivan rejects (as question begging) a statement in the first schema of Vatican II's Constitution on the Church: "Since this same magisterium is the ministry of salvation by which men are taught the way they must follow in order to be able to attain to eternal life, it therefore has the office and the right of interpreting and of infallibly declaring not only the revealed law but also the natural law, and of making judgments about the objective conformity of all human actions with the teaching of the Gospel and the divine law."[42] Sullivan thinks it significant that this claim did not appear in later drafts which led to *Lumen gentium* or any other Vatican II document.

If the omission of this argument from the mature work of Vatican II is to be taken as significant, however, the significance might well be that the phrasing "not only the revealed law but also the natural law" makes a false contrast between revelation and the norms of natural law.[43] Moreover, the development of *Lumen gentium* between the first and second session left behind all sorts of things which were in the initial, rejected schema.[44] Hence, in the absence of evidence, such as interventions criticizing certain points, that particular changes implied the Council's rejection of a position, such omissions should not be considered significant.

Sullivan also claims that there is "evidence that the term *res fidei et morum* was not understood at Vatican I to embrace all possible questions of natural morality."[45] He adduces this evidence when he considers and rejects another argument for the view that the magisterium can teach specific moral norms infallibly. Sullivan formulates this argument: "The magisterium is infallible in matters of faith and morals: but particular norms of the natural law are matters of morals; therefore the magisterium can speak infallibly about them." Sullivan rejects this as "rather simplistic," because "it ignores the difference between what is revealed and what is not revealed with regard to morals."

By itself, this statement of Sullivan's would merely repeat what he needs to prove. So he seeks to establish the point by appealing to Bishop Gasser's response to a proposal to substitute "principles of morals" for *res morum* in the definition of papal infallibility. Sullivan cites the second of two reasons why the *Deputatio de fide* rejected this proposal: "Moreover, principles of morals can be other merely philosophical principles of natural morality [*alia mere philosophica naturalis honestatis*], which do not in every respect pertain to the deposit of faith."[46] Sullivan thinks this portion of Gasser's comment an "illuminating proof" of his thesis.

However, the first reason Gasser gives for rejecting the proposed amendment is an even more illuminating disproof of Sullivan's thesis:

Sed etiam hanc emandationem non potest admittere Deputatio de fide et quidem partim quia vox ista esset omnino nova, cum vox *res fidei et morum,* doctrina fidei et morum sit notissima, et unusquisque theologus scit quid sub his verbis sit intelligendum. (But the *Deputatio de fide* cannot accept this amendment either, partly because that expression would be wholly new, while the expression *res fidei et morum,* for doctrine of faith and morals is very well known, and every theologian knows what ought to be understood by these words.)[47]

The theological periti of Vatican I plainly knew what every theologian knew. J. Kleutgen and J. B. Franzelin were leading *periti* of Vatican I; both participated in the session of the *Deputatio de fide* where Gasser's responses to the proposed amendment were determined.[48] But Sullivan himself says that these two theolgians were among those who "asserted that the whole of the natural law is revealed, without making any distinction between the basic princi-

ples and more particular norms." Thus, theologians Gasser knew
well included specific moral norms under "faith and morals."

Had Vatican I accepted the amendment which was thus rejected, Sullivan would have had some real support. For the amendment, proposed by Archbishop Yusto of Burgos, was intended to
restrict the scope of the infallible teaching authority to principles,
in order to exclude moral determinations which depend on matters
of fact that are not revealed.[50] But this argument, which is close to
Sullivan's, must not have seemed cogent to the *Deputatio de fide*,
for they rejected Yusto's proposed amendment.

But if Gasser's remarks cannot be read as excluding specific
moral norms from the object of the infallible magisterium marked
out by the phrase "faith and morals," what could the *Deputatio de
fide* have meant by "merely philosophical principles of natural
morality, which do not in every respect pertain to the deposit of
faith"? I think a clue to the answer is in the phrase *naturalis
honestatis*, which Sullivan translates "natural morality." The translation is not bad, but it facilitates Sullivan's argument in a way that
the Latin does not. For *naturalis honestatis* does not mean the same
thing as *naturalis legis*, and the two expressions have different
connotations.

Honestas does refer to morality, but it means moral uprightness
(not moral goodness *or* badness) and it connotes the social value of
upright character, which merits honor. There is a body of philosophical moral literature concerned with *honestas*. It includes, for instance, Castiglione's *Courtier* and Chesterfield's *Letters to His Son*.
This genre mixes morals in the strict sense with social conventions,
etiquette, and practical techniques for getting ahead. The philosophical principles *naturalis honestatis* found in works of this genre
might be included in the reference of "principles of morals." But for
the most part such "principles of morals" have little to do with the
deposit of faith. They pertain to it only to the extent that they touch
on matters of faith and morals. For example, when Chesterfield
explains how to conduct extramarital affairs discreetly, the immorality of fornication and adultery pertains to the deposit of faith, but
the honorable way of engaging in that immorality does not.

When Gasser spoke of "alia mere philosophica naturalis honestatis, quae non sub omni respectu pertinent ad depositum fidei,"

he may well have meant principles of morals of that sort. In any case, the first reply to the proposed amendment, which Sullivan ignores, makes it clear that "faith and morals" in Vatican I means what every theologian at the time meant by it—what Kleutgen meant by it.

VI

What Vatican I meant by "morals" is extremely important because that Council used "faith and morals" in specifying the authority of the pope teaching *ex cathedra,* and in its definition Vatican I identified the object of papal infallibility with that of the Church. Thus, Vatican I implicitly defined the infallibility of the Church as extending to matters of "morals." And this implicit definition should be taken to mean what Vatican I in fact meant by it. But Vatican I included in the reference of "morals" what theologians of that time included—specific moral norms. It follows that the reference of "faith and morals" in Vatican I's implicit definition of the infallibility of the Church ought to be taken to include specific moral norms.

But even if they bow to the evidence that Vatican I included specific moral norms in the reference of "faith and morals," those who wish to exclude such specific norms from the object of infallibility will argue that Vatican I has not definitively rejected their position. Since all theologians at the time thought the Church could teach infallibly on such questions, this was not then at issue. Hence, the Council did not consider this issue, and so the common theological view of the time cannot have settled it.

I grant (not concede) that Vatican I did not definitively teach that the Church's competence to teach infallibly extends to specific moral norms. Still, Ford's and my view that contraception falls under "faith and morals" as the phrase is used by Vatican I and Vatican II in their statements of conditions for infallible teaching finds support in the documents, while Sullivan's contrary view finds none.

Furthermore, by citing passages in four previous documents as comparable to its own teaching, Vatican II itself provides guidance on the correct interpretation of the conditions for infallible teaching by the ordinary magisterium. One of the documents cited is Vatican I's revised schema for the second constitution *De ecclesia Christi,* together with Kleutgen's commentary.[51] The schema would have defined the infallibility of the Church as extending to "all those points which in matters of faith or morals are everywhere held or handed down as undoubted under bishops in communion with the Apostolic See, as well as all those points which are defined, either by those same bishops together with the Roman pontiff or by the Roman pontiff speaking *ex cathedra.*" Kleutgen's commentary makes it clear that "morals" here refers to specific moral norms. Indeed, he argues at length that the Church can teach infallibly on new moral questions, with respect to which revelation says nothing implicitly or explicitly, because the answers to such questions are closely connected with revelation.

Ford and I, not wishing to press Vatican II's reference to Kleutgen, said that although the note might refer to his whole commentary, it does not seem this reference "ought to be read as an endorsement of Kleutgen's entire commentary, yet the commentary remains a very authoritative guide to what the proposed text of Vatican I meant." My view remains the same: Vatican II perhaps meant its teaching to be read in the light of Kleutgen's whole commentary; but even if it did not, that commentary specifies the meaning of Vatican I's schema, to which Vatican II refers.

One of the arguments Kleutgen uses for the extension of infallibility to the Church's whole moral teaching is that it would be utterly at odds with her divinely constituted role of mother and teacher if with utmost gravity and severity she misled the faithful as to what is right and wrong.[52] This argument is like one Sullivan criticizes, drawn from the so-called minority report of Paul VI's commission on birth regulation:

> . . . there is no possibility that the teaching itself is other than substantially true. It is true because the Catholic Church, instituted by Christ to show men the sure road to eternal life, could not err so atrociously through all the centuries of its history. The Church cannot substantially err in teaching a very serious doctrine of faith or morals

through all the centuries—even through one century—a doctrine constantly and insistently proposed as one necessarily to be followed in order to attain eternal salvation. The Church could not substantially err through so many centuries—even through one century—in imposing very heavy burdens under grave obligation in the name of Jesus Christ as it would have erred if Jesus Christ does not in fact impose these burdens. The Catholic Church could not in the name of Jesus Christ offer to the vast multitude of the faithful, everywhere in the world, for so many centuries an occasion of formal sin and spiritual ruin on account of a false doctrine promulgated in the name of Jesus Christ.[53]

It was this argument that Ford and I meant to improve upon by our study. Hence, I do not claim it was perfect. However, Sullivan's criticisms scarcely do it justice.

Sullivan thinks this argument "is based on the grave consequences of erroneous moral teaching by the Church."[54] Having thus oversimplified it, Sullivan offers two answers.

First, if the argument were sound, "it would also have to be true that the Church has never erred when it has taught something to be gravely sinful."[55] Sullivan insinuates that this test of history could not be passed, but leaves the issue to historians.

But the argument sets a higher standard, "a doctrine constantly and insistently proposed as one necessarily to be followed in order to attain eternal salvation." This standard is more precisely expressed in Vatican II's formula: "agree in one judgment as that to be held definitively." While the test of history set by Sullivan's reformulation of the standard might not be passed, the test set by the more adequate formulation can be. Ford and I showed that neither of the two main counterexamples suggested by John T. Noonan, Jr.—the supposed requirement of procreative purpose to justify marital intercourse and the condemnation of usury—tells against Vatican II's conditions for the infallibility of the ordinary magisterium.[56]

Second, Sullivan argues that scandalous conduct by leaders of the Church certainly has caused great spiritual harm, which God has permitted. It cannot be shown that erroneous moral teaching would cause greater spiritual harm. Hence, we cannot know that God has not permitted the spiritual harm arising from erroneous moral teaching.[57]

Here Sullivan confuses infallibility with impeccability. The argument he criticizes does not assume that we can know how much harm God will permit sinful leaders of the Church to do. Hence, the harm caused by scandalous conduct is irrelevant. The argument is that the Church herself, divinely established and assisted to teach the truth humankind needs for salvation, could not act in her universal magisterium so defectively as to accomplish precisely the opposite of her mission. If the Catholic Church is what she claims to be, she cannot have been misleading the faithful through the centuries by erroneously telling them that certain kinds of acts are absolutely and gravely wrong.

VII

Having dealt with the position he rejects, Sullivan devotes the last section of his chapter on the infallibility of the ordinary magisterium to the opinion that no specific moral norm can be infallibly taught. He claims this is the view of "the majority of Catholic moral theologians today"[58] and that "most of the Catholic theologians who have written on this question in recent years" subscribe to it.[59] Thus, although he also summarizes some of the arguments offered for this view, Sullivan primarily relies on the authority of other theologians who hold it.

This appeal to the authority of other theologians is unsound in three ways. First, within theology, opinions no more weigh in an argument than do scholarly opinions in any other field of scholarship. As in any intellectual discipline, the weight of theological opinions is no greater than the evidence and arguments offered for them. Second, Sullivan begs the question by appealing to these opinions to complete his argument against us, for we have made our case against these same opinions.

Third, the appearance of theological consensus in favor of the opinion Sullivan adopts is only that. There are two substantial bodies of theological opinion. Which is the majority, which the minority? Who knows? Richard A. McCormick, S.J., writing in 1984 of those who support the Holy See's defense of Catholic teaching, says: "There are growing numbers of reactionary theologians who support this type of thing with insistence on a verbal conformity that is utterly incredible to the modern—and, I would add, open—mind."[60] I dislike McCormick's adjectives, but am glad he sees the tide is turning.

According to Sullivan's summary, the "majority" view admits the possibility of infallible teaching concerning basic principles of natural law and of authoritative pastoral guidance on concrete problems. But it holds that specific norms of natural law "are neither formally nor virtually revealed" and that they cannot be deduced from revealed truths. The argument is that we arrive at concrete norms by shared reflection on experience; the process is inductive rather than deductive.

Sullivan adds that specific norms cannot be shown to be necessarily connected with revelation. Here the argument is based on the rule of Canon Law that nothing is to be considered infallibly defined or declared unless this is manifestly the case. Sullivan thinks this puts an impossible burden of proof on anyone who would try to show that a particular moral norm falls within the secondary object of infallibility.[61]

In these arguments, Sullivan uses language which seems to narrow the class of moral norms which he claims cannot be infallibly taught. For instance, he says: "The concrete determinations of the natural law with regard to the complex problems facing people today are neither formally nor virtually revealed." Again, he refers to the "concrete and complex problems of modern man."[92] Such language might lead one to think of problems such as the morality of nuclear deterrence or in vitro fertilization.

However, granted (not conceded) that the solutions to such problems do not pertain to revelation, that does not entail that revelation neither contains nor requires any specific moral norm. Yet that is Sullivan's thesis. If it were not, one could grant his thesis but point out that contraception, adultery, abortion, and so on are not "complex problems of modern man," but fairly straightforward and perennial problems.

Sullivan's argument that specific moral norms cannot pertain to revelation if they depend upon shared reflection on experience not only assumes that all specific norms must be reached in this way, but that divine revelation can only be unfolded deductively. As I explained in section three, that assumption would preclude the development of doctrine.

When Sullivan invokes the rule of Canon Law that nothing is to be considered infallibly defined or declared unless that is manifestly the case, he evidences a confusion, widespread among the theologians who share his view, between teaching infallibly proposed in solemn definitions and teaching infallibly proposed by the ordinary magisterium. For that rule of Canon Law refers to the former, not the latter.[63]

Sullivan ends the chapter by summarizing arguments for the thesis "that the concrete norms of the natural law simply do not admit of such irreversible determination"—that is, truth which would permanently preclude any need for substantial revision.[64] The basic argument is one already used: that specific moral norms are reached by shared reflection upon experience. Sullivan thinks that passages in *Gaudium et spes,* 16, 33, and 46, which speak of searching for solutions to problems, support this thesis. He also says that the open-ended character of experience is such that moral absolutes are impossible: "We can never exclude the possibility that future experience, hitherto unimagined, might put a moral problem into a new frame of reference which would call for a revision of a norm that, when formulated, could not have taken such new experience into account."[65] Finally, he involves the opinion of Karl Rahner that the dynamism of human nature precludes specific moral norms with permanent validity.[66]

The passages in *Gaudium et spes* which Sullivan cites clearly support the view that *some* moral questions call for shared reflection on experience, admit of no ready answers, and baffle everyone, including popes and other bishops. There are complex, fresh problems, such as how to order modern technology and industry to the common good, how to avoid the holocaust without surrendering to tyranny, and so forth. But *Gaudium et spes* makes it clear that there are at least some specific moral norms whose truth permanently precludes the possibility of substantial revision:

> Contemplating this melancholy state of humanity, the Council wishes to recall first of all the permanent binding force of universal natural law and its all-embracing principles. Man's conscience itself gives ever more emphatic voice to these principles. Therefore, actions which deliberately conflict with these same principles, as well as orders commanding such actions, are criminal. Blind obedience cannot excuse those who yield to them. Among such must first be counted those actions designed for the methodical extermination of an entire people, nation, or ethnic minority.[67]

Obviously, genocide is a much greater immorality than contraception or adultery. However, the norm forbidding genocide is a specific moral norm. Indeed, this norm would not have been articulated without reflection upon some recent experience.

Again, the argument that the ongoing, open-ended character of experience precludes permanently true specific moral norms might be true with respect to *some* norms. But the argument only succeeds if someone establishes a theory of moral norms which shows the impossibility of moral absolutes. Many who deny moral absolutes think proportionalism is such a theory. However, there are strong reasons for considering proportionalism indefensible. In a recently published volume, I state these reasons. In the same work I criticize Rahner's claim that the dynamism of human nature precludes specific moral norms with permanent validity.[68]

VIII

Vatican II's conditions for infallible teaching by the ordinary magisterium include that the teaching be proposed *tamquam definitive tenendam*—as to be held definitively. Sullivan criticizes two of the four considerations Ford and I offer to show that this condition has been met in the case of the received teaching on contraception. To follow this argument, one must bear in mind a basic point: This requirement cannot mean that the infallible teaching of the ordinary magisterium must be expressed in the language of solemn definition. For the bishops dispersed throughout the world cannot define anything and do not use the language of solemn definition in their day-to-day teaching.

In his basic treatment of the infallibility of the ordinary magisterium, Sullivan refers to Salaverri's preconciliar treatise on ecclesiology for the meaning of "as to be held definitively." According to Salaverri, bishops propose something to be held definitively only "when, with the highest level of their authority, they oblige the faithful to give irrevocable assent to it."[19]

Ford and I say that what is to be held definitively is to be accepted with an assent of certitude, as undoubted.[70] Is not such an assent "irrevocable?" It might seem so, for one who assents to something as certain does not consider that assent recallable or reversible. However, "irrevocable" is often used in legal contexts, and so it can mislead by connoting a formality not characteristic of submission to the ordinary magisterium—a formality usually not present in a Christian's assent of faith, although it can be, as when an adult convert professes the faith. Thus, "irrevocable" suggests, misleadingly, that bishops never propose anything to be held definitively without consciously acting *as* authorities and formally demanding that the faithful obey *as* subjects.

Is there any reason to think that Vatican II intended to refer only to instances of teaching involving such formality when it said that the position must be proposed as to be held definitively? Sullivan supplies none. Against it is that holding something definitively either is or is like assenting to it with faith. (The motive will not be that of divine faith if the point pertains to the secondary object of infallibility.) But without formalities, bishops in their ordinary teaching frequently propose revealed truths to be held with faith. Hence, they can propose without formalities other truths to be held definitively.

Logically, this can happen because the certitude of one's assent is neither identical with nor necessarily related to the level of authority at which a teaching is proposed or the severity of the obligation to assent. A bishop can limit himself to gentle persuasion in communicating a truth he considers to pertain to faith. For instance, a bishop might not invoke his authority or demand "irrevocable assent" if he is trying to reconcile opposing groups who think that only the Latin Mass is valid and only Mass in the vernacular is valid. Even if he believed the validity of both a truth to be held definitively and wished people to accept it as such, the bishop might not say so.

Sullivan also quotes comments of Karl Rahner, S.J., on *Lumen gentium*, 25. Rahner makes three points bearing on the meaning of "as to be held definitively." First, he says that the draft of 10 November 1962 did not include the clause "*tamquam definitive tenendam*, which is very important in judging the intention of the final text." Second, Rahner says that "an absolutely strict and irreformable assent must be explicitly called for." Third, he argues: "It has often been assumed in the past, with practical effects, that a doctrine is irreformable in the Church simply because it has been generally taught without clearly notable contradiction over a considerable period of time. This view runs counter to the facts, because many doctrines which were once universally held have proved to be problematic or erroneous, and is fundamentally unsound."[72]

The fact that the November 1962 draft did not include *tamquam definitive tenendam* is significant, but not in the way Rahner's comment suggests. For this qualification was introduced when "in handing on the revealed faith" was replaced with "teaching on matters of faith and morals" to avoid *restricting* the infallibility of the episcopal body to points proposed to be believed as divinely revealed.[72] The phrase was not chosen to tighten what would otherwise have been a looser requirement.

Rahner gives no argument and offers no basis in the Council's documents for his requirement that "an absolutely strict and irreformable assent must be explicitly called for." The reasons for questioning Sullivan's introduction of "irrevocable" from Salaverri apply here too. Of course, there are times when assent is called for explicitly, namely, when the extraordinary magisterium solemnly defines a proposition. The word "irreformable" also appears in this context, for it properly qualifies a definition rather than an act of assenting. Vatican I, for example, speaks of the "irreformable" definitions of popes teaching ex cathedra.[73] Rahner tends here to reduce the requirements for infallible teaching by the ordinary magisterium to those for solemn definitions, and thus to leave no room for the infallibility of the ordinary magisterium.

As to the third point, I agree with Rahner in rejecting the view that "a doctrine is irreformable in the Church simply because it has been generally taught without clearly notable contradiction over a considerable period of time." This formulation is too loose; it omits the requirement that the teaching be proposed as certain. Moreover, as already explained, it is not exact to say that a doctrine infallibly taught by the ordinary magisterium is "irreformable."

IX

Ford and I stated as follows what we think is meant by "as to be held definitively":

> The genesis of the text makes clear that what is demanded if the exercise of the ordinary magisterium is to be infallible is that a judgment be proposed for acceptance with an assent of certitude, similar to the assent of divine faith, but not necessarily having the same motive as has the latter assent. The formula in the second schema *De ecclesia Christi* of Vatican I, which Vatican II cites as comparable with its own teaching, refers to points held or handed down *as undoubted*. Thus, "to be held definitively" clearly excludes cases in which a bishop proposes a view as a safe and probable opinion, but only as such.

> A point of teaching surely is proposed as one to be held definitively if a bishop proposes it in the following way: not at his option but as part of his duty to hand on the teaching he has received; not as doubtful or even as very probable but as certainly true; and not as one which the faithful are free to accept or to reject but as one which every Catholic must accept.[74]

When Sullivan specifically criticizes our arguments that the teaching on contraception has been proposed "as to be held definitively," he recalls his account of this requirement based on Salaverri and Rahner, quotes the second paragraph of Ford's and my explanation without the first, and then says: "Now it seems to me that there is a very real difference between authoritative teaching which calls upon the faithful to give their assent to it as certainly true, and the kind of teaching which proposes a doctrine as irreformably true and calls for an irrevocable assent."[75]

By "irreformably true" and "irrevocable assent," Sullivan again tends to set a standard met only in the case of solemn definitions. But he realizes he needs some argument to show that "as to be held definitively" means more than "as certainly true." So he quotes a passage from John Reed, S.J., who recognizes not only infallible teaching both in solemn definitions and by the ordinary magisterium, but authoritative teaching which falls short of infallibility. Reed points out the distinction between infallibility and certainty:

> In matters of conduct, a doctrine which is not taught with the plenitude of infallibility may still be taught with certainty, in the sense of moral, practical, certitude, so as to exclude any solidly probable opinion to the contrary here and now, i.e. with the effect that at a given time a particular mode of conduct is certainly licit or certainly illicit, without the abstract question of its relation to right order being definitively closed. Infallibility excludes the absolute possibility of error. Certitude, in the sense of moral, or practical, certitude, excludes the prudent, proximate fear of error.[76]

The point Reed makes here is sound. However, the way he puts it is confusing.

Reed's point is that popes and other bishops can provide authoritative moral guidance, even when they are not absolutely certain that the guidance they give is true. In such cases, they obviously should be morally certain—sure beyond a reasonable doubt. Given such guidance, the faithful have the duty of religious assent and obedience. (Notice, however, when such guidance is that a particular kind of action is licit, it frees rather than burdens consciences.)

But Reed's way of putting his point can mislead. By contrasting what is taught with "the plenitude of infallibility" with what is taught with "moral certitude," Reed both suggests that these are direct opposites and that there is nothing between them. However, there is another category.

In their day-to-day teaching, bishops do not individually teach "with the plenitude of infallibility," even when they hand on revealed truths which call for the assent of faith. Rather, they simply teach truths—those which are revealed as such, those closely connected with revelation as certain, and those they consider sufficiently probable and important as safe judgments to accept and follow. Infallibility supervenes on acts of day-to-day teaching if all the conditions are met. But the bishops in teaching and the faithful in accepting their teaching usually do not reflect upon the supervening infallibility. Thus, doctrines taught infallibly by the ordinary magisterium are not "taught with the plenitude of infallibility." Only solemn definitions are proposed in that way.

Hence, *what is taught with the plenitude of infallibility* and *what is taught as only morally certain* are not the only categories. A bishop might propose an implicitly revealed truth to be held with faith, yet his teaching would not be infallible if the truth had not been defined and had not yet been proposed by many other bishops. Again, a bishop can propose moral teachings already infallibly taught as if they were only morally certain, because he happens to be unclear about their status.

In any case, bishops can propose teachings as more or less certain. To propose something as "morally certain" is one way of proposing it as probable enough to follow in practice. That would not meet the requirement set in *Lumen gentium,* 25, as Ford and I explain it: The teaching must be held and handed down "as undoubted," proposed "not as doubtful or even as very probable but as certainly true," not as a "safe and probable opinion" but as a "judgment to be held definitively."

X

Ford and I offer four considerations to show that the teaching on contraception was proposed as a norm to be held definitively.

The first of these we called a "negative" point: "We know of no evidence—and Noonan points to none—that anyone handed on the received teaching as if it were a private opinion, a merely probable judgment, or a commendable ideal which the faithful might nevertheless blamelessly choose to leave unrealized. The teaching always was proposed as a received and certain part of the obligatory moral teaching of the Church."[77] Obviously this point is not entirely negative. Sullivan ignores it; Ford and I considered it basic.

The next consideration we advance pivots on the fact that the teaching on contraception concerns grave matter:

> Second, the teaching is that acts intended to impede pro-creation are in species gravely evil—that is, are the matter of mortal sin. This fact . . . makes clear the unqualified character of the intellectual assent demanded for the teaching. When the Church proposes a moral teaching as one which Christians must try to follow if they are to be saved, she a fortiori presents the teaching as one which must be accepted as certain. The magisterium permitted no differing opinions about the morality of contraception, and so probabilism was inapplicable. Thus the condition under which the teaching was proposed left no room for doubt in the matter.[78]

Sullivan calls this our "principal argument" to show that the sinfulness of contraception was taught as a moral norm to be held definitively: "They base this claim primarily on the fact that the magisterium condemned contraceptive behaviour as gravely sinful."[79]

But Sullivan does not deal with the statement of the argument quoted above, where we actually make our case. Instead, he selects a one-sentence summary from an answer to an objection much later in the article: "To propose a norm excluding some kind of act as mortally sinful is to propose a teaching to be held definitively."[80] This summary is overly compact; I admit that, considered by itself, it is not sound.

The first point Sullivan makes is that a teaching could be proposed that something is morally certainly gravely illicit without that meaning (in Reed's language) that "the speculative question is definitively closed."[81] I concede this point and now say (contrary to Ford's and my summary of the argument): To propose a norm excluding some kind of act as mortally sinful need not be to propose a teaching to be held definitively. The content of the teaching and the kind of assent called for are at least logically distinct. A bishop could propose a norm excluding some kind of act (for example, working in an H-bomb factory) as mortally sinful but expressly propose that norm as probable rather than as certain. (But a conscientious bishop would not say *without qualification* that something is mortally sinful if he had the least doubt about it.)

Sullivan sums up his case on this point: "It is one thing to teach that something involves a serious moral obligation; it is quite another to claim that this teaching is now absolutely definitive, and demands an irrevocable assent." He thinks our argument "would practically rule out any ordinary, noninfallible exercise of the Church's teaching authority on moral issues."[82] Here Sullivan restates the point I concede—that teaching about grave matter is not necessarily proposed as certain—within the framework of his interpretation, which tends to reduce the conditions for infallible teaching by the ordinary magisterium to those for a solemn definition.

Although I concede that teaching about grave matter need not be proposed as to be held definitively, still I can complete the consideration Ford and I advanced by supplying a missing premise. We should have pointed out a norm for Catholic teachers on which St. Alphonsus and several other doctors of the Church insist: Catholic teachers never should unqualifiedly assert anything to be grave matter unless they are certain it is.[83] This norm for pastors and teachers is almost always observed, because most try hard to avoid putting unnecessary burdens on the faithful. Hence, where grave matter is involved, the whole body of bishops in communion with the pope never will agree in unqualifiedly proposing a norm unless they consider it certain—to be held definitively.

Thus, I admit that there is no necessary logical relationship between the grave matter contained in a norm and the certain assent called for by those who teach it. But I deny that any sin was included all over the world in Christian lists of mortal sins unless the norm excluding that kind of act was received, held, and handed on as an inescapable requirement of God's plan for Christian life—not merely as "morally certain" but as undoubted—to be held definitively.

XI

The third consideration Ford and I advanced to show that the norm concerning contraception was proposed to be held definitively points to another set of facts: "Third, the insistent repetition of the received teaching in recent times when it was called into question outside the Catholic Church often included and always implied the proposition that this is an obligatory teaching, one which every Catholic must hold even though it is denied by other Christians."[84] Sullivan ignores this consideration, as he does the first.

He goes on at once to the fourth consideration we advanced: "The other argument Ford and Grisez use to show that the doctrine on contraception was being taught as to be held definitively is that it was often proposed as a divinely revealed moral norm."[85] He then quotes the first and last paragraphs of this consideration:

> The teaching on the morality of contraception often was proposed as a moral norm divinely revealed. Since it was proposed as revealed, a fortiori it was proposed as a teaching *to be held definitively.* We prescind from the question whether the evidence alleged to show that the condemnation of contraception is divinely revealed does or does not show this. The point we wish to make is simply this: when one who is proposing a teaching appeals to divine revelation to confirm the truth of what he proposes, he implicitly calls for an assent of divine faith, and thus proposes the teaching as one to be held definitively.[86]

If one considers the explicit appeals made to Gen 38:9–10 together with the implicit appeals made to the same passage, to Rom 1:26–27, and to the Ten Commandments, one realizes that most who handed on the Catholic teaching on contraception claimed the authority of Scripture, which they believed to be the authority of divine revelation, in support of this teaching. Whether one thinks this claim was valid or not—a question we are not considering here—no one can deny that those who made it proposed the teaching on behalf of which they made it as a moral norm *to be held definitively*.[87]

Sullivan's criticism of this argument is brief:

> Now it seems to me that if this argument were valid, it would eliminate practically all ordinary, non-definitive teaching by the magisterium. For, whenever any appeal was made to Scripture in support of what was being taught, this would automatically become definitive teaching. Are we to conclude that the popes, who regularly appeal to Scripture in their encyclicals, have in all such cases been proposing their doctrine as definitively to be held?[85]

It seems to me this criticism involves two confusions.

First, Sullivan here introduces the phrases "non-definitive teaching" and "definitive teaching." This language shifts the focus from the kind of assent called for to the teaching which calls for assent, and again suggests that the subject of discussion is teaching by solemn definitions. Actually, acceptance of Ford's and my argument would not "eliminate practically all ordinary, non-definitive teaching by the magisterium." It would merely mean that the part of this ordinary moral teaching which all the bishops in communion with the pope agree in proposing as certain has been taught infallibly—although lacking solemn definitions it is not "definitive teaching."

Second, the argument Ford and I make does not entail that whenever the popes appeal to Scripture in their encyclicals they are proposing their doctrine as to be held definitively. For instance, in *Humanae vitae* there are sixteen references to New Testament texts, but none of them is employed to found or support the central argument and conclusion.[89] The same thing is true of most uses of Scripture in encyclicals.

But in the detailed argument between the two paragraphs Sullivan quotes, Ford and I show that Scripture texts usually have been used precisely to found or support arguments for the conclusion that contraception is morally wrong. Today everyone is much more cautious than people once were about using proof texts, and Ford and I prescind from the question whether the use of Scripture texts to certify the teaching concerning contraception was sound. But we say that when Catholic teachers claimed that God himself tells us that contraception is wrong, they proposed that norm as something divinely revealed, and thus called for an assent of faith. And that is the clearest way of proposing something *tamquam definitive tenendam*.

This consideration, it seems to me, is the decisive one. It explains why Christian teachers held not only this norm but other specific norms bearing on sex and innocent life, and proposed them to the faithful as obligatory standards for Christian living. They agreed in one judgment and proposed it so firmly because they held the common body of moral teaching, centering on and elaborating the Ten Commandments, with divine faith.

XII

In a general audience on Wednesday, 18 July 1984, John Paul II reflected on the status and ground of the norm excluding contraception:

The Church teaches this norm, although it is not formally (that is, literally) expressed in Sacred Scripture, and it does this in the conviction that the interpretation of the precepts of natural law belongs to the competence of the Magisterium. However, we can say more. Even if the moral law, formulated in this way in the Encyclical *Humanae Vitae*, is not found literally in Sacred Scripture, nonetheless, from the fact that it is contained in Tradition and—as Pope Paul VI writes—has been "very often expounded by the Magisterium" (*HV*, n. 12) to the faithful, it follows that this norm *is in accordance with the sum total*

> *of revealed doctrine contained in biblical sources* (cf. *HV*, n. 4).
> 4. It is a question here not only of the sum total of the moral doctrine contained in Sacred Scripture, of its essential premises and general character of its content, but of that fuller context to which we have previously dedicated numerous analyses when speaking about the "theology of the body."
> Precisely against the background of this full context it becomes evident that the above-mentioned moral norm belongs not only to the natural moral law, but also to the *moral order revealed by God*: also from this point of view, it could not be different, but solely what is handed down by Tradition and the Magisterium and, in our days, the Encyclical *Humanae Vitae* as a modern document of this Magisterium.[90]

Here the Pope makes at least three points: The fact that the norm excluding contraception is in accord with the sum total of revelation *follows from* its being contained in tradition and its often being expounded by the magisterium; the norm belongs to the moral order *revealed by God;* and it *could* not be different.

These three points clearly imply that the norm concerning contraception has been infallibly taught by the ordinary magisterium, that at least some specific moral norms do fall under "faith and morals," and that one can argue from the way a norm is held and handed on to its pertaining to revelation. Ford's and my view and that taken by the Pope come to the same thing. John Paul II has made a significant personal contribution: a scripturally based "theology of the body" which provides fresh evidence that Catholic teaching not only on contraception but on other questions concerning sex, marriage, and innocent life is rooted in divine revelation.

The view that revelation includes no specific moral norms goes against the convictions of Christians down through the centuries. If one sets aside the twentieth century and considers the entire previous Jewish and Christian tradition, its massiveness and unity are overwhelmingly impressive. For example, not only no Catholic but no other Christian and no Jew ever would have dared to say of adultery and killing the innocent anything but: These are wicked things, and they who do them, unless they repent, can have no part in God's kingdom. Contrary contemporary theological speculation has the burden of showing that even until yesterday the whole People of God grossly misunderstood his wise and loving commands.

Notes

1. Francis A. Sullivan, S.J., *Magisterium: Teaching Authority in the Catholic Church* (New York: Paulist Press, 1983).
2. See John C. Ford, S.J., and Germain Grisez, "Contraception and the Infallibility of the Ordinary Magisterium," *Theological Studies,* 39 (1978), 259–61.
3. DS 3011/1792; my translation.
4. *Lumen gentium,* 25; my translation.
5. See Ford-Grisez, 265–69; Sullivan, 131–36.
6. Ford-Grisez, 263–86.
7. *Lumen gentium,* 25; my translation.
8. Ford-Grisez, 287.
9. Sullivan, 143.
10. *Ibid.*; Ford-Grisez, 280–87.
11. Richard A. McCormick, S.J., "Notes on Moral Theology: 1983," *Theological Studies,* 45 (1984), 95, seems to have been misled.
12. Sullivan, 144.
13. *Ibid.*
14. *Ibid.*
15. *Ibid.*
16. *Ibid.*, 144–45.
17. *Ibid.*, 145.
18. Ford-Grisez, 287–90.
19. Sullivan, 145.
20. *Ibid.*, 131.
21. Ford-Grisez, 268–269.
22. Sullivan, 133.
23 *Ibid.*, 134.
24. See Karl Rahner, S.J., in Herbert Vorgrimler, ed., *Commentary*

on the Documents of Vatican II (New York: Herder and Herder, 1967), 1:212.

25. See J. H. Walgrave, "Doctrine, Development of," *New Catholic Encyclopedia,* 4:940–44.

26. Sullivan, 18.

27. Ford-Grisez, 272–73.

28. Sullivan, 138, quoting *Gaudium et spes,* 50.

29. *Ibid.*

30. *Gaudium et spes,* 89.

31. *Ibid.,* 50–51.

32. *Ibid.,* 51, n. 14; DS 3716-18/2239-41.

33. Sullivan, 152.

34. *Ibid.,* 137.

35. *Ibid.,* 148, in the subheading.

36. *Ibid.,* 152, 227–28 (n. 46).

37. Karl Rahner, *Nature and Grace: Dilemmas in the Modern Church* (London: Sheed and Ward, 1963), 51–52. Rahner later joined in ignoring the existence of the ordinary magisterium: *Theological Investigations,* vol. 11, *Confrontations I,* trans. David Bourke (New York: Seabury Press, 1974), 270.

38. See Germain Grisez, *The Way of the Lord Jesus,* vol. 1, *Christian Moral Principles* (Chicago: Franciscan Herald Press, 1983), 873.

39. Richard A. McCormick, S.J., *Notes on Moral Theology: 1965 through 1980* (Washington, D.C.; University Press of America, 1981), 700; cf. 528–44, 684–97, 748–57.

40. Sullivan, 128–29.

41. See T. López Rodriguez, " 'Fides et mores' en Trento," *Scripta Theologica,* 5 (1973), 175–221; Marcelino Zalba, S.J., " 'Omnis et salutaris veritas et morum disciplina': Sentido de la expresión 'mores' en el Concilio de Trento," *Gregorianum,* 54 (1973), 679–715.

42. Sullivan, 140–41.

43. *Dignitatis humanae,* 14, does not make this contrast. The Council's n. 36 (Abbott n. 57) refers to an address of Piux XII on the formation of the Christian conscience; he makes it clear that natural law also pertains to revelation.

44. The original schema used "head of the college of bishops" to specify the authority of the pope in ex cathedra teaching—see Rahner, in Vorgrimler, ed., *Commentary on the Documents of Vatican II,* 1:212. Did Vatican II's change mean it teaches the opposite?

45. Sullivan, 140.

46. *Ibid.*

47. J. D. Mansi et al, ed., *Sacrorum conciliorum nova et amplissima collectio,* 52:1224.

48. Kleutgen ("Peters") was *relator* for that *Deputatio* session: Mansi, 53:270–72.

49. Sullivan, 137, 226 (n. 23).

50. Mansi, 52:854; also 986, 1130, 1132, 1228.

51. Ford-Grisez, 271.

52. Mansi, 53:327.

53. Sullivan, 141–42; Ford-Grisez, 302.

54. Sullivan, 141.

55. *Ibid.,* 142.

56. Ford-Grisez, 294–98.

57. Sullivan, 142.

58. *Ibid.,* 149.

59. *Ibid.,* 152.

60. Richard A. McCormick, S.J., "Notes on Moral Theology, 1983," 84.

61. Sullivan, 150.

62. *Ibid.*

63. This is clear enough even in the 1917 Code Sullivan quotes (150, 227 n. 44), but even clearer in the 1983 Code, where "or declared" is omitted (Can. 749.3).

64. Sullivan, 151.

65. *Ibid.,* 152.

66. *Ibid.*

67. *Gaudium et spes,* 79.

68. *Christian Moral Principles,* 141–71 (critique of proportionalism); 859–60 and 869 n. 62 (critique of Rahner's claim about the dynamism of human nature).

69. Sullivan, 125–26.

70. Ford-Grisez, 275.

71. Sullivan, 126.

72. Ford-Grisez, 267.

73. DS 3074/1839.

74. Ford-Grisez, 275–76.

75. Sullivan, 146.

76. Quoted, *ibid.*

77. Ford-Grisez, 281–82.

78. *Ibid.,* 282.

70. Sullivan, 147.

80. *Ibid.*; Ford-Grisez, 295.

81. Sullivan, 147.

82. *Ibid.*

83. S. Alphonsus Maria de Ligorio, *Theologia Moralis,* ed. L. Gaudé (Rome: Typographia Vaticana, 1905–9), 1:456: "Ad hoc igitur ut actio aliqua sit graviter illicita requiritur certitudo prout docet omnes"; and he goes on to cite St. Raymond, St. Antoninus, and Benedict XIV. He often repeats this point and provides additional citations: 1:51, 70, 445; 2:53, 747–48; 3:627.

84. Ford-Grisez, 282.

85. Sullivan, 147.

86. Ford-Grisez, 282; Sullivan, 147–48; he deletes "Fourth" from the beginning.

87. Ford-Grisez, 284–85; Sullivan, 148.

88. Sullivan, 148.

89. See Joseph A. Komonchak, "*Humanae Vitae* and Its Reception: Ecclesiological Reflections," *Theological Studies,* 30 (1978), 251.

90. John Paul II, "General Audience of 18 July," *L'Osservatore Romano* (Eng. ed.), 23 July 1984, 1.

Authority & Conscience

Avery Dulles

This article originally appeared in *Church* in 1986.

The tension between authority and conscience arises in many areas of life—for example, in the citizen's relationship to political authority, in the scholar's relation to academic authorities, and in the believer's relation to the church. In fact, the problem is likely to emerge anywhere that authority asserts itself and is thought to impose an obligation to assent or obey. Thus a child might feel justified in disobeying its parents, or a soldier in refusing to follow the command of an officer. When we hear about conflicts of this kind, our sympathies are torn between respect for the rights of conscience and impatience with those who fail to heed the voice of authority. The liberal spontaneously identifies with the dissident; the conservative spontaneously sides with the guardians of conformity and order.

According to the Catholic ethical tradition, conscience is the ultimate subjective norm of all human action. By conscience I do not here mean a blind feeling or instinct but a personal and considered judgment about what one ought, or ought not, to do or to have done. By calling conscience the subjective norm, moral theologians intend to distinguish it from the objective norm, which is frequently described as right reason, that is, reason that apprehends the objective order of things, including the will of God as manifested through nature and revelation. A person's conscience can be out of phase with what is objectively right. In such a case the individual will not be guilty for following the voice of conscience, but may be guilty for having failed to form that conscience by utilizing the necessary means. Conscience, therefore, is not autonomous. It cannot speak clearly unless it has been properly educated. When we are in doubt about whether our conscience is correct we have an obligation to seek guidance and instruction.

Without denying the normative value of conscience for the individual, public authority must also defend the rights of persons who might be injured by others seeking to follow the dictates of an erroneous conscience. The fact that a man thinks he ought to commit a murder does not imply the right to carry out such a crime. The state seeks to deter criminal actions, however well intended, and even uses force to restrain criminals from doing what they may feel conscientiously obliged to do. Thus the rights of conscience are far from absolute.

Most societies, of course, try to keep physical compulsion to a minimum. They try to educate members of the community so that each will have a moral judgment that supports the common good. Rather early in life, individuals are subjected to education that will socialize them into the group. The young are trained by parents and teachers in whose selection they have little or no choice. But through such training their freedom is nurtured so that later they can make mature and principled choices. Without social formation we could have only an infantile and stunted freedom. The members of every social group form their personal moral norms with some dependence on the group and its authorities. Among the authorities are the rituals and stories of the group, its customs, its prevalent axioms, its legal and literary classics, its heroes, and its living teachers. Authority is the voice of those who are presumed to be able to furnish reliable guidance. Just as we turn to lawyers, doctors, and investment counselors in their respective spheres of competence, so we turn to specialists to guide us in making moral decisions. But we remain morally free to disregard the experts and go against their recommendation, if we judge that they have erred. As the general reaction to the Nazi "crimes against humanity" illustrated, obedience is no excuse for doing what offends against an upright conscience.

The relationship between authority and personal judgment may be described as dialectical. That is to say, the two are neither identical nor separable. Our personal convictions about what is right and wrong are at least partially shaped by what the community and its leaders have taught us, and on the basis of those convictions we determine whether to follow the community's authorities in a given instance. To the extent that we have been successfully socialized into the community, our free and spontaneous judgments about right and wrong tend to coincide with the rules and expectations of the community.

Cases of conflict are the exception rather than the rule. Yet such cases do arise. In the area of civil life we are familiar with the phenomena of loyal dissent and conscientious objection. An enlightened government with a tradition of civil liberties makes provision for the rights of those who feel bound in conscience not to serve as combatants in a given war, or not to undergo blood transfusions. Yet there are limits to what people are permitted to do in the name of conscience. As I have already indicated, they are not permitted to trample on the rights of other persons or to jeopardize the common good.

In the academic world similar conflict situations sometimes occur. The school or university maintains the right to select professors who will impart the ideas and values that it regards as educational. Faculty members, on the other hand, insist on their right to communicate the convictions they have reached on the basis of serious research and reflection. To protect both sets of rights as far as possible, universities have adopted elaborate procedures for hiring, promotion, and dismissal. Sometimes respect for academic freedom compels them to retain faculty members of whose teaching they disapprove—a procedure that the academic world regards as preferable to giving the administration discretionary authority to dismiss otherwise competent professors whose ideas are deemed unacceptable.

These introductory remarks about political and educational institutions can greatly help us to understand the subject of "Church Authority and Freedom of Conscience." The problems in each case are similar, and yet also profoundly different. The analogies between the church and institutions such as the secular state and the independent university are helpful only to a limited extent, because the church, while it has the features of a human society, is very different in its purposes, origins, and means. Neither the state nor the independent university, at least as conceived in our American tradition, is committed to any substantive set of beliefs about the ultimate nature of reality. The state is a community of people willing to live together under the same laws, even though they may vehemently disagree in their philosophies and theologies. The academy is a community of scholars committed to adhere to certain methods of investigation and communication, but not necessarily sharing any common convictions about the way things are. The church, however, is by nature a society of faith and witness. It exists only to the extent that it continues to adhere to a very specific vision of the world—one centered on Jesus Christ as Lord and Savior. Unlike any secular organization, the church has a deposit of faith that must be maintained intact and transmitted to new members. Thus the church cannot accommodate the same kind of ideological pluralism that is acceptable in the secular state or university.

A second difference flows from the origin of the church. Unlike the secular state, the university, or any other institution on the face of the earth, the church, according to Christian belief, has been established by the action of God in Jesus Christ. The members of the church, including the highest officeholders, are not free to change in a substantive way the beliefs, structures, purposes, and forms of worship of the church. They are trustees, obliged to safeguard the trust committed to them.

Third, the church differs from other societies in the means whereby it discharges its mission. Unlike the secular state and many other organized groups, the church, at least in modern times, does not use physical coercion. It has no prisons and does not execute persons convicted of crimes such as heresy. It uses only the "sword of the spirit," which works through love and persuasion and does not impose even spiritual penalties except in the hope of bringing about repentance and reform. The Declaration on Religious Freedom adopted at Vatican Council II, in asserting these principles, cautiously admitted that in the history of the church "there have at times appeared ways of acting which were less in accord with the spirit of the gospel and even opposed to it" (*DH* 12).

The church also has at her disposal special aids not available to other societies. It has received from apostolic times inspired Scriptures and inspired traditions as expressions of its faith and guideposts for future development. Christ, moreover, has promised to remain with the community and its official leaders to the end of time. "Behold, I am with you all days, even to the close of the age" (Mt 28:20). In the Catholic tradition the hierarchy is considered to be included in the promises originally directed by Christ to the apostles, such as "Whoever hears you hears me" (Lk 10:16) and "As the Father has sent me, I send you" (Jn 20:21). The confidence in the continuing presence of Christ in the church and its hierarchy profoundly affects the attitudes of believing Catholics toward ecclesiastical authority. They are convinced that in submitting to popes and bishops as teachers and rulers, they are submitting to Christ and to God.

When we think of authority in the church, we must surely include Scripture and tradition, popes and bishops, but the system of authorities is in fact much more complex and extensive. As Vatican II clearly taught, Scripture and tradition were not committed only to the hierarchy, but to the church as a whole (*DV* 10). All the members of the church share in the priestly, prophetic, and royal offices of Christ and therefore have their own part to play in the mission of the church (*AA* 2). Thanks to a supernatural sense of the faith which characterizes the people of God as a whole (*LG* 12), believers can find reliable guidance in turning to the community of faith. As Cardinal Newman pointed out in his celebrated article "On Consulting the Faithful," even popes have been accustomed to seek out the opinions of the Christian people before they define matters of doctrine. Quoting Hilary of Poitiers as a witness, Newman maintained that at times the ears of the faithful have been holier than the hearts of their bishops. Thus, when we think of the authorities available to the Catholic Christian, we should not overlook the consensus of the faithful themselves.

Still another source of authority in Catholicism is that of theologians. The Catholic church has always had a deep resepct for learning and intelligence. It has conferred on outstanding theologians the titles of Father or Doctor of the Church. John Wycliffe in the fourteenth century and Martin Luther in the sixteenth century were censured because, among other things, they failed to respect the authority of the theological schools. In the late Middle Ages and in early modern times, university faculties of theology exercised a true magisterium, rendering ecclesiastically recognized judgments as to the orthodoxy or heterodoxy of new opinions. Although theological faculties no longer exercise such an independent magisterium, they have continued to collaborate very closely with popes and bishops in making judgments about heresy and in drawing up official doctrinal formulations.

The relationship between the hierarchy and the theologians, at least as it stands in modern times, can be clarified by a distinction between official and personal authority. The popes and bishops, as members of the hierarchy, enjoy authority by virtue of their status or position in the church. Their statements have authority not so much because of their personal wisdom and prudence as because of their sacramental ordination and the office they hold. With theologians the reverse is true. Whatever authority they enjoy accrues to them not primarily because of their position but rather because of their reputation for learning and acumen. Even their scholarly degrees and academic appointments are significant merely as presumptive signs of personal ability.

Once the distinction is understood it becomes apparent why theologians are normally used as consultants by popes and bishops. The authority of office does not simply take the place of personal authority. Rather, it requires for its proper exercise that the office-bearer either be a personal authority or make use of others who have personal authority. Otherwise the authority of office will be brought into disrespect, to the great detriment of the church. The authority of office is a kind of gift or charism which, if utilized well, enables the officeholders to draw upon the knowledge and wisdom that is present in the whole community, including the scholars, and bring this to a focus, as it were. In so doing, the hierarchy is able to formulate the church's faith in an official way, and to make judgments about the compatibility of current opinions with that faith.

In its official statements the hierarchical magisterium sometimes imposes a given formulation as an apt expression of the truth of the gospel. Sometimes it condemns a misleading formulation as contrary to that truth. And sometimes it makes judgments of a permissive character, stating not that a given opinion is true but that it may be held and is not to be condemned as heretical. Thus the magisterium serves as an agency for protecting the legitimate freedom of theologians to speculate about the truth without harassment from rival theological schools.

When the hierarchy is faced by a conflict of opinions in the church, it does not always succeed in achieving a perfectly adequate response. Broadly speaking, two kinds of mistake are possible—excessive permissiveness and excessive rigidity. It is hard to know which of the two errors has done more harm.

The first of the two errors was more common at certain earlier periods in history, when communication between Rome and the other churches was difficult. During the first half of the Middle Ages, when there was little contact between Rome and Constantinople, the Eastern and Western churches developed different ways of thinking about subjects such as the Trinity; the two groups drifted apart until they finally ceased to be able to recognize each other's formulations as orthodox. Then again, before the Reformation, theological pluralism in Northern Europe ran to excess. For example, some Nominalist theologians professed an inordinate optimism about human nature, holding that even without grace human beings could perfectly observe the moral law and perform meritorious acts that God would be obliged to reward. Reacting against this, some Augustinians held that human nature had been so corrupted by the Fall that it was impossible for human beings to do anything but sin unless God's grace were to take hold of them, so to speak, by main force. Although doctrinal issues were not the sole cause of the Protestant Reformation, it is possible that the tragic split could have been averted had the excessive pluralism been held in check by a timely exercise of church authority. The price of unity, it may be said, is perpetual doctrinal vigilance.

After the sixteenth century, the Roman magisterium did practice vigilance, but in some cases it was inclined to condemn new opinions without sufficient deliberation. A famous example is the Galileo case. More recently, in the first decades of the twentieth century, the Roman Biblical Commission issued a whole series of decrees that proved, with the passage of time, unduly restrictive.

For a generation or so, Catholic biblical scholars were severely hampered in their dealings with colleagues from other traditions on the basis of new scholarly discoveries. Fortunately, in the pontificate of Pius XII, the restrictions were eased, and the result has been an unprecedented flowering of Catholic biblical scholarship.

In retrospect, it seems clear that the reactions of the Roman magisterium to new developments in the physical and historical sciences were excessively defensive. But that was not so clear at the time. When the new theories first arose, the faith of many Catholics was troubled. Perhaps by its conservatism in these matters the hierarchy did in fact shield the faith of many Catholics who would have been shaken by the new advances, and gave a needed space of time in which the compatibility of the new science with the old faith could be discerned. Many liberal Protestants, who impetuously embraced the latest hypotheses, ended up by watering down their faith, or even losing it entirely.

We must recognize, therefore, that there can be such a thing in the church as mutable or reformable teaching. The element of mutability comes from the fact that such teaching seeks to mediate between the abiding truth of the gospel and the sociocultural situation at a given time and place. For example, the condemnations of usury in the Middle Ages were based upon valid moral principles, but were linked, more than was recognized at the time, to a precapitalist economy. Once the shift to capitalism had been made, the moral teaching had to be modified. Other changes in doctrine were linked to new astronomical discoveries, (such as the overthrow of the Ptolemaic system), new biological theories (such as evolutionism), new methods in historical criticism, and new developments in politics.

Changes such as those just mentioned have led to important shifts in Catholic doctrine, even within recent memory. Vatican II approved of new attitudes toward biblical studies, religious freedom, and ecumenism. Those who have lived through these changes have learned how important it is not to confuse reformable doctrine with the content of the faith itself.

At this point we may raise again the question of conscience. In any response to magisterial teaching conscience is of course involved. Two questions must be asked: Can we conscientiously assent, and can we conscientiously do other than assent?

The answer will be different according to the kind of teaching involved. In some instances, rather rare, the church invokes her infallible teaching power. Practically speaking, this happens only in matters close to the heart of Christian faith, after much consultation and deliberation, where there has been a virtually unanimous consensus for a long period of time. In such cases the faithful are under strong pressure to assent, for the church has committed itself to such a degree that to reject the definition is in effect to reject the church itself. An outright denial of a recognized dogma or other infallible teaching is tantamount to a renunciation of the Catholic faith, and entails a rupture of communion.

On the other hand we must recognize that a given individual may experience considerable anguish in yielding assent, even to a dogma. A poorly educated Catholic, or one strongly influenced by the secular mentality of the day, may feel compelled to say; I do not understand the meaning of this dogma, or if I understand it correctly I do not see how it can be true, but I trust that if it were better explained to me I might be able to find meaning and credibility in it. Such a reaction, though far from ideal, could be an honest one, compatible with an upright conscience. A person who reacted in this way could still be considered a Catholic Christian.

Most of the difficulty arises in the sphere of noninfallible teaching, which, as we have seen, is reformable. Such teaching is not proposed as the word of God, nor does the church ask its members to submit with the assent of faith. Rather, the church asks for what is called in official documents *obsequium animi religiosum*—a term which, depending on the context, can be suitably translated by "religious submission of the mind," "respectful readiness to accept," or some such phrase. This term actually includes a whole range of responses that vary according to the context of the teaching, its relationship to the gospel, the kind of biblical and traditional support behind it, the degree of assent given to it in the church at large, the person or office from which the teaching comes, the kind of document in which it appears, the constancy of the teaching, and the emphasis given to the teaching in the text or texts. Because the matter is so complex, one cannot make any general statement about what precisely amounts to "religious submission of the mind." (See on this subject Ladislas Orsy, S.J., "Reflections on the Text of a Canon," *America,* May 17, 1986, pp. 396–99.)

Normally, the response of the Catholic to official but noninfallible teaching will be something more than a respectful hearing and something less than a full commitment of faith. Unless one has serious reasons for thinking that the magisterium has erred in the particular case, conscience will prompt one to submit on the basis that the magisterium is generally trustworthy. Some have compared the guidance of the magisterium in such matters to that of a doctor or lawyer, but the differences are important. The doctor or lawyer is not divinely commissioned and the content of such professional advice would normally have little relation to salvation. Because of the promise of Christ to be with the pastors of the church when they teach in the area of faith and morals, we have special assurances that in following them we are not being led astray.

With respect to noninfallible teaching, therefore, there are two possible errors. One would be to treat it as if it were infallible. Such an excessive emphasis could overtax the individual's capacity to assent and could lead to a real crisis of faith in the event of a later change of doctrine. The opposite error would be to treat noninfallible magisterial teaching as though it were simply a matter of theological opinion. This would be an error for the reasons already explained. The hierarchy is not just a group of theorists, but a body of pastors who are sacramentally ordained and commissioned as teachers of the faith.

Which of the two errors is the greater temptation for American Catholics? In the generation before Vatican II, when they were still something of a foreign enclave, American Catholics gloried in their obedience to their clergy and to Rome. An exaggerated conformism still persists in certain circles. But the more prevalent danger today is that of excessive distrust. Charles Dickens, in 1842, identified this as an American trait:

> One great blemish in the popular mind of America, and
> the prolific parent of an innumerable brood of evils, is

Universal Distrust. Yet the American citizen plumes himself upon the spirit, even when he is sufficiently dispassionate to perceive the ruin it works; and will often adduce it, in spite of his own reason, as an instance of the great sagacity and acuteness of the people, and their superior shrewdness and independence.

When he remonstrated that this trait had bad effects on public life, Dickens received invariably the same reply: "There's freedom of opinion here, you know. Every man thinks for himself, and we are not to be easily overreached. That's how our people come to be suspicious." Turning a little later to the subject of religious dissent, Dickens observed that it would be impossible to have an established church in America. "I think that the temper of the people, if it admitted of such an Institution being founded amongst them, would lead them to desert it, as a matter of course, merely because it *was* established." (See Charles Dickens, *American Notes*, [London: Oxford University Press, pp. 244–49]).

Since Vatican II a certan number of Catholics in this country, having become thoroughly Americanized, resent any interference with their freedom to think as they see fit. When confronted by anything less than a solemn dogmatic pronouncement from Rome, they are inclined to respond: "This teaching is not infallible; I do not have to believe it." Such Catholics might do well to ask themselves whether it is really better to believe less rather than more, and to be defiant rather than trusting. Do their critical attitudes in fact correspond to the ideas of humility, concord, and submission that are so powerfully commended in the New Testament?

In the normal case conscience and authority are not opposed. Conscience is not a law unto itself, but seeks by its very nature to be conformed to the law of God. Conscience therefore bids one to recognize authority, and authority, in turn, educates one's conscience. Only through a perversion of speech does conscience come to be coupled with dissent and authority with abuse. Conscience and authority normally concur because both are given by the same God as helps for knowing what is to believed and done.

Even when all of this has been said, it still remains true that there are cases in which a person's conscience will permit or re-

quire the nonacceptance of some reformable teaching. Vatican II
in effect admitted this by employing as prominent experts a number of theologians whose views had been suspect during the pontificate of Pius XII. Without explicitly contradicting previous papal
doctrine, the council took many positions that in fact corrected
what had been previously taught.

Did Vatican II teach the legitimacy of dissent from noninfallible teaching? It did so implicitly by its action, we may say, but not
explicitly by its words. The theological commission responsible for
paragraph 25 of the Constitution of the Church refused to make
any statement, one way or the other, about dissent.

A step beyond the council was taken by the German bishops
in a pastoral letter of September 22, 1967, which has been quoted
on several occasions by Karl Rahner. This letter recognized that in
its effort to apply the gospel to the changing situations of life, the
church is obliged to give instructions that have a certain provision-
ality about them. These instructions, though binding to a certain
degree, are subject to error. According to the bishops, dissent may
be legitimate provided that three conditions are observed. (1) One
must have striven seriously to attach positive value to the teaching
in question and to appropriate it personally. (2) One must seriously ponder whether one has the theological expertise to disagree
responsibly with ecclesiastical authority. (3) One must examine
one's conscience for possible conceit, presumptuousness, or selfish-
ness. Similar principles for conscientious dissent had already been
laid down by John Henry Newman in the splendid chapter on
Conscience in his *Letter to the Duke of Norfolk* (1874).

A year after the German bishops, the United States hierarchy,
on November 15, 1968, took up the question of licit dissent from
noninfallible doctrine on the part of theological scholars. Their
pastoral letter, entitled *Human Life in Our Day*, fundamentally
agreed with the German letter except that it went somewhat further in dealing with the *expression* of theological dissent. It laid
down three conditions: (1) The reasons must be serious and well-
founded; (2) the manner of the dissent must not question or impugn the teaching authority of the church; and (3) the dissent must
not be such as to give scandal. The American bishops added, as

had the German bishops, that even responsible dissent does not excuse one from faithful presentation of the authentic doctrine of the church when one is performing a pastoral ministry in her name (USCC ed, p. 19).

In view of collective pastoral letters such as those of the German and American bishops' conferences, it now seems impossible to deny that dissent from the noninfallible magisterium is sometimes licit. For to deny such liceity would be to dissent from the teaching of these documents, which lay down conditions under which such dissent may be permitted. Anyone who wants to reject the teaching of these documents on dissent is thereby dissenting from the noninfallible magisterium, and thus confirming that very teaching.

It is by no means accidental that documents such as these two pastorals should have been issued several years after Vatican II, for the council by its doctrinal shifts ineluctably raised the question of licit dissent. These pastorals do not solve all the problems. Difficult questions can arise as to whether a given teaching is fallible or infallible and whether the conditions for legitimate dissent have been met. Distinctions have to be made between internal dissent, private dissent, public dissent, and organized dissent.

It is relatively easy to justify internal (or tacit) dissent, for there are cases in which Catholics of good will find themselves simply unable to accept certain teachings of the magisterium. It is more difficult to justify the expression of dissent, but as we have seen, the United States bishops do admit that this can be licit under certain conditions. If the dissent is expressed only privately, for example, in letters or memoranda circulated to a limited number of persons, there is little danger that the faithful will be misled and the public disedified. But there may be occasions when the dissenter has the right, and even the conscientious obligation, to go public. If theologians such as Yves Congar and John Courtney Murray had not publicly manifested their disagreement with certain official teachings, it is far less likely that Vatican II, under their influence, would have adopted new positions on subjects such as ecumenism and religious freedom. Another consideration is that in the world of our day it is often very difficult to keep one's communications private.

Dissent is said to be "organized" when a deliberate effort is made to influence public opinion against a decision of the magisterium. Richard A. McCormick has pointed out that organized dissent of this kind carries with it special risks and hence demands special warrants. Among the risks he lists the following: it tends to polarize scholars and hierarchical teachers in opposition to each other; it tends to undermine the confidence of the faithful in their pastors; it tends to politicize the church and to discourage truly personal reflection, and finally, it tends to associate theology with the popular media rather than with serious scholarship. The special warrants for such dissent, according to McCormick, are two: (1) Other forms of less sensational dissent are ineffective and (2) the circumstances are such that unopposed error would cause grave harm (cf. *Theological Studies* 30 [1969] 652). Provided that both these conditions are verified, a theologian might feel conscientiously obliged to conduct a campaign of organized dissent, but it is almost inevitable that others would deplore this action and seek to make it ineffective. The church can rather easily tolerate internal or privately expressed dissent, but it can scarcely help but oppose public and organized dissent to the extent that this would in effect set up a second magisterium in opposition to that of the hierarchy.

Some very difficult cases regarding dissent arise in connection with theological education. It is often said, with good reason, that the faithful are entitled to have official Catholic doctrine presented to them in a fair and favorable light. But such presentations can be made at various levels. In catechetical instruction the teacher is expected to present the doctrine of the church rather than the opinions of private theologians. But the case is not so simple in higher education. University students, especially at the graduate level, have the right to know the difference between reformable and irreformable teaching. With regard to the former, as Professor Francis A. Sullivan, S.J., of the Gregorian University has recently stated, they have the right to know that there are dissenting positions, and a right to know the arguments on both sides. (See NC News Service for May 6, 1986.) A professor who adheres to the official teaching must be able to present the objections fairly, and one who questions the official teaching must be able to present them in a favorable light. A professor who fails on either score is deficient by academic standards.

There is always a temptation for church authorities to try to use their power to stamp out dissent. The effort is rarely successful, because dissent simply seeks another forum, where it may become even more virulent. To the extent that the suppression is successful, it may also do harm. It inhibits good theology from performing its critical task, and it is detrimental to the atmosphere of freedom in the church. The acceptance of true doctrine should not be a matter of blind conformity, as though truth could be imposed by decree. The church, as a society that respects the freedom of the human conscience, must avoid procedures that savor of intellectual tyranny.

Where dissent is kept within the bounds I have indicated, it is not fatal to the church as a community of faith and witness. If it does occur, it will be limited, reluctant, and respectful. Those who, in their zeal for orthodoxy, would wish to suppress dissent by coercive measures, might advantageously meditate on the gospel parable of the good grain and the weeds. When asked by the servants whether the weeds should be uprooted, the Master replied: "No; lest in gathering the weeds you root up the wheat along with them. Let both grow together until the harvest" (Mt 13:28–30). The mistaken doctrines of hierarchical teachers and of theologians can alike be considered weeds, but it is not easy, at any given moment, to discern exactly which doctrines are mistaken. For this reason it is often necessary to allow both to survive, and to pray that the Holy Spirit will give clarity of insight so that God's truth may in the end prevail.

Dissent in the Church

Michael Novak

This article originally appeared in *Catholicism in Crisis* in 1986.

What are the proper roles and limits of dissent? What are the demands of orthodoxy? These have become, once again, basic questions for all Catholics.

"No longer can we speak about the perennial theology or the perennial philosophy," writes one distinguished American Catholic theologian, whose work and practice I very much admire. "There are many different and acceptable theological approaches within the Catholic faith tradition." He adds; ". . . *some theologies are inadequate,* but nevertheless the Church must recognize a plurality of possible theologies within one Catholic faith" (italics added). Thereby hangs a problem.

I agree with my colleague that there are many possible theologies. I also agree that "some theologies are inadequate." Should these not be criticized accordingly?

I also heartily assert that theologians need elbow room. But bishops, and above all the Bishop of Rome, have as their own appointed task to "confirm the faith of the brethren," that is, to make narrower judgments than the expansive judgments of theologians. It is important, even crucial, for theologians to have room to err. Bold and original investigations, even when admixed with error, uncover new ways of thinking and new angles for casting light upon the revelation of God entrusted to the Church. Tradition is not only a gerund—the *tradita* that are passed from generation to generation—but a noun: the *traditio,* the living stream, that grows with an inner principle of organic life.

Even the traditional view of heresy establishes this point. The heretic, it has always been said, has hold of part of the truth, often an important and neglected part, which needs to be recovered. It is, therefore, a crucial part of the teaching ministry to discern what is true from what is false, even in the most deceptive and attractive of heresies. Otherwise, the Church would merely stagnate or else be blown about by every "spirit of the times." It is never easy to interpret "the signs of the times." To fail in such discernment would render the Church regularly unfaithful to the Faith entrusted to it. Catholic life demands many sacrifices; if made in the name of a false faith, such sacrifices would represent sadly wasted human energies.

Theologians need room to err. That is why we do not base our lives upon the teachings of theologians. Their errors, despite themselves, can nonetheless be fruitful for the body of the Catholic people. The chances they take, the specific neuroses to which intellectuals are prey, and the odd angles of vision they assume, often serve the Lord's ironic purposes. We theologians do our best, in the hope that even our errors will serve to shed reflected light upon the truths to which we struggle to be faithful.

In this sense, a pluralism of theologies and of philosophies is vitally necessary to the Church. In our own time, a good example is given in the life of Karol Wojtyla, the theologian. Trained profoundly in the work of St. Thomas Aquinas and St. John of the Cross, to whose work he dedicated the labors of his doctoral dissertation, Karol Wojtyla also studied closely the works of contemporary personalists and phenomenologists, then rather suspect in Roman circles. He also made Marxist thought, especially on work and on collectivism (ideas he found to be bogus), the object of intense and rigorous study. These pluralistic philosophical and theological efforts prepared him admirably for the teaching office he was eventually to assume, with such a commanding brilliance that even his foes, within and without the Church, have been compelled to admire it.

How could such a pope be against "pluralism," of which he has been so admirable a practitioner? His own justification for private property, broader participation in workplace decisions, a regulated market system, and a personalist rather than a collectivist theory of work, is both faithful to the Catholic tradition and remarkably original in the annals of Catholic thought. Such originality could not have been reached if theologian Wojtyla had earlier worked solely in one intellectual tradition alone.

On the other hand, not everything about Thomism, St. John of the Cross, personalism, or phenomenology is to be mistaken for a full report on authentic Catholic faith. Discernment is indispensable. Discernment means not only guidance by the Holy Spirit during a lonely intellectual struggle, amid conflicting currents and in darkness, but also a learned facility for singling out the felicitous expression closest to the true meaning intended by the Creator. Such discernment is a rare gift. That is why the prayer of St. Thomas Aquinas, a model for theologians, still touches us.

Creator, beyond any words of ours to describe!

Most gloriously You have disposed all parts of the whole universe. You are the true source of light and wisdom, You are their first and final cause.

Pour out now, I beg you, a ray of Your clear light upon my murky understanding, and take from me my doubly dark inheritance of sin and ignorance. You who inspire the speech of little children, guide and teach my tongue now, and let the grace of Your blessing flow upon my lips. Grant me a sharp discernment, a strong memory, a methodical approach to study, a willing and able docility; let me be precise in interpretation and felicitous in choice of words.

Instruct my beginning, direct my progress, and bring my work to its proper finish: You, who are true God and true man, living and reigning forever!

If St. Thomas, a Teacher of the Church, renowned seven hundred years after his death for his calm, unruffled clarity of thought, could not trust his own work to "hit the mark," how can any of the rest of us?

It is not disgrace for a theologian to err in half or more of his sentences, or to misstate again and again the essential heart of the matter. On the contrary, it is a great joy to hit the bull's-eye only once or twice in a lifetime, and in that small way to make an original and genuine contribution to the life of the historical community of which one is so small a part.

Why, then, should a theologian or a philosopher be distressed to be found in error here or there? What else ought mortals to expect? In the sight of the Lord, intellectuals are not giants. Clear fidelity to the truths we seek to express is such a rare achievement that we must be content to have achieved, as Aristotle put it in another context, a "tincture of virtue." For the most part, even at our best we merely repeat, more or less well, what the great minds of the past tutored us to discover on our own. Particularly in matters of human nature and destiny, it would be astonishing if we were to discover something wholly original, beyond the ken of the greatest of our ancestors.

This is not to say that knowledge does not progress. St. Thomas Aquinas, for example, far more clearly articulated the workings of human "will," which Aristotle only darkly grasped, if at all. A thousand other fresh and illuminating distinctions have been added to our patrimony by hundreds of our predecessors. Yet knowledge in matters of faith and morals, unlike knowledge in modern sciences, has a remarkable constancy, even in the clearer light of new distinctions and new methods. To simplify the reality only a little: in medicine and other modern scientific work, new breakthroughs into the unknown occur constantly; in the humanities, by contrast, movement is rather from the known to the more accurately known. Progress in the sciences is quite different from progress in the humanities. The sciences constantly overturn earlier scientific classics. Humanists constantly cite the humanistic classics for evidence that they are on the right track, still retaining their indispensable universality.

To the one side, in matters of faith, there is the danger of "non-historical orthodoxy." This is the failure to respect the concrete texture of human history, with all its angularity, new points of view, and new "horizons" of intellectual insight and judgment. The grip of a certain "non-historical orthodoxy" was decisively broken at Vatican II. But to the other side lies the opposite danger, "neo-doxy," the failure to respect what is abiding in human nature and history, in the hot lust for what is "new."

"Historical consciousness" is a relatively new discovery. It must not be forgotten, though, that Aristotle explicitly recounted the historical narrative of Greek philosophy of which he saw himself a part, and Thomas Aquinas often recounted how and where he differed from his predecessors. On the one hand, then, in the humanities, one must be constantly aware of one's roots and one's true place in the history of inquiry. On the other hand, historical consciousness must not be surrendered to "historicism," in which there lies *nothing but* a "diversity of approaches based on historical and cultural differences." That way lies pure relativism. If the human mind is not capable of rising above the subjectivity of individual thinkers and the prejudices of the spirit of its times, then fidelity to God's Word is impossible across the ages, and philosophers can enjoy no real communion across cultures and down the centuries. Even "the development of doctrine" would then be only an illusion.

At the high point of Vatican II, it was my lot to coin the phrase "non-historical orthodoxy" in my report on Vatican II, *The Open Church* (1964), and to write an early article on "Catholic Education and the Idea of Dissent" (*Commonweal,* April 27, 1962). In self-criticism, I must now note that at that time (more so in the article than in the book) I concentrated upon what was *new,* underemphasizing what was *traditional,* in the search for light.

If one re-reads T.S. Eliot's pregnant essay, "Tradition and the Individual Talent," one sees how what is true for the humanities in general, and for the poet in particular, is also true for the theologian and the philosopher. Humanists try to shed light that is *both* original and highly individual—but upon the human condition as it was, is, and will be. In this sense, their work is always both individual and traditional. Were we only to illuminate what is new, our work would speedily become "dated" and "old-fashioned." It would not rise to the level of the classics, and would have failed to plumb the depths of what is universally human. To write only of our own culture or of our own age is not to write of humankind, but only of a passing moment. In Rome, the jesters of the fountains smile because they have seen many generations come and go before those mocking mouths of theirs, that spew everflowing streams of water.

One reason why there *is* a perennial philosophy (and a perennial theology), in fact, is that some thinkers have managed, in an exemplary way, to observe both the permanent and the passing in human experience. By contrast, others manage to grasp only the passing or only the permanent, testifying so to their own incompleteness. Some texts do live perennially. Among these are both the Word of God and those philosophies fashioned most like unto it. These are precious to the human race. It is one of the disgraces of the intellectual life of our era that the very existence of a perennial philosophy is now denied.

There is a second vein of difficulty. An ironic feature of contemporary American life is that many intellectuals who deny the legitimacy of liberalism in economics affirm it in intellectual commerce. They desire "pluralism" and an "unfettered intellectual marketplace of ideas," while railing against "unfettered markets" in the exchange of goods and services. They are liberal in intellect, illiberal in economics. They are not wrong to note that, in order to function at all, economic markets must be regulated both by morality and by law. But they *are* wrong in failing to observe the difference between the free marketplace of ideas in some realms, and crucial constraints upon the liberty of ideas in other realms.

Note, for example, the crucial difference between those fields that serve pure inquiry and those that also serve the human community in some significant institutional embodiment. Just because some medical doctors stand ready to testify that laetril is a cure for cancer, it does not follow that medical science so affirms. Freedom of thought is indispensable to scientific investigation. But so, also, is stringent and authoritative peer review. And so, also, even allowing for excessive rigidity on some occasions and excessive leniency on others, is the Food and Drug Administration. In medicine, there are enthusiasts, quacks, and profiteers, whose practices require a certain fettering. Why should it be different in theology? (I leave philosophy aside, for on the whole, blessedly, philosophers do not institutionalize their teachings. They count themselves lucky to achieve tenure and a lively readership.)

Theologians, and philosophers who so choose, aim not only to have original thoughts but also to serve the indispensable intellectual needs of an historical community. These two aims are often placed in tension. In a living community, a community (in Newman's phrase) of "real assents," there is typically a lag between fresh notional clarity and its real appropriation in the lives of members of the community. This "time lag" becomes a crucial factor in realistic community life. That is why original genius is often not widely recognized until generations have come and gone. New ideas must be assimilated until they have become as common as common sense.

During their lifetimes, original minds typically face resistance, are sometimes hated, and may be persecuted even in petty ways. Such a fate is not easy for the timid. A desire to be in tune with the up-to-date spirit of their age, to be respected by their peers (and competitors), is very strong. Often even great minds try their best to make concessions, to phrase matters in ways not too shocking, to coax their peers along. For many decades, Bernard Lonergan made a practice of not answering his critics, and not publishing his exploratory essays, in order to avoid such temptations.

On matters of dissent, furthermore, as culture differs from culture, so temptations differ. Our own culture highly values the "new" and the "improved," not only in the "news" industry, but also in an intellectual community driven by imperatives of invention, discovery, and creativity. North American culture is based upon the premise that the cause of the wealth of nations is intellectual creativity. In American universities, as legislation establishing the land-grant colleges shows with particular clarity, the purpose of inquiry is to discover new knowledge. In most fields a doctoral dissertation must be justified in terms of the new knowledge it aims to produce. This conviction is natural to a biblical people; it is the vocation of Christians and Jews to imitate the Creator by unlocking the secrets the Creator has hidden within creation. This conviction is not universally embodied in universities.

There are universities in Latin America, for example, that are 300 years old, yet cannot point to a single original idea that they have ever produced. Their purpose, on the contrary, a purpose quite noble in itself, has been to transmit a tradition of culture; and, in addition, to convey to students new knowledge discovered elsewhere. By contrast, the orientation of American intellectual life is a special hazard to theologians and to the "itching ears" of the news industry. There is a temptation to judge intellectual work less by whether it is true than by whether it is new.

In a liberal culture, then, it may be more difficult than in other cultures for theologians and philosophers to admit that they work within a tradition. It may be harder for them to admit that even their original achievements are, in the end, no more than a new angle of light upon perennial reality. They face a pervasive temptation to disguise what is traditional in their teaching, to pose as rebels or revolutionaries, and to stress what is "new" (or, these days, "prophetic"). Thence derives the cultural power of *neo-doxy*. Thence, too, derives the temptation to be dismissive towards even the *idea* of a perennial philosophy.

In fact, as Julian Benda made clear in *La Trahison des Clerques*, intellectuals who spend so many hours within the world of their own minds are peculiarly prone to be the very first to abandon the living springs of the tradition that gave them life. We fall in love with our own creations. We are all too quick to find our predecessors wrong. We can hardly help imagining that we are the voices of "a new age," as if the world of truth begins with our discoveries (or with Vatican Council II!).

A third strand in the cultural perplexity of contemporary intellectual life among Catholics in America is the confusion between the democratic virtues and the Catholic virtues. It is quite proper to be a strong supporter of the virtues of democratic capitalist societies. Such are the virtues necessary for and proper to societies at once democratic in their political institutions, capitalist in their economic institutions, and pluralist in their moral-cultural traditions. These are lovely virtues. They are as important to the human race, in the dimension of social life, as the Greek virtues of delight in intellectual and artistic form; the Roman virtues of law, administration and *pietas;* the knightly virtues of courtesy, compassion, and charity; the virtues of the gentleman articulated so brilliantly by Cardinal Newman; and the particular virtues of other peoples of the human race.

By contrast, the specifically American virtues are but poorly understood even by Americans themselves. As Jacques Maritain pointed out, we are better at doing what we do than in articulating it as a theory. (Another French Catholic philosopher of culture, Alexis de Tocqueville, has probably expressed the American virtues better than any American.) The specifically American virtues add something precious to the patrimony of the human race and to the Church Universal. But they are not identical to the virtues specific to *Catholic* living.

To mention the obvious first, Catholics freely bind themselves to an authority over matters of faith and morals vested in the Bishop of Rome, in a way their fellow Americans (Protestant, Jewish, and other) do not. The American system permits Catholics freely to do so. Further, it grants them the liberties of free citizens to argue in public for their own distinctive views. Still, Catholics value "authority," even in a general sense, in a way that for many of their fellow citizens it is a matter of honor to resist.

Each American, *qua* American, wishes to say that he or she is independent, autonomous, able to pursue individual happiness as each sees fit. It is no contradiction of this claim for some to choose to realize this independence, autonomy, and individual happiness in a communal, theonomous, and rooted way through fidelity to the Catholic (or any other) faith. Still, between the virtues of democratic capitalist living and the virtues of Catholic living, there is a healthy and fruitful tension. The two sets of virtues may impregnate and fertilize each other, but they are as likely to be in daily tension as husband and wife. They may be in union, but each is also distinct—as the other will be certain to point out.

It is the constitutional right of every American *qua* American, for example, to form his or her own conscience, even in dissent from all other consciences. It is, in fact, the natural right of every human person to do so. ("Unless a man hate father, mother, wife, or children for My name's sake, he is not worthy of Me. . . .") Still, dissent in the American sense is different in character from the dissent of Catholics from the teachings of the Church. To become a citizen of the United States is not to pledge unity in faith, only to swear to preserve and defend the Constitution of the United States. But for a Catholic to dissent from the teachings of the Church is to cut a vital spiritual tie. To become an American is to accept outward institutions of political economy, and to embrace in one's civil behavior the limited American "Proposition" (as John Courtney Murray, S.J., aptly called it). It is not to pledge one's entire soul to a faith. By contrast, to be a Catholic is to tie oneself to a community based upon commitment to God's Word, as defined and protected institutionally in a special way by bishops and by the pope. To dissent spiritually from this faith is, *qua* Catholic, by so much to die.

Thus, the commitment of a U.S. Catholic to abide by and to defend the Constitution of the United States is only analogous to his or her commitment to the Catholic faith. To breach the first is traitorous, to breach the second is to be unfaithful. The commitment of a U.S. citizen is but a temporal, worldly commitment, explicitly understood to be "under God." By contrast, the commitment of a U.S. citizen to the Catholic faith is a commitment to God. The U.S. Constitution asks of its citizens a precisely limited commitment, allowing unprecedented room to dissent in every other sphere. By contrast, Catholic faith asks of its adherents that they love and serve God with their whole hearts, their whole minds, and their whole soul. Its teachings suffuse every aspect of life, as fire suffuses an ingot. To shield part of one's life from that teaching is to leave part of the soul dead.

Nonetheless, there has grown up since Vatican II a new ecclesiology. Its aim is to protect Catholics from "death by slow degrees"; its aim is pluralism, if not individual choice. This new ecclesiology, usually informal rather than formal, holds that "the Church is the people of God, a community of equal disciples." Here I cite the same theologian as earlier, who continues: "For example, the Holy Spirit dwells in all the faithful, and through baptism all share in the priestly, ruling and teaching functions of Jesus." The consequence? "As a result, the teaching function of the total Church cannot be absolutely identified with only the hierarchical teaching office." But what happens in practice? "In practice, there can be no doubt that the temptation is strong to reduce the Church to just the hierarchical offices that should exist in the service of the Church."

In this new ecclesiology, the individual believer is master, hierarchical officers are servants. The "community" is imagined to be egalitarian: "a community of equal disciples." It is proper to stress the whole community, the whole people; but egalitarianism goes much too far. Catholic faith is not simply a Chinese menu, from which each selects a preference; nor is it the hierarchy only; but its unique separation of roles and powers in one Body is not well expressed as "equality."

In this new ecclesiology, to recognize the unique teaching office of the hierarchy is regarded as a "temptation"; that is, as heresy. The new orthodoxy requires egalitarianism and decentralization. "The New Code of Canon Law does not really decentralize the Church." The new national conference and synods of bishops "have really not functioned as a true exercise of collegiality, for they have functioned merely as a consultative body to the pope." The new ecclesiology is much more Catholic than the pope. "Collegiality will not exist in reality until a bishop or group of bishops can say publicly: "Holy Father, we love you. We respect you as a holder of the Petrine office in the Church. But in this matter you are wrong.' "

In principle, further deductions follow. What is true of the Petrine office in the Church must also be true, *a fortiori*, of a lesser offices of conferences of bishops and individual bishops. Now "the equal disciples" can say to their bishops: "Bishops, we love you. We respect you as holders of episcopal offices in the Church. But in this matter you are wrong."

Further, the "equal disciples" are now entitled to say to each other: "Brother, sister, I love you. I respect you as holders of the priestly, ruling, and teaching functions of Jesus. But in this matter you are wrong."

Thus the new ecclesiology outlines a church composed spiritually of a community of one, gathered in no *ecclesia* at all. The priestly, ruling, and teaching functions of Jesus have been located in each single dissenter. Each is his or her own priest, ruler, and teacher.

In the eyes of this "new" ecclesiology, the linchpin to the "old" ecclesiology is the authority vested in Peter. Take that away and the new ecclesiology is vindicated. Turn St. Peter's Basilica into a museum, and hire "a servant of the people" to show up from time to time for the acclamation of cheering throngs, who have come to see the "dear Holy Father," who is so often wrong, and for whom being right or wrong in matters of faith and morals no longer makes a difference.

"In a sense," my admired exponent of the new ecclesiology writes, "the most crucial question today concerns the limits of pluralism and dissent." He adds: "but the discussion of this crucial issue cannot take place until the hierarchical teaching office recognizes the possibility of dissent." Unconditional surrender, then discussion.

But, of course, there is already immense room in the Catholic body for dissent. The U.S. Catholic bishops, e.g., painstakingly distinguished in their pastoral letters on nuclear arms and the economy between matters of faith and morals, binding on all Catholics, and matters of fact and concrete judgment on which, quite properly, persons of good will disagree.

Look. If to be a Catholic is to dissent on critical matters of faith and morals, what is the point of celibacy, strict Catholic teachings on chasity, Catholic social teachings, the Catholic tradition on peace and war, the condemnation of abortion, the difficult notion of Jesus as both God and man, the Petrine office, the eucharist as the real presence of the real God, and the communion of saints? If our communion is really solipsism, covered over by the good fellowship of shaking hands in church, forget it. There are in this world more attractive communities. The communities that now meet in our parishes do not meet because we are in most important matters likeminded. On the contrary, we are in strenuous disagreement with one another's politics, moral sensibilities, artistic tastes, and even manners. What unites us is a transcending, authoritative faith in an embodied Church, one Body with many different roles and functions, charisms and responsibilities. Ours is not an egalitarian church. It is a hierarchical church, with one head, the Vicar of Christ. If we did not think that to be apart from that head were to be like an ingot without fire, who for a minute would get up to go to the seven a.m. mass?

The principle of authority raises an urgent question for Catholic universities. A university, like the Church itself, has a vocation to universality. The ideas, habits, and values that animate it extend across times and cultures, as the Church does. Both the university community and the Church, however, depend on leadership, out-

lining current priorities and making wise decisions about boundaries. An institution is finite; no one institution can do everything.
Insofar as a university is Catholic, it serves two historical communities; that of the university and that of the Church. The spirit of
inquiry in the university must be free, but it must also include
among its many inquiries those that clarify, defend, and advance
the special pilgrimage on which the Church is launched. It would
be odd if its purpose were to be served by abandoning the faith in
whose name its inquiries have been launched. It would be odd if
outsiders were to ask: "But how do modern eugenics, nuclear
weapons, computers, theories of mind, etc. alter the Catholic
faith?", only to be told that no one any longer cares to take that
faith seriously enough to offer a thorough answer. The Catholic
faith is also an historical and dynamic fact, whose importance to
the future of this planet grows clearer every day. Even many who
are not Catholic want the Church—need the Church—to be faithful to itself, and not simply buckle at every gust of contemporary
wind. A Catholic university unfaithful to the Catholic faith does
not well serve even those who are not Catholic. Catholic faith is
itself a crucial voice in the universal pluralism.

For theologians, there must be elbow room aplenty. Intellectuals must take intellectual risks. From time to time, some of us
lose our way; others drink water poisonous to our brains. In all
cases, ours is to *propose*. In my healthy community, there must be
others who *dispose*. If the people of the United States were ruled
by the faculty of Harvard rather than by all the other names in all
the telephone books of the nation, and by the persons of common
sense whom all elect, the nation long since might have perished at
the Hudson. The faculty of Harvard *ought* to be dissenters from
the rest of their fellow citizens. Their task is lonely exploration.
Their service to the community is vital, which is why the community so heavily endows their labor. That, too, is why the Catholic
community pays the salaries of its theologians, whose work so
much nourishes the community, even when that work (as much of
it necessarily must be) comes to be rejected over time. Intellectuals
have a perennial habit of following two or three premises all the
arduous way to an absurd conclusion. Even in this, they illuminate

the crux of the matter. They themselves thus help the community to decide against them. To be an intellectual is a noble, but a fragile, task.

In some ways, furthermore, the American experience has blazed new trails for the Catholic experience. U.S. institutions of religious liberty turned out to be (although for John Courtney Murray, S.J., who mapped the way, after considerable personal pain) one such new path. In matters of political economy, American secrets are still blazing a trail for Catholic social thought, particularly in institutional matters: secrets of public-spiritedness; of voluntary cooperation; of economic creativity and unprecedented human enterprise; of the due balance among political, economic, and moral-cultural institutions, and of the new virtues appropriate to each. However that development may turn out, those involved need not believe their efforts have been in vain, even should the hierarchical offices of the Church, for our time or forever, reject their efforts.

The Catholic community, like every other living community, most urgently needs dissenters. It especially needs dissenters whose dissents are provisional. It needs dissenters who try to be as honest, as clear, and as broad of view as a person can, recognizing the while that it is the *unequal* office of the college of bishops, and the still more *unequal* office of the Bishop of Rome, to render practical judgment upon any dissenter's efforts. We also serve who only err. Our *intention*, even when we seem to stand in arrogant dissent, is to serve the entire living Body, in which our function is but one of many, decidedly not the function of the Head. The God who made us made us to seek His truth. If His truth is what we serve, there is no possible way to lose, even if we are unfairly judged, or even if we err, along the way.

What has gone wrong in recent decades is that many dissenters have come to claim a certain quasi-infallibility, according to which *they* pass judgment and wait impatiently until the bishops and the popes docilely obey. Dissenters today conduct their own Inquisition in the press, pointing fingers at Cardinal Ratzinger and Pope John Paul II for *their* mistakes. Dissenters have no call to be blushing violets. They should make good arguments and state them openly. But in the Catholic Church, as in the field of medicine, there is "peer review," and in the Catholic Church the bishops and the pope have no peers. Theologians serve the whole community. To offer their service well, they must be free and bold, and have elbow-room aplenty. But they should also accept, in all humility, and with a sense of loyalty and affection, the lowliness of all they do, *sub specie aeternitatis.*

Norms of Licit Theological Dissent

National Conference of Catholic Bishops

This excerpt originally appeared in *Human Life in Our Day*, 1968.

There exist in the Church a lawful freedom of inquiry and of thought and also general norms of licit dissent. This is particularly true in the area of legitimate theological speculation and research. When conclusions reached by such professional theological work prompt a scholar to dissent from noninfallible received teaching the norms of licit dissent come into play. They require of him careful respect for the consciences of those who lack his special competence or opportunity for judicious investigation. These norms also require setting forth his dissent with propriety and with regard for the gravity of the matter and the deference due the authority which has pronounced on it.

The reverence due all sacred matters, particularly questions which touch on salvation, will not necessarily require the responsible scholar to relinquish his opinion but certainly to propose it with prudence born of intellectual grace and a Christian confidence that the truth is great and will prevail.

When there is question of theological dissent from noninfallible doctrine, we must recall that there is always a presumption in favor of the magisterium. Even non-infallible authentic doctrine, though it may admit of development or call for clarification or revision, remains binding and carries with it a moral certitude, especially when it is addressed to the universal Church, without ambiguity, in response to urgent questions bound up with faith and crucial to morals. The expression of theological dissent from the magisterium is in order only if the reasons are serious and well-founded, if the manner of the dissent does not question or impugn the teaching authority of the Church and is such as not to give scandal.

Since our age is characterized by popular interest in theological debate and given the realities of modern mass media, the ways in which theological dissent may be effectively expressed, in a manner consistent with pastoral solicitude, should become the object of fruitful dialogue between bishops and theologians. These have their diverse ministries in the Church, their distinct responsibilities to the faith and their respective charisms.

Even responsible dissent does not excuse one from faithful presentation of the authentic doctrine of the Church when one is performing a pastoral ministry in Her name.

We count on priests, the counsellors of persons and families, to heed the appeal of Pope Paul that they "expound the Church's teaching on marriage without ambiguity"; that they "diminish in no way the saving teaching of Christ," but "teach married couples the indispensable way of prayer . . . without ever allowing them to be discouraged by their weakness" (*Humanae Vitae*, 29). We commend to confessors, as does Pope Paul, the example of the Lord Himself, Who was indeed intransigent with evil, but merciful towards individuals.

The Document of the German Bishops Addressed to All Members of the Church Who Are Commissioned to Preach the Faith[1]

The West German Bishops

This excerpt originally appeared in English in Karl Rahner, *Theological Investigations*, 1976.

At this point a difficult problem arises, calling for realistic discussion. It is one which today more than formerly threatens either the faith of many Catholics or their attitude of free and unreserved trust towards the teaching authorities of the Church. We refer to the fact that in the exercise of its official function this teaching authority of the Church can, and on occasion actually does, fall into errors. The fact that such a thing is possible is something of which the Church has always been aware and which she has actually expressed in her theology. Moreover she has evolved rules of conduct to cater for the kind of situations which arise from this. This possibility of error refers not to those statements of doctrine which are proclaimed as propositions to be embraced with the absolute assent of faith, whether by a solemn definition on the part of the Pope, a general council, or by the exercise of the ordinary *magisterium*. Historically speaking it is also incorrect to maintain that any error has subsequently arisen in such dogmas as proclaimed by the Church. This is of course not to dispute the fact that even in the case of such a dogma, while we must uphold its original meaning, it is always possible and always necessary for a development in our understanding of it to take place, involving a progressive elimination of any misinterpretations which may perhaps have been attached to it hitherto. Nor should we confuse the question which we have raised here with the manifest fact that side by side with the immutable divine law there is also a human law in the Church which is subject to change. Changes in this latter have from the outset nothing to do with error. At most they raise the question of how far some juridical decision in the remote or recent past was opportune.

Now let us consider the possibility or the fact of error in nondefined statements of doctrine on the part of the Church, recognizing that these themselves in turn may differ very widely among themselves in their degree of binding force. The first point to be recognized resolutely and realistically is that human life, even at a wholly general level, must always be lived "by doing one's best according to one's lights" and by recognized principles which, while at the theoretical level they cannot be recognized as absolutely certain, nevertheless command our respect in the "here and now" as valid norms of thinking and acting because in the existing circumstances they are the best that can be found. This is something that everyone recognizes from the concrete experience of his own life. Every doctor in his diagnoses, every statesman in the political judgments he arrives at on particular situations and the decisions he bases on these, is aware of this fact. The Church too in her doctrine and practice cannot always and in every case allow herself to be caught in the dilemma of either arriving at a doctrinal decision which is ultimately binding or simply being silent and leaving everything to the free opinion of the individual. In order to maintain the true and ultimate substance of faith she must, even at the risk of error in points of detail, give expression to doctrinal directives which have a certain degree of binding force and yet, since they are not *de fide* definitions, involve a certain element of the provisional even to the point of being capable of including error. Otherwise it would be quite impossible for her to preach or interpret her faith as a decisive force in real life or to apply it to each new situation in human life as it arises. In such a case the position of the individual Christian in regard to the Church is analogous to that of a man who knows that he is bound to accept the decision of a specialist even while recognizing that it is not infallible.

At any rate any opinion which runs contrary to a current statement of doctrine on the part of the Church has no place in preaching or catechesis, even though the faithful may, under certain circumstances, have to be instructed as to the nature of, and the limited weight to be attached to, a current doctrinal decision of this kind. This is a point which has already been discussed. Anyone who believes that he is justified in holding, as a matter of his own private opinion, that he has already even now arrived at some better insight which the Church will come to in the future must ask himself in all sober self-criticism before God and his conscience whether he has the necessary breadth and depth of specialized theological knowledge to permit himself in his private theory and practice to depart from the current teaching of the official Church. Such a case is conceivable in principle, but subjective presumptuousness and an unwarranted attitude of knowing better will be called to account before the judgment-seat of God.

It belongs intrinsically to the right attitude of faith of any Catholic seriously to strive to attach a positive value to even a provisional statement of doctrine on the part of the Church, and to make it his own. In secular life too far-reaching decisions have to be taken on the basis of fallible findings on the part of others, which have been arrived at according to their best lights. And it is no less true in Church matters that the individual need not feel any shame or diminishment of his own personality if in his findings he relies upon the Church's teaching even in cases in which it cannot be accounted as definitive from the outset. It is possible that in specific cases the development of the Church's doctrine proceeds too slowly. But even in arriving at a judgment of this kind we must be prudent and humble. For in any such development of doctrine within a Church made up of men subject to historical conditions time is needed. For it cannot proceed any faster than the task permits of preserving the substance of the faith without loss.

We do not need to fear that in adopting positions of the Church in the manner described we are failing to respond to the claims of our own age. Often enough the serious questions raised for us by our own age, and which we are called upon to answer on the basis of our faith, make it necessary for us to think out the truths of our faith afresh. It is perfectly possible that in this process fresh points will come to be emphasized. But this is not to call the faith itself in question. Rather it contributes to a deeper grasp of the truths of divine revelation and of the Church's teaching. For we are firmly convinced, and we see that experience confirms us in this, that we need neither deny any truth for the Catholic faith, nor deny the Catholic faith for the sake of any truth, provided only that we understand this faith in the spirit of the Church and seek always to achieve a deeper grasp of it.

Note

1. The text was published by the Secretariat of the Conference of German Bishops in the autumn of 1967 as a semi-private document and disseminated at diocesan level. Hence it is relatively difficult to achieve access to it. cf. *Herder-Korrespondenz* 21 (1967), col. 549.

Dissent and the Catholic Religion Teacher

William Levada

This article originally appeared in *Origins* in 1986.

For Catholic religion teachers to teach their students "responsible dissent" from the teachings of the church is not only undesirable and self-defeating, but not in conformity with the requirements of Catholic faith, Archbishop William Levada said in an April 2 address given at the National Catholic Educational Association annual convention, held in Anaheim, Calif. "Our students," said Levada, who is scheduled to be installed as archbishop of Portland, Ore., Sept. 22, "need to have the assurance that the church is indeed a reliable teacher and guide. In my judgment, that is an assurance which we all . . . ought to give willingly and convincingly." In his address Levada discussed the distinction between infallible and non-infallible authoritative church teaching, public vs. private dissent, conscience and the "sensus fidelium." He faulted some current discussion of the right to dissent for going about the "task of theological discernment in questions of faith and morals much as we engage in debate about political policies. . . . I would say that Catholic theology does not recognize the right to dissent if by that we mean adopting conclusions which are contrary to the clear teachings of the authoritative, non-infallible magisterium and presented to the public in such a way as to constitute

133

equivalently an alternative personal magisterium." The text of his address follows.

This lecture has a double connection with the National Catholic Educational Association: In the first place, it is part of the program of the 1986 NCEA national convention; and second, it has its genesis in two brief articles published in the May 1985, NCEA magazine Momentum titled "The Magisterium and the Catholic Educator: Two Views."

My interest in these brief (one-page) articles was drawn not only by their content but also by their manner of presentation. The "two views," each written by an NCEA staff person, were presented on facing pages. What struck me when I read them was their fundamental disagreement regarding the task of the religion teacher and catechist.

The manner of presentation thus seemed to me to constitute a sort of paradigm of the way in which much of our teaching of religion seems to go on today. "Here is one view, the teaching of the church," we seem to say. Opposite that we say, "Here is another opinion, representing the viewpoint of several theologians or my own personal conviction" as the case may be. "Here they are— take your pick."

But if the presentation of intelligently thought out and respectfully articulated contrasting points of view is to serve a useful purpose, it seems to me, it would be important not simply to present such opposing views, but to analyze them, engage in dialogue about them and evaluate them.

I take it this is what the editors of Momentum intended to do, for the two-page presentation is accompanied by this note: "The NCEA staff welcomes the views of Momentum readers on this subject and will publish brief, signed statements in future issues, space permitting." In accepting the implicit invitation to dialogue given by the editors of Momentum, I was not able to follow up regarding any particular response that may have been made to these "two views." But I do want to assure the NCEA staff that I am making this presentation in a spirit of dialogue and evaluation, precisely with a view to helping Catholic educators for whom this exchange of opinions was presented to make an appropriate evaluation of the issues involved in this discussion.

In order to give you some flavor of the exchanges of views which I have taken as a springboard for my remarks, let me provide a brief description which I hope will be faithful to the basic thrust and purpose of the authors. While both articles express genuine sympathy for the situation of the Catholic teacher of religion and catechist, their conclusions regarding the role of the religion teacher are strikingly different.

One suggests, "It is my conviction that the overwhelming majority of our Catholic school teachers and parish catechists are totally dedicated to Christ and to his church and have no desire or motive but to present its teachings to their students as faithfully and attractively as possible. Given our cultural situation, this is not always easy." And the article goes on to say that the teacher "is called to form students in the mind of Christ and to help them develop right consciences in keeping with the church's authentic teaching as presented by the bishops in union with the pope."

On the other hand, the facing article takes a much different approach: Using the 1984 New York Times abortion ad as an introduction, the article contrasts two different perceptions of the role of magisterium and of authority in the church—on the one hand, church teaching is seen as the sole preserve of the bishops; on the other, church teaching should reflect a "sense of the faithful." The article continues: "The controversy about the differing views on the teaching magisterium clearly has significant implications regarding the role of U.S. Catholic educators. Is our role that of facilitators of persons, enabling our students to form correct consciences in order to make critical decisions and act with integrity as fully responsible human beings? Or is one of the basic premises of Catholic education the imposition of certain answers on our students?"

Practically, the author goes on to say, "we acknowledge the commonly recognized understanding that the universal ordinary magisterium of the church has a role in guiding the faithful—our students—in the formation of their consciences. What we are concerned about is the interrelationship between this role/authority of the teaching magisterium of the church as it is presently being acted out on some levels and our role as Catholic educators in the fully human development of our students. As we teach our students the importance of dialogue and respectful dissent, as well as responsible assent to authority, the magisterium can reinforce these teachings by exercising its authority in a manner which will encourage thoughtful, proactive contributors to the life of the church and the future human community."

Now it occurs to me that the suggestion that it is the role of the Catholic educator to teach our students "respectful dissent" from the magisterium is quite mistaken; hence it will be the purpose of my remarks in this presentation to illustrate why I believe such a position and the premises from which it is drawn are not correct. And I do this as a contribution to the dialogue initiated by the NCEA with these articles, in the hope that others who may have read them and pondered upon them as I did will find these remarks useful.

FAITH

As I begin to engage in dialogue on this delicate issue, I want to clarify some ground rules which might otherwise remain presumed but I think necessary to make explicit here. Sometimes I fear that we do not do justice to our dialogue because we fear that by disagreeing with another person or by indicating that someone else's conclusion may be wrong we are somehow impugning that person's motives. I consider it a given in dialogue within our church that all partners to the dialogue share the virtues of faith, hope and love given by the Spirit and, furthermore, that we all share the desire to spread the good news of God's kingdom.

With regard to religious educators and catechists, this "common ground" is inspiringly summed up in the apostolic exhortation by Pope John Paul II, *Catechesi Tradendae* ("Catechesis in Our Time," 6), when he addresses the role of the catechist:

"Christocentricity in catechesis also means the intention to transmit not one's own teaching or that of some other master, but the teaching of Jesus Christ, the truth that he communicates or, to put it more precisely, the truth that he is. We must therefore say that in catechesis it is Christ, the incarnate Word and Son of God, who is taught—everything else is taught in reference to him—and it is Christ alone who teaches—anyone else teaches to the extent that he is Christ's spokesman, enabling Christ to teach with his lips. Whatever be the level of his responsibility in the church, every catechist must consistently endeavor to transmit by his teaching and behavior the teaching and life of Jesus. He will not seek to keep directed toward himself and his personal opinions and attitudes the attention and consent of the mind and heart of the person he is catechizing. Above all, he will not try to inculcate his personal opinions and options as if they expressed Christ's teaching and the lessons of his life. Every catechist should be able to apply to himself the mysterious words of Jesus: 'My teaching is not mine, but his who sent me.' St. Paul did this when he was dealing with a question of prime importance: 'I received from the Lord what I also delivered to you.' What assiduous study of the word of God transmitted by the church's magisterium, what profound familiarity with Christ and with the Father, what a spirit of prayer, what detachment from self must a catechist have in order that he can say: "My teaching is not mine!' "

The problem lies not with our desire to do Christ's will, but with its application to the teaching of the church and with our responsibility as teachers to propose to our students the church's teachings.

In the first place, it must be noted that the teacher of religion is dealing with a question of authority. While the philosopher may reason to the existence of God, the believer knows and accepts the God who reveals himself by the assent of faith which is based on the authority of that same God who reveals. Reductively, the Catholic Christian religion comes to us through reliable witnesses ("faith comes by hearing"), whose ultimate credibility rests in the reliability of the witness, Jesus Christ.

Now it is the very nature of the response of faith which we as humans are called to make to God, who reveals himself to us, that we are free to respond or not, in a way in which we are not free to assent to the mathematical proposition 2 and 2 equals 4. The reason for this would ultimately rest in the fact that the revelation of a personal God to creatures made in his own image and likeness involves a dialogue of love, in which the God who freely creates and reveals invites the free response of love and commitment on the part of those he has sent his Son to redeem.

What God reveals to us—that Jesus Christ is true God and true man, that he has redeemed us by his life, death and resurrection, that his Spirit lives on in and with his church to guide us in the knowledge of all truth—are surely truths, but truths which we must accept not on our conviction but on the authority of him who reveals them to us. Hence, every person remains free to choose not to believe.

I mention the central place of authority in the response of faith to God revealing himself for two reasons. First, because the bumper sticker which says "Question Authority" is but one indication of a cultural mind-set which the religion teacher encounters in today's student and which compounds the problem of the catechetical task. I mention it secondly to underline a traditional datum of Catholic theological tradition, namely that although from the human point of view the response of faith can never exclude all possibility that the contrary might be so, the truths which one knows because God has revealed them and accepts on his authority can be embraced with a certitude which is complete. In other words, we can know with absolute certainty that these things are true because of the authority of the God who reveals them—God who by very definition is alien to the possibility of deceiving us. Hence the fundamental question for religion and faith is not, Did God really know what he was talking about? but, Did God really reveal himself to me/us?

If this discussion seems to be reaching back to matters too fundamental to be useful to our discussion, I want to relate it at this point to the above-mentioned Momentum article, which set up a disjunction between the development of "full human beings" and the "imposition of certain answers" on our students. I am not here to defend the teacher who answers every legitimate and sincere question with "Don't be a heretic" or "Because the church says so." But the very notion of faith in God does create a separation between the freethinker and the believer precisely on the issue of whether the believer surrenders his human freedom to another (in this case, God) by believing, by his faith.

The journey of faith which the religion teacher makes with the student is not designed to force a decision of faith, but rather to explore why the decision to believe is reasonable, why it does not offend against but rather enhances our rational nature. It does so precisely because through faith we come to a grasp of the real truth about human nature—the truth of the very meaning of human existence. This truth which God reveals about us human beings is reliable, and it is knowledge which we can not have as freethinkers. Not only is God's revelation not an "imposition of certain answers" on our students (and ourselves as believers), as if it were something foreign, but rather it is the new and definitive insight into what it means to be fully human. At the same time, this faith response, involving a decision of our free will, is not some kind of "blind obedience"; instead it should be accompanied by all of the rational explanation of which our human intellect is capable, precisely to pose the questions and explore the possibilities about the fact of God revealing (which always presents itself in a way that allows us to ask the question, But what if it were otherwise?) and to explore in an ever deeper way the meaning of this revelation in order to understand it better and thus come to a fuller grasp of the real truth about our human condition.

AUTHORITATIVE TEACHING

I have felt it necessary to deal briefly with the fundamental question of "the obedience of faith" (cf. Rom. 16:26; *Dei Verbum*, 5) in order to place our subsequent discussion of religious authority into a proper theological perspective. I do so in particular because the author of the Momentum article seems to confuse questions and explorations in matters of faith with "responsible dissent." As I hope to point out, questions are a natural and inherent part of the rational human being's growth toward the assent of faith, but dissent is a decision not to grow any further in the direction of the God who reveals himself in and through Christ and his church. For dissent would seem to say, "Not what the church says, but what I say." While we all remain free to make such a choice, the decision not to believe or not to follow the guidance given in the doctrine of the Catholic Church, taught with the promised assistance of the Holy Spirit, instead of ensuring that "full humanity" which is rightly the legitimate goal of us all, rather prevents us from achieving it.

If we appreciate the dynamics of our faith, of the difficulties we experience in the midst of a materialist and secularized world in coming to know and accept God's revelation to us—especially since revelation is not about some abstract set of truths but involves a commitment of our lives to what is good and the avoidance of what is evil, according to a standard which is itself revealed in the person and cross of Jesus Christ—then we can see that the purpose of the church is always to persuade us to believe, to present the truths of the faith in the most attractive way possible, to show us precisely why the response of faith leads us to be able to realize our full humanity. It is Jesus who continues to fulfill the mission for which his Father sent him: in the church, his body, in which the biblical witness to God's revelation in Christ, written under the inspiration of the Holy Spirit, is handed on in the deposit of faith by the living tradition of the church and with the promised assistance of the same Holy Spirit. This Holy Spirit guides the church into an ever-deeper understanding of revealed truth in the life of the church—in its prayer and work—in response to the preaching of the apostles and their successors, the bishops.

Two important passages of the Constitution on Divine Revelation, which the fathers of the extraordinary Synod of Bishops in 1985 recently called "too neglected," are especially pertinent here:

"The tradition that comes from the apostles makes progress in the church, with the help of the Holy Spirit. There is a growth of insight into the realities and words that are being passed on. This comes about in various ways. It comes through the contemplation and study of believers who ponder these things in their hearts. It comes from the intimate sense of spiritual realities which they experience. And it comes form the preaching of those who have received, along with their right of succession in the episcopate, the sure charism of truth . . . The Holy Spirit, through whom the living voice of the Gospel rings out in the church—and though her in the world—leads believers to the full truth and makes the word of Christ dwell in them in all its richness" (No. 8).

"The task of giving an authentic interpretation of the word of God, whether in its written form or in the form of tradition, has been entrusted to the living, teaching office of the church alone. Its authority in this matter is exercised in the name of Jesus Christ. Yet this magisterium is not superior to the word of God, but is its servant. It teaches only what has been handed on to it. At the divine command and with the help of the Holy Spirit, it listens to this devotedly, guards it with dedication and expounds it faithfully. All that it proposes for belief as being divinely revealed is drawn from this single deposit of faith" (No. 10).

We should note in particular in these citations that the whole church, and each of us believers, is called to continue to grow in the understanding of our faith. This should give us some reassurance as Catholic educators when our students seem to balk at and resist understanding or accepting some aspect of church teaching. The path of human growth is not necessarily a straight one, but may take some byways and find a few cul-de-sacs out of which it will have to retrace its steps. Moreover, Vatican II has pointed out the interrelatedness of the Holy Scriptures, tradition and the church's magisterium in forming and handing on the deposit of faith.

INFALLIBLE AND NON-INFALLIBLE TEACHING

Up until now I have not explored the distinction between the infallible teaching of the church's magisterium and its authoritative, non-infallible teaching; this distinction is at the heart of current discussions about dissent from church teaching. To dissent from infallibly proclaimed teachings, knowingly and deliberately, is considered by the church to be heresy and excludes one from the communion of the faith. But the refusal to accept the authoritative teaching of the church, even when this is not proclaimed infallibly, also implies a separation from full communion with the church teaching, believing and practicing its faith, although such separation does not necesarily exclude one from the church.

The reason for this lies in the nature of the guarantee given to infallible and non-infallible teaching in the church. When some doctrine is infallibly taught, we may know with absolute certainty that God intends us to believe the teaching in question. When a doctrine in faith and morals is taught as certainly true, but not infallibly proclaimed, our minds are not given an absolute guarantee that God intends to bind us to believe it. But we are given the assurance that the Holy Spirit is guiding the authorized teachers in the church to enable them to propose what we must know and do for the sake of our salvation as Christians.

What would allow us to separate ourselves from this church teaching given with the promised assistance of the Holy Spirit? Nothing trivial, to be sure. For we can rightly presume that such teaching is correct.

But suppose I am a person who is truly expert in the area touched upon—perhaps a theologian or a scientist—and I find some discrepancy between church teaching and my view of the matter. If the question is infallibly taught, I am obliged to submit my judgment to the doctrine proposed, guaranteed by the Holy Spirit, and accept the fact that through further exploration and study I shall find out where I have been mistaken or why this belief is at least not contrary to human reason.

But if the matter is taught as certain, but without the unconditional guarantee which is contained in an infallible church judgment, I may think that the reasons for my view are so persuasive as to allow for a conditional response, i.e., to allow me to withhold my assent to this doctrine (which has been proposed as the truth) to test my reasoning, e.g., by reporting my conclusions to church authorities or submitting them to the judgment of my peers. This is a classic case of what Catholic theology has traditionally meant by "dissent."

At the Second Vatican Council the question of assent to and dissent from church teaching was referred to in Paragraph 25 of the Constitution on the Church (*Lumen Gentium*):

"Among the more important duties of bishops, that of preaching the Gospel has pride of place. For the bishops are heralds of the faith, who draw new disciples to Christ; they are authentic teachers, that is, teachers endowed with the authority of Christ, who preach the faith to the people assigned to them, the faith which is destined to inform their thinking and direct their conduct; and under the light of the Holy Spirit they make that faith shine forth, drawing from the storehouse of revelation new things and old (cf. Mt. 13:52); they make it bear fruit and with watchfulness they ward off whatever errors threaten their flock (cf. 2 Tm. 4:14). Bishops who teach in communion with the Roman pontiff are to be revered by all as witnesses of divine and Catholic truth; the faithful, for their part, are obliged to submit to their bishop's decision, made in the name of Christ, in matters of faith and morals, and to adhere to it with a ready and respectful allegiance of mind. This loyal submission of the will and intellect must be given, in a special way, to the authentic teaching authority of the Roman pontiff, even when he does not speak *ex cathedra,* in such wise, indeed, that his supreme teaching authority be acknowledged with respect, and sincere assent be given to decisions made by him, conformably with his manifest mind and intention, which is made known principally either by the character of the documents in question, or by the frequency with which a certain doctrine is proposed or by the manner in which the doctrine is formulated."

While the passage itself does not mention dissent, the background to the discussion of this section at the Second Vatican Council does refer more directly to our question.

During the preparation of this constitution, several bishops asked about the status of a person who felt in good faith he could not accept one or other teaching of the authoritative but non-infallible magisterium. The council's theological commission suggested that these bishops consult the theological authors expert in this area. The viewpoint of these authors can be summed up as follows:

The Christian who has a point of doctrine proposed to him for his belief by an infallible definition must give an assent of mind and will which is unconditioned precisely because he can know that the guarantee of the Holy Spirit, which excludes any possibility of error, is a part of its being proposed for his belief. When non-infallible teaching is proposed for our assent, we are asked to give full submission of mind and will to a doctrine which is proposed by the church's authentic teachers, who are assisted by the Holy Spirit so that the church may come to the full knowledge of the truth and be guided to right conduct in our Christian lives. Because this teach-ing has not been infallibly proposed, we cannot know absolutely that the possibility of error is excluded; we can, however, pru-dently proceed to assent and accept this doctrine because the Holy Spirit is presumed to be guiding the church's shepherds in its articu-lation. But because the proposition of certain but non-infallible teaching does not include the absolute guarantee of its truth, it is possible to justify the withholding of assent by a person who has arrived at truly convincing reasons, free from personal bias, which lead him to believe that the teaching in question is not correct.

In this case such a person (for example, the theologian or scientist we mentioned earlier) would want to clarify the issues with the church's authorized teachers, with a view to helping fur-ther the discussion of the matter and to developing a new or re-vised position, and/or submit it to the judgment of his peers, whose comments and insights should help to clarify the question in doubt. Such withholding of assent or "personal dissent" is by its very definition an exceptional and rare event in regard to the authorita-tive, non-infallible magisterium, which enjoys the presumption of truth—all the more so because it not only involves a personal judgment about some teaching which is connected intimately to the deposit of faith, but it also implicitly contains a judgment that such teaching has not enjoyed the presumed assistance of the Holy Spirit. Hence it is a judgment not only about some doctrine but about the church and its magisterium itself.

This is an important point to keep in mind since some contem-porary discussion about the "right to dissent" seems to ignore the ecclesiological presuppositions of authoritative church teaching and goes about the task of theological discernment in questions of faith and morals much as we engage in debate about political policies. The suggestion that we should teach our students about "responsible dissent" fails to take into account our first responsibil-ity as Catholics to assent to the teachings as proposed to us as certainly true by the church's magisterium. It further fails to note that the church's teaching is not one opinion among many nor a snap judgment, but is made precisely on the basis that such a teaching alone can faithfully correspond to the tradition contained in the deposit of faith. To dissent from such a teaching would require a thorough acquaintance with the basis upon which such teaching is founded.

QUESTIONS ABOUT DISSENT SINCE VATICAN II

Once we have grasped the issues involved in "dissent" as they appeared at Vatican II, we will be in a better position to judge the legitimacy of some more recent developments.

Some discussions about dissent fail to recognize that not everything that the church teaches infallibly has been infallibly defined. Because of the work of the ecumenical councils through the centuries, we can know about many truths of our faith that they have been infallibly defined: the divinity of Christ, the necessity of receiving the sacrament of penance for the forgiveness of mortal sins committed after baptism, that the pope is infallible as a teacher of faith and morals to the same extent that the church is an infallible teacher and so forth. Even about these infallibly defined truths of our faith, there are still further questions to be asked, further developments to be explored, new ways of formulating the truth contained in the infallible definitions, etc. But there are other doctrines of faith which are also a part of the infallibly taught patrimony of our church's tradition: the virginity of Mary, the bodily resurrection of Jesus and moral truths (such as the evil of abortion, which the Second Vatican Council calls "an abominable crime"); abortion, for example, is an instance of the biblical moral norm contained in the commandment "Thou shalt not kill." While we may know that many moral norms are part of the deposit of faith, it can be difficult to arrive at a precise formulation of them (an infallible "definition") because of the changing technological data which often affect the human acts in question.

For this reason the use of the simple dichotomy infallible and non-infallible teaching can be misleading. One cannot simply presume that any church doctrine which has not been infallibly defined (that is, identifiable in the definitive decisions of an ecumenical council or in a papal definition, such as the dogmas of the immaculate conception or the assumption of the Blessed Virgin Mary) is not in fact contained in the infallible teaching of the church's universal ordinary magisterium, which is described by Vatican II in these words:

"Although the bishops, taken individually, do not enjoy the privilege of infallibility, they do, however, proclaim infallibly the doctrine of Christ on the following conditions: namely, when, even though dispersed throughout the world but preserving for all that among themselves and with Peter's successor the bond of communion in their authoritative teaching concerning matters of faith and morals, they are in agreement that a particular teaching is to be held definitively and absolutely" (*Lumen Gentium*, 25).

Sometimes the word *dissent* is used—improperly, in my view—to describe the work of theological research and of scholars who are exploring the frontiers of some issue with hypothetical, speculative, and hence tentative, conclusions. It seems to me that such explorations do not properly fall within the area of dissent when they are presented as hypothetical and not as pastoral norms which can be followed in practice (for example, in the moral order) or as substitutes for the accepted understanding of church dogmas. If more theological research were presented in this speculative and hypothetical fashion, I personally believe that there would be less tension about dissent in the church today.

The key issue for the theologian, it seems to me, is the recognition of the methodology of theology as a science. If theology is going to be faithful to its own internal discipline, it must recognize the place of revelation and faith, and the assistance of the Holy Spirit in its guidance of the magisterium. For the theologian who judges that he may withhold assent from some authoritative, non-infallible church teaching, the methodology of Catholic theology requires that he explore the issue and report his findings in such a way as not to call into question the role of the magisterium of the church.

This leads to a final important distinction in the discussion on dissent, namely between private and public dissent. The personal or private dissent described above theoretically remains open to achieving a fuller understanding of the issue in such a way that will allow one to remain in harmony with the church's teaching authority. Whether it is the theologian's own view or the formulation of church teaching which is modified, the process can properly be seen in the context of the growth in a fuller understanding of the truths of our faith toward which the Holy Spirit is constantly leading the church.

On the other hand, public dissent, in which one proposes a personal opinion or conclusion which directly contradicts some teaching of the church's non-infallible, authoritative magisterium, is no longer a step on the path of dialogue toward a growth in understanding of church teaching. Rather, it contains a decision to place one's own judgment on a par with that of the magisterium and implicitly suggests that the question or doubt which has led one to withhold assent or dissent has now become an answer which one offers to others to accept and imitate as a legitimate position for a Catholic believer.

If such a person is a teacher (for example, a theologian or catechist), it is difficult to see how the decision to substitute a doctrine proposed by the teaching church by a conclusion proposed on one's own authority will not subvert the student's continued grasp of and eventual assent to the truths which the church teaches. Hence the person who dissents publicly, that is, who presents conclusions as a decision at which they have arrived in contradiction to the teaching of the church, must also understand that this decision implies a certain separation from the tradition of the church which is handed on in the magisterium under the guidance of the Holy Spirit for the belief of the Christian faithful.

(I do not include in this public dissent the explorations of theological scholars and researchers when discussion of their speculative theological conclusions takes place in a way which becomes public *per accidens* or is popularized in a way that is not within their own control.)

To sum up this discussion on dissent, I would say that Catholic theology does not recognize the right to dissent, if by that we mean adopting conclusions which are contrary to the clear teachings of the authoritative, non-infallible magisterium and are presented to the public in such a way as to constitute equivalently an alternative, personal magisterium.

It is important to note that this discussion applies to teaching on faith and morals, and not to the area of the many prudential judgments that popes and bishops are daily required to make in the governance of the church. For example, after World War II, Pope Pius XII forbade Catholics to vote for the Communist Party under pain of excommunication. While the penalty was severe, this judgment did not and could not involve the kind of assent which one is obliged to give to the certain teachings of the church because it did not involve a question of faith and morals. For another example closer to home, the American bishops have consistently taught the evil of abortion as part of the universal ordinary magisterium. But their prudential judgment some years ago to support the Hatch amendment as a political strategy did not and cannot oblige the "submission of mind and will," because it was not a teaching on faith and morals.

The medieval discussion about what to do in the case of a pope who lapses into heresy or who teaches mistakenly as a private theologian makes it clear that popes and bishops are not immune from error per se. The promised assistance of the Holy Spirit is given to their teaching insofar as the pope teaches as the supreme pastor and shepherd of the universal church, and the bishops teach in union with him those things that we must believe and do for the sake of our salvation.

Another of the confusing issues which is related to the question of dissent is that of conscience. In much popular discussion conscience is used as a synonym for one's own opinion and as such becomes a counterpoint to the teaching of the church. This is an improper understanding of the notion of conscience in Catholic tradition, which understands conscience as a faculty of discernment by which one is led to judge here and now what course of action to take—what to do or not to do in a specific and concrete case—taking into account all that one has learned, the particular circumstances, etc. In a particular case conscience may make a determination which in hindsight turns out to be mistaken, either through lack of proper information or the pressures of the situation. Or one may persist in a mistaken conscience through peer pressure or the example of many other Christians who seem to do or omit something "in good conscience," etc.

As disciples of Christ in a highly secularized world, every Christian is faced with difficult choices of conscience. A right conscience, which has been educated to know God's will through the teaching of the church, through discipline and a conscientious exercise of its decision-making power, should be the goal of every Christian. Unfortunately today the lack of clear teaching, as well as the presentation of dissenting or contradictory opinions as legitimate, have caused a true crisis of conscience for many persons and have contributed greatly to the dulling of conscience as an effective function to guide us in the choice of the good and the avoidance of evil. Lack of a right conscience not only takes its toll in lowering personal moral standards, but also greatly desensitizes people to the perception of social evil and to their responsibilities in its regard.

In any case, it is not correct to think that one can oppose one's own conscience to the teaching of the church. As the Second Vatican Council says in the Declaration on Religious Liberty (No. 14):

"In forming their consciences the faithful must pay careful attention to the sacred and certain teaching of the church. For the Catholic Church is, by the will of Christ, the teacher of truth. It is her duty to proclaim and teach with authority the truth which is Christ and, at the same time, to declare and confirm by her authority the principles of the moral order which spring from human nature itself."

The obligation of forming a right conscience is a basic demand inherent in our discipleship of Christ. While it is true that conscience is subjectively the final arbiter in any particular decision we must make, it is also the constant teaching of our church's tradition that no one can exempt himself from the formation of a correct and right conscience, for which the revelation of God as handed on in the teaching of the church is indispensable.

Finally, we need to say a word about the *sensus fidelium* or "sense of the faithful," which is sometimes presented as an alternative magisterium. The Vatican Council, in the Constitution on the Church (No. 12), speaks about the "appreciation of the faith of the whole people, when 'from the bishops to the last of the faithful' they manifest a universal consent in matters of faith and morals. By this appreciation of the faith (called the *sensus fidei*), aroused and sustained by the Spirit of truth, the people of God, guided by the sacred teaching authority (magisterium) and obeying it, receives not the mere word of men but truly the word of God." In Catholic tradition, the *sensus fidelium* is not another channel for the teaching of the Holy Spirit in the church apart from the magisterium; it is rather the instinct of the believing people about what God has revealed and taught in and through his church, so that people everywhere and in every age can be said to know and share in the same Catholic faith.

Sometimes statistical results of polls among Catholics (both practicing and non-practicing) are cited as evidence that there is a *sensus fidelium* which stands in contrast with the teaching of the church's magisterium. For example, last summer Our Sunday Visitor carried the results of a Gallup Poll which had posed the question, "Do you think it is wrong for a man and a woman to have sex relations before marriage or not?" Of the Catholics who responded (50 percent described themselves as regular Massgoers), 33 percent said they believe premarital sex to be wrong, while 59 percent saw it as acceptable. (That compared to 39 percent of Americans at large who identified premarital sex as wrong and 46 percent of Protestants polled in the same poll who indicated its unacceptability.) On the other hand, in 1969, 72 percent of the Catholics who responded to the poll said they thought premarital sex was wrong. Does this poll constitute a *sensus fidelium?* Has the Holy Spirit guided the *sensus fidelium* from 1969 to 1985 into a total reversal of values? Such a notion strikes me as suspect.

Rather than accuse the Holy Spirit of lack of fidelity to the Gospel, it seems to me that we should analyze the data as indicating the enormous invasion of secular values—I might say values directly opposed to the Gospel and inimical to discipleship in Christ and to authentic apostolic service—which have overwhelmed the resources of many of our Catholic families, our Catholic religious education programs and, indeed, our Catholic Church life in this area. It would not be correct to justify one's dissent on the grounds that the Holy Spirit needs it in order to correct what one's personal judgment cannot accept or sees as erroneous in church teaching.

The effective teaching of Catholic faith in today's culture, especially in the United States and other highly secularized nations, will require the Catholic educator to be clear and persuasive in discussing and presenting the teachings of Catholic faith in a way that will make them not only attractive but able to be seen ultimately as the meaning of personal human existence in the world.

Without the cultural supports of past ages, this task is even more challenging than it has ever been. The teacher will have to model his or her own growth in faith into the fullness of truth in a convincing way. In my opinion it would be counterproductive to follow a suggestion like that in one of the "two views" published in Momentum last year, that we teach our students "responsible dissent" from the teachings of the church.

I hope I have shown this to be not only undesirable and self-defeating but, in fact, not in conformity with the requirements of Catholic faith. Our students need to have the assurance that the church is indeed a reliable teacher and guide. In my judgment that is an assurance which we all—bishops, Catholic teachers of religion and catechists—ought to give willingly and convincingly, confident that the Lord in promising his Spirit to the church indeed had us and our students in mind.

Dissent in the Church

Daniel Pilarczyk

This article originally appeared in *Origins* in 1986.

An analysis of levels of church teaching, the assent called for to church teaching, kinds of dissent and some catch phrases associated with controversies on dissent are included in the June 6, 1986, pastoral letter on dissent by Archbishop Daniel Pilarczyk of Cincinnati. "I do not like controversy in the church. I wish we did not have to deal with it. That is not a very realistic wish, though, if one looks back through the church's history," Pilarczyk writes. In his analysis, he concludes at one point: "It is simply not true to suggest, as some seem to, that whatever is not formally defined as infallible is subject to full and open debate in the church or, for that matter, that all the church's teachings require the same degree of faith assent." Every church teaching, says Pilarczyk, "implies a decision, a decision about public church order, a decision about what teachers in the church are to say and do. The church does not put forth a teaching and let it find its own way as best it can." Public dissent, he adds, "always involves deliberate refusal, even if for conscientious reasons, to carry out an order from church teaching authority." May theologians dissent from non-infallible church teaching? "Under certain circumstances they may, perhaps they must. But when they do so, they do so at their own risk, subject to a final determination by church authority." Pilarczyk's pastoral letter follows.

Over the past few months, there have been several items in the news dealing with dissent from church teaching. An advertisement in the New York Times claimed that disciplinary action taken by certain agencies of the Holy See against persons who disagreed with church teaching about abortion was unjust in that it violated these persons' right of free speech.

Then came the news that a professor of moral theology at the Catholic University of America was under investigation by the Congregation for the Doctrine of the Faith because he holds that under certain circumstances contraceptive acts, homosexual acts, and even abortions are morally justifiable.

Reactions to these news items have been varied and vocal. There have been calls for punishment as well as demands that the rights of individual Catholics be defended against church bureaucracy. Petitions have begun to circulate, encouraging people to join in declarations of public solidarity with the Holy See or expressing their concern for the rights of the theological community. A certain amount of anger was expressed against our own Catholic Telegraph for even printing this news!

People wonder what is going on. Many are confused.

The purpose of this brief letter is to offer to the faithful of the archdiocese some help in coming to grips with this issue of dissent from church teaching. My intent is neither to provide a complete theological treatise on church teaching and on theological dissent from that teaching nor to treat every aspect of the present controversies. Likewise, I do not intend to impute guilt to individuals or offer suggestions to higher church authority about how the situation should be handled. I merely offer some pastoral reflections with the hope that they will help people put the issues into some kind of appropriate perspective.

I will divide what I have to say into four parts:

1. How the church teaches and the kind of assent to the teaching the church calls for.

2. What church authority is saying in the act of teaching.

3. Dissent and its implications.

4. Some specifics which have surfaced in the course of the present controversies.

1. How the Church Teaches

Please note that "church teaching" in the context of this letter means the teaching of the pope and of the bishops in communion with him when they write or speak in their capacity as official spokespersons for the church. This constitutes official Catholic teaching. Because a certain position is taught by a large number of theologians does not necessarily make it church teaching. There can be, and often is, a difference between what some Catholics teach and what is official Catholic teaching. In this letter I am talking about official Catholic teaching.

Church teaching tells us what we must believe and what we must do in order to be saved, in order to be part of Christ's life, in order to be a member of Christ's people, the church. Church teaching is not something the pope and the bishops make up, but rather something which reflects, clarifies and explicates the teaching of Christ himself. The ultimate source of church teaching is the teaching of Christ.

However, not everything which the church teaches is of equal weight or authority, and not everything calls for the same degree of acceptance on the part of the faithful. There are at least three kinds, three levels of church teaching.

—One level is constituted by those teachings which the church has formally and specifically defined as being so much a part of revelation that their truth is guaranteed by God himself, and that they simply cannot be wrong. These are formally defined, infallible truths such as the divinity of Christ and the reality of his human nature.

—A second level of teaching is constituted by those truths about faith and morals which are proposed as certainly true, even though they have not been the object of a specific and formally infallible definition. There are truths which have been consistently, conscientiously and deliberately taught by the pope and the bishops in communion with him as being absolute and obligatory. They include such matters as the responsibility of bishops to proclaim the Gospel and the prohibition of deliberately taking innocent human life.

—The third category—ordinary, non-infallible teaching—consists of teaching which the church proposes as true, though not defined as infallible and not necessarily unchangeable. It includes such matters as the teaching that workers have the right to organize into labor unions or that society has the responsibility to see that appropriate employment is available to all its citizens. The level of teaching represents the ordinary teaching level of church authority; and, while it is not infallible, it is the fruit of mature consideration and reflection on the part of theologians and church authority, and enjoys the regular guidance from the Holy Spirit which Christ promised to his church.

Just as there are different levels of teaching in the church, so also there are different levels of assent to the teaching which the church calls for from its faithful. When a teaching has been formally defined as infallible, the church expects that all the faithful will accept the teaching as a condition for church membership. A person who does not believe, for example, that Jesus is God is simply not a Catholic Christian. That which is infallibly taught but not formally defined calls for acceptance as certain. When it comes to the third level of teaching, that of the ordinary, non-infallible magisterium, the church calls for its members to accept and follow the teaching "with religious submission of mind and will" (*Lumen Gentium*, 25).

The church teaches with authority at every level and authoritatively calls for a response from the faithful at every level even though the intensity of the expected response varies with the level of the teaching. It is simply not true to suggest, as some seem to, that whatever is not formally defined as infallible is subject to full and open debate in the church or, for that matter, that all the church's teachings require the same degree of faith assent.

2. What the Church Is Saying When It Teaches

When the church teaches at any of the various levels I have outlined above, it is actually saying two distinct things. The first is, "This is true and is in accord with divine revelation. All of our members are to accept this and/or to behave in this particular way." The second thing the church is saying in this official teaching is particularly addressed to those who are responsible for delivering church teaching. These include catechists, theologians (who, in fact, spend much of their time teaching), preachers, writers and other "public" persons within the church. To them, church authority says, "We want you who teach under the auspices of the church to present this teaching to your public as true and as binding in accord with the level of authority with which it is presented."

Every time the church teaches, therefore, it is dealing with these two elements—the articulation or enunciation of the teaching; and also with the demand that the teaching be presented in the church as church teaching. Every church teaching implies a decision, a decision about public church order, a decision about what teachers in the church are to say and do. The church does not put forth a teaching and let it find its own way as best it can. Rather, the church views all of its teaching as a kind of project, as something to be "done," as an activity in which its whole delivery system is to be involved.

3. Dissent

In this context, dissent is the nonacceptance or rejection of a church teaching. There are two levels on which dissent must be considered.

The first is dissent by individual Catholics who find that they cannot in conscience accept or act on a given church teaching. Conscience is that faculty of the spirit which enables us to apply moral principles to the concrete situation in which we find ourselves. For example, I know that it is wrong to steal, but I have to apply that truth to my specific situation as I fill out my income tax forms. Conscience does not lead us to decide what we want to do but what we ought to do, and we are always obliged to follow our conscience because our conscience tells us what is right and wrong here and now.

However, if we believe in any kind of objective moral teaching whatsoever, it is clear that conscience can be correct and it can also be incorrect. We have to follow it, no matter what, but we have the obligation to try to have a conscience which is correct. One element of a correct conscience is a set of correct principles to build from, principles which provide the premises on which to base our specific conclusions. Another way of saying this is that we have the obligation of seeing that our conscience is correctly formed. As Catholic believers we have committed ourselves to operating from the principles taught by the church, and we must therefore carefully strive to incorporate the church's principles into our personal moral decision-making process.

If, in a given case, I find myself unable to accept the moral principles which the church teaches or I am convinced that the expected application of those principles is simply wrong in this case, I must, of course, follow my conscience. At the same time, though, I must continue to strive to assimilate, understand and make operative in my faith and my behavior the principles of Catholic teaching. Responsibility for forming our conscience correctly never ceases.

Conscience is complicated. So is individual conscientious dissent from church teaching. It is dangerous and oversimplified to tell ourselves or other people, "Just go ahead and do what you think is right." There is more to it than just that.

The second level at which dissent must be considered occurs when someone who has assumed teaching responsibility in the church finds that he or she cannot personally accept certain points of the church's teaching. Here we are dealing not only with conscientious choices in the life of an individual, but with a public responsibility owed toward the church. This person must not only come to grips with what he or she is to believe, but also with what he or she is to teach.

Teachers in the church (catechists, theologians, preachers, etc.) have several possible alternatives from which to choose. One is to submerge their personal doubts and teach what the church teaches on the grounds that the authority of the church outweighs their personal views. Another is to keep quiet about their personal doubts and also to keep silent about the church's teaching on the matter. A third is to oppose the church's teaching openly.

Supposing, as one must, that those who dissent from church teaching do so on conscientious grounds, the fact still remains that those who choose not to teach what the church wants taught or who publicly oppose church teaching even when it is a question of non-infallible doctrine are not in compliance with the church's "public order decision" about this particular teaching, namely, that it is to be taught as true and binding in accord with its own level of authority. Public dissent always involves deliberate refusal, even if for conscientious reasons, to carry out an order from church teaching authority.

In regard to such public dissent, whether it takes the form of refusing to teach what the church wants taught or the form of offering public opposition to such teaching, church authorities have heavy responsibilities toward Christ and the church community. They must treat the dissenters with understanding and fairness, while at the same time safeguarding official Catholic teaching. They can exercise these responsibilities in many ways.

—They can keep quiet and wait to see what happens. Sometimes it will turn out that the teaching in question is open to a better formulation. In the case of non-infallible teaching it may become clear that the teaching should be changed. On the other hand, it often happens that dissenting opinions of theologians are examined in a scholarly way by their peers in the theological community, are demonstrated to be untenable and are thus taken care of without the intervention of church authority.

—Another option is to invite the dissenter to consider his or her lack of compliance with church teaching and church policy, and to change his or her mind about dissenting.

—Still another option on the part of church authority is to demand that the dissenter publicly retract the dissenting opinion. (The use of this option entails some danger in our American culture in that it tends to push the dissenter into the posture of the underdog and make him or her look like a hapless victim of harsh authority figures. "Retract" and "recant" are highly charged words in our society.)

—If a case is serious enough and if the points of theological dissent are numerous enough, church authority can decide that the person is so far out of compliance as to have forfeited his or her right to be called a Catholic theologian. (This is not saying that the theologian is personally bad or is excluded from the love of Christ. It only says that the church does not want to be represented in its teaching by that person.)

—Of course, if the matter of dissent is a point of infallibly defined doctrine, the church authority can take the ultimate step of cutting the dissenter off from the church by a declaration of excommunication.

4. SOME SPECIFICS

I now offer some reflections on three catch phrases which have surfaced rather frequently in the controversies of dissent which we have been reading about.

Freedom of Conscience
Some time ago I received a letter from someone who did not like something I had said. "In case you are not aware of it," the letter said, "Vatican II gave us freedom of conscience so we will never again have to listen to guys like you." A rather radical interpretation of Vatican II, I thought.

Freedom of conscience is primarily a matter of the relationship of the individual with civil government. Freedom of conscience means that no civil government has the right to demand any kind of religious compliance from its citizens. This freedom of conscience has been one of the treasured foundational concepts of our republic since its beginning.

Freedom of conscience, however, does not mean that it is morally acceptable for a Catholic to believe or do whatever he or she chooses within the church. There are teachings which the church demands that its members accept. There are standards of moral behavior which the church expects its members to strive to observe. The church cannot compel anybody to believe anything or to do anything. But the church can say that refusal or inability to accept what the church teaches, at least on certain basic matters, may be an indication that the person should not be in the church to begin with.

Freedom of Speech
This too is a political concept. As an American citizen I am free to say just about anything I choose. I can say that the presi-

dent is a scoundrel and that all the laws passed since 1932 are detrimental to the common good and should be repealed. That is my right as a citizen and nobody can take away my citizenship for exercising it. It is confusing, though, to try to introduce this political concept into other contexts.

Within the church, I am not free to say what I like and at the same time claim to be a member in good standing. This is particularly true if I represent the church as a catechist, teaching theologian, preacher or in any other sort of public capacity. As such, I am expected to comply with the church's requirements for public order, and if I choose not to do so, I cannot take refuge in a plea of exercising free speech. Not even the pope has, within the church, the right of unlimited free speech which exists in civil society. Like all the rest of us, he is bound by the truths of revelation and is simply not free to deviate from them.

Right of Theologians to Dissent from Non-Infallible Teaching

Here we are at the nerve center of the whole present controversy. Theologians have a special responsibility in the church and perform a special service to the church. As teachers they are called to teach what the church teaches as true and binding. But they also have a specific role as theologians. This special role calls them to explore the implications of church teaching, to investigate it, to refine it, to probe it, to push back its horizons. If not all church teaching is guaranteed to be infallible, then some of it could be fallible, reformable, conceivably even incorrect. It is part of the theologian's responsibility to speak to church teaching which he or she conscientiously believes to be inexact or erroneous.

Unless theologians take seriously their whole responsibility, very little progress in our understanding of the truths of revelation would be made.

At the same time, if we speak of "the right to dissent," we run the risk of seeming to say that certain people in the church are allowed to deal with church teaching and church policy about teaching in whatever way they see fit, as a matter of right. Rather than ask about a theologian's right to dissent from church teaching— even non-infallible teaching—we might do better to ask how much dissent church authorities should tolerate, how much is permissible. After all, dissent from church teaching and church policy should always be the exception, the extraordinary situation.

In their 1968 pastoral letter "Human Life in Our Day," the bishops of our country wrote a brief section on theological dissent (nos. 49–54). They do not speak of a "right" to dissent, but they offer some norms of "licit" theological dissent. They say, "The expression of theological dissent from the magisterium is in order only if the reasons are serious and well-founded, if the manner of the dissent does not question or impugn the teaching authority of the church and is such as not to give scandal" (no. 51). I take these criteria to be the "outer limits" that the church is willing to tolerate. Thus, any dissent that is not seriously founded, that does undermine the authority of the church and that turns people away from doing good (which is what scandal means) is clearly out of bounds.

But even within these limits it is not clear to me that everything is acceptable as a matter of right. After all, what is at issue here is a refusal, for whatever reason, to accept the directives of church leadership about what is to be taught in the name of the church. Church authority may tolerate such refusal for any number of reasons. In some cases church authority may eventually decide to modify the teaching if it is a teaching that admits of modification.

But church authority also has the right and the responsibility to make a prudent judgment, case by case, about the limits of such tolerance. At some point, church authority may perceive itself compelled to say, "We have listened. We have tried to understand. But now we do not believe it is good for the church for this to continue. Your dissent is no longer tolerable."

May theologians, then, dissent from non-infallible church teaching? Under certain circumstances they may, perhaps they must. But when they do so, they do so at their own risk, subject to the final determination by church authority.

5. Conclusion

As I come to the close of these reflections, I am aware that there are many issues I have not treated. One is the question of discerning at which level of authority a given teaching is presented by the church.

Is the church's teaching on contraception, for example, something that has been so consistently, consciously and deliberately taught that it is proposed as certainly true, absolute and obligatory; or is it at the level of ordinary non-infallible teaching that admits of change?

Another issue is the question of the development of church doctrine. How does it grow and mature and what is the role of the faith of church members in that process?

Then there are the practical questions connected with the work of theologians. How are theologians to carry on their work of probing and exploring without seeming to establish themselves as a distinct authority over against popes and bishops? How can theologians responsibly ask questions about church teaching when their every utterance is likely to be the subject of newspaper headlines?

Another matter I have not treated is the sense of struggle that accompanies the teaching and understanding of church doctrine: the struggle of church authority to remain faithful to the teaching of Christ and to maintain church order, the struggle of the theological community to refine church teaching in accord with new scholarly insights and new social and scientific situations, the struggle of all the church's members to accept and carry out the demands of our Catholic faith. Sometimes this struggle manifests itself in a centuries-long process of earnest reflection, sometimes in the joining of ranks against an attack from without, sometimes as a sharp controversy within the church.

I do not like controversy in the church. I wish we did not have to deal with it. That is not a very realistic wish, though, if one looks back through the church's history. A couple of things are clear to me however. One is that in all controversy we have to treat everybody with the charity and love that Christ expects his members to offer one another. This includes persons on the right and on the left of the theological spectrum, dissenters and church authorities, theologians, catechists, bishops and cardinals.

Another is that it is the Lord's church, not ours, and that he is much busier in it and much more influential in it than any of us. He can also see a lot more clearly than we can. He loves more effectively than we do. That is a source of great hope for me.

A third is that everyone involved in these controversies needs the support of the prayers of the entire church. Please pray, then, for those who teach in the church, for those who teach in the name of the church, for theologians, for students, for church authorities, for those who write and for those who read. Somewhere in there I hope that you will also include a remembrance of me.

The Magisterium and Theological Dissent

Roger Mahony

This article originally appeared in *Origins* in 1986.

"In my opinion, it is (a) blurring of roles in the realm of pastoral practice that has resulted in the current tensions between the magisterium and some theologians," Archbishop Roger Mahony of Los Angeles said in an address Oct. 16 at the University of Southern California. Along with Father Charles Curran, he addressed an audience of more than 1,000 on dissent in the church. Mahony said that he believes the church must exercise its most "diligent teaching authority" when theologians propose personal theories as pastoral practice. Mahony said he hoped his address would not reinforce "the image of the church as a merely juridical structure." He said it is "not only or even primarily" the bishop's role to control. "He must also facilitate." Despite the negative image of bishops held by some people, Mahony said that bishops are "not overinclined to be restrictive. The greater danger, I suspect, is that we may be too permissive." The church, "if it is to stand for anything, has to have some common doctrine that is respected, and put into practice by its members," said Mahony. His full text follows.

I am very pleased to accept the invitation of your dean to share with you my views on the teaching ministry of the church. The teaching office of the bishop has been strongly emphasized by the Second Vatican Council and is briefly but clearly set forth in the new Code of Canon Law. Canon 386 declares:

"(1) The diocesan bishop is bound to present and explain to the faithful the truths of the faith which are to be believed and applied to moral issues, frequently preaching in person; he is also to see to the careful observation of the prescriptions of the canons concerning the ministry of the word, especially those concerning the homily and catechetical formation, so that the whole of Christian doctrine is imparted to all.

"(2) Through suitable means he is strongly to safeguard the integrity and unity of the faith to be believed while nevertheless acknowledging a rightful freedom in the further investigation of its truths."

Notable in this canon, as in the teaching of the council, is the primary emphasis given to the preaching ministry of the bishop. As a preacher, he has the responsibility to proclaim the good news of the Gospel and to present the person of Jesus Christ, the crucified and risen savior, in an engaging and challenging way.

In my ministry as a priest and a bishop I have become increasingly convinced that authority in the church is best served when we bishops focus our attention on Christ and on God, and allow juridical rights and obligations to flow from our discipleship with the Lord. The Synod of Bishops that met in Rome last fall (1985) recognized this approach. In their Final Report the bishops said:

"Perhaps we are not free from all responsibility for the fact that young people, in particular, regard the church critically as a mere institution. Have we not put the idea into their heads by talking too much about reforming external church structures and too little about God and Christ?"

I hope that in trying to adhere to my assigned topic this evening I shall not be reinforcing the image of the church as a merely juridical structure rather than presenting it as a community of men and women embarking together on an exciting journey of faith. Still it must be recognized that the church, as a visible society, must have institutional structures and that they can be of great service for the proclamation of the Gospel and for preventing the message of Christ from being distorted by arbitrary interpretations.

One other point in the canon I have quoted deserves to be

emphasized. When in its second part the canon turns to the bishop's responsibility to safeguard the integrity of the faith, it immediately adds that the rightful freedom of theologians to inquire into doctrinal questions must be respected. Although an authentic teacher of the faith, the bishop is not merely an "ecclesiastical policeman."

His task is not only or even primarily to control. He must also facilitate. He must enable others to perform their ministries in the diocese. I think it only fair to say that bishops commonly enjoy a cordial and cooperative relationship with theologians and with others engaged in the ministry of the word. Church history shows, if I am not mistaken, that authority functions best when bishops and theologians work in harmony, as they generally do.

I am pleased that here in our own Archdiocese of Los Angeles there is now a theological commission comprised of outstanding professional theologians—priests, lay men and women—to guide and assist me with current theological concerns.

I cannot think of any major dispute in which the conflict has been between the hierarchy and the theologians as such. In every doctrinal quarrel known to me, there has been a division within the theological community itself. Very often the hierarchical magisterium has found itself in the position of trying to mediate between rival theological schools.

Occasionally, however, some theological opinion has to be ruled out as incompatible with the Christian message. Such a ruling has to come from the pope or the bishops.

Our American culture, quite rightly, puts a high value on freedom and has a corresponding distrust for any restrictive exercise of authority. Freedom is in fact closely related to human dignity as proclaimed in the Gospel. Jesus tells us, "If you live according to my teaching, you are truly my disciples; then you will know the truth, and the truth will set you free" (Jn. 8:32). In its teaching ministry the church strives to liberate its members from domination by passions or worldly forces that would blind their minds or chain their wills. If the church sometimes seems to be stern in its discipline, this is only for the sake of leading its members to that true freedom which Christ has purchased for us all.

Championing freedom in the world, the church fosters freedom in its own household. The Second Vatican Council taught that freedom is to be respected as far as possible and curtailed only when and insofar as necessary (cf. *Dignitatis Humanae,* 7). This principle, as I understand it, applies as much to the church as to the political society. Because of our esteem for freedom, we bishops generally prefer to say yes rather than no to any serious request. In spite of our negative image in some minds, we are not overinclined to be restrictive. The greater danger, I suspect, is that we may be too permissive. From time to time we need to be reminded of Paul's admonitions to Timothy and Titus that they must correct and reprove false doctrines and defend the faith against any abridgement or contamination.

To set the right context for any discussion of teaching authority and dissent, it is crucial to keep in mind that the church differs in many ways from secular societies and agencies. Although debate and exploration surely have their place in the church, the church is not a debating club or a society of explorers.

Most fundamentally, it is a community of faith and witness, one that worships God in Jesus Christ and seeks to live in close union with its risen Lord. The church is sent into the world to bear witness, both by word and example, to its divinely given message. It cannot justify its existence unless it remains solidly rooted in the faith that gave it birth.

From the earliest days Christians recognized the importance of an authoritative teaching body for the maintenance of inner unity. Christ imposed upon the apostles and their successors the tasks of disseminating his full doctrine and making disciples of all nations. He assured them that he would remain ever present to assist them in their work. Paul continually exhorts his converts to submit humbly to the teachers set over them and to avoid every trace of factionalism. The dangers of partisanship and polarization were manifest in Paul's day, as they are in ours.

In the first three centuries the unity of the church continued to depend on its structured hierarchical leadership. Clement of Rome, Ignatius of Antioch, Irenaeus and Tertullian all insist on the authority of the bishops who stand in the apostolic succession. Where this authority was maintained, the church exhibited a remarkable unanimity which was, to the early apologists, a sign of its divine origin. Let me illustrate this with several characteristic quotations.

Irenaeus, writing late in the second century, speaks as follows:

"Having received this message and this truth, the church, although scattered through the whole world, keeps them carefully, as if she inhabited a single house. She unanimously believes them as if she had but one heart and one soul; she preaches them as if she had but one tongue. The languages of the world are many, but the force of tradition is one and the selfsame. . . . The sun, God's creature, is one and the selfsame in the world. So likewise the preaching of the truth is the light that shines everywhere and enlightens all who wish to know it" (*Adv. haer.* 1.10.2; SC 264: 158–60).

Tertullian, a generation later, describes the church as "a body all of whose members are conjoined by the bond of a single faith, unity of discipline and concord of hope" (*Apol.* 39: 1; CC 1:150). In spite of the wide diversities between East and West, he declares, Christians are not divided. "They and we have one faith, one God, the same Christ, the same hope and the same baptismal sacrament. Let me say it once and for all: We are one church" (*De virg. vel.* 2.2; CC 2:1210).

Irenaeus and Tertullian both explain the marvelous unity of the church by pointing to the role of the bishops who stand in the apostolic succession. Cyprian, my third witness, is of the same mind. Writing toward the middle of the third century, he anticipates the modern doctrine of collegiality. He writes:

"The episcopate is one; it is a corporation in which each member possesses title to the whole (*cuius a singulis in solidum pars tenetur*). The church is likewise one, although she is spread abroad and multiplies with the increase of her progeny. Even so the sun has many rays but one light; a tree has many branches but one life, drawn from a single tenacious root; and, when many streams arise from one source, unity is preserved by reason of the origin even though many diverse bodies of water flow from the abundance of the spring" (*De cath. eccl. unit.* 5; CSEL 3:214).

In all these metaphors Cyprian is insisting that the unity of the church depends upon that of its episcopate, which is itself grounded in the See of Peter as the source from which unity takes its rise.

The unity in doctrine that resulted from these structures was never merely abstract or theoretical. It had a clear impact on the ways in which Christians behaved. One of the earliest apologists, the anonymous author of the Letter to Diognetus, contrasts the values and practices of Christians with those of their pagan neighbors. Christians, he says, marry and have babies as others do, but they do not destroy their infants. They share a common table but not a common bed (*Ad Diogn.* 5: 6–7; PG 2: 1173).

Tertullian makes a similar point in his counterattack on the church's persecutors:

"Now for us Christians murder is forbidden on all counts, and we are forbidden to terminate the life of the womb once the blood has been drawn for the conception of the child. To prevent the child from being born is merely premature murder: It makes no difference whether one takes the life of one already born or stops it on its way to birth. What is to be born is already human; the full fruit is already present in the seed" (*Apol.* 9. 8; CC 1: 90).

I give these quotations not in order to raise the specific questions of extramarital intercourse and abortion, which are still relevant today, but to make the more general point that the church, if it is to stand for anything, has to have some common doctrine that is respected and put into practice by its members.

The principles that governed the church's common life in the early centuries must continue to be operative in subsequent ages, for the permanence of the church, as Cardinal Newman perceived, implies continuity in its doctrinal principles. From the very beginnings, Newman observed, Christians felt bound "to defend and to transmit the faith which they had received, and they received it from the rulers of the church; and, on the other hand, it was the duty of those rulers to watch over and define this traditional faith." The truth of the faith, Newman goes on to say, is something independent of all the members of the church; it is something definite, formal and obligatory (*Essay on Development,* Chap. 7, sec. 5, no. 3).

The vision of the church which comes down to us from the fathers through writers such as Newman is no longer unchallenged. It stands in some tension with the modern mentality, which favors freedom of inquiry, experimentation and expression. Modern journalism, politics and university practice all seem to be based on the premise that truth wells up from below, through a process of trial and error, and is not to be sought in any kind of revelation, authoritatively transmitted.

The church is no stranger to the modern world. One of the main purposes of the Second Vatican Council was to establish a new and better relationship between the church and that world. The aim was not and could not have been to blur the distinctive witness of the church or to dissolve its unity and continuity. But it was felt that the church, without detriment to its own proper identity, could achieve a better relationship with its present cultural environment. Just as Paul became a Jew to Jews and a Greek to Greeks in order to gain all to Christ, so the church could adapt its apostolate to a variety of cultures.

Quite evidently the church today in a country such as our own cannot depend entirely on ideas and institutions shaped in other times and places. It needs open-minded scholars who, with full loyalty to the Catholic heritage, approach current questions with modern methods and techniques. While every effort will be made to reach solutions that harmonize with Catholic teaching, it will occasionally happen that a scholar may become convinced, on the basis of personal research and reflection, that certain past or recent statements of ecclesiastical authorities stand in need of revision. The question then arises, May the theologian dissent, privately or publicly, from the currently received doctrine?

This question admits of no simple yes or no answer. We have to consider in detail what is being challenged and how. Church pronouncements are not all on the same level of authority. They may be ranked all the way from the solemn dogmatic pronouncements of popes and ecumenical councils at the top to casual statements of bishops and Curial officials at the bottom. To assess the obligatory force of a teaching one would have to consider carefully who issued it, in what kind of pronouncement, how emphatically, how frequently, for how long a period, on what grounds and with what kind of support or reception from other authorities. It would be an oversimplification to say either that Catholics must submit to all the teaching statements of the church authorities or that they are entitled to dissent from anything not infallibly taught. But it would not be an exaggeration to state that as Catholics we are expected to give our internal and external, private and public, assent to magisterial teaching that is clearly within our time-honored tradition.

In practice it is very rare that anyone who claims to be a Catholic simply denies a dogma of the faith. Father Hans Küng, who had serious questions about infallibility, did not see himself as departing from the clear teaching of the First Vatican Council, and for this reason he has never been declared a heretic. Even though he is no longer an ecclesiastically approved teacher of Catholic theology, he remains a priest in good standing.

Far more common is the case in which a theologian, on the basis of scholarly research and reflection, diverges from a doctrine that has been taught without the special guarantee of infallibility. Such a dissent may at times be justified, but the justification will be more difficult if the docctrine is taught by high authority, with great emphasis and deliberation. One may think, in this connection, of a doctrine taught by a succession of recent popes and set forth in encyclicals that were intended to put an end to previous controversy.

Even in cases such as this, dissent cannot be totally ruled out. Provided that the statement is not uttered with the unconditional guarantee of infallibility, which must be proved and not presumed, error cannot be excluded as out of the question. Dissent, consequently, would not involve a separation from the Catholic communion. But church authorities might have good reason for placing restrictions on persons who try to use their position in the church to gain credibility for the opposition.

In the realm of dissent one must distinguish between different cases. At one extreme one could imagine an individual who, in spite of sincere efforts, felt unable to assent interiorly to what the hierarchy was teaching on a given point. Such a person might remain silent or share his difficulties with a few friends or counselors. Private dissent of this kind is readily tolerated by the church.

At the other extreme would be a dissent that was organized with a view to forming a party or pressure group working for a change in church doctrine or for official recognition of an alternative position. In view of their commission as teachers, bishops who personally supported the current teaching would feel obligated to resist such an assault on the received doctrine. They would object to the formation of what amounts to a second, competitive magisterium of dissenting theologians.

Between these two imaginary cases, representing private dissent and organized dissent, one can think of a whole spectrum of intermediate cases. I cannot discuss them all in the context of this present paper. Let me say only that there are certain circumstances in which the advocacy of dissent is clearly inappropriate.

One obvious case would be the sermon. Since preaching is a public act performed in the service of the church, the preacher may not use the pulpit to contradict the official teaching. Much the same is true of catechists and catechisms, to the extent that their very purpose is to present the approved doctrine of the church rather than the personal views of a particular author.

To this I would add that seminary teaching is another sensitive area. Without being overprotective, bishops will want to see to it that their seminarians receive formation for their future ministry under the most favorable circumstances. If major elements of church teaching are contested in the classroom, seminarians may later find it difficult to support and implement that teaching in their pastoral ministry. On the other hand, it is well for seminarians to be familiarized with the objections against current doctrine so that they can deal sympathetically with Catholics who find difficulty in assenting.

If these restrictions on the expression of dissent are admitted, one may wonder whether the theologian is anything more than an apologist for whatever the hierarchy is teaching. To present and explain the actual teaching of the church is indeed an important part of the theologian's task but, as I have already suggested, theology has a critical and creative role in grappling with new and unsettled questions. A new development of doctrine, when it begins to emerge, may be hard to distinguish from a deviation. What appears as dissent may eventually prove to have been a contribution to a more adequate formulation of the faith. In our own Catholic theological history, the example of usury is well-known. Just as industries have chemistry laboratories and governments have planning divisions, so the church needs a research arm in which difficult questions are raised and new ideas are debated.

Normally such proposals are set forth in theological conferences and written up in specialized publications for the scrutiny of peers. If a somewhat venturesome theory is put before the general public in the popularized form, the author would be well-advised to warn the reader that the opinion is a personal one that is being submitted to the judgment of the church. When certain Catholic theologians confidently assert the popes and bishops are teaching error, they appear to put their own judgment above that of the hierarchical magisterium and in so doing inevitably discredit the latter. Their attitude does not seem consonant with the reverence due to ecclesiastical authority and with the avoidance of factionalism. But the irresponsible behavior of a few should not prejudice the case. It is still possible for dissenting opinion, proposed in a positive and creative manner and within the norms of legitimate dissent, to be of service in the church's quest for deeper understanding.

A church that opened its pulpits and theological chairs to persons of every opinion would lose all credibility. It would have surrendered its claim to be the body which Christ had commissioned to teach in his name.

In my opinion, the church must exercise its most responsible and diligent teaching authority when a single theologian or group of theologians proposes their personal theory as pastoral practice for the members of the church community. I believe that in these cases the theologian(s) have seriously moved beyond their role of theologian and have usurped the role of pastor held by the bishops and the pope. In my opinion, it is this blurring of roles in the realm of pastoral practice that has resulted in the current tensions between the magisterium and some theologians.

The church, then, recognizes that in the course of scholarly theological work it is possible at times for legitimate dissent from non-infallible Catholic teaching to arise. When such dissent occurs, however, it does not replace authentic Catholic teaching but remains dissent from it. Nor does the dissenting opinion reduce the authentic teaching to being itself just another opinion.

Confronted with a dissenting opinion, authentic Catholic teaching remains what it is: authentic Catholic teaching.

It is misleading and wrong, therefore, to describe a situation of dissent, even legitimate dissent, from authentic church teaching as if it were only a matter of diversity or plurality of opinions in the church. Because of the apostolic origin and the hierarchical structure of the church, the teaching of the magisterium is not simply one theological opinion alongside others; it is, rather, church doctrine. And if proper respect is to be paid to church doctrine, it must first of all be acknowledged as what it is.

In individual cases church authorities may find it difficult to decide whether a given opinion may be taught under ecclesiastical auspices. If an unfavorable judgment is reached after long and painstaking investigation by competent authorities, the faithful should accept it very seriously. They should not assume without solid evidence that the theologian's rights have been violated.

The importance of the church's pastoral office becomes more evident day by day. The press and electronic media are often not able or willing to express all the sensitivities, nuances or distinctions necessary in the issues explored. Thus, many times they express ideas in catch phrases or titles, such as "conservative" or "liberal." Or they attempt to explore all the issues only in a confrontational way, rather than an objective difference of opinion. So often our Catholic people do not read religious journals or publications. Thus they unwittingly begin to consider these questions in oversimplified terminology.

Even theologians in university situations are likely to be overinfluenced by the reigning ethos of academic freedom. It therefore becomes more necessary than ever for the church to have firm authority structures so as to preserve its rich and ancient heritage and to address new problems in the light of Christ.

Let me conclude by echoing the message of our Holy Father, Pope John Paul II, to the theologians of the United States during his pastoral visit in 1979:

"And here I want to say a special word of gratitude, encouragement and guidance for the theologians. The church needs her theologians, particularly in this time and age so profoundly marked by deep changes in all areas of life and society. The bishops of the church, to whom the Lord has entrusted the keeping of the unity of the faith and the preaching of the message—individual bishops for their dioceses; and bishops collegially, with the successor of Peter for the universal church—we all need your work, your dedication and the fruits of your reflection. We desire to listen to you, and we are eager to receive the valued assistance of your responsible scholarship" (Oct. 7, 1979, The Catholic University of America, Washington, D.C.).

The Holy Spirit continues to be very present within the church, and the tensions which arise from time to time in the history of our church cannot lessen the power of Christ's promise: "And know that I am with you always, until the end of the world!" (Mt. 28:20).

I am optimistic about the continuing working relationship of the pope and bishops with our theologians, and as a member of the body of Catholic bishops I feel privileged to share in this challenging and sometimes demanding mission. I do so with the humble realization that I shall have to render an account of my service to the Lord himself.

Thoughts on Freedom, Conscience and Obedience

Michael Pfeifer, O.M.I.

This article originally appeared in *Origins* in 1986.

How are freedom, conscience, faithfulness and obedience interrelated for members of the church? Bishop Michael Pfeifer, OMI, of San Angelo, Texas, discussed that question in a pastoral letter issued Oct. 31. "The formation of conscience involves us in a constant dialogue with God's scriptural revelation, with the ongoing tradition and official teaching of the church. It also implies a dialogue with our experience and understanding of the daily demands which face us as individuals and as a community," Pfeifer said. He examined matters related to the formation of conscience, official church teaching, the role of the pope and the role of theologians, as well as the task the ordinary member of the church faces in reconciling conscience, freedom and authority. Pfeifer's text follows.

In recent years the official teaching of the church has come before the public on a number of issues. These statements have frequently aroused a certain controversy, both within the church and outside. Recently one of our brothers, a famous theologian, has been told that he may no longer represent us as a teacher of theology. The reason which has been given is that his public views on several matters, especially in the area of morality, are too different from the church's official teaching to qualify him as one of our public spokesmen.

This is not the place to examine the particular issues of the case. It would be even less proper to take sides here. However, the publicity and the seriousness of the decision have caused many of us to ask ourselves some questions—questions about freedom, about conscience, about faithfulness and obedience. I would like to share some reflections with you about these aspects of our lives as followers of Christ, as Catholics.

FREEDOM

At the very heart of God's scriptural revelation and his dealings with humanity is the clear and ringing message that God has made us free. There is a hope in the Creator's gift that we should come in freedom to love God and to seek union with him above all else. Our whole lives—all of our efforts, all of our relationships, indeed, all that we are—should finally be a confession of that love. The only love that God wants is a love that is freely given from the heart. No sacrifice, no rule keeping, no other artifact or attitude can substitute, and no one else may force our decision. In the final analysis, this gift is our power for good and evil, for life or death.

FAITHFULNESS

If we are created so radically free by God, how can anyone tell us what to believe? How can anyone finally command how we are to behave?

No one can. God will not, even though he awaits our free, loving response. Even what we call God's commands are given to those who have responded to the call to be his own. We learn that we must believe what God has revealed after having begun to learn who God is. In any case, we are constantly choosing for or against God and the pattern which emerges in our day-to-day choices displays the degree of our fidelity to God. We can take an important clue to the meaning of human faithfulness by considering God's own free faithfulness. The Scriptures remind us time and again that it is God who is faithful even when the people are unfaithful; our faithfulness is a reflection of God's. God's revelation is adapted to our capacity to receive it; God's action is limited by fidelity to the great covenants, in fact, to all of the divine promises and callings.

Our faithfulness as Christians is not lived in a vacuum, but rather it expresses our continuing journey to God as God's chosen ones. God is faithful to the choice of his people; our very identity as God's chosen ones is expressed in our faithfulness to the implications of having been called, chosen and graced.

CONSCIENCE

The name we have given to that faculty, that place, that secret tribunal which God will not violate and no other power can coerce, is conscience. Here is the place whereby we discern right from wrong in a spirit of striving to be faithful to God's natural law and the gospel teaching of Christ in the concrete circumstances of everyday life. Here is that place where we finally choose to activate the implications of our Christian call in our lives.

FORMATION OF CONSCIENCE

Since that is so, it is clear that our conscience must be well-formed, that is, knowledgeable and practiced, in seeking God's will. The formation of conscience involves us in a constant dialogue with God's scriptural revelation, with the ongoing tradition and official teaching of the church. It also implies a dialogue with our experience and understanding of the daily demands which face us as individuals and as a community. Prayer for the guidance of the Holy Spirit is of vital importance in the process of conscience formation.

GUIDANCE

This is where such language as "official teaching of the church" becomes significant. There is much about our faith which is prior to church teaching. We have the natural law, which tells us to do good and avoid evil which we know from reason, and also the Ten Commandments. What about divine revelation, which is the law of God, and how this binds the whole church? It cannot be changed because it is God's word and not ours. Sometimes the words of Scripture are not absolutely clear. In order to understand what is called for, one must seek out an application or interpretation of the Sacred Scriptures for our daily lives.

Bishops

Throughout Christian history this interpretation, this guidance whereby the ancient text is applied to the present, has been the work of the bishops. Indeed early bishops, because they were theologians, were often chosen precisely because they had shown an ability to offer this kind of guidance. The unity of the church requires bishops to seek to teach "with one voice" in their teaching efforts. The most important teachings of the bishops of the church are those of an ecumenical council in which the bishops of the church teach together in union with the pope.

The Pope

Since Vatican Council I in 1870, the position of the pope as chief teacher has been defined, clarifying his authority and those moments when he teaches infallibly, i.e., he cannot err in doctrine of faith and morals. Not all statements of the pope are infallible, but his official teaching in union with the other bishops is without doubt the best guidance for arriving at truth. At times, teaching will originate not only from the pope, but also from one or more of the Vatican congregations charged with special responsibility and under the authority of the pope. These are teachings of lesser authority, and there are several different levels of this lesser authority. However, all of them are "official" teaching in that they are public, addressed to the whole church and therefore command serious attention. Not only the most formal teachings, then, but also those teachings of lesser authority are part of the formation of conscience of any member of the church.

THEOLOGIANS

Throughout history there have been certain members of the church who have given themselves over to the study of Scripture and of the Christian tradition. Though not bishops—not necessarily even clerics at all—these persons assist the church and its official teachers by seeking to offer careful and mature reflection on our faith and its implications. These theologians are also teachers in the church. They are recognized on the basis of their mastery of the disciplines and are meant to be active collaborators in the church's theological ministry of teaching. In fact, it has very often been the case even today that official teaching in the church has been directly based on the initial study, reflection and teaching of these specialists. For example, the process used by the U.S. Catholic bishops in the formulation of the pastoral letters on peace and the economy was greatly enhanced by the study, research and wisdom of good and sound theologians. Their writings and teaching also form a part of the teaching of the church, and they participate in the assistance that is given to us all in the formation of our Christian conscience.

WHAT HAPPENED TO FREEDOM OF CONSCIENCE?

If all official teaching binds the conscience of a member of the church, where is the freedom—and where is the responsibility—of the individual person? Are we simply to do what we're told and count on church authorities always to be right? If not all teaching is the final word on a subject, can't we do what we think is right until the authorities reach a final conclusion and teach it as certain?

God's gift of freedom entails the responsibility to seek sincerely after all that is good. The gift of intelligence similarly entails the responsibility to seek the truth in all things. As already stated, freedom and responsibility cannot be replaced by authority in the

Christian life. Official teaching cannot replace the responsibility of Catholics to seek the truth in those teachings and to give their assent to that truth. And no one of us can simply sit back and wait for church authorities or theologians to figure things out or to make up our minds for us. This responsibility and freedom is nowhere more evident than in the areas where no final assurance can be given that God's own truth has been found.

In such cases, today as always, the church offers its guidance to the whole community according to the best available resources at its disposal. One can always rely on this official teaching *at least* not to lead us astray, even if a final word cannot be given. It is this assurance which obliges Catholics to open themselves to what is taught, ready to give assent and obedience. But just as the teaching is not final, both church authorities and Catholics in general must be open to ongoing exploration and even revision when greater clarity emerges. This ongoing exploration is carried out especially by theologians, specialists in the disciplines which are required.

At times the work of theologians leads in directions which *seem* to be contradictory to the stated teaching. Historically some apparent "contradictions" have led to greater refinement in official teaching while at other times it has been impossible to reconcile the two points of view. This should not surprise us since what we seek is a clearer vision of God's own truth. In such cases it could be that both points of view accurately describe a part of the mystery, but neither actually provides a comprehensive view. In these instances church authorities can demand that the theologian in question cease to publish his or her views for the sake of the unity and peace of the church. In no way is this a final judgment on the *question* at issue, but only a warning that a certain point of view seems irreconcilable with what has been taught thus far.

Where Does This Leave the Ordinary Person?

In all cases of non-infallible teaching we retain the responsibility to seek truth and goodness in our own lives. Official teaching must be addressed to the whole Catholic world. For that reason it cannot take into account the specific circumstances of each person who seeks sincerely to hear the church's guiding word and to live accordingly. The well-formed conscience will always strive to be based on the gospel principles of Christ and on the best teaching of the church. Prayer, study, reflection and consultation are of vital importance in conscience formation. This process should be followed before one would make an exception for oneself. But such a decision also implies openness to ongoing reflection and perhaps reconsideration in light of new teaching or new circumstances.

In the United States perhaps we have not been as concerned as we might about helping Catholics to resolve their consciences on disputed issues. More adults than ever are involved in theological study—either through parish programs or religious education or in Catholic universities, colleges and seminaries. But still only a small minority of Catholics are working toward a more adequate adult theological understanding of the New Testament and of the church's teachings. Moral questions belong not in a context of simple legal demands alone, but in a much broader context of God's loving covenant with believers asking faithfulness and generosity from us in the light of God's promises of fullness of life. Without such a context, much of the beauty and power of divine teaching will be lost upon those who struggle to understand the church's rulings. God's call to freedom is above all a call to fulfill as completely as possible an authentic image of our humanity.

CONCLUSION

It is God who has made us free. Our use of that freedom will finally constitute our ultimate choice for or against God and neighbor. The Lord Jesus has lived out human freedom and love of God in a human life to reveal to us the richness and faithfulness of God's love. The Holy Spirit urges us and strengthens us to seek that free love in our daily lives. Our participation in this covenant, this plan of salvation, is grounded in our baptism and participation in the church, which is the body of Christ. Our sincere and faithful membership, then, is one sign of our choice for God in response to grace. The church, for its part, seeks to offer assistance to those striving for truth and love. Membership implies that we take this assistance seriously; our humanity forbids that we simply resign from the struggle and insist that others make our choices for us. This calls for sincere searching on the part of all of us for the truth and for the way of goodness.

The Price of Orthodoxy

Rembert G. Weakland, O.S.B.

These articles originally appeared in the *Catholic Herald* in 1986.

St. Paul was interested not only in spreading the Good News but also in maintaining its integrity. This concern characterized the early Christian community, too. For example, in the letter to the Colossians it is written: "See to it that no one deceives you through any empty, seductive philosophy that follows mere human traditions, a philosophy based on cosmic power rather than on Christ" (Colossians 2:8).

One can imagine how difficult it must have been in those early decades of Christianity to find the right words and concepts to capture the significance of Christ's mission and especially his death and resurrection. Remember how the writers searched for the right equivalent of a simple word like "love?" "Eros" was too sensual; "philia" too philosophical; "agape" had to be chosen. No wonder scholars today talk of various New Testament theologies!

The letter in Pauline style that emphasizes the concern for the integrity of the message most strongly is the letter to Timothy. Holding fast to sound doctrine is the keynote of the advice given to this young leader. Titus gets similar advice in the letter addressed to him. Both show the concern in the early church for maintaining the purity of the gospel message as handed down.

But a tension seems built into the system and has been found in all ages and places. Bad doctrine ultimately leads to bad conduct derived from it, and all religions—as sublime as they may be— have had to deal with aberrations.

The problem of orthodoxy is difficult in itself but becomes even more complicated because the church always exists in a particular historical context and not in some abstract world. Civilization continues to raise new problems and challenges that the church must face up to. Repeating old formulas does not answer new problems; they demand new thinking in the light of held truths.

John Henry Newman in the last century, struggling much with this problem, wrote some of his most illuminating essays on the development of dogma. He developed a careful analysis of the criteria for keeping continuity, but with progress.

He knew that the glory of the Catholic Church, as distinct from fundamentalism, has been its willingness (at times, it is true, with much hesitation, doubt and reluctance) to accept truth wherever it comes from and to integrate it with revealed truth, but only after a long struggle to work out apparent contradictions.

So, for example, the early church had to struggle against the Hellenistic and Roman cultures with their Platonic philosophical base, arriving at a synthesis in the West in the Fourth century with St. Augustine. The Middle Ages saw the influx of philosophy, especially Aristotelian, and it took a St. Thomas Aquinas in the 13th century—after considerable debate—to show the integration of that new thinking.

Humanism in the Renaissance in the 16th century, rationalism in the Enlightenment in the 17th and 18th centuries—all posed problems for the church.

Perhaps the conflict that seems closest to us is the integration of the truths of science with the biblical accounts, a conflict acrimoniously fought out earlier in this century. (We still see this struggle going on in some religious groups after it has been put to rest in Catholicism.)

Today's challenges to the church, on the other hand, come mostly from psychology and the human sciences. In fact, it is not by accident that the troubled territory today is sexuality and its relationship to the whole of human behavior, that is, moral issues.

The fervor for orthodoxy often came and went in the church; but, strangely enough, such a fervor was also often characteristic of the most fertile growth periods within the church. People were excited about and cared about religion. What is important is that these struggles in history led to growth, but also to division.

In honesty one has to admit, too, that in these struggles many human beings were treated inhumanely and with excessive cruelty. The Inquisition and the periodic witch hunts for heretics were not the most glamorous part of the history of the Catholic church. On the contrary, too many innocent people suffered. It does no good to poor Galileo to vindicate and exonerate him today. This list, alas, is endless.

Unfortunately, such periods also produced, in addition to the cruelty mentioned, fear. In such an atmosphere, amateurs—turned theologians—easily became headhunters and leaders were picked, not by their ability to work toward a synthesis of the new knowledge and the tradition, but by the rigidity of their orthodoxy, so that often second-rate and repressive minds, riding on the waves of that fear, took over.

Religion under such circumstances then can become an ideology that tolerates no obstacle and that values ideas more than people. And more about that next week.

When we read of the cruelties of the Spanish Inquisition, we say to ourselves that that was another world, far from our own, one tainted as much by political ambitions as by religious fervor. To us it seems like a bad dream. There are, however, more subtle prices to pay in the continuous struggle to be faithful to the faith handed down to us but at the same time to accept the true advances of our civilization.

The history of the church in the U.S.A. was affected in a vital way by the modernist controversies at the turn of the century. These controversies are closer to home and have left lasting effects on us.

In the first decade of the century, during the pontificate of Pope Pius X, seminaries were closed, theological periodicals were suppressed, a network of "informers" in each diocese was organized, oaths were repeatedly taken, intellectually rigid bishops were appointed, and fear and distrust were everywhere in the U.S.A. Fr. Andrew Breen (who died in 1938) of St. Francis Seminary here in Milwaukee was himself involved in these unfortunate disputes.

When I entered the monastery of St. Vincent in Latrobe,

Pennsylvania, as a young high school student in 1940, the tales were still being related about the dispersal of the monk-scientists to various parishes during that decade and the cessation of all experimentation that had made the monks famous in their fields. The retired pastor of the hometown parish I came from had been one of those scientists. The new generation of scholars in the monastery talked much of that atmosphere of fear that lasted into the period of the Second World War.

Theology in the seminaries during these 50 years was taught from textbooks that were repeatedly reprinted without reflections on the new currents that were rising in Europe. When I returned from Rome in 1951 after doing my theology there, I heard much criticism about the new things I had been taught—all of them considered by my American classmates as novel and suspect. These European currents, I was to learn later, led up to Vatican Council II, for which the church in the U.S.A. was so totally unprepared.

The theological suppression of the first decade of the century and the fears it instilled resulted in a total lack of theological creativity in the U.S.A. for half a century. It also left us unprepared for the dramatic changes of the sixties. We are only now again coming to life and only now producing in the areas of biblical exegesis and theology world-renowned scholars.

Some could say we have been spared in this way some of the theological turmoil of the forties and fifties. The fact that during that time such theologians as Yves Congar, Henri de Lubac and Teilhard de Chardin were silenced seems to have had little effect on us. Even the fact that our own John Courtney Murray was not permitted to publish went unnoticed by most in the church.

Most of these theologians were rehabilitated and vindicated by Vatican Council II. In the meantime they demonstrated much humility and a strong faith. (Sometimes it seems a long life is the way to see oneself and one's ideas finally accepted!)

The desire to maintain the purity and integrity of doctrine will always be with us. No church could long stand if every new idea were to be accepted as a part of faith. On the other hand, the church must always face up to the challenges of the times and the new discoveries about the universe and the human person. Her doctrine never finds a full verbal expression as it grows in new insights and understanding.

On the negative side of this pursuit for purity of doctrine is the need to avoid the fanaticism and small-mindedness that has characterized so many periods of the church in its history—tendencies that lead to much cruelty, suppression of theological creativity and lack of growth.

Is there a better way of proceeding? Has history taught us anything?

Pope John XXIII thought there might be when, in his famous opening speech of Vatican Council II, he said:

"Often errors vanish as quickly as they rise, like fog before the sun. The church has always opposed these errors. Frequently she has condemned them with the greatest severity. Nowadays, however, the spouse of Christ prefers to make use of the medicine of mercy rather than that of severity. She considers that she meets the needs of the present day by demonstrating the validity of her teaching rather than by condemnations."

Was good Pope John being naive? Many, I fear, think so.

Part Two

CANONICAL ASPECTS

Church Teaching Authority in the 1983 Code

John P. Boyle

This article originally appeared in *The Jurist* in 1985.

The publication of the new Code of Canon Law[1] on January 25, 1983, by Pope John Paul II completed a program for the reform and renewal of the church announced on January 25, 1959, by Pope John XXIII. The central event of that program, the Second Vatican Council, completed its work on December 8, 1965, an event to be marked in 1985 by an extraordinary meeting of the Synod of Bishops. This new governance structure aptly symbolizes both the achievements and the still unfulfilled promise of Pope John's program of *aggiornamento*.

It has long been apparent that the progress of reform and renewal is not a straight line. The first event of Pope John's program, the Roman Synod of 1960, was not notably successful. The constitution, decrees and declarations of Vatican II were the result of compromises among the bishops that were needed to achieve the substantial consensus that supported the council documents. A careful study could no doubt chart inconsistencies in the implementing of the council documents which often reflect inconsistencies in the documents resulting from the compromises.

The long process of revising the 1917 Code of Canon Law called for by Pope John XXIII has paralleled the implementation of the council legislation. It is to be expected that the new code reflects the work of the council and the post-conciliar period, including its inconsistencies.

The focus of this study is the teaching authority of the Church.

Moreover, it is a study of historical and theological aspects of the new code's treatment of church teaching authority. Major attention will therefore be given to Book Three of the new code, *De Ecclesiae Munere Docendi*. But brief attention must also be given to other sections of the code if the theological aspects of the revised code are to appear clearly. I will therefore give some attention to Book Two, *De Populo Dei*, for its ecclesiology.

In fact the organization of the new code itself reflects the work of the council. While the 1917 codification made use of Roman law concepts to organize the canons into books dealing with persons, things, processes, and crimes and their penalties, the new code begins with the Church as the people of God, then deals with the Church's functions (*munera*) of teaching and sanctifying (it was found impractical to have a single section on the *munus regendi*),[2] before dealing with temporal goods and processes. The influence of *Lumen gentium* is pervasive.

The revision process was governed by fundamental principles formulated by the code commission and then discussed and approved by the Synod of Bishops in 1967.[3] Several are of interest for this study. Number three, for example, prescribes that in addition to justice, the new code is to include attention to other virtues, including charity, temperance, moderation, humanity, etc. Number four, without mentioning the teaching of the council on episcopal collegiality, prescribes that greater power of dispensing from the general laws of the Church is to be given to bishops. Number five enunciates the principle of subsidiarity in the government of the Church, and points to the need for decentralization and a healthy autonomy of particular churches, though it warns against the formation of national churches. Number six asserts the fundamental equality of all members of the Church, though there is a diversity of functions (*munera*) and offices. The principle also asserts that power in the Church is to serve and to safeguard the rights of persons. Number seven asserts the need for procedures in the Church to safeguard rights.

The principles, even though their concern is juridical, have a clear basis in the teachings of the council. Vatican II reversed tendencies in ecclesiology in particular which had been developing since the Reformation. Ecclesiology before the council was rightly described by Yves Congar as "hierarchology."[4] The reigning model of the Church was heavily juridical and institutional.

Without denying the need for the church institution, Vatican II first defined the Church in *Lumen gentium* as mystery or sacrament. Then it went on to speak of the Church as the people of God who are fundamentally equal in virtue of their baptism and profession of faith in Jesus Christ. This people of God shares in various ways in the *triplex munus Christi* as prophet, priest and shepherd-king: the offices of Christ are also the offices of his Church. Only after asserting this fundamental equality of the whole people of God did the council go on to speak of the specific offices of the hierarchy and the laity.

In addition to reasserting the reality of the Church as a people which shares in various ways in the offices of Christ, the council forcefully asserted the doctrine of episcopal collegiality and the co-responsibility of the whole body of bishops, the pope included, for the universal Church, without prejudice to the definitions of papal primacy and infallibility of the First Vatican Council.

Vatican II's view of the work of the Church is elaborated in many of its documents, including those on the missions and education. But the Pastoral Constitution on the Church in the Modern World deserves special mention here along with the modern papal documents which have developed a strong teaching on human rights. I have already drawn attention to the fundamental principles of the revision of the code which give special attention to the enunciation of rights and to the function of church authority in protecting them.

The revision of the code could only take place after the council had done its work. We must attend throughout this study to the way in which the teaching of the council finds its way into the new code of law.

I.

GENERAL THEOLOGICAL THEMES IN BOOK TWO

With these preliminary remarks, I turn first to Book II[5] of the new code, *De Populo Dei,* to note the impact there of the conciliar teaching on the Church. The book includes canons 204–746—nearly a third of the entire code. Part I of the book deals with the faithful, canons 204–329. The first two titles deal with obligations and rights, first setting out obligations and rights of all the faithful, then obligations and rights of the laity. Here I intend only to call attention to those canons which touch on the teaching office of the Church. Many of the canons were brought into the code from the 1980 draft of the proposed *Lex Ecclesiae Fundamentalis*[6] when the decision was made not to issue the *LEF* as a separate document. The notes to the draft indicate *LG* as the source of many of the canons.

Among the canons of Title I which define the rights and obligations of all the faithful, canon 211 points of the obligation of every believer to announce the good news. Canon 212 emphasizes the obligation of the faithful to obey the magisterial and pastoral decisions of their pastors. But section two of the same canon notes the right of the faithful to make their needs and desires, especially spiritual ones, known to their pastors. Section three notes the right and at times the obligations of the faithful to make their opinions known to their pastors on matters that pertain to the good of the Church. Indeed they have the right and even the obligation to make these opinions known to others of the faithful, taking care to preserve the integrity of faith and morals, due reverence toward their pastors, the common good, and the dignity of persons. Such caveats appear frequently in the code along with the statement of rights.

Canon 213 enunciates a right of the faithful to receive from the pastors spiritual goods, especially from the Word of God and the sacraments.

Canon 217 asserts a right to formation in the faith. Canon 218 on the basis of *GS* 62, asserts the right of those who are engaged in the sacred sciences to enjoy freedom of research and to make known prudently their views in their area of expertise, saving a due submission to the teaching authority of the Church, surely a cautious but important statement for theologians.

Canon 220 asserts the right of every person to a good name and to the preservation of privacy.

Title II enumerates the rights and obligations of the laity.

Canon 225 declares the obligation of the faithful to participate in the spreading of the gospel. Canon 229, §2 announces their right to be educated in the sacred sciences, to attend classes and to receive academic degrees from ecclesiastical faculties and universities. Section three of the canon asserts their ability (the term "right" is not used) to be appointed to teach the sacred sciences and to receive the requisite canonical mandate to teach.

Title III of Part I, Book II, canons 232–293, deals with clerics and their education. In the section on seminaries, canon 252, §3 directs that seminarians be taught doctrine, especially under the tutelage of St. Thomas. Canon 253, §1 directs that only those persons are to be appointed teachers of philosophy, theology and canon law who have received the licentiate or the doctorate from a faculty or university recognized by the Holy See.

Canon 215 enunciates the right of all the faithful to form associations for purposes of piety or charity or for the promotion of the Christian vocation in the world. In Title V canon 301, §1 requires that associations "which propose to present doctrine in the name of the Church" must be erected by a competent church authority. We will return to these canons.

Part II of Book II is entitled "The Hierarchical Constitution of the Church," and its first section is "On the Supreme Authority of the Church." Chapter one is entitled "On the Roman Pontiff and on the College of Bishops."

An introductory canon (c. 330) states that pope and bishops constitute a single college as did Peter and the other apostles.

There is in the following canons 331–341 an unmistakable emphasis on the prerogatives of the Roman Pontiff and the dependence upon him of the body of bishops if it is to perform any truly collegial act. This subordination of episcopal authority is exemplified by the code's treatment of the synod of bishops in chapter two, canons 342–348. The code has dropped the phrase of Paul VI's constitution *Apostolica sollicitudo* describing the synod as "representing the whole Catholic episcopate" and has placed it alongside the college of cardinals and Roman Curia among the structures which assist the Roman Pontiff in the discharge of his primatial duties.

Attention might also be drawn here to the distinction which is made both in the council documents and in those actions of the episcopate which are strictly "collegial" and thus involve the entire worldwide episcopate, and those actions which are described as "conjoint," such as local synods and councils and the various episcopal conferences. While the council documents offer a clear theological account of the basis for collegial action, there is little theological basis offered for conjoint action in spite of the council's endorsement of the tradition of synodical government in the Church (*CD* 36).[7] The problem may lie in part in the council's unstated habit of equating the "college" of bishops, the "body" of bishops, and the "order" of bishops.

It seems to me[8] that the acknowledged authority of local and regional synods and councils in the Church is unintelligible if the episcopal order does not imply a basis for conjoint action in a way in which the council's highly restrictive definition of "college" does not.[9] Given the tradition that by ordination a man is received into an already functioning "order," the ordained is joined by multiple bonds with those who also have received from ordination both the episcopal *munera* and the means of grace to discharge them. To say this is not to diminish the importance the council rightly attaches to hierarchical communion among all the bishops, but it points to the fact that if "collegial" actions are only those of the college of bishops as a whole, including the pope as the head of the college, there are other bonds joining bishops which are rooted in their ordination and which encourage or require joint action. The notion that between the whole body of bishops, including the pope, which can perform collegial actions, and the individual diocesan bishop there are only cooperative arrangements with utilitarian value—even if that be considerable—does not seem at all adequate. The very traditional notion rooted in the theology of orders is that ordination means reception into an already constituted *ordo* of bishops who must work together.

Part II, section two of Book Two of the new code deals with particular churches and their groupings. Among other things the code lays down regulations for provincial and plenary councils and for diocesan synods. While the law requiring review by the Holy See of the acts of such councils remains, it is notable that some of the suffocating regulations of the 1917 code governing particular councils are gone.[10] It can also be noted that the new canon 445 states explicitly that such councils enjoy the power of governing (*regiminis*) but also that they are to act for the increase of the faith, to direct morals and to deal with matters of discipline. References in the old canon 290 to removing abuses and to settling disputes have been dropped. It may be notable that the new canon makes no reference to the office of teaching nor to matters of doctrine as being among those in which disputes might be settled by particular or plenary councils. The emphasis in the code appears to be on the disciplinary role of such councils.

Chapter four, canons 447 to 459, deals with episcopal conferences, one of the most significant structural innovations in the new code and one directly dependent upon the conciliar teaching on episcopal collegiality. Although institutions like the National Catholic Welfare Conference had been in existence in the United States in some form since the time of the First World War, and the American bishops had met together each year, the episcopal conference is a permanent institution of conjoint action which brings together not only bishops of each nation, but with the approval of the Holy See can also bring together larger groupings of bishops such as the bishops of Latin America.

The canons not only deal with such matters as the membership and organization of the conferences, but they also spell out the circumstances in which the conferences can legislate and the approval of the Holy See that is needed for such legislation (c. 455). It might be noted here that canon 135, §2 prohibits the delegation of legislative power at levels inferior to the Holy See, a norm of importance for the functioning of the committees and other organs of an episcopal conference.

Canon 455, §4 takes care to point out that the individual diocesan bishop retains full competence to speak and act on all matters on which the conference has not been authorized to legislate. The president of the conference cannot speak in the name of all the bishops in such a case unless each and every one has consented.

The new structure has predictably raised questions both about its relationship to the central authority of the Church and about the relationship of the bishops' collective responsibility and actions to the responsibility and action of the individual diocesan bishop.[11]

Legislation in the code is essentially that of the council decree *Christus Dominus* and the 1966 motu proprio *Ecclesiae Sanctae* of Paul VI. The theological basis for the episcopal conference is not really in question, even if there is some difference of opinion about the limits of conjoint action and individual actions by bishops.

It is apparent from this brief review that the new code reflects in broad outline the ecclesiology of Vatican II. It sees the Church as the people of God, though it states the responsibilities and rights of the people of God with frequent caveats and repeated reminders of the obedience owed to hierarchical authority, especially the pope. The collegial structure of the episcopacy is stated, although the role of the episcopal college in teaching and governance of the universal Church remains rather undeveloped except for ecumenical councils. Subsidiary governance structures have been strengthened by the new episcopal conferences—but cautiously and with much emphasis on supervision and approval by the Holy See. The synod of bishops is in place, but its role is emphatically subordinate to the pope and only consultative to him. The office of bishops, especially of the pope, as teachers in the Church is set out but not developed in Book II.

So we turn now to Book III, *De Ecclesiae Munere Docendi*.

II.
Introductory Canons of Book Three

Book III contains canons 747 to 833. The new book is a revision of Book III, part 4, of the 1917 code *De Magisterio Ecclesiastico*, which included canons 1322 to 1408. Each code contains five titles and covers roughly the same range of topics, with one notable exception: the new code includes a title on the missionary activity of the Church which did not appear in any form in the 1917 code. The topics within the book have been reordered somewhat, and the section which dealt only with books has been expanded to include the whole range of the mass media.

Because the interest of this study is limited to the theological underpinnings of canons on church teaching authority and their historical development, I will deal in greater detail with the introductory canons of the book, canons 747–755, which correspond to canons 1322–1326 of the 1917 code.

Canon 747

The new canon's first section takes over and abbreviates slightly the old canon 1322 asserting the right of the Church to proclaim the gospel. Its conciliar sources are in *LG* 25, *DV* 8, and 9 and 10, and *IM* 3. The final phrase asserting the Church's independence of any human power is taken from the old canon 1322, §2.

The second section states a broad claim for the competence of the Church to proclaim "always and everywhere moral principles, even those of the social order, and to make judgments about anything whatsoever pertaining to human beings to the extent that the fundamental rights of the human person or the salvation of souls demands it." This part of the canon has been brought into the code from the 1980 draft schema of the *LEF* which cites *GS* 76 as its source. The material did not appear in the 1969 or 1971 schemata of the *LEF*.

The competence claimed for church teaching authority in this canon appears so sweeping that it may be useful to compare the canon with n. 76 of *GS* which reads in part:

> There are indeed, close links between earthly affairs and those aspects of man's condition which transcend this world. The Church herself employs the things of time to the degree that her own proper mission demands. Still she does not lodge her hope in privileges conferred by civil authority. Indeed, she stands ready to renounce the exercise of certain legitimately acquired rights if it becomes clear that their use raises doubt about the sincerity of her witness or that new conditions of life demand some other arrangement. But it is always and everywhere legitimate for her to preach the faith with true freedom, to teach her social doctrine, and to discharge her duty among men without hindrance. She also has the right to pass moral judgments, even on matters touching the political order, whenever basic personal rights or the salvation of souls make such judgments necessary. In so

doing, she may use only those hopes which accord with the gospel and with the general welfare as it changes according to time and circumstances.[12]

I cite this text at length because the adaptation made of it for the new code has altered considerably the content of the council text, and even more dramatically its tone. The notes of modesty with which the council surrounded its statement of the Church's role are gone.

GS said that the Church has the liberty (1) to proclaim the faith, (2) to teach its social doctrine, (3) to carry out its task without hindrance, (4) to make moral judgments even about the political order when (a) the fundamental rights of the person or (b) the salvation of souls demanded it—but using only appropriate means.

The code has made some notable adaptations: (1) proclamation of the faith is presumably stated in canon 747, §1; (2) teaching social doctrine has become "enunciating moral principles even about the social order"—a broader formulation than the "political" order mentioned by the council; (3) reference to carrying on the Church's function has been dropped, perhaps as too broad in the immediate context of the teaching office; (4) making moral judgments has become "making judgments on any human affairs," and in place of *when* the fundamental rights of the person demand it has become *to the extent that* the fundamental rights of the person or the salvation of souls demand it.

If one compares this statement with a strong preconciliar one such as Pius XII's *Magnificate Dominum mecum,*[13] both the scope and the line of reasoning are interestingly different. Rejecting the claim that the power of the Church is limited to the sacristy or the church, while the world belongs to the laity, Pius XII insisted that the power of the Church is not limited to the strictly "religious" sphere, but extends to the natural law, to the whole range of its material, to teaching it, interpreting it and applying it, precisely to the extent that it is a *moral* law. The pope reasoned that the Church was to be the guide and guardian of the way to a supernatural end which could not be reached without observance of the natural moral law. Pius XII cited Pius X's insistence that the "social question" was a moral question and thus within the teaching competence of the Church.[14]

Neither *GS* 76 nor the new code mentions natural law; both appeal to the rights of the person and the salvation of souls, this latter an echo of a long tradition enunciated by Pius X and Pius XII. But in fact there has been a remarkable development of natural law doctrine in the Catholic Church from the classic formulation of natural law which is presented in John XXIII's *Pacem in Terris* (1963) to the personalism of Paul VI's *Populorum Progressio* (1967), with *GS* (1965) a crucial transition point.[15]

Both *GS* and the code distinguish between teaching and judging. The code asserts that the Church can enunciate moral principles even about the social order and make moral judgments about "any human affairs whatsoever (*quibuslibet rebus humanis*)." The difference is of some importance, given the discussion among Catholic theologians about the competence and levels of authority of church teaching when it speaks on the one hand about moral principles and on the other makes specific moral judgments about concrete situations and problems.[16]

What appears to be the more common opinion today attributes greater authority to the enunciation of principles than to the making of specific judgments. This important distinction has been incorporated into the American bishops' pastoral letters on war and peace and on the economy.[17] The importance of the distinction may be even greater, given the decentralized way in which teaching authority is exercised in the Church since Vatican II.

In sum then, the claim of Canon 747, §2 is indeed strongly put and its appeal to the human person as the basis of the Church's competence to teach the moral law is a recent development. But in substance the canon does not seem to go beyond the preconciliar teaching of Pius XII in its claims for the competence of church teaching authority.

Canon 748

The canon asserting the human obligation and right to seek and embrace religious truth is a recasting of canons 1322, §2 and 1351 of the 1917 code, with an interesting shift of emphasis from the rights of the Church so often emphasized in the nineteenth century controversies with the lay state, to the rights of the human person so much emphasized in recent teaching. An echo of *Dignitatis humanae* 2 is here, too.[18]

Canon 749

This canon on infallible teaching authority is derived from the old canon 1322, §2, but the canon has been expanded with material from *Lumen gentium* 25. Section one deals with papal infallibility, section two with the infallibility of the college of bishops. Section three restates canon 1323, §3 to the effect that nothing is to be considered defined infallibly unless the intention to define is manifest.

It is of theological interest to note that in the 1969 and 1971 drafts of the *LEF,* there was a subsection of this canon on the infallibility of the people of God in believing, from *LG* 12. In the revisions a strong reference to the directive role of the magisterium was first inserted and finally the entire subsection was deleted. I will return to this.

Canon 750

The canon which defines what must be believed *de fide* restates the old canon 1323, §1 with the addition of a phrase from *Dei Verbum* modifying the source text from Vatican I to make it clear that there is a single deposit of faith committed to the Church and transmitted in scripture and tradition. Only the divine revelation which is the content of the deposit of faith and proposed as such by the Church is to be believed *de fide divina et catholica.* But there are two interesting additions to the old canon. The first appears to be a vestige of the draft *LEF* on infallibility in believing and the *sensus fidei.* In the 1969 draft of the *LEF,* the canon spoke of the *sensus fidei* by which the Holy Spirit leads the people of God to adhere faithfully to the word of God once given to the saints, to penetrate it more fully in right judgment, and to apply it to life more fully—under the leadership of the magisterium, to be sure. All this was from *LG* 12 and *DV* 10. In 1971 that text was combined with another which spoke of infallibility in believing when the whole people displays its consent on a matter of faith and morals, a text also from *LG* 12. But in the 1980 draft of the *LEF* all references to the consent of the faithful were dropped. What remains is footnoted to *LG* 25 and *DV* 10, to which it gives an interesting reverse twist: *LG* 25 states that the assent of the faithful to the infallible definitions of the pope or the college of bishops with the pope can never be lacking because of the work of the Holy Spirit preserving the unity of the Church. In the new code the adherence in faith of the faithful to the teaching proposed by the pope and bishops manifests the fact that there has been an infallible exercise of teaching authority. There is no mention of *LG* 12 or of infallibility in believing, but what there is is an interesting and rare example of "reception" in the new code.[19]

The second addition to the canon is reminiscent of the old canon 1324 and the Vatican I Constitution on Faith and Reason *Dei Filius* from which it was taken. It states that everyone is bound not only to adhere to teaching which is *de fide* but also bound to avoid any teaching contrary to that which has been taught *de fide*. The difference suggests the traditional notions of primary and secondary objects of infallible authority.[20]

Canon 751

The canon defines heresy, apostasy and schism in a form somewhat more compact than the old canon 1325, §2. The pope moved the canon to this position from its former position as canon 755 in the final schema approved by the code commission, a move of no apparent doctrinal import.

Canon 752

Citing *LG* 25, this canon requires religious obedience of intellect and will ("respect" is not strong enough for *obsequium*) to the authoritative teaching of the pope or bishops even if they do not intend to make a definitive and thus infallible judgment. To the draft text, little changed since the 1969 schema of *LEF,* the code commission's final schema and the published code add an injunction parallel with that of canon 750 regarding matters of faith: the faithful are to avoid doctrines which do not accord (*quae . . . non congruant*) with authoritative but not infallible teaching.

Neither the body of the canon nor the injunction even hint

that official teachers might commit their authority in various degrees to which various levels of assent might be appropriate, although the canon deals with non-definitive teaching. I shall say more of this when I comment on the related penal canon 1371.

It is noteworthy that canon 752 has no parallel in the old code. Its appearance together with a penal canon is evidence of a significant development in the notion and role of an ordinary magisterium in the Church, especially the ordinary, authoritative but not infallible magisterium. The absence of a parallel canon in the 1917 code is curious, since the term "ordinary magisterium" was used in 1870 by Vatican I.[21]

Canon 753

A revision of canon 1326 of the old code, the canon asserts the teaching authority of bishops over their own people, whether they teach alone, in particular councils, or in their episcopal conference. To their authoritative teaching, religious obedience (*obsequium*) of intellect and will is owed. The text again derives from *LG* 25 and puts the episcopal *magisterium*, whether single or conjoint, in parallel with earlier statements about papal and conciliar teaching authority. The clear assertion of the authority of conjoint teaching of bishops in their councils or conferences is significant in the light of recent questions raised about the *munus docendi* of episcopal conferences.[22]

Canon 754

The canon, derived from the old canon 1324, has been considerably expanded and specified. It emphasizes the duty of the faithful to obey the docrinal decisions of legitimate church teaching authority—the pope and bishops are mentioned explicitly. Given the antecedents of the canon in the old code and the sources of the old canon 1324 in the epilogue of the constitution *Dei Filius* of Vatican I, and recalling the nineteenth century disputes over the authority of the Roman congregations in doctrinal matters,[23] the thrust of the canon is to lay emphasis on the congregations, even though they are not mentioned. Once again, while the college of bishops is mentioned along with the Roman Pontiff, the fact that there are now no organisms other than a general council for a strictly collegial act of teaching by bishops leaves the emphasis on the Roman authorities.

The reference in the canon to "legitimate ecclesial authority" appears broad enough to include committees or other agencies of the episcopal conferences, but that possibility is foreclosed by canon 135, §2, which forbids the delegation of legislative authority by any but the supreme authority. A recent application of this discipline came from the Congregation for the Defense of the Faith[24] which cited canon 135, §2 to forbid episcopal conferences to delegate their conjoint responsibility for the approval of catechisms to committees of the conferences.

Canon 755

The canon reverses the discipline of the old canon 1325, §3 which forbade Catholic participation in ecumenical discussions without special permission. With obvious dependence on *Unitatis redintegratio,* the canon points to the obligations of the college of bishops and the Apostolic See to promote the ecumenical movement, and then in section two, asserts the right of the pope and the bishops, including the episcopal conferences, to regulate Catholic participation by laying down norms.

Now that more than twenty years have passed since the council published the Decree on Ecumenism, it may be useful to draw attention to the historic significance of this canon, since it marks the end of an era in theology and the life of the Church that extended back to the time of the Reformation. The change has had implications for various areas of the code such as those which deal with mixed marriages, common worship, and the like. Ecumenism may also be a good example of a movement in which the particular churches in the United States and elsewhere have taken a significant number of initiatives, often under the auspices of the conference of bishops. The doctrinally important bilateral dialogues in the U.S. are a good example. Thus have important doctrinal initiatives of the council both reenforced and been reenforced by Vatican II's revisions of church governance structures which encouraged the principle of subsidiarity.

Summary Comments

At the end of this series of canons, some summary comments are in order.

First, a summary of the canons on teaching and the assent owed to it: canon 750 deals with infallible teaching to which the assent of faith is owed; canon 751 defines the related crimes. Canon 752 then deals with the religious assent of mind and will that is owed to authoritative but not infallible teaching. Canon 753 deals with the authority of the teaching of bishops singly or conjointly and the assent owed to it. Then canon 754 deals with the teaching of other competent authority, *de facto,* it would appear, the Roman congregations in spite of the mention of constitutions and decrees of the Roman Pontiff and the college of bishops.

Second, some summary notes on the theology of these first canons of book III. First we should observe what is not here, and that is the use of the *munus propheticum* as an organizing principle so conspicuous in *Lumen gentium's* treatment in turn of the people of God, the hierarchy, and the laity. Without a meaningful reference to *LG* 12 or 35, in which the council discusses the *munus propheticum* of the whole people of God and of the laity, Book III on the *munus docendi* is in fact a legal treatise *de magisterio ecclesiastico,* i.e. on the hierarchy, in which the only role of the rest of the people of God is to give assent. The words are not used, but the *ecclesia docens* and *ecclesia discens* of nineteenth and twentieth century ecclesiology seem to be alive in these canons.[25]

That observation is reenforced by the purely passive notion of reception reflected in canon 750.

The repeated demand for assent to magisterial teaching of various kinds which runs through the canons from 750 to 754 creates serious theological questions. It is one thing to insist on the assent of faith to teachings presented as revealed doctrine which are or could be proposed so definitively as to be infallibly true. But it is something else to insist in so undifferentiated a way on religious assent of mind and will to teachings of quite varied content and authority for which no such demand for the assent of faith is made—and for which in some cases no such claim could be made, because revelation is not the warrant for the teaching.

These degrees of authority, clearly reflected by the tradition of theological notes, together with the undeniable fact that church teaching authority changes its mind or is corrected in its teaching, makes the absence of any modesty in these claims seem, as Yves Congar has put it, "excessive and unreal."[26]

Of course, a code of law is not a theological treatise, and it is well known that the council's theological commission, responding to amendments to *LG* 25 that would have made the text explicit in acknowledging the possibility of respectful dissent, referred the issue to "approved authors."[27] But the matter is troublesome when church legislation is framed in such broad terms, and the concern deepens when the canons of Book III become the basis for penal legislation in Book VI.

Episcopal collegiality has fared better. Canon 753 affirms the teaching role not only of diocesan bishops but of episcopal conferences. However grudgingly, the code grants the possibility of what has become an important reality in the Church since the council: the decentralized exercise of teaching authority, especially through the work of bishops' conferences. It suffices to mention the influential statements of the Latin American bishops at Medellin and Puebla as well as the American bishops' pastoral on war and peace. F. X. Winters has noted the various approaches of conferences of bishops in the West to issues of nuclear weapons use and the emergence of some consensus—a fascinating example of interaction among bishops' conferences and of a new role played by the Holy See.[28]

Implementing the principle of subsidiarity, of course, requires many prudential judgments about the level at which doctrinal solicitude will be exercised and church teaching presented. Honest differences of opinion are to be expected.

In addition to the issues of ecclesiology, the canons also reflect a renewed theological anthropology, especially in canon 747, §2 with its emphasis on the human person and human rights as the basis for church teaching competence.

The same canon also reflects a position on an important issue in theological ethics, the role of the natural moral law. Other canons raise questions of moral agency and relationship of that agency to authority.[29] Yves Congar has also helpfully drawn attention to the fact that when the relationship of church authority and assent is being discussed, there must always be a third term, the authority of the Word of God itself. *Dei Verbum* 10 reflects this conviction in its assertion that the magisterium is to serve the Word of God. When matters of natural moral law are at issue, the third term is truth itself.[30]

III.
PARTICULAR ISSUES IN BOOK III

After noting the more general theological themes of the code in the first section of this article and commenting more extensively on the introductory canons dealing with the teaching task of the Church in the second section, I intend in this third section to survey the several titles of Book III more briefly, noting only those things that are of theological interest.

Ministry of the Divine Word

Title one deals with the ministry of the divine word, beginning with some introductory canons (cc. 756–761). The topic is not new, but the council gave it new prominence in *Dei Verbum* and in other documents. Here a bit of the code's ecclesiology appears. The bishops are said to have the *munus* of preaching the word (c. 756); pastors have the *officium* of announcing the good news; and deacons are to serve the ministry of the word (c. 757). Religious give testimony to the word by their consecrated lives and are appropriately (*convenienter*) asked to assist in the announcing of the good news by the bishop (c. 758). The laity are witnesses to the good news by their words and the example of their Christian lives—this in virtue of their baptism and confirmation. They can also be called to assist bishops and priests in exercising the ministry of the word (c. 759).

Too much ought not be made of the rather inconsistent use of *munus* and *officium* in these texts; they are based on conciliar texts which do not use the terms consistently. But the code commission did pass up the chance to introduce some clarity. There is no explicit reference in the drafts to *LG* 35, though the use of "witness" for the role of the laity may well have come from there. A reference in the 1980 *LEF* to the need for a "mission" if the laity are to exercise the ministry of the word of God *in nomine Ecclesiae* has been omitted. Again the code has avoided the council's use of the *munus propheticum* as a way of relating the roles of the hierarchy and the laity as members together of the people of God. In addition, the regular insertion of canons referring to religious between those referring to bishops, priests and deacons, and those referring to the laity suggests a conscious assimilation of religious to the clergy and a separation of the clergy and religious (especially the latter) from the laity which the council avoided by emphasizing their common membership in the people of God.

Preaching

Chapter one of Title I deals with preaching the Word of God (cc. 762–772). Canon 766 reverses the old canon 134, §2 by permitting the laity to preach if it seems necessary or useful, but canon 767, §1 reserves the homily to the priest and deacon, since it is a part of the liturgy. How successful that distinction will prove to be in practice remains to be seen. There is strong encouragement for homilies, even at daily Masses, from *Sacrosanctum Concilium* 2. There is also a notable emphasis in canon 768, §2 on preaching the social doctrine of the Church with its emphasis on the dignity and liberty of the human person. Its source is in *Christus Dominus* 12.

Catechetics

Chapter two, canons 773–780, is on catechetics. Much of the revision in this and the following sections on schools is inspired by *Gravissimum educationis*. There is a notable emphasis on the role of parents in the religious formation of their children here and elsewhere in the code. The chapter also has a series of canons outlining the catechetical responsibilities of various levels of church leadership. Religious are included in canon 778, which was added after the 1977 draft of Book III.

Canon 775 is noteworthy for the detailed directives it gives for the approval of catechisms. Its provisions reflect regulations issued earlier by Vatican congregations. The CDF recently called attention to several documents containing such regulations.[31] They include (1) *The General Catechetical Directory* issued by the Congregation for the Clergy;[32] (2) the decree *Ecclesiae pastorum* of the CDF on the prior censorship of books, published in 1975;[33] (3) a 1980 response of the CDF to *dubia*.[34] In addition, material from the *General Catechetical Directory* was included in the exhortation *Catechesi tradendae*,[35] for example nn. 49–50 on the nature of catechisms.

The over-all impact of the regulations has been apparent since the publication of the *Directory* in 1972. Number 133 of the *Directory* is a very forceful statement on the primatial prerogatives of the pope in the exercise of his *munus docendi et regendi* in the whole Church. The pope can exercise his *munus* by freely choosing to act either alone or collegially, and if he acts alone he can do so either personally or through the Roman congregations.[36]

Number 134 then asserts the authority of the Congregation for the Clergy over catechetics, including its authority to review and approve catechetical directories and catechisms and programs of preaching prepared by the bishops' conferences.[37]

These regulations have been taken into the new canon 775, which has no parallel in the 1917 code. It need hardly be said that the requirement for *prior* Roman approval of catechetical texts approved by the conferences of bishops for their countries is not consistent with the fifth guiding principle for the revision of the code, which emphasized subsidiarity. On the contrary, it is a significant expansion of centralized control of doctrine and catechetical instruction in the Church. There is more of this in Book III.

Missions

Title II of Book III, canons 781–792, is entitled "On the Missionary Activity of the Church"; it is remarkably large because it has no antecedents in the 1917 code and represents an important new emphasis in the council's understanding of the Church. The new title depends most heavily on the Vatican II decree *Ad gentes*. Canon 781 states that evangelization is a fundamental duty (*officium*) of the people of God in which all Christians participate in various ways. Much of the title spells out and orders that variety. Canon 789 is also of importance: it defines the missionary task as the planting of the Church among a people or a group which is discharged by sending preachers of the gospel until the new church is fully constituted; i.e., it is able to carry on the task of evangelization itself, with its own resources adequate to the task. The emergence of many "new churches," especially from the developing countries, into the life of the universal Church, is one of the striking phenomena of the period since Vatican II, and the definition of missionary activity is an important corrective to tendencies to leave particular churches in former colonies in permanent dependence upon foreign resources and personnel, whose links with colonial governments often made Christian missions suspect. These are important developments for a more decentralized exercise of teaching authority.

Catholic Education

Title III, canons 793–821, deals with Catholic education—with the conspicuous exception of seminaries. Legislation regarding seminaries has been located in the new code in Book II in the section dealing with the education of clerics, canons 232–264. It is no surprise that the revision here is much influenced by *Gravissimum educationis*. With that decree, the code emphasizes the right of parents to direct the education of their children, including their religious formation. It also asserts the right of parents to help from the state in providing that education (c. 793).

Chapter one of Title III, canons 796–806, is on schools, a term which refers to institutions below the university level. Most of the canons have no antecedents in the old code.

The chapter is another in a long series of protests by the Church in the 19th and 20th centuries against the monopoly on education claimed by the modern state.[38] The Church's position emphasizes the rights of parents as well as the rights of the Church as an institution. Canon 800 asserts the right of the *Church* (which in context seems to mean the institution or the hierarchy) to establish and to oversee schools in any discipline at any level. Section two of the same canon exhorts the *faithful* to favor such schools by supporting their establishment and maintenance. The formulation of the canon better reflects the way in which the debate with the modern state has been carried on than the ecclesiology of *Lumen gentium*.

Other canons, e.g. canon 804, which assert the right of the

bishops to supervise the teaching of religion and to designate teachers of religion even in state schools, are foreign to the American context. Their presence in the code reflects arrangements in force elsewhere in virtue of concordats and is a reminder of problems being faced by the Church in other places.

Chapter two, canons 807–814, deals with Catholic universities and institutes of higher studies, and chapter three, canons 815–821, with ecclesiastical universities and faculties—i.e., those which are directly dependent upon the Holy See. Throughout the title there is a remarkable emphasis on hierarchical control of teaching, especially theological teaching, in the Church. It does not seem to me that this emphasis can be explained entirely as a reflection of the Church's determination to maintain the independence of its schools in the face of pressures from the state.

The mechanisms of control appear in various places and they take several forms. One example is the insistence in the code that a "Catholic" school is one directly dependent upon Church authority or at the very least approved by that authority in writing (c. 803). Canon 808 declares that no university, even if it is indeed Catholic (*etsi reapse Catholica*) may use the name "Catholic" without the consent of the competent church authority. Canon 803, §3 says the same of other schools. Canon 816 prescribes that the ecclesiastical faculties and universities can be erected only by the Holy See or at least must be approved by it. Over such institutions the Holy See exercises direct supervision; it must approve the statutes of each institution and also its program of studies. Recall canon 301, §1 which requires approval of lay associations which propose to present doctrine in the name of the Church.

A second form of control is that exercised over the appointment of teachers. Canon 805 gives to local ordinaries for their dioceses the right to nominate or at least approve teachers of religion along with the right to remove or to demand the removal of the unfit. Canon 812 requires that teachers of theological disciplines in any institution of higher learning must have a canonical "mandate"—a term which has replaced the older "canonical mission" in the new code. Canon 818 applies the same rule to teachers in ecclesiastical faculties. The constitution *Sapientia Christiana*[39] further requires that teachers in pontifical faculties must not only have the canonical mandate but that before they are given the mandate as tenured or full professors they must receive a *nihil obstat* from the Holy See.

A related form of control can be found in the statement of canon 817 that only degrees conferred by ecclesiastical universities or faculties erected or approved by the Holy See can have canonical effects. In the old code (c. 1378) the effects included the right to wear certain regalia and, more importantly, the right to preferential treatment in appointment to certain offices and benefices. In addition, the old canon 1366 laid down the policy that *ceteris paribus* teachers with doctorates from universities and faculties recognized by the Holy See were to be preferred in appointing seminary faculty. The new canon 253, §1 requires that *only* those with such degrees be appointed to seminary faculties. Article 16 of the *ordinationes* attached to *Sapientia Christiana* specifies that the "suitable doctorate" required by article 25 of the constitution must be a canonical doctorate if the field is one of the sacred sciences. The same point is made, with explicit reference to "canonical effects," in number 7 of the *ordinationes.*

Much of this legislation has its origins in the struggles of the Church in the nineteenth and twentieth centuries which are discussed below in the appendix. In places where the Church carries on its educational role only with difficulty, the provisions of the code are properly perceived as bulwarks against the state.

In the Anglo-American world, where the Church enjoys broad freedom to establish and direct schools at all levels, though also without government financial support in the United States, the mechanisms of control tend to be perceived in the academic world more as threats of manipulation than defenses against governmental pressure.[40]

Books and Other Media

Title IV, canons 822–832, deals with the mass media and with books in particular. The sections dealing with the media are of course inspired by *Inter mirifica.* Since that decree has been widely regarded as the weakest of the documents of the council,[41] it is a pity that the revisers of the code ignored the fine instruction *Communio et progressio* issued in 1971 by the Pontifical Commission for the Instruments of Social Communication.[42] Its treatment of public opinion in the Church, a topic treated very gingerly in canon 212, and its arguments for openness in the handling of information would have been a useful counterweight to the tendency of the code to accentuate hierarchical vigilance and approval.

Much of Title IV is devoted to the reformed discipline for the censorship of books, which is taken from the 1975 decree *Ecclesiae pastorum* of the CDF. The reform has retained prior censorship, but for a narrower range of books, including translations of the Scriptures, catechisms and textbooks in the sacred sciences. Other categories of books are no longer covered, and it can be noted that the Index of Forbidden Books lost its juridical force in 1966.[43]

The impact of the reform ought to be to encourage the publication of works in the sacred sciences which do not present themselves as texts and which therefore would be freer in presenting theological opinions or discussing *questiones disputatae*, the sort of theological research commended by canon 218. Whether this will happen will depend in large measure on the way in which the new discipline is administered.

The reformed discipline for the prior censorship of books takes on added significance if one considers that it is one area in which the status of adult members of the people of God creates interesting problems and opportunities. Title I of Book III is entitled "The Ministry of the Word of God" and the canons on catechetics appear as its chapter two—immediately after the chapter on preaching. The emphasis is clearly on formation in the faith. A clean distinction between the presentation of the core doctrines and practices of Christianity and "theology" may be easier to maintain when children are being catechized than when adults are. The questions of the searching adult may require responses in the form of books which blur the clear lines of the canons, precisely because they probe the limits of officially formulated statements of the faith. There are ecclesiological issues here too (including subsidiarity) because of the tension between hierarchical solicitude for sound doctrine and the flexibility that is needed pastorally by those who must carry on the task of planting and nurturing the faith.

Profession of Faith

Title V of Book III (c. 833) deals with the profession of faith which various persons in the Church (pastors, diocesan officials, seminary teachers) are required to take before entering upon an office or beginning a major church synod or council. The formula for the prescribed oath was revised and simplified[44] in 1967. The new canon 833 is a revision of canons 1406–1408 of the old code.

The 1967 revision of the required oath brought to an end an era which included the suppression of Modernism in the Catholic Church and the requirement that a stringent oath against Modernism be taken on numerous occasions by teachers and pastors in particular.[45] The simplicity and serenity of the new formulas contrast sharply with those they replaced.

IV.

PENALTIES AND THE TEACHING OFFICE

Other sections of the code also have legislation affecting the exercise of the teaching office. For example, in Book VI, on penalties in the Church, canon 1371, §1 prescribes a "just penalty" (*justa poena*) for those who violate canon 750 by teaching doctrine that has been condemned by the Roman Pontiff or an ecumenical council (see the old canon 2317). But the canon adds something: the crime of violating canon 752 by pertinaciously rejecting doctrine taught by the authoritative but not infallible magisterium.

Here then is a new crime: dissent from the ordinary, non-infallible magisterium. Its inclusion in the code apparently is the result of a papal intervention, since the second part of the first number of the canon was in none of the drafts of the code, including the code commission's final approved schema. Most of the canon is a restatement of the old canon 2317. Its second section prescribes the same "just penalties" for those who disobey the legitimate orders of the Holy See, their ordinary or superior, and who persist in their disobedience after they have been warned; all this is a restatement of the old canon 2331.

The development of the new canon 1371 is interesting. The 1973 schema of Book VI proposed a canon dealing with cases not of formal heresy but with the teaching of doctrines condemned with some lesser censure than heresy. (Both the new code and the old penalize formal heresy with an excommunication *latae sententiae.*) The 1973 draft mentioned both doctrines *condemned* by the Roman Pontiff or an ecumenical council and also doctrine *taught* by them (*doctrinam . . . traditam*). The draft did not enumerate possible penalties as the 1917 code did: removal of faculties to preach or hear confessions, removal from any sort of teaching office, and others which might be included in a judicial sentence or administrative decree or be needed to repair scandal. In 1977 the draft canon was revised. Penalties which in the first draft were permitted (*puniri potest*) were made mandatory (*puniatur*), and the text was revised to eliminate mention of doctrine taught by the Roman Pontiff or an ecumenical council, thus limiting the crime to the pertinacious teaching of condemned doctrine. This amended text was approved by the Commission for the Revision of the Code and transmitted to Pope John Paul II.

The addition of the phrase referring to the teaching mentioned in canon 752 was apparently made by the pope.

The breadth of the new crime is striking. The 1917 code had penalties for heresy or the teaching of condemned doctrines just mentioned. Each case that carried a penalty seemed to suppose a formal condemnatory action. By contrast, the teaching mentioned by canon 752 embraces a great range of papal or episcopal teaching. Since canon 752 explicitly mentions teachings of the episcopal college, and some formal action by the pope is required for a "collegial act" (c. 377, §2), the practical effect of the canon is likely to be restricted to papal teaching.

But the teaching of what has come to be known as the "ordinary" magisterium[46] takes many forms and implies the commitment of teaching authority in various degrees, as *LG* 25 acknowledges. The new canon simply flattens distinctions worked out over centuries in the tradition of theological notes and raises serious questions about the legitimacy of any dissent whatever from the teaching of the ordinary magisterium. The canon is made even vaguer by the substitution of "just penalty" for the more specific formulation of the old canon 2317—even if its penalties seem draconian.

A PRELIMINARY EVALUATION

The new Code of Canon Law presents something of a puzzle. It reflects at important points the inconsistencies of the underlying conciliar documents and of the period of implementation which has followed the council. The great themes of the Second Vatican Council, especially of its ecclesiology, are in the new code. The *triplex munus Christi,* which served the council as an organizing pattern, is in the new code too. So is the doctrine of episcopal collegiality which is so important to the implementation of subsidiarity and which undergirds episcopal conferences and other structures of the particular churches and their groupings since the council. The role of lay Christians receives more attention than before.

I should also call attention to the new emphasis in the code on the preaching of the Word of God and the spreading of the good news by evangelizing those who have not heard it and catechizing those who are already members of the Church. The use of the mass media in the Church's varied teaching tasks is strongly encouraged. Parents' rights to educate their children in the faith are given new expression. Human rights emerge as a theme of the Church's teaching that is to be given special emphasis in the modern world.

A code of law must give much attention to the ordering of the Church's tasks, and that means attention to institutional structures. But if the law succeeds in structuring the teaching tasks, then it may well be the instrument by which new energy is channeled to the *munus docendi* in its various facets.

Inevitably, however, the special responsibilities of the hierarchy for the teaching office get greatest attention in the new code. And there is the repeated and rather nervous insistence on the prerogatives of the hierarchy and the submission owed to it that commentators have noted.[47] In Book III there has been a significant step toward increased and centralized hierarchical control of theological teaching. Unfortunately that increased control seems inconsistent with the principle of subsidiarity and is introduced with little provision for the protection of rights. Concern for both was to be a fundamental principle for the revision of the code, based on important theological themes of Vatican II.

The life of the Church late in the twentieth century will be different from that of other periods. Already we have seen evidence of a more decentralized exercise of magisterial authority. Adaptations needed to meet the needs of the teaching office at every level in new situations are still being made, as the worldwide travels of the pope show.

The new code provides some new structures and some important new emphases. The test of experience lies ahead.

APPENDIX: AN HISTORICAL NOTE
ON THE NOTION OF A MANDATE TO TEACH

John A. Alesandro has noted that the introduction into the new code of the requirement of a canonical mandate to teach theology is a shift from the norms of the 1917 code.[48] Two things are especially prominent: the code undertakes to make all theological institutions dependent upon ecclesiastical authority[49] and in doing so, it shifts from what had been a system of negative vigilance to a system of positive deputation.[50] Moreover, theological teaching is to be dependent upon the Church to insure fidelity to the magisterium.[50]

Alesandro is, of course, correct. But a look at the system of controls in place over a longer period suggests that in some respects the shift represents an attempt to return to an older system of hierarchical controls over the teaching of theology. In this appendix I will briefly trace the medieval system of controls and what replaced it in the nineteenth and twentieth centuries.[52]

Beginning with the earliest indication of papal concern for education in the arts, a decree of Eugene II (circa 826), a series of church decrees emerged directing the establishment of schools by monasteries and cathedrals to provide facilities for the education of both clergy and needy laity. The decrees included papal bulls giving exempt status to the institutions which developed into the medieval universities. Most of the schools were at least originally under the direction of the local bishop and the members of the chapter of canons attached to the cathedral or a collegiate church. In time the direction of the lower schools was put in the hands of one of the canons, who was designated *scholasticus* or *magischola,* while the emerging higher schools were under the direction of the chancellor of the bishop. It was these officials who issued the *licentia docendi* without which no one could teach in the medieval schools.[53]

It is true that there was also an interest by secular rulers in institutions of learning and that at times lay rulers issued the *licentia docendi* or issued decrees creating the *studium generale* whose degrees brought with them the *ius ubique docendi*. But as Rashdall's editors note, "By the end of the twelfth century the ecclesiastical sanction behind the license to teach was undisputed."[54] However imperfectly the system may have worked, the notion that the Church controlled teaching in all fields, not just in theology, was solidly established.

It should be noted in particular that the granting of the license to the holder of a degree from an institution of pontifical right meant acknowledging a right to teach any place in Christendom. The license from other institutions carried with it the right to teach only in the area to which the school's founder's authority extended, which meant in most cases the local diocese.

There is a surprising lack in the decrees of popes and councils of the theological rationale for this system. But the function of the school in Christendom was nicely put by a thirteenth century German writer:

> His siquidem tribus, scilicet sacerdotio, imperio et studio, tanquam tribus virtutibus, videlicet vitali, naturali et animali, sancta catholica ecclesia spiritualiter vivificatur, augmentatur et regitur.[55]

The view of Christendom taken by the Gregorian Reform included both ecclesiastical and civil government as part of a single whole over which the pope presided. While many papal acts taken regarding universities seem to be acts of canonical importance only, the theological rationale underlying them left no part of medieval life free of the superintendency of the Church and especially of the pope. That this included the teaching of theology goes without saying.

The Reformation and rise of the modern state changed the medieval world over time, and the final blow to the system came with the French Revolution and the Napoleonic wars. By the middle of the nineteenth century the Church found that it had lost the direction of schools at every level in much of Europe, and was unable to control institutions for the training of the clergy or to control the teaching of religion, even in places where that teaching was ostensibly Catholic. The new omnicompetent state claimed the right to appoint teachers, prescribe books, and superintend education including religion.[57] It was to this situation that the bishops of Germany addressed themselves in 1848.

The bishops met in Würzburg in October, 1848, with their theological and canonical advisors. What emerged was the first formal demand to the modern state that those who taught Catholic theology (or religion in lower schools) must have from the bishop not the historic *licentia docendi* but what the bishops called a *missio canonica*. Thus in their sixth session they said:

> Episcopi Germaniae declarant, nemini in ullo omnino scholae genere docendae religionis catholicae munus mandari posse, cui hujus rei potestas ecclesiastica missione rite facta non sit.[58]

To those teaching theology in Germany the bishops wrote:

> Episcopi Germaniae, pro ea fiducia, quam in publicis theologiae professoribus collocant, plane sperant fore, ut illi, non solum tanquam sacerdotes, sed etiam tanquam sanctarum disciplinarum doctores, semper se ab Ecclesia missos et docendi potestate instructos existiment, ob eamdam ipsam rem se, ex divino et ecclesiastico jure, adversus Ecclesiae auctoritatem, qua funguntur Episcopi, reddendae muneris sui rationi conditione teneri perpetuo recordentur.[59]

This statement was drafted by Ignaz von Döllinger of Munich, amended by Archbishop Johann von Geisel of Cologne, and adopted unanimously by the assembled bishops.

The Würzburg meeting of the German bishops was an attempt

to establish for the German church the sort of national structures which the National Assembly at Frankfurt had proposed in the political sphere. The bishops' concern for schools was a response to the National Assembly's constitutional provisions that would have made schooling a virtual monopoly of the state.

As Döllinger put it, "The most important thing is to assert the principle that teachers of religion are to be appointed by bishops."[60] Döllinger also asserted the right of the Church to establish schools of its own at every level—but that is not our principal concern here.

What is of interest is the rationale given for the claim being made. Not all the bishops or their advisors agreed on that. The right of the Church to establish schools which taught subjects other than theology was warmly debated. Döllinger and others argued for the right on the basis of the right of association or the right to educate.

The chief spokesman, though not the only one, for an emphasis on the mission of the Church was the archbishop of Munich, Karl August von Reisach.[61]

Reisach argued that the right of the Church to establish and operate schools is grounded in its "mission to bear witness to the truth."[62] He said that if faith and morals are endangered in the world, then the Church has the right to operate schools in any subject area, to see to it that the one truth is promoted in everything. Reisach's insistence on the one truth was a rejection of a right to teach error. Therefore, only the teacher of truth has the right to teach, and that meant the Church.

It is Reisach, too, who provided the clearest rationale for the demand that teachers of religion and theology have a "canonical mission." The notion of a "canonical mission" has been familiar in the Western Church since the medieval controversies over lay preaching by the Waldensians and others.[63] In the highly juridical ecclesiology of the nineteenth century Roman School in which Reisach was trained, the notion of a "mission" was supported by an understanding that as the bishops were sent (*missi*) by Christ, so priests or others had to be sent to teach religion or theology. In this ecclesiology any other authority, whether the state or private persons, is simply incompetent to authorize teachers of theology or instructors of the young in their faith. Such teachers must be sent by a bishop.

It seems to me that the notion of "mission" urged by Reisach, with the juridical cast that it had taken on in counter-Reformation theology, is consistent with but goes beyond many of the claims made for the requirement of a *licentia docendi* in the earlier period. Indeed it is striking how little theological rationale is offered for the medieval papal and conciliar legislation regarding the *licentia*. The role of the papacy as the ultimate juridical authority in Christendom was well established, and according to some of its defenders, the ultimate authority was also the source of all inferior authority. In that medieval context the requirements for a *licentia docendi* fit very well. Congar has many times called attention to this *juridicizing* of Western ecclesiology in the Gregorian reform.[64]

The nineteenth century adopted the rationale used in the Lateran Councils against the claim of charismatic preachers to have their authorization directly from God. The proof text was Romans 10:15: "How shall they preach unless they be sent?" After Würzburg, the bishops, with strong papal support, insisted that no one *teach* religion unless he be sent.

In the 1983 Code of Canon Law the term *missio canonica* adopted at Würzburg which had been taken over into a number of concordats and into the papal constitutions *Deus scientiarum Dominus* (1931) and *Sapientia Christiana* (1979) governing pontifical faculties, has been dropped in favor of the less technical term "mandate."[65] That term was used in connection with discussions of the nature of Catholic Action. Its use avoids the issue of the relationship of holy orders and canonical missions. It is asserted in the new code that all who teach theology, clergy or lay, are to have the mandate. In the case of seminary teachers, the new code demands that seminary teachers have the license or the doctorate from a pontifical faculty or at least from one recognized by the Church (c. 253, §1). *Sapientia Christiana*, article 27, §2 prescribes that teachers in pontifical facilities be approved by the Holy See (*nihil obstat*) prior to their appointment with the canonical mandate. In each case the approval or authorization can be withdrawn by the authority which granted it, following the procedures prescribed by the

statutes of the faculty or the institution. Institutions not of pontifical rank commonly do not have such statutes, which means that no
process is prescribed for withholding the mandate or withdrawing
it.

Although some have suggested that the new code ought not to
be understood in the light of local legislation that preceded it,[66] the
literature on both the *nihil obstat* and the *missio canonica* as they
were found in 19th and 20th century concordats appears indispen-
sible for interpretation. It suffices to note as an example the agreement of authors on the subject that a serious offense would be
needed to justify the withdrawal of the *missio canonica*.[67]

Earlier I noted that in many places in the world, where the
Church's right to educate and to operate schools is not respected,
the mechanisms for church control of teaching, especially of theology, were and are perceived as a needed defense against the pretensions of the state.

But Alesandro has noted, on the basis of the *relatio* of the
code commission secretariat, that a significant shift has taken
place. Explaining a proposed change in the 1980 draft code which
eliminated the suggestion that theological faculties should be established by the Church even in universities it does not control, the
commission's *relatio* said,

> Facultates Theologiae Catholicae ut Ecclesiae Magisterio
> fideles re vera maneant, debent ab Ecclesia dependere.[68]

That statement says plainly that what had begun as a way of defending the rights of the Church against the pretensions of the state has
now become an internal mechanism to insure hierarchical control
of the teaching of theology.

There is no doubt in the Catholic tradition that the church
hierarchy has special responsibilities for the integrity of the Christian message. But Alesandro is surely right in raising doubts about
the wisdom of the pervasive shift in the new code from a system of
negative vigilance to one of positive deputation. For one thing, the
new system seems to imply a greater responsibility of the deputiz-
ing bishop for the work of a theologian than seems desirable. For
another the system seems to echo the view of *Si diligis*[69] that no

one teaches theology except *vi missionis*. I certainly do not question the right and the need for the church hierarchy to oversee the teaching of theology, especially in the Church's own institutions. But oversight is one thing, even if it includes the right to require that errant theologians be removed; the notion that all teaching of theology is but an extension of hierarchical teaching authority is something else, a claim that would absorb the charism of theology into the authority of hierarchical office. On both historical and theological grounds such a claim seems insupportable.[70]

There are also important practical problems. The apparatus of hierarchical control which the code puts in place is so vast and cumbersome that it seems unlikely to succeed in the long run. The machinery may be invoked in selected instances, but one can wonder whether bishops will long be interested in the details of every academic appointment in theology. If the code is ignored or circumvented in the majority of the cases, it can only heighten the impression of arbitrariness in those cases in which the law is invoked, especially if the result is the denial or withdrawal of the mandate. The possibility of abuse or the appearance of abuse is increased by the fact that the code prescribes no canonical process for the granting, withholding, or withdrawal of the mandate. By contrast, *Sapientia Christiana*, article 30, prescribes that the statutes of each ecclesiastical faculty are to set out the process to be followed and notes that rights of teachers, the institution, the students and the church community are to be protected.[71]

1. *Codex Iuris Canonici auctoritate Ioannis Pauli pp. II promulgatus* (Libreria Editrice Vaticana, 1983). Page references in this article will be to the *Code of Canon Law, Latin-English Edition* (Washington: CLSA, 1983).

2. See Thomas J. Green, "The Revision of Canon Law: Theological Implications," *Theological Studies* 40 (1979) 601.

3. "Preface to the Latin Edition," *Code of Canon Law, Latin-English Edition*, p. xxi—xxii.

4. Yves Congar, *Lay People in the Church* (Westminster, Newman, 1965), p. 45.

5. Book I of the code is not considered here, since it deals with technical canonical matters.

6. Pontificia Commissio Codici Iuris Canonici Recognoscendo, *Lex*

Ecclesiae Fundamentalis seu Ecclesiae Catholicae Universae Lex Canonica Fundamentalis (Rome, April 24, 1980).

7. See the discussion in Avery Dulles, "What Is the Doctrinal Authority of a Bishop's Conference?" *Origins* 14 (1985) 528–534.

8. On "ordo" and "college" see Bernard Botte, O.S.B., "Collegiate Character of the Presbyterate and Episcopate," *The Sacrament of Holy Orders* (Collegeville: Liturgical Press, 1962), pp. 74–97, esp. pp. 83–96.

9. See "Nota explicativa praevia" to chapter three of *LG.* Text in *Acta Synodalia Concilii Oecumenici Vaticani Secundi*, 4 vols. in 25 parts (Vatican City, 1971–80) III, 8: 11–13. See also the commentary on the note by Joseph Ratzinger in *Commentary on the Documents of Vatican II*, ed. Herbert Vorgrimler (New York: Herder & Herder, 1967), I: 297–305.

10. On the older regulations on provincial and plenary councils, see commentary by James Provost in *The Code of Canon Law: A Text and Commentary*, ed. James A. Coriden, Thomas J. Green and Donald E. Heintschel (New York: Paulist, 1985), pp. 356–362.

11. See Henri deLubac, *The Motherhood of the Church* (San Francisco: Ignatius Press, 1982), pp. 257–273; and critical comments by Cardinal Joseph Ratzinger, prefect of the CDF, reported in *The Catholic Messenger*, May 30, 1985, p. 6.

12. Translation from *The Documents of Vatican II*, ed. Walter M. Abbott (New York: American Press, 1966), pp. 288–289. It may be important to keep the original Latin text in mind: "Res quidem terrenae et ea, quae in hominum condicione hunc mundum exsuperant, arcte inter se iunguntur, et ipsa Ecclesia rebus temporalibus utitur quantum propria eius missio id postulat. Spem vero suam in privilegiis ab auctoritate civili oblatis non reponit; immo quorundam iurium legitime acquisitorum exercitio renuntiabit, ubi constiterit eorum usu sinceritatem sui testimonii vocari in dubium aut novas vitae condiciones aliam exigere ordinationem. Semper autem et ubique ei fas sit cum vera libertate fidem praedicare, socialem suam doctrinam docere, munus suum inter homines expedite exercere necnon iudicum morale ferre, etiam de rebus quae ad ordinem politicum respiciunt, quando personae iura fundamentalia aut animarum salus id exigant, omnia et sola subsidia adhibendo, quae Evangelio et omnium bono secundum temporum et condicionum diversitatem congruant." *Acta* IV/7: 300.

13. *AAS* 46 (1954) 666–667.

14. Ibid., pp. 671–672.

15. The personalist emphasis is continued in the statements of Pope John Paul II. See, for example, *Redemptor hominis*, n. 12 (*Origins* 8 [1979] 632), and part two (ibid., pp. 633 ff.).

16. See John P. Boyle, "The Magisterium and the Natural Law," *CTSA Proceedings* 34 (1979) 189–210; and Francis J. Sullivan, *Magisterium: Teaching Authority in the Catholic Church* (New York: Paulist, 1983), pp. 138–152.

17. See the "Letter on War and Peace," part one, *Origins* 13 (1983) 2, and the first draft "Letter on the American Economy," part two, introduction, *Origins* 14 (1984) 358.

18. See David Hollenbach, S.J., *Claims in Conflict: Retrieving and Renewing the Catholic Human Rights Tradition* (New York: Paulist, 1979).

19. On reception see Yves Congar, "La 'Réception' comme réalité ecclésiologique," *Revue des sciences philosophiques et théologiques* 56 (1972) 369–403; the discussion in Sullivan, pp. 109–117; and the important discussion of the topic in the context of contemporary ecumenism by Cardinal J. Willebrands in *Origins* 14 (1985) 720–724.

20. On the primary and secondary objects of infallibility, see Sullivan, pp. 127–138.

21. On the growth of the magisterium in the 19th and 20th centuries, see Yves Congar, "A Brief History of the Forms of the Magisterium," in *Readings in Moral Theology, No. 3*, ed. Charles E. Curran and Richard A. McCormick (New York: Paulist, 1982), pp. 325–328; and J. Boyle, "The 'Ordinary Magisterium': Toward a History of the Concept," *The Heythrop Journal* 20 (1979) 380–398 and 21 (1980) 14–29.

22. See Dulles (note 7, above) and the comments of Cardinals deLubac and Ratzinger cited in note 9.

23. See Herbert Jedin, ed., *Handbuch der Kirchengeschichte*, VI/1 (Freiburg: Herder, 1971), pp. 507–515 and 683–695.

24. *AAS* 76 (1984) 47.

25. See Yves Congar, *Die Lehre von der Kirche vom Abendlandischen Schisma bis zum Gegenwart, Handbuch der Dogmengeschichte*, III/3d (Freiburg: Herder, 1971), p. 65.

26. Congar, "A Brief History," p. 327.

27. See *Acta* III/8: 88, and Sullivan, pp. 166–173.

28. Francis X. Winters, "Nuclear Deterrence Morality: Atlantic Community Bishops in Tension," *Theological Studies* 43 (1982) 427–446, and the sequel, "After Tension, Detente: A Continuing Chronicle of European Episcopal Views on Nuclear Deterrence," *Theological Studies* 45 (1984) 343–351.

29. The problem arises when authority seems to substitute itself for that personal moral judgment without which authentic moral agency seems impossible. See Boyle, "The Magisterium," p. 205.

30. See Yves Congar, "Sur la trilogie Prophète-Roi-Prêtre," *Revue des sciences philosophiques et théologiques* 67 (1983) 113, n.; and Brian Tierney, "'Only the Truth Has Authority': The Problem of Reception in the Decretists and in Johannes de Turrecremata," in *Law, Church and Society: Essays in Honor of Stephen Kuttner,* ed. Kenneth Pennington and Robert Somerville (Philadelphia: University of Pennsylvania Press, 1977), pp. 69–96.

31 *AAS* 76 (1984) 46.

32. *AAS* 64 (1972) 97–176.

33. *AAS* 67 (1975) 281–284.

34. *AAS* 72 (1980) 756.

35. *AAS* 71 (1979) 1277–1340.

36. *AAS* 64 (1972) 173.

37. Ibid., p. 173.

38. See James Bowen, *A History of Western Education,* III: *The Modern West: Europe and the New World* (New York: St. Martin's Press, 1981); see also the "Syllabus of Errors," n. 45, cited in DS 2945 for a statement of the position against which the Church reacted.

39. *AAS* 71 (1979) 469–499, with *Ordinationes,* pp. 500–521.

40. See, for example, the criticisms of the "Initial Report of the Task Force Committee on the Draft of the Canons of Book Three: The Church's Teaching Mission," ed. James A. Coriden (Washington: CLSA, 1978).

41. See the very negative judgment of Karlheinz Schmidthus in Vorgrimler, I: 94–95.

42. *AAS* 63 (1971) 593–656.

43. *AAS* 58 (1966) 445.

44. *AAS* 59 (1969) 1058.

45. Text in DS 3537–3550.

46. See note 21.

47. See, for example, the "Initial Report" cited in note 40, above.

48. John A. Alesandro, "The Rights and Responsibilities of Theologians: A Canonical Perspective," in *Cooperation Between Theologians and the Ecclesiastical Magisterium,* ed. Leo J. O'Donovan (Washington: CLSA, 1982), p. 107.

49. Ibid., p. 105, n.

50. Ibid., p. 108.

51. Ibid., p. 105, n.

52. For what follows, see H. Flatten, "Missio Canonica," in *Verkündigung und Glaube: Festschrift für Franz X. Arnold,* ed. Theodor Filthaut und Josef Jungmann (Freiburg: Herder, 1958), pp. 123–141;

Hugo Hellmuth, "Die missio canonica," *Archiv für katholisches Kirchenrecht* 91 (1911) 448–476 and 601–637; Georges Bourbon, "La licence d'enseigner et le rôle de l'écolâtre au Moyen Age," *Revue des questions historiques* 19 (1876) 513–553; Gaines Post, "Alexander III, the *licentia docendi* and the Rise of the Universities," in *Haskins Anniversary Essays in Mediaeval History,* ed. Charles H. Taylor and John E. LaMonte (Boston and New York: Houghton Mifflin, 1929), pp. 255–277; Alexander F. Sokolich, *Canonical Provisions for Universities and Colleges: A Historical Synopsis and a Commentary,* Canon Law Studies, 373 (Washington: Catholic University of America Press, 1956); Hastings Rashdall, *The Universities of Europe in the Middle Ages,* new ed. by Frederick M. Powicke and Alfred B. Emden, 3 vols. (Oxford University Press, 1936).

53. The medievals had a double system of approval of teachers. The approval of the body of masters was given when the candidate had demonstrated competence. Then the *licentia docendi* was granted by the chancellor—who, it should be noted, was not a member of the faculty but an "outsider" to the university. But it should also be noted that the chancellor was forbidden by repeated papal decrees to withhold the *licentia* from any competent person who asked for it. The reason for this demand on the part of the popes was the tendency of the masters to organize themselves into guilds and erect obstacles to the entry of new members to the guild. It was the role of the chancellor to keep open the entryway to teaching status. The popes fought another battle to secure the admittance of members of the new mendicant orders, Franciscans and Dominicans, to the theological faculty at Paris. See Rashdall, I: 278–293 (Paris) and I: 221–231 (Bologna). At first, the doctors of Bologna granted the *licentia* themselves, but Rashdall observes: "This unfettered liberty of the Bologna doctors was, however, out of harmony with hierarchical ideas; it was contrary to the general principle of canon law which claimed for the Church a certain control over education; and it was contrary to the analogy of the schools north of the Alps, particularly of the great University of Paris, where the *licentia docendi* had always been obtained from the chancellor of the cathedral church. Accordingly, in 1219 Honorius III, himself a former Archdeacon of Bologna, enjoined that no promotion to the doctorate should take place without the consent of the Archdeacon of Bologna, who was probably the head of the chapter school as well as the chapter itself. The innovation was accepted without opposition . . ." (I: 221–222). "Hierarchical ideas" rather than explicit theological warrants were at work. See also the "note" in Rashdall, I: 20–24, which insists that the granting of the *licentia* was an ecclesiastical act and cites the protest of Marsiglio of Padua against it as a usurpation of secular authority.

54. Rashdall, I: 21. In Karl Bihlmeyer and Hermann Tückle, *Church History II: The Middle Ages* (Westminster: Newman, 1963), it is reported that of 44 universities founded before 1400, 31 had papal as well as royal charters and 21 had only papal charters. The authors comment: "There can be no doubt of the predominantly ecclesiastical character of the medieval university: the consent of the pope as supreme guardian of the faith was necessary for the institution to exist and only with his approval could the *facultas ubique docendi* be conferred; theology took precedence over all the other branches of learning, most of the teachers were clerics who derived their maintenance from ecclesiastical benefices, and the feast of the patron saint was solemnly celebrated *in corpore*" (p. 323).

55. Cited in Rashdall, I: 23. The statement is attributed to a "German patriot (probably Alexander of Roes, in the year 1281)."

56. See Walter Ullmann, *The Growth of Papal Government in the Middle Ages* (London: Methuen, 3rd ed., 1970); and Rashdall in the "Note" cited in note 53, above.

57. See Bowen, cited in note 38, above.

58. *Acta et Decreta sacrorum conciliorum recentiorum* (*Collectio Lacensis*) (Freiburg: Herder, 1889), V, col. 969b.

59. Ibid., col. 971–972.

60. Ibid., col. 1020a.

61. On Reisach, see Boyle, "The Ordinary Magisterium," p. 386.

62. *Collectio Lacensis*, col. 1026b.

63. See DS 809.

64. See Yves Congar, "The Historical Development of Authority in the Church: Points for Christian Reflection," in *Problems of Authority*, ed. John M. Todd (Baltimore: Helicon, 1962), pp. 119–156.

65. See Yves Congar, review of *Cooperation* in "Sur la trilogie," p. 113, n. See also the discussion by Aldo del Monte in *Il Decreto sull Apostolato dei Laici* (Turin-Leumann: Elle-di-Ci, 1966), p. 278, n.

66. Ladislas Orsy, "Note: The Mandate to Teach Theological Disciplines: Glosses on Canon 812 of the New Code," *Theological Studies* 44 (1983) 476–488, esp. p. 477.

67. Reinhard Lettman, "Das bischöfliche 'Nihil Obstat' für die Lehrtätigkeit an theologischen Fakultäten staatlicher Universitäten in Deutschland," *Investigationes Theologico-Canonicae* (*Festschrift Wilhelm Bertrams*) (Rome: Gregorian University Press, 1978), pp. 285–287.

68. Alesandro, p. 105, n.

69. *AAS* 46 (1954) 314–315.

70. See the discussion in Sullivan, pp. 196–204.

71. As this study was being done, the Congregation for Catholic

Education circulated a "Proposed Schema (Draft) for a Pontifical Document on Catholic Universities" dated April 15, 1985. Its proposed norms, which every Catholic institution of higher learning would be required to incorporate into its statutes, demand *inter alia* links of the institution to the church hierarchy (art. 3 with others). Every institution would be required to submit quinquenial reports to the congregation (art. 21); the "Catholic identity" of the institution is given much emphasis; a procedure for the removal of teachers who are unfit for various reasons, including doctrinal integrity, is to be established (art. 26). Although the draft document in part simply repeats the requirements of the new code, its intention clearly is to strengthen hierarchical controls over higher education under Catholic auspices, using the provisions of *Sapientia Christiana* as a model.

Reflections on the Text of a Canon

Ladislas Orsy, S.J.

This article originally appeared in *America* in 1986.

In the Code of Canon Law, promulgated in 1983, there is a special section—entitled "The Teaching Office of the Church"—with several new canons in it. This article will focus on one of them. As always, new rules reflect new problems in the church; they are responses to emerging needs.

The problem of religous respect or submission to noninfallible teaching is with us more than ever before in history. Many factors have contributed to this situation. The progress in understanding and defining the scope and limits of the infallibility of the church, and of the role of the pope and of the episcopal college in exercising it, led to questions about the significance of their noninfallible pronouncements. Further, our age has produced many new questions concerning faith and morals to which there are no obvious answers in Christian tradition. The church itself must reflect and search, even make provisional statements, before it can come to a definitive judgment. Also, particularly since the 19th century, there has been a shift in the exercise of the teaching office of the See of Rome; besides acting as judges in doctrinal disputes, the popes have assumed a greater initiative in clarifying Christian traditions in relation to new questions, which understandably has led to an expansion of noninfallible teaching.

In approaching the problem, history—and very recent history at that—has taught us to be cautious. Within living memory we have seen how some theologians, once silenced and penalized, have come to play a major role at Vatican II; we have seen also how noninfallible positions and pronouncements have been quietly reversed by the same council. Be that as it may, the problem of how to respond to noninfallible teaching is with us, and will remain so for a long time to come. New questions concerning faith and morals will continue to be addressed to the church. The church, not having the gift of sudden enlightenment, will seek answers as it can—through any honest means or method that faith and reason can find, such as prayer, reflection, disputes or debates. This is a complex and unique process in which every member of the social body must play its own proper part. It is not to be compared to any kind of political operation; it is the way the living body of Christ on earth seeks understanding.

The purpose of this article is not to describe that process in all its details; far from it. It merely wants to point toward the complexity of the process, and does so on the basis of somewhat limited but still authentic information taken from the new Code of Canon Law.

Canon 752 is concerned with this specific issue: "When the pope or the episcopal college in the exercise of their authentic teaching office [*magisterium*] affirm [declare, enunciate] a doctrine concerning faith or morals without intending to proclaim it with a definitive act, [on the part of the faithful] no assent of faith but religious respect [in Latin: *obsequium;* compliance? submission?] of mind and will is due. The faithful, therefore, should avoid what is not congruent [*non congruit*] with such a doctrine."

The canon draws a sharp distinction between a doctrine that has been proclaimed with a definitive act, and a doctrine that has not been so affirmed. The former is really part of the profession of the faith of the church, even if it is not explicitly in any creed; the latter is not, although it is not lightly spoken. In the first case, the church has committed itself with a certainty that only faith can give; in the second case, it is still on the way toward such a certainty.

Accordingly, the canon says, the faithful must exercise discretion. If the church has committed itself, they too, in order to be one with the church, must do the same with an assent of faith. Such an assent is a surrender to God, revealing Himself and His kingdom to us—a surrender ultimately on the testimony of the Spirit, not on the strength of any argument.

If the church has not committed itself with an act of faith, the faithful, to be one with the church, must not do it either. Their response to the words of the teaching authority must be religious *obsequium*—a term that I provisionally translate as "respect" with the warning that its meaning certainly goes beyond a simple respect for another opinion, as we shall see later. Such a "respect," however, is not, and cannot be, a surrender to God speaking; it is a response to the church searching. Since there is a human element in this search, there must be one in the response, too. Arguments given by the teaching authority play their role.

In concrete cases, the distinction between the two types of doctrine, and consequently between the two types of response, may not be so clear as the canon makes it (law has a genius for simplifying issues in view of action); but the theoretical soundness of the distinction is not canceled out by the practical problems of its application.

At any rate, it is clear that the law asks for religious *obsequium* in response to noninfallible teaching, but it is not clear as yet what exactly this *obsequium* means. Since it is a response to noninfallible teaching, we should go beyond the field of law to have a better understanding of it, and see what the church is doing in so teaching.

Noninfallible teaching is intimately connected with the church's search for a better understanding of the evangelical message. John the Evangelist reports that Jesus said at His last supper: "I have yet many things to say to you but you cannot bear them now. When the Spirit of truth comes, he will guide you into all the truth" (Jn. 16:13). That is, the Lord did not give the full understanding of the truth to the apostles, or to the primitive church. Rather, He set the believing community on the path toward it where it has remained ever since, searching, struggling, articulating: faith seeking understanding.

There is the paradox of the church: It is endowed with divine gifts and it is subject to human limitations; it is in possession of the truth and it has to seek the truth.

This search is the task of the whole church. Vatican II could not have been more explicit about it: "The body of the faithful as a whole, anointed as they are by the Holy One (cf. Jn. 2:20,27), cannot err in matters of belief. Thanks to a supernatural sense of the faith that characterizes the People as a whole, it manifests this unerring quality when 'from the bishops down to the last member of the laity,' it shows universal agreement on matters of faith and morals. For, by this sense of faith which is aroused and sustained by the Spirit of truth, God's People accepts not the word of men but the very Word of God (cf. 1 Th. 2: 13). It clings without fail to the faith once delivered to the saints (cf. Jude 3), penetrates it more deeply by accurate insights and applies it more thoroughly to life. All this it does under the lead of a sacred teaching authority to which it loyally defers" (Dogmatic Constitution on the Church, No. 12).

The search belongs to the whole body; all, head and members, should take part in it; all together, they should arrive at a fuller understanding of the mystery. In this process, a delicate and complex pattern of rights and duties arises. They are not juridical relations, but they are no less real for that.

The faithful have a right to be informed correctly, as far as possible, concerning what point of doctrine belongs to the core of our Christian beliefs and what does not. In the first case, their response ought to be a surrender to the Word of God, alive in the church. In the second case, it must be a religious *obsequium*, an attitude essentially different from an act of faith. This distinction is vital. If there is no surrender to God's invitation to believe, the "sacrament" of the Word of God cannot become alive in the life of the hearer; if there is an assent of faith when it is not due, a serious crisis of faith may arise later if the doctrine stated needs to be corrected, completed or perhaps abandoned. Many of the faithful experienced such a "crisis of faith" after Vatican II because "the teaching of the church has changed." In truth, our faith has not changed. The root of the crisis was in earlier misinformation. Points of doctrine that required an assent of faith and theological opinions that did not were indiscriminately proposed by less than well informed preachers as "the teaching of the church," and when the council reaffirmed the essential doctrines and modified or abandoned other theological opinions, the crisis followed inevitably.

Further, if the faithful have the capacity to penetrate the mysteries by accurate insights, and to apply the evangelical teaching more thoroughly to their lives on the strength of their baptismal consecration, they must have the right, not only to reflect in silence, but also to discuss their insights in the community. In this process, those who have the mandate to teach authentically also have the duty to listen; the episcopal college with the pope presiding can indeed be enlightened by the rest of the faithful. This duty to listen does not take away their right to be judges of the authenticity of the insights and applications proposed; for this, they have the assistance of the Spirit through their ordination. They can bring the search to a close, but as long as they have not done so, the search should go on.

The process of "faith seeking understanding" must be marked by truth and freedom. By truth: As far as possible, all preaching and teaching should carefully distinguish between doctrine to which the assent of faith is due and doctrine that must be "respectfully received" but without such an assent. By freedom: The capacity to penetrate the mysteries with deeper insights and apply them more thoroughly to life was given to the whole church. Hence, as far as it is possible, all should have the opportunity to contribute to the process. But this should be "under the lead of a sacred teaching authority," that is, under the successors of Peter and of the other apostles. Their insights have a special standing, due to the gentle assistance of the Spirit, even while they are searching. To confine this help only to the moment of their final judgment would be incorrect. Yet, the divine assistance in the searching stage is not so strong that their insights could not be completed or corrected.

This brings us to a better understanding of the text of the canon that speaks of a religious respect, *obsequium* of mind and will. The word cannot be given an easy and standard meaning. When the search for understanding is at its very beginning and the statements of the teaching authority are somewhat tentative (as they were, no doubt, in the case of the earliest declarations of the Biblical Commission), *obsequium* may not mean more than respectful listening and reflection on what has been "officially" stated—knowing that the church as a whole is still far from a final commitment. The scope for freedom must be great at that stage. When the search for a full understanding comes close to a clear vision and the minds and hearts in the church converge "from the bishops down to the last member of the laity," religious respect may well mean submission since the community is on the threshold of a surrender in faith.

We are in a better position now to raise the question about the meaning of "dissent" from noninfallible teaching. I wish that word "dissent" had never been used! It is too simple to carry the shades of meaning that a complex reality postulates. After all, as long as the pope and bishops have not committed themselves and consequently have not bound the rest of the church, all are on the way toward the full truth. If "to dissent" means to offer at that stage particular insights that are different from the insights of those who are exercising teaching authority, we are not talking so much of dissent as of contribution toward common assent that should eventually emerge from the search for "all the truth." Should the "dissenter" claim that he alone has the light, he would deny the communitarian nature of the search. Should the dissenter be unduly silenced, his valuable contribution may be lost.

Now it is easier to understand the last clause of the canon: "The faithful, therefore, should avoid what is not congruent with such a doctrine." Undoubtedly, it is not a call for an assent of faith. It is a call for *obsequium,* as it is fitting and due according to the nature of the case. At times, the voicing of a different opinion can be most congruent because it advances the search and thus helps to clarify the doctrine further; it would not be difficult to show that some of the writings of Cardinal Newman would fall into this category. At times it can be incongruent because it has little positive to offer and it disrupts the church; Archbishop Marcel Lefebvre's "dissent" from the noninfallible teaching of Vatican II would be a good example of this.

Two more ambiguities should be cleared up here: one is about "ordinary magisterium," another about "official teaching."

"Ordinary magisterium" had been used originally, especially in theological textbooks published before Vatican II, to describe infallible teaching by ordinary means; that is, not through an ecumenical council or solemn papal definition, but through constant affirmations over a long period of time. The response of the faithful to such "ordinary magisterium" ought to be an assent of faith. The mystery of the Assumption could be singled out as having been taught in this way before its solemn definition.

In more recent times, however, "ordinary magisterium" has acquired a new significance and an essentially different one at that. It is used more and more to mean noninfallible teaching as described in the second part of this canon: authentic but not definitive. The response can only be "religious respect."

Admittedly, in concrete cases the dividing line between the two meanings can be blurred, but it can be clear as well. Not to perceive this distinction may easily lead to an incorrect response.

"Official teaching" is a somewhat vague and all-embracing expression. It can mean a formal definition by an ecumenical council just as much as it can refer to an instruction by a Roman congregation. There is no way of saying what in a precise case the response to a piece of "official teaching" should be without a close examination of the source of the teaching and of its content.

That much for theory. Now some practical consequences can be drawn.

Simple statements—such as "a noninfallible statement can never bind" or "the official teaching always binds, infallible or not"—should be avoided. They do not do justice to a complex process. The particular importance of an issue, the progress already made, the weight of the reasons offered for a response—all such elements should be taken into consideration before the nature of a response to a particular point of teaching can be determined. While no "assent of faith" is ever due before a definitive proclamation, religious *obsequium* should be given, but in a degree that cannot be defined a priori; it may bind us to a respectful consideration of the teaching in one case, to readiness for submission in another case.

There should be an effort on the part of the church to educate the faithful in the understanding of these admittedly complicated matters. It can be done best by steadily explaining the nature of the church: a human community endowed with divine gifts, in possession of the truth and in the process of searching for a better understanding of it. To know and to love the church, the faithful must grasp, not only that it is of divine foundation, but that it is operating under human limitations. The Word of God has been handed over to human beings. No one should say that all this is too sophisticated for the ordinary faithful. They see the human side of the church anyway; the teachers' and preachers' task is to bring sense into what often appears as "not fitting for the church."

There should be no undue dichotomy between theory and practice. If the highest teaching authority, be it an ecumenical council, or the college of bishops, or the pope, has not committed itself with an act of faith to a particular belief, the faithful should not be compelled to do so either in the practical order. This may happen if a noninfallible doctrine is enforced by heavy disciplinary measures, or by an exclusion from offices, or by the denial of the sacraments to those who respect, but as yet have not adopted, the official position. Any such action would mean requiring an assent of faith in practice when it is not due in theory.

There are two ways of sinning against the teaching authority of the church: by downgrading it, or by upgrading it. To downgrade it means to deny the weight of authority that is present in a proclamation; to upgrade it means to project a strength into an official affirmation that the teacher himself has not put there. For instance, if someone said that the council's Dogmatic Constitution on the Church is a mere exhortation, he would sin by downgrading an important conciliar document; or if someone said that the *Syllabus of Errors* of Pope Pius IX consists of dogmatic definitions, he would sin by upgrading the theological value of the statements contained in it. There is no virtue in either of these excesses; there is, however, an infidelity to the intention of the respective authors in both cases. In other terms, we are bound to give to every point of doctrine as much authority as the church has granted to it; neither less, nor more. Then, and then only, are we rooted in truth.

Finally, a most important conclusion that puts everything that has been said in this article into the right context: In the canon we examined, both the "assent of faith" and the "religious *obsequium*" appear as if they were legal obligations. In truth, they are the gifts of the Spirit. No one can surrender to God unless moved to do so by the Spirit. No one can responsibly participate in the church's search for a deeper understanding of the mysteries unless prompted to do so by the Spirit. The canon describes rather than prescribes the manifold gifts that enable the Christian community to respond to God's unfolding revelation.

Theological Pluralism
and Canonical Mandate

John J. Strynkowski

This article originally appeared in *The Jurist*.

In 1964 during the discussions regarding the exercise of papal primacy as the document on the Church was being prepared, Paul VI proposed an amendment to the text which would state that in his action the Pope is "answerable to the Lord alone." The Theological Commission studied the proposal and responded as follows: "The Roman Pontiff is also bound to revelation itself, to the fundamental structure of the Church, to the sacraments, to the definitions of earlier councils and other obligations too numerous to mention."[1]

It will be the purpose of my presentation to demonstrate that theology is so inextricably bound up with the life and activity of the Church that the requirement of a *missio canonica* or any sort of mandate for the teaching of theology in institutions of higher learning will have to be interpreted by bishops, theologians and canonists in the light of the necessary existence of theology within the Church. It will also be my aim to show that since theology has never been nor ever can be monolithic, *missio canonica* or any other sort of mandate for teaching theology must respect the fundamental pluralism of theology and be interpreted by it.

I do not have to say that I approach this task with some anxiety. Although I welcome the opportunity to engage in a dialogue with canonists, I must confess my limitations most especially with regard to canon law, its interpretation and its implementation. Further, even though the new Code has been published, it remains somewhat problematic how the mandate to teach will be interpreted. But I hope that what I say will make some small contribution to our understanding of the role of theology within the Church and thus will be helpful no matter what the Code requires. Although as a result of the October, 1981 meeting of the Commission for the Revision of the Code the term *missio canonica* in the draft canon then numbered 767 was replaced by *mandatum,* I will make use of the former concept from time to time for the purposes of my argument. The canon now reads: "Those who teach the theological disciplines in any institute of higher learning whatsoever must have a mandate from the competent ecclesiastical authority."[2]

In recent years the discussion of the relationship between the magisterium and theologians has become quite lively with an abundance of statements from both sides. It was, for example, the subject of a meeting of the International Theological Commission in 1975. The conclusions reached at that meeting were published in the form of theses in 1976.[3] To read only some of the literature on this topic is sufficient to gain the impression that an at least implicit presupposition to the discussion is that there is an inevitable antagonism between the magisterium and theologians. Such of course is the undoubted premise of the mass media and many Catholics. The very repetition of the need to collaborate that is made so frequently by both sides witnesses perhaps to an underlying sentiment of unavoidable mutual opposition.

Although such a sentiment and presupposition may be the fruit of some bitter conflict in recent decades, what cannot be neglected is the fundamental datum of history and experience of the Church that there is more which unites the magisterium and theology than separates them. To quote the International Theological Commission, " . . .it is neither necessary nor possible to establish a hard and fast separation between them."[4] It is obvious, first of all, that both serve the same Word of God and stand under it. They both must have recourse to the way in which that Word has been proclaimed, celebrated and understood through twenty centuries and in a variety of traditions, rites and schools. The gifts of both, as all gifts in the Church, are meant for its up-building.

But there is an even more profound unity. The task of the magisterium is to proclaim authoritatively what belongs authentically to the profession of faith. But such proclamation in its fullest sense is not a mechanical repetition of time-honored formulae. It presupposes some understanding and insofar as there is understanding there is already some theology, be it only perhaps in a rudimentary and non-reflexive manner. A principle enunciated by Cardinal Newman continues to be valid: "As intellect is common to all men as well as imagination, every religious man is to a certain extent a theologian. . . ."[5]

The Scriptures themselves, which are the very source of all magisterial proclamation and theological effort, demonstrate the essential link between kerygma and theology. Such a basic statement of the primitive apostolic message as "Jesus is Lord" presupposes and is imbued with a theology. It presupposes the legitimacy of applying a divine name to a concrete human being. The very name "Lord" carries the weight of previous usage in belief and worship.

The Gospels themselves are products of communities of reflection and witness to growth in the understanding of the experience of Jesus. How impoverished would our own understanding be if we did not have one of those Gospels? The Scriptures lead us to the discovery of the Word of God through a diversity of perspectives emerging from a variety of situations in which the earliest communities found themselves. The Scriptures contain the Word of God within an interweaving of theologies and that Word is not to be found apart from those theologies.

Subsequent proclamations of the teaching authority of the Church have similarly presupposed theology and been imbued with at least the fruit of theological discussion. The Councils of Nicea and Trent had to resolve the theological question whether it was appropriate to use non-Scriptural words like "consubstantial" and "transubstantiation" to describe beliefs of the Church. It is only too evident from history how many doctrines of the Church came to be proclaimed authoritatively only after centuries of discussion among theologians. But discussion means diversity of approach and opinion, and through the difference of theologies consensus (though never unanimous even up to the moment of proclamation) gradually developed. In the latter part of the fourth century as the Church moved closer to the affirmation of the divinity of the Holy Spirit, there were still some who held that such a belief could be maintained privately but should not be preached publicly. Magisterial proclamation reflects growing theological consensus and contains some theological understanding. That understanding may not be fully adequate nor complete, but it is the task of historians, theologians and the magisterium in subsequent generations to determine what was time-conditioned and what was permanent. The fact remains, however, that there was some understanding.

The magisterium, then, is not without a theology in its authoritative proclamation. Nor is there any theology without some proclamation of the Word that it serves. Precisely because theology serves the Word its every essay into understanding will involve some proclamation—not as authoritative as that of the magisterium nor as direct, perhaps, as that of preaching. But it does have an authority that comes from the success of its effort to relate doctrines to the Word of God and the contemporary human and ecclesial situation, and it can have the directness of preaching through the power and clarity of its insight. Systematics and communications are the last two of Lonergan's eight functional specialties within theology, but specialization does not mean mutual exclusion. Even the most esoteric essay can be proclamation.

It is on that basis that I have a bit of difficulty with a comment made recently by Avery Dulles: " . . .one may say that the functional specialty of the ecclesiastical magisterium is judgment; that of the theologian is understanding."[6] From the perspective of specialization that is accurate, but the fact remains that the magisterium does not exercise its responsibility without some understanding and the work of the theologian is not without proclamatory effect.

Magisterium and theology are inextricably interwoven. Why then the antagonism? It is the result of the failure of some on both sides to recognize the mutuality and complementarity of their responsibilities. A bishop has a theology and either canonizes it as doctrine or does not want to admit that it is a theology. Similarly a theologian canonizes his positions as doctrine or will not allow for other schools of thought. In both cases dialogue comes to an end. But I hope it has become clear that constant dialogue between the magisterium and theologians is not an option for the Church but a necessity. It is only through such dialogue that each side can fulfill its responsibilities adequately. Without growth in their theological understanding the preaching and teaching of bishops run the risk of stagnation and lose the benefits of accuracy and clarity that can come through such understanding. On the other hand, theologians need dialogue with the magisterium as part of the ecclesial context of tradition, celebration and praxis that is necessary for their work if it is to be service to the Word in the Church. A stellar example of such dialogue is the Second Vatican Council and its aftermath. The contribution of theologians to that magisterial action is beyond question and that action in its turn has spurred further theological reflection.

Insofar as the magisterium and theologians recognize their need for each other, then dialogue will proceed more smoothly. That does not mean it will be without tensions. The Church has never been free of doctrinal and theological tension nor will it ever be until it has passed over into the Kingdom of Heaven. To be without tension would be death. All growth in understanding is a process requiring conversion—intellectual conversion that not infrequently brings with it the demand for moral and spiritual conversion for which not all are ready at the same time. Conversion is never easy nor painless because it demands surrender of established patterns of thought and action. On that basis alone there will never be perfect agreement. But the very responsibilities of bishops and theologians will create tension, too. For example, a bishop concerned for the unity of the diocese will be reluctant to pursue a certain line of theological thought that in the circumstances of that local church might create division; or a theologian on the basis of his or her historical research and for the sake of the truth will criticize the theological presuppositions and implications of a position taken by a bishop or a bishops' conference. Yet the dialogue must continue because such tension can be creative and from it the truth established with greater clarity and certainty.

It is in the context of mutual need, constant dialogue and creative tension that the question of mandate can now be discussed. But there is still a further difficulty which has to do with the very notions of mandate and *missio canonica* themselves. There is no clear and simple definition of them. This can be illustrated by looking at their usage in documents of Vatican II. In n. 24 of the Decree on the Apostolate of the Laity we read:

> Because of the demands of the common good of the Church, moreover, ecclesiastical authority can select and promote in a particular way some of the apostolic associations and projects which have an immediately spiritual purpose, thereby assuming in them a special responsibility. Thus, making various dispositions of the apostolate according to circumstances, the hierarchy joins some particular form of it more closely with its own apostolic function. Yet the proper nature and individuality of each apostolate must be preserved, and the laity must not be deprived of the possibility of acting on their accord. In various documents, this procedure of the hierarchy is called a mandate.
>
> Finally, the hierarchy entrusts to the laity some functions which are more closely connected with pastoral duties, such as the teaching of Christian doctrine, certain liturgical actions, and the care of souls. By virtue of this mission, the laity are fully subjected to higher ecclesiastical direction in the performance of such work.[7]

It is obvious from this text that the change in canon 812 from "*missio canonica*" to "*mandatum*" can be interpreted as somewhat of an improvement. But in the conciliar text itself it is important to note that although the mandate does identify an apostolate more closely with the hierarchy, yet that apostolate does not thereby surrender its own nature, individuality and initiative.

A second text is taken from n. 17 of the Decree on the Missionary Activity of the Church: "It is to be hoped that, where it seems opportune, catechists who are duly trained will receive a 'canonical mission' in a publicly celebrated liturgical ceremony. In this way they can serve the faith with greater authority in the eyes of the people." It is evident from this passage that the "greater authority" of the catechists comes from a closer identification with the Church by means of public commissioning within a liturgical celebration.

That celebration would be presided over by an ordained minister and so I suppose the conclusion could be drawn that the closer identification is actually with the hierarchy. But that need not be so. The statement cannot be read in such a way as to contradict other statements of the Council regarding bishops and priests as representatives of the local and universal Church and the laity as possessing a prophetic and teaching responsibility by virtue of baptism. Thus the statement could also be interpreted in the sense of more explicit identification with the prophetic role of the entire Church, and the canonical mission thus be seen as public confirmation of an already existent responsibility flowing from baptism and decision by the individual and community.

Of course this is somewhat reminiscent of the current debate concerning lay ministries. Are they simply the consequence of baptism, or do they also require some recognition and/or commissioning by the Church through ordained ministers? If it is the former, then all action becomes ministry. I myself wonder if it is not better to use the word "gift" as the unique service to which each baptized person is called and for which each is empowered through the sacraments. I would reserve the word "ministry" for those whose particular gift is to engage in some more intensely public service. The gift flows from baptism but its particularly public character requires some form of recognition by an ecclesial community and its official leadership. Such recognition can take many forms and need not involve a public commissioning or celebration.

The story of Paul's conversion and mission in the Acts of the Apostles can be helpful in this regard. There is no question that he is considered to receive his ministry directly from the Lord; yet it is not finalized without human intervention and intermediaries. His vision of the Lord is complemented by the imposition of Ananias' hands and by his baptism (Acts 9:3–19). His call to mission comes from the Holy Spirit through the prophets and teachers at Antioch who impose hands on him and Barnabas before sending them off (Acts 13:1–3).

These parenthetical considerations will not be without usefulness in the consideration of mandate for theologians. But two more passages from Vatican II must be considered. The first is from n. 7 of the Decree on the Ministry and Life of Priests.

> All priests, together with bishops, so share in one and the same ministry of Christ that the very unity of their consecration and ministry requires their hierarchical communion with the order of bishops. . . . By reason of the Holy Spirit which is given to priests in sacred ordination, bishops should regard them as necessary helpers and counselors. . . . On account of this communion in the same priesthood and ministry the bishop should regard priests as his brothers and friends. . . . Priestly obedience animated with a spirit of cooperation is based on the very sharing in the episcopal ministry which is conferred on priests both through the sacrament of orders and the canonical mission.

Canonical mission is seen within the context of communion. While it is the foundation of obedience together with ordination, it does not do away with the unique contribution that each priest can and should make within that communion, especially by way of counsel and thus by way of the dialogue that is thereby required. This contribution itself is based on the work of the Spirit within the priest.

The second text is from n. 24 of the Dogmatic Constitution on the Church: "The canonical mission of bishops can come about by legitimate customs which have not been revoked by the supreme and universal authority of the Church, or by laws made or recognized by that same authority, or directly through the successor of Peter himself. If the latter refuses or denies apostolic communion, a bishop cannot assume office." When seen in conjunction with the second note of explanation placed at the end of *Lumen gentium,* this statement would seem to indicate that canonical mission is a juridical expression of communion. But communion is a far deeper reality than the mission, as is also that mission which the bishops receive from Jesus Christ. In the first paragraph of n. 24 of *Lumen gentium* we read: "To the Lord was given all power in heaven and on earth. As successors of the apostles, bishops receive from Him the mission to teach all nations and to preach the gospel to every creature. . . . " Nor does *missio canonica* suppress the "variety of local churches" which "is particularly splendid evidence of the catholicity of the undivided Church" (LG 23).

What I am suggesting is that the notions of *missio canonica* and mandate are quite complex. They cannot be understood in such a way as to deny or undervalue the very nature of the Church in its diversity of gifts and traditions. They must be seen, on the contrary, as an expression of communion. Both these notions are forms by which the unity of the church is concretized, but they do not suppress the uniqueness of individual gifts that come from the sacraments and the Holy Spirit.

In interpreting the mandate that is to be given to theologians the argumentation can proceed *ex analogia*. There is further ground for this in the very statement on *missio canonica* found in *Sapientia Christiana:* "Those who teach disciplines concerning faith or morals, must receive, after making their profession of faith, a canonical mission from the chancellor or his delegate, for they do not teach on their own authority but by virtue of the mission they have received from the Church."[8] It seems to me that this text is not without obscurity, since there is no reason to interpret the word "Church" as referring only to the hierarchy. That would be contrary to Vatican II itself. In that case the word "authority" does not refer to the personal competence of the theologian but refers rather to the responsibility which he has from and to the Church.

Canonical mission could thus be seen as the expression of the authority which the theologian enjoys not only on the basis of his competence, but also because he exercises the responsibility of theological understanding which is necessary for the Church within the context of ecclesial communion. This would be supported by article 12 of *Sapientia Christiana* which states that the chancellor "fosters . . . communion with the local and universal church."[9]

It could thus be said that canonical mission from an ecclesial authority is granted on the basis of an already accepted mission from and within the entire ecclesial community and is an expression of that mission. It does not make the theologian nor un-make him by co-opting him into the "system." It is a sign that the theologian is an essential and necessary part of the Church and that the Church is an essential and necessary source and context of his work.

This it seems to me is the way in which mandate can be interpreted. The theologian is what he is by virtue of his gifts through baptism and the Spirit, and of his competence. Mandate is an expression of the fact that he is necessary to the Church and the Church necessary to him. It is a sign of communion among bishops, theologians and the rest of the Church.

I have not gone into practical questions concerning mandate. To whom is it to be given and on what basis? From whom would it be taken and on what basis? It seems to me that no matter what the answers to these questions, they must be developed collegially. No one Ordinary by himself is an adequate judge of orthodoxy, although it does fall to him to grant or remove mandate. If Ordinaries take collegiality seriously, they will not want to make judgments concerning orthodoxy by themselves. National and regional bishops' conferences in collaboration with professional theologians should draw up the criteria regarding mandate. Theology is too essential to the Church for it to be subject to the opinion of one man.

I hope I have shown that the mandate need not in itself be seen in a negative light. It need not and cannot be interpreted as a suppression of the theological enterprise. It can and should be seen as an expression of that communion which binds bishops and theologians in the Church and indeed could be a stimulant for greater dialogue to the benefit of both and the entire Church.

Notes

1. See Karl Rahner, "Commentary on *Lumen gentium*, Chapter III," in *Commentary on the Documents of Vatican II*, ed. Herbert Vorgrimler, I (New York: Herder and Herder, 1967), p. 202.

2. The Latin text of canon 812 in the promulgated Code reads: "Qui in studiorum superiorum Institutis quibuslibet disciplinas tradunt theologicas auctoritatis ecclesiasticae competentis mandatum habeant oportet."

3. They are available in English translation: *Theses on the Relation-*

ship Between the Ecclesiastical Magisterium and Theology (Washington: USCC Publications Office, 1977).

4. Ibid., p. 2.

5. See his *A Grammar of Assent* (Westminster, MD: Christian Classics, 1973), p. 98.

6. Avery Dulles, "The Two Magisteria: An Interim Reflection," *Proceedings of the Catholic Theological Society of America* 35 (1980): 163.

7. Translations of Vatican II documents are taken from *The Documents of Vatican II,* Walter M. Abbott, general editor (London: Geoffrey Chapman, 1966).

8. Article 27, i. Translation from *Origins* 9/3 (June 7, 1979): 39.

9. Ibid., p. 38.

Part Three

ACADEMIC ASPECTS

Academic Freedom and Catholic Institutions of Higher Learning

Charles E. Curran

This article originally appeared in the *Journal of the American Academy of Religion.*

Academic freedom in Catholic higher education in the United States has once again become an important theoretical and practical issue. This paper will discuss the question in three progressive stages. The first part will summarize briefly and explain the historical development which culminated in the middle 60's with the strong endorsement of academic freedom for Catholic universities. The second part will discuss the threats to academic freedom which have recently come from new and proposed Vatican legislation. The third part will propose reasons why the Catholic Church itself should recognize the academic freedom of Catholic institutions of higher learning and of Catholic theology in these institutions.

I.
Historical Overview and Explanation

This essay makes no pretense to propose a definite history of the relationship between Catholic higher education and academic freedom. Higher education in the United States has insisted that the college and university must be a free and autonomous center of studies with no external constraints limiting its freedom. No authority external to the university, be it lay or clerical, can make decisions which have a direct impact on the hiring, promoting, tenuring, and dismissing of faculty members. The existing literature on Catholic higher education usually points out that before 1960 it was generally accepted that Catholic higher education could not and would not accept the full American sense of academic freedom (Gleason). From the Catholic side the two most in depth studies of academic freedom in the 1950's rejected the American concept of academic freedom (Donahue, Tos). Ecclesiastical authority, from which there is no appeal, can and should settle controversial questions in the academy. Non-Catholics also did not expect Catholic universities to accept academic freedom. Robert M. MacIver, the director of the American Academic Freedom Project housed at Columbia University, in his influential *Academic Freedom in Our Time* (1955), used statements by Catholics to illustrate the religious line of attack on academic freedom (134–146).

However, in the 1960's change came quickly and somewhat dramatically. In 1965 Gerald F. Kreyche published a paper in the *National Catholic Education Association Bulletin* that called for Catholic institutions to accept full academic freedom. The most evident sign of change was "The Land O'Lakes Statement" signed in 1967 by twenty-six leaders of Catholic higher education in the United States and Canada. According to this statement, "To perform its teaching and research functions effectively, the Catholic university must have a true autonomy and academic freedom in the face of authority of whatever kind, lay or clerical, external to the academic community itself" (336). The changing times of the 1960's are well illustrated by the actions of the College Theology Society, which is the small professional society founded by teachers of theology in Catholic colleges. At its meeting in 1967 the society endorsed the 1940 statement of the American Association of University Professors and of the Association of American Colleges on academic freedom and tenure. However, the year before, this society had defeated a motion to endorse the same statement (Rodgers: 28–30).

Since the 1960's the leaders of Catholic higher education in the United States have generally strengthened their support of and committment to institutional autonomy and academic freedom. A very few Catholic colleges have opposed this trend.

Why this change at this time? In retrospect, there are a number of factors that influenced and helped bring about the dramatic change. In my judgment cultural, theological, and educational factors all supported the change.

From a cultural perspective American Catholics entered into the mainstream of United States life and culture in the post-World War II era. Throughout the nineteenth century and the first part of the twentieth century, the Catholic Church in the United States was primarily an immigrant church. The question was often raised: Could one be both Catholic and American at the same time? Rome often feared that the Catholic Church in the United States was becoming too American and would lose its Roman Catholicism. The condemnation of Americanism in 1899 was an expression of that anxiety. On the other hand, many Americans felt that Catholics could never really accept the American political and cultural ethos. The primary sticking point was the United States emphasis on political and religious freedom. Official Catholic teaching denied religious freedom and could only tolerate as second best, and not fully endorse, the American understanding of the separation of church and state.

By the time of World War II immigration had dwindled. Catholics were patriotic supporters of their country during the war. After the war, on the home scene Catholics entered more and more into the mainstream of American life and culture. On the international scene, the United States and the Roman Catholic Church became the two bulwarks of the free world in the struggle against communism. Note that there is a negative aspect to all this which resulted in the failure of American Catholics at times to criticize their country and its policies. However, Catholics were becoming very much at home in the United States of the 1950's.

Two events in the 1960's illustrated the fundamental compatibility between being Catholic and being American. In 1960 a Catholic, John F. Kennedy, was elected President of the United States. The conventional wisdom was that a Roman Catholic could never be elected President of the United States. Kennedy's election thus put to rest forever what had been a generally accepted axiom in American political life until that time. Roman Catholic acceptance and endorsement of the United States political system with its emphasis on religious freedom and the separation of church and state came at the Second Vatican Council in 1965. The Council's Declaration on Religious Freedom recognized the need for religious freedom. Thus, the chasm between being Catholic and being American was overcome. Again, one must note the danger of Catholicism's losing any critical view of United States structures, ethos, and policies. The ultimate Catholic acceptance and appreciation of the principles of United States higher education with their emphasis on the autonomy of the institution and academic freedom must be seen in the light of this broader context of the relationship between being Catholic and being American.

The theological factors influencing the acceptance of academic freedom by American Catholic higher education in the 1960's are associated with developments that occurred at the Second Vatican Council (1962–1965). The most significant theological development was the already mentioned acceptance of religious freedom. There can be no doubt that Catholic thought has traditionally given more importance to order than to freedom. In the realm of political ethics, Catholic teaching opposed much of the eighteenth and nineteenth century developments precisely because of their emphasis on freedom. Individualistic liberalism and freedom were the primary targets of much Catholic opposition. In the nineteenth and early twentieth century, Catholics were strong opponents of political freedom. However, in the twentieth century the social structures changed. No longer was the threat coming from proponents of individualistic freedom, but now from the theoretical and practical tenets of totalitarianism. In the light of the new threats of fascism, nazism, and communism (with the recognition that Roman Catholicism was always more fearful of the totalitarianism from the left), Roman Catholic teaching and theology began to defend the freedom and rights of individuals. The first full-blown statement in defense of human rights in official Catholic social teaching appeared only in Pope John XXIII's 1963 encyclical *Pacem in Terris* (par. 11–27). The growing appreciation of freedom in the Catholic tradition found its greatest obstacle in the older teaching denying religious freedom. However, the Second Vatican Council was able to accept religious freedom on the basis of the dignity of the human person. In the light of the growing emphasis given to freedom in Roman Catholic self-understanding and the acceptance of religious freedom, it was much easier for American Catholics to recognize the importance of and need for academic freedom.

The Second Vatican Council, in keeping with the Catholic tradition, recognized the autonomy of earthly institutions and cultures provided that autonomy is properly understood. Created things and society enjoy their own laws and values which must be developed, put to use, and regulated by human beings. In this light, one can more readily accept the American institutions of higher learning with their insistence on the autonomy of the institution. Catholic institutions of higher learning thus serve the church by being colleges and universities in the American sense of the term. Colleges and universities should not be changed into catechetical schools or seen merely as a continuation or extension of the pastoral teaching function of the bishops.

In the light of the Second Vatican Council, the self-understanding of Catholic theology itself changed. The manualistic neoscholasticism, which was in vogue immediately before the Second Vatican Council, tended to see theology as an extension of the teaching role of the pope and bishops with the need to explain and confirm this teaching. However, the general theological shift at Vatican II, especially the acceptance of historical consciousness, made theology conscious of a role that did not involve merely the repetition, explanation, and defense of church teachings. The very historical process that was the experience of the Second Vatican Council showed the creative role of theology and the need for theology to constantly probe the meaning of faith in the contemporary cultural and historical circumstances. The theologians who had the greatest effect on the council had been disciplined and suspect before the council itself. Theology is called to have an important role in bringing about change in Catholic thought and life.

Changes in the area of education itself also affected the Catholic community's willingness to accept institutional autonomy and academic freedom. In 1955 John Tracy Ellis published what is now recognized as a classical essay in which he questioned the failure of Roman Catholicism to contribute to the intellectual life of the United States. Many others (e.g., O'Dea, Ong) took up the challenge of this essay and explained its ramifications. Catholics had been entering into leadership roles in many areas of American life, but their intellectual contribution was little or nothing. Perhaps the very fact that such a question could be raised and thoroughly discussed showed the growing maturity of American Catholicism. These discussions inevitably led to questions about Catholic higher education.

Many changes began to occur in Catholic higher education in the 1950's and 60's. Catholic colleges and universities were generally established by religious communities of women and men. The professors were often members of religious communities, and Catholic lay professors had little or no say in the functioning of the administration. The presidents and chief academic officers often were appointed by the religious community from among its own members. Boards of trustees were either nonexistent or heavily composed of members of the religious community. The college or university was often seen as an extension of the religious community and its pastoral mission.

The structure gradually gave way to new and different structures by the 1970's although some of the remnants of the older structure continued to exist. In general, one can describe these changes as an attempt at a greater professionalization of the role and the structure of Catholic institutions of higher learning.

In the 1960's more lay people were functioning as professors and administrators. Some of these had been trained at the best American institutions of higher learning and brought with them the standards and operating procedures of the American academy. Catholic institutions began to put more emphasis on graduate study and research so that they became more conscious of the need for institutional autonomy and freedom. In striving for academic acceptability and excellence, Catholic institutions were only too willing to accept the American understanding of the academy and the regulations proposed by accrediting associations. Catholic institutions wanted to be good colleges and universities.

However, Catholic college and university leaders were conscious that many American institutions of higher learning had begun as church sponsored institutions but had ceased to have any relationship with the founding church. Catholic educators wanted their institutions of higher learning to be both Catholic and American. They frequently discussed the ways of safeguarding a Catholic identity and at the same time insisted on the academic freedom and institutional autonomy of American higher education.

Today, the faculty and administration of Catholic institutions are heavily lay. The boards of trustees that run these institutions are free and independent from the founding or sponsoring religious community. Presidents in these institutions often continue to be religious or clerics, but they operate in a very different manner from the immediately post-World War II era.

What might be described as the professionalization of Catholic higher education in general also took place with regard to the teaching of theology and religion on Catholic college campuses. Theology courses were traditionally required in Catholic institutions, but before 1960 they were frequently taught by people who did not have doctoral degrees. It was often thought that the mere fact of religious profession or priestly ordination was a sufficient training for teaching theology. The first national meeting of the Society of Catholic College Teachers of Sacred Doctrine (later called the College Theology Society) was held in 1955. One of the primary concerns of this group was the poor quality of undergraduate theology courses and the need for a greater professionalization. Accrediting agencies had been critical of Catholic theology courses. The founders of this new society recognized the legitimacy of these criticisms and wanted to raise the standards of such theology and religious programs to reach the standards for other faculties and courses in Catholic colleges and universities (Rodgers: 11–20).

This emphasis on a greater professionalization in Catholic higher education in general and in the teaching of theology influenced the move of Catholic higher education to accept the American academic standards and principles. All these reasons helped to explain the seemingly dramatic change which occurred in Catholic higher education in the 1960's with the acceptance of institutional autonomy and academic freedom.

II.
Threats to Academic Freedom

There is no doubt that the mainstream of Catholic higher education is firmly committed to academic freedom and institutional autonomy. There is also ample evidence that the leaders of

Catholic higher education in the United States have convinced the American Catholic bishops of the importance of such characteristics. In 1980 the United States Catholic bishops issued their first pastoral letter on Catholic higher education, "Catholic Higher Education and the Pastoral Mission of the Church." The letter recognizes some inevitable tensions but maintains that "Academic freedom and institutional independence in pursuit of the mission of the institution are essential components of educational quality and integrity. . . . " (380) "We shall all need to recall and to work for that 'delicate balance . . . between the autonomy of a Catholic University and the responsibilities of the hierarchy.' There need be no conflict between the two" (381).

However, the Roman Curia has been unwilling to accept the American insistence on academic freedom and institutional autonomy. These differences have come to the surface over the years in the relations between American Catholic higher education and the Vatican Congregation for Catholic Education. Three recent instances of legislation or proposed legislation for the universal church basically deny the role of institutional autonomy and academic freedom for Catholic institutions of higher learning.

In 1979 Pope John Paul II issued *Sapientia Christiana,* an apostolic constitution promulgating new norms for ecclesiastical faculties, that is, those institutions and schools that give Vatican accredited degrees. In the United States there are very few such faculties or institutions, with the department of theology at The Catholic University of America in Washington, D.C. being the best known example. According to these norms, Catholic theologians in these faculties teach in the name of the church and need a canonical mission from church authorities. Church authorities existing outside the academy thus have the power to give and to withdraw this mission or license to teach.

The 1983 Code of Canon Law proposed for the entire Latin Catholic Church in canon 812 maintains: "It is necessary that those who teach theological disciplines in any institute of higher studies have a mandate from a competent ecclesiastical authority" (Coriden: 575). This canon provides that a church authority, external to the academy, can and should make decisions directly involving the hiring, promoting, and dismissal of faculty in theological disciplines. At the present time it seems that this canon has not been applied in the United States, but it is definitely on the books.

Third, in April 1985, the Vatican Congregation for Catholic Education sent out a "Proposed Schema (Draft) for a Pontifical Document on Catholic Universities" containing proposed norms for all Catholic institutions of higher education throughout the world. These proposed regulations build on canon 812 with its call for a competent ecclesiastical authority to give a mandate to all who teach theological disciplines in any institution of higher learning. This canon is incorporated within a broader framework emphasizing church control over these colleges and universities.

Negative reactions from the leaders of Catholic higher education to these recently proposed norms have been swift and sharp. The Association of Catholic Colleges and Universities has sharply criticized the proposed norms. The leaders of Catholic higher education in the United States are striving to keep the identity of Catholic institutions, but they cannot accept the Vatican's understanding of what that identity entails. According to a report sent to the Vatican by the Association of Catholic Colleges and Universities, "The real crux of the document is perceived by many to be the assertion of a power on the part of the bishops to control theologians. . . . What is proposed here is contrary to the American values of both academic freedom and due process both of which are written into most university statutes and protected by civil and constitutional law" (703). What will happen? Will the leadership of Catholic higher education in the United States convince the Roman Congregation for Catholic Education to change its proposed norms and allow institutional autonomy and academic freedom? Only time will tell. In the past, these same leaders tried to change the proposed canon law of the church but were unsuccessful.

The present canon 812 was first proposed in the 1977 draft of the new canon law. At that time the leaders of Catholic colleges and universities in the United States strongly objected to the proposed canon and tried to have it changed. The Association of Catholic Colleges and Universities, the Catholic Theological Society of America, and a joint committee of bishops and college and university presidents all urged that the canon be deleted. Some United States and Canadian bishops tried to convince the commission for the new code to delete this canon. On April 18, 1982, delegates of the Association of Catholic Colleges and Universities met with the pope himself to try to convince him not to promulgate this canon. But the canon remained (Coriden: 575–576).

What will happen now? Will the recently proposed norms be accepted? Will the present canon 812 begin to be applied in the United States? Only the future will give answers to these pressing questions. However, it is incumbent upon Catholic scholars to develop convincing reasons in favor of the autonomy of Catholic institutions of higher learning and of the academic freedom of such institutions and especially of Catholic theology.

III.
Defense of Academic Freedom for Catholic Institutions and for Catholic Theology

Different types of arguments can be proposed to support the need for academic freedom in Catholic institutions of higher learning and especially for the academic freedom of Catholic theology. Leaders in Catholic higher education have already pointed out the practical ramifications of the proposed legislation. Such legislation in practice would probably destroy the system of Catholic higher education in the United States as we know it today. At the present time, Catholic higher education receives government funding, especially in the form of grants and loans to students as well as funds for research. The Supreme Court has ruled that government funding for Catholic grammar and high schools is unconstitutional but not for Catholic colleges and universities. Catholic higher education accepts the principle of academic freedom and does not proselytize or catechize as do grammar and high schools under Catholic auspices. If the existing and proposed legislation for Catholic higher education is enforced, then the courts could very well rule unconstitutional all aid to Catholic higher education since these institutions would no longer accept the autonomy of the university and academic freedom. Thus the very existence of Catholic higher education is in jeopardy.

One cannot dismiss the significance of this practical argument.

However, practical reasons should not be the primary consideration. From an ethical perspective, it might be very true and necessary at times not to accept funding from other sources if this is contrary to one's own basic principles. At the very minimum, the practical consideration is secondary, and a more convincing reason is needed to justify the autonomy and academic freedom of Catholic higher education. The real issue is the academic freedom of Catholic theology.

The ultimate and necessary justification for the academic freedom of Catholic institutions of higher learning and especially for Catholic theology in those institutions is that such academic freedom is for the good of the church. This is the justification for academic freedom in secular society. Such freedom does not exist just for the good of certain academics and for academic institutions but is ultimately for the good of society itself and is justified precisely because of this reason.

Does academic freedom, especially that of theology, in Catholic institutions of higher learning ultimately work for the good of the Roman Catholic Church? Can the church with an authoritative hierarchical teaching office really accept academic freedom as compatible with and even helpful for the good of the church? I believe the academic freedom of Catholic theology in institutions of higher learning is ultimately for the good of the church.

The mission of the church is to make the word and work of Jesus present in the light of the contemporary historical and cultural circumstances. Creative fidelity must characterize the church. Creative fidelity is an apt description because the church cannot merely repeat what was said in previous generations. The word and work of Jesus must be appropriated by every age and culture.

Catholic self-understanding grounds the need for creative fidelity. The Catholic tradition has always rejected the axiom, "the scripture alone." By insisting on the scripture and tradition despite some aberrations, the Catholic self-understanding recognizes the need to make the word of God manifest in the changing situations of time and space. One cannot just cite the scripture and repeat what has been said in the past, but the word of God must be appropriated, understood, and lived in the light of the present. The early church saw the need to understand God and Jesus in the light of the Greek philosophical understanding of persons and natures. Some claimed that the church could not teach that there are three persons in God and two natures in Jesus because these concepts and terms are not found explicitly in the scriptures. However, the total church insisted on understanding the word of God and appropriating it in its own age.

The Catholic Church has also insisted on the importance of human reason. According to this tradition, faith and reason can never contradict one another. Reason can help us to know better and understand our faith and the actions that spring from faith. In fact, Catholic moral teaching on specific actions has been based primarily on human reason and not directly on faith. Thus the Catholic tradition with its emphasis on scripture and tradition as well as on faith and reason insists on the characteristic of creative fidelity to the word and work of Jesus.

With this self-understanding, the Roman Catholic church has always recognized and given great significance to the role of theologians. The total church could not carry out its mission of creative fidelity without the work of theologians. Theology should be expected to be on the cutting edge of the mission of creative fidelity. Theologians will often be like the scouting party that goes out to explore before the whole group passes through. Theology prepares the way for development and the ongoing appropriation of Christian thought and action. However, some theologians will also tend to stress the fidelity aspect and will be very cautious about new developments. There is no one role for theology in general to play, but the work of theologians is necessary for the total mission of creative fidelity of the church itself.

However, what is characteristic of Roman Catholicism is the role of the hierarchical teaching office in the church. It is precisely because of the existence of an authoritative teaching office in the church that many would argue against the legitimacy of academic freedom for Catholic theologians. But it is important to understand how the authoritative teaching office of pope and bishops functions.

First, the authoritative teaching office or magisterium is itself subject to the word of God and the truth according to the Constitution on Divine Revelation of Vatican II (n. 10). This teaching authority with the help of the Holy Spirit discerns the truth and the word of God. This understanding coheres with the basic Catholic tradition that morality is intrinsic. Something is commanded because it is true and good and not the other way around.

Second, there are different levels of authoritative church teaching. Some teachings are by their nature core and central to the faith, whereas other teachings are more removed from the core of faith. Contemporary Catholic ecclesiology and canon law accept the distinction between infallible teaching, which calls for an assent of faith on the part of the faithful, and authoritative, noninfallible teaching, which demands the religious respect of intellect and will. Even in infallible teaching, Catholic self-understanding recognizes the possibility and even the need to deepen, improve, and develop the teaching, which is one of the functions of theologians. Noninfallible teachings, according to a document of the German bishops, "involve a certain element of the provisional even to the point of being capable of including error" (Rahner: 86). It is generally accepted that such authoritative, noninfallible teaching enjoys a presumption of truth in its favor. However, such teaching has been wrong in the past, and the presumption always cedes to the truth. Thus, all must recognize that the role of Catholic theology is not merely to repeat and defend official church formulations.

Third, the hierarchical teaching office is not identical with the total teaching function of the church. The primary teacher in the church is the Holy Spirit. All the baptized share in the teaching role of Jesus just as they share in the priestly role, but there still exists a hierarchical teaching function and a hierarchical priestly function. Such a view does not claim that the church is a democracy, but it does recognize a pluralistic theory of teaching authorities which can and should serve as mutual checks and balances.

Fourth, the pastoral role of the hierarchical teaching office and the teaching function of theologians are somewhat independent and complementary. The hierarchical teaching function is conferred with an office in the church and has the promise of the assistance of the Holy Spirit to discern the truth. The theological teaching function rests on the faithful scholarship of the individual and the community of scholars. The theologians' teaching function is not merely derivative from or an extension of the hierarchical teaching office. Yes, the theologian must give due assent to official hierarchical teaching, but the teaching role of the theologian differs from the pastoral teaching role of pope and bishops.

Fifth, history reminds us of the existence and importance of the somewhat independent and complementary teaching role of theologians. The apostolic church gives a distinct role to *didaskoloi* who teach in their own right and not merely as delegates of the *episkopoi* or *presbyteroi*. In the Middle Ages there was a magisterium of doctors or theologians in the church. The term magisterium referred primarily to theologians and not to pastors. Theological faculties exercised an independent teaching authority. In some ecumenical councils theologians had a deliberate vote. Even at the Second Vatican Council the somewhat independent and complementary role of theologians stands out when one studies what the council accomplished.

In this connection it should be noted that the understanding of the role of the theologian proposed here does not confuse the role of the theologian with that of the pastoral teaching office in the church. The teaching office of pope and bishops deserves a respect which of itself is not due to the teaching of theologians. To the pastoral teaching office of pope and bishops even in noninfallible matters one owes a religious respect of intellect and will. However, it still could be that noninfallible teachings are erroneous and that infallible teachings need to be improved and deepened. Likewise, such an understanding does not call for two magisteria in the church but recognizes the role and limitations of the official hierarchical teaching office.

In the United States context, the academic freedom of the academic theologian is a very legitimate way to safeguard the somewhat independent and complementary role of the theologian in the teaching function of the Roman Catholic Church. But what about the mistakes that theologians will make? It is inevitable that theologians will make mistakes, but there are three important safeguards to protect against the mistakes that will be made.

First, theological debate, like all scholarly debate, seeks the truth. In the critique and give and take of theological discussion, one hopes to come to the truth. Such discussion and mutual criticism constitute the means that the academy itself presents to help safeguard the search for truth. The Catholic Church has known vigorous theological debate over the years. In fact, at times that debate has gone too far and offended against Christian charity and even the unity of the church. Manuals of theology even acknowledged a special type of hatred—*odium theologicum*—theological hatred—because of the vehemence with which some theological debates have been carried on in the church.

A second safeguard against the danger of theological mistakes and abuses is found in the right of the hierarchical magisterium to point out what it judges to be theological error and ambiguity. At times the hierarchical magisterium may judge that such interventions are necessary to safeguard faith. All have to recognize that this could be a necessary and apt use of the hierarchical teaching office. In pointing out the errors and ambiguities of a theology or of a particular theologian, this action of the hierarchical magisterium would have no direct effect on the role of the individual theologian in the academy. Academic freedom means that no external authority, lay or clerical, can make decisions affecting the hiring, promoting, tenuring, and dismissing of faculty members. However, the hierarchical teaching office can safeguard the faith of its members through such an intervention if it deems it necessary and helpful.

A third safeguard against theological mistakes and abuse is found in the recognized academic norm that even a tenured professor can be dismissed for incompetency, but the judgment of incompetency must be made by academic peers in accord with academic due process. Competency demands that a Catholic theologian theologize within the Catholic faith parameters. A Catholic theologian who does not believe in Jesus or does not accept a role for the pope in the church could rightly be judged to be incompetent. However, this judgment must be made by academic peers and in accord with academic due process and not by church authorities external to the academy.

There will never be a perfect solution to the tensions between the role of the hierarchical teaching office and the role of the theologian. The tension between these roles is rooted ultimately in the tension of creative fidelity to the word and work of Jesus which is the characteristic mission of the whole church. A living church and a living tradition will always know and experience tensions.

Theology is necessary for the life of the church, and it serves the church in general and the hierarchical teaching office itself. Academic freedom protects the role of some theologians and gives them the freedom to make their necessary contribution to the life of the church. Theologians will make mistakes and might even abuse this academic freedom, but there are safeguards to protect against the damage that such mistakes might cause the church. The academic freedom of the academic theologian in the long run is good not only for the church but for the hierarchical teaching office in the church. The teaching office will be more credible in the light of the recognition of the academic freedom of Catholic theologians.

The academic freedom of Catholic theologians and of Catholic colleges and universities must ultimately be justified as being for the good of the church itself. This section has attempted to make such a case for academic freedom. I think the vast majority of Catholic theologians writing today would agree with the role of theology described here. However, at the present time official church documents and legislation do not seem to be willing to accept this role of the Catholic theologian as proposed here. In the midst of these tensions, it is all the more necessary to develop and to strengthen the arguments for the acceptance of the academic freedom of Catholic theology and of Catholic institutions of higher learning on the basis of their contribution to the good of the Catholic Church itself.

References

Association of Catholic Colleges and Universities
  1986   "Catholic College and University Presidents Respond to Proposed Vatican Schema." *Origins* 15:697–704.

Congregation of Catholic Education
  1985   "Proposed Schema (Draft) for a Pontifical Document on Catholic Universities." *Origins* 15 (1986):706–711.

Coriden, James
   1985   "The Teaching Office of the Church." In *The Code of
           Canon Law: Text and Commentary,* edited by James A.
           Coriden, Thomas J. Green, and Donald E. Heintschel. New
           York: Paulist Press.

Donahue, Charles
   1952   "Freedom and Education: The Pluralist Background."
           Thought 27:542–560.
   1953   "Freedom and Education: The Sacral Problem." *Thought*
           28:209–233.
   1954   "Freedom and Education, III: Catholicism and Academic
           Freedom." *Thought* 29:555–573.

Ellis, John Tracy
   1955   "American Catholics and the Intellectual Life." *Thought*
           30:351–388.

Gleason, Philip
   1967a   "Academic Freedom: Survey, Retrospect and Prospects."
           National Catholic Education Association Bulletin 64:67–74.
   1967b   "Academic Freedom and the Crisis in Catholic Universi-
           ties." In *Academic Freedom and the Catholic University,*
           edited by Edward Manier and John W. Houck. Notre
           Dame, IN: University of Notre Dame Press, pp. 33–56.
   1968   "Freedom and the Catholic University." *National Catholic
           Education Association Bulletin* 65:21–29.

Kreyche, Gerard F.
   1965   "American Catholic Higher Learning and Academic Free-
           dom." *National Catholic Education Association Bulletin*
           62:211–222.

Land O'Lakes Statement
   1967   In *The Catholic University: A Modern Appraisal,* edited by
           Neil G. McCluskey, Notre Dame, IN: University of Notre
           Dame Press, 1970.

MacIver, Robert M.
   1955   *Academic Freedom in Our Time.* New York: Columbia Uni-
           versity Press.

O'Dea, Thomas F.
  1958   *American Catholic Dilemma: An Inquiry into the Intellectual Life.* New York: Sheed and Ward.

Ong, Walter J.
  1957   *Frontiers in American Catholicism.* New York: Macmillan.

Pope John XXIII
  1963   *Pacem in Terris.* In *Renewing the Earth: Catholic Documents on Peace, Justice and Liberation,* edited by David J. O'Brien and Thomas A. Shannon. Garden City, NY: Doubleday Image Books, 1977.

Pope John Paul II
  1979   *Sapientia Christiana.* In *Origins* 9:34–45.

Rahner, Karl
  1976   *Theological Investigations* XIV: *Ecclesiology, Questions in the Church, the Church in the World.* New York: Seabury Press.

Rodgers, Rosemary
  1983   *A History of the College Theology Society.* Villanova, PA: The College Theology Society.

Tos, Aldo J.
  1958   *A Critical Study of American Views on Academic Freedom.* Ph.D. thesis, The Catholic University of America.

United States Catholic Bishops
  1980   "Pastoral Letter: Catholic Higher Education and the Church's Pastoral Mission." *Origins* 10:378–384.

Statement of Presidents
of Leading Catholic Universities
# of North America
on the Schema for a Proposed
Document on the Catholic University

1. Presidents of fourteen (14) leading Catholic universities of North America (listed below) are sympathetic to the fundamental purpose of the proposed pontifical document on Catholic universities. We understand this purpose to be the clarification of the distinctively Catholic character of our institutions. Surely, if the Catholic university is to fulfill its mission, then its sense of Catholic identity must be clear and confident.

2. We also recognize and share the concern reflected in the Schema that authentic Catholic doctrine be communicated in compelling fashion, and not be confused with speculative opinions.

3. Finally, we fully support the important mission assigned by the Schema to the Catholic university: to be a place of dialogue between religious faith, on the one hand, and science (reason) and culture, on the other, as well as a promoter of values (Proemium, IV).

4. Unfortunately, we believe that the Schema, if published in its present form, would not promote these important objectives. In fact, the publication of this Schema would, in our judgment, actually cripple the present efforts of our North American universities to fulfill the mission the Schema describes.

5. Secularistic critics of Catholic education would find that their most searing critiques of Catholic universities had been confirmed by the Vatican itself. For if the relationship of these universities to the Church, as defined in this Schema, must necessarily involve control by the Church, then Catholic universities cannot respect academic freedom, and cannot enjoy true

institutional autonomy. Any contractual obligations entered into by such institutions would be subject to the approval or disapproval of Church authorities outside of the university. This, at least, would be the view of most of the academic communities in North America and a good part of our general public.

6. Our critics would charge that such direct ecclesiastical control means that our institutions are not universities at all but places of narrow sectarian indoctrination; hence they have no right to claim public monies to support what would be described as their proselytizing mission. If such a view prevailed in our courts, then decades of sacrifice by generations of faculty, students, and benefactors of Catholic universities in North America would have been squandered.

7. There are any number of specific points in the Schema that need revision. We want to emphasize, however, that the single most important problem in the present document is this recurring insistence that any authentic Catholic university must be under the jurisdictional control of ecclesiastical authorities. In Chapter 3 of the norms, four different categories of Catholic university are identified, but all of them contain the notion of ecclesiastical control. For this reason none of them fits the actual situation of the vast majority of Catholic universities in North America. We believe that another category of Catholic university must be recognized.

8. Ordinarily, our universities are not canonically erected but are chartered by the state; they are governed not by the local ordinary but by an independent board of trustees, which is generally composed of a majority of lay people and often includes at least some non-Catholics.

9. Nonetheless, we believe our institutions are authentically Catholic universities. They are Catholic not only in their original tradition but in their continuing inspiration. Although not under direct Church control, they provide a broad range of opportunities for Church influence.

10. The pastoral efficacy of this influence is unquestioned. One thinks, for example, of the important role Catholic universities in North America have played in the discussion of the recent

pastoral letters of the Catholic bishops of the United States. One thinks also of the lively sense of faith reflected in the well-attended student liturgies that take place in our university Churches. The success of these efforts and others, however, depends on the recognition of the Catholic university's special character as a university.

11. The Catholic university is a Church-related academic community. It relates to the mission of the Church, but not as a seminary, nor a parish nor a diocese nor as anything but a university. It is important to affirm the Catholic identity of our universities, but it is also important that they be authentic universities.

12. If our universities accepted as part of their self-definition the relationship between the Church and the university described in the Schema, then the credibility that they have earned over many years would be quickly eroded. Furthermore, many of the juridical provisions in the present draft, which subject the structures and processes of Catholic universities to external Church control, would expose our institutions to damaging litigation concerning contractual obligations and possible claims of discrimination in personnel matters. In the light of the principle of ascending liability, the affirmation of a juridical link between the universities and the hierarchy of the Church could make our bishops vulnerable to such litigation as well.

13. One of the most important values to be protected in an authentic university is academic freedom. If theology is to be granted the same academic integrity of other disciplines, theologians also must enjoy authentic academic freedom. We realize that in the case of theology, a special problem exists, since the orthodoxy of Catholic doctrine is also an important value to be preserved. The tension between a theologian's academic freedom and the legitimate pastoral concern for doctrinal orthodoxy certainly deserves particular attention. In our judgment, however, the approach taken in the Schema to this complex issue does not respect this tension. If the university is to be a place of dialogue between faith on the one hand and reason and culture on the other, then the academic freedom of the theologian must be recognized and respected. Otherwise Catholic theology would not enjoy the academic respect of other disciplines.

14. How should the Church then exercise its responsibility to pro-
    tect doctrinal orthodoxy? As is the case in other academic disci-
    plines, erroneous theological opinions are often corrected by
    the self-criticism of the scholarly theological community. It also
    may be necessary, on occasion, for Church authorities to make
    a forthright statement that a particular theological position is
    inconsistent with authentic Church teaching.

15. Episcopal affirmations of Catholic doctrine will be recognized
    to be the legitimate exercise of the right of any community of
    faith to define the content of its own belief. This kind of episco-
    pal statement could not fairly be interpreted as a violation of
    academic freedom. No attempt would be made to interfere with
    the autonomy of the academic community, since no authority
    external to the university would attempt to impose sanctions on
    a faculty member because of the intellectual opinions he or she
    might hold. In fact, the tension between the concern of Church
    authority for doctrinal orthodoxy and the academic freedom of
    the theologian can be a creative tension, if the distinctive yet
    complementary roles of bishops and theologians are properly
    understood and respected.

16. Because we are personally and collectively committed to the
    important mission of the Catholic university, we are all the
    more concerned that the good intentions of the proposed docu-
    ment not be subverted by provisions that do not take into suffi-
    cient account the pluralism of cultures and political systems in
    which Catholic universities exist around the world. Further-
    more, in the case of the Catholic universities of North America,
    the present Schema ignores the pluralism that exists within our
    institutions, where many non-Catholics work side by side with
    Catholics and where the methodologies of different academic
    disciplines demand their own proper respect.

17. With particular reference to the institutional autonomy of the
    university and the academic freedom of the theologian, we
    believe that the formulations of the 1972 document on "The
    Catholic University in the Modern World" were far more suc-
    cessful in addressing these important issues than the present
    Schema. In the continuing discussion and revision of this
    Schema, we trust that the 1972 document and the experience

from which it emerged will be given careful attention. Failure to do so, we fear, can result in serious, if not fatal, damage to the very institution the pontifical document seeks to promote: the Catholic university of today.

Rev. William Byron, SJ, President
Catholic University of America, D.C.

Rev. Norman Choate, CR, President
University of St. Jerome's College, Canada

Rev. John Driscoll, OSA, President
Villanova University, PA

Brother Raymond L. Fitz, SM, President
University of Dayton, OH

Rev. Thomas Fitzgerald, SJ, President
St. Louis University, MO

Dr. Author E. Hughes, President
University of San Diego, CA

Rev. Timothy Healy, SJ, President
Georgetown University, D.C.

Rev. Theodore M. Hesburgh, CSC, President
University of Notre Dame, IN

Rev. Robert A. Mitchell, SJ, President
University of Detroit, MI

Rev. J. Donald Monan, SJ, President
Boston College, MA

Rev. Joseph O'Hare, SJ, President
Fordham University, NY

Rev. John P. Raynor, SJ, President
Marquette University, WI

Rev. William J. Rewak, SJ, President
University of Santa Clara, CA

Rev. John T. Richardson, CM, President
DePaul University, IL

The Catholic College
Versus Academic Freedom

Edward J. Berbusse

This article originally appeared in *Homiletic and Pastoral Review* in 1986.

In recent years many administrators and professors at Catholic colleges have been speaking in favor of "Catholic presence" on the campus, while permitting heterodox teaching to mount an offensive against the Church within its very walls. The individual teacher, it is said, can give his Christian witness; but the college, as an institution, must exert no guidance or control on faculty or student opinion. Consequently, Catholic colleges have awakened to find their faculties of teaching, their student-organized lectures and campus press in contradiction to the very Christian commitment of the college. Living facilities, also, have been opened to deviant life-styles which affront the founding purpose of the institution. Under pressure, many Catholic administrators have made the fatal and irrevocable decisions of allowing all ideas and manner of living free expression in their campus-city. It has become a city of man, in which freedom becomes the absolute, and Catholic teaching and morality fight for survival against this secularized assault on the Kingdom of God. The confusion arises from the belief that academic freedom is the ultimate value in any academic institution. It is forgotten that the college is in pursuit of Truth; that there are surer guides to Truth than mere uninhibited freedom.

Unwittingly, some Catholic colleges have adopted the philosophy of the New Left which has an inbred enmity toward any establishment, especially one with a Catholic identity. The slogan, "free speech," becomes the arbiter of all speech and behavior; and, as it exerts its absolute permissiveness, it simultaneously denies freedom to those who oppose it. We remember the sit-ins and "free speech" demonstrations at the University of California, Berkeley, in 1964, where the voices of reason and order were silenced. As one student leader there said: "The Great Sit-in was a strong-arm, uncivil, disruptive act, justified by the need to struggle for a free university."[1] The Catholic college has felt these same pressures, and many have capitulated to their dictation. "Moral" pressure has made it unpopular to speak in support of the Church; restriction of inter-parietal privileges is said to be a denial of maturity and freedom; and the roster of speakers strongly features those who attack papal infallibility, ridicule our Lady, and encourage pornography under the title of "emancipation from sex inhibitions." In trying to prove itself super-free, the Catholic college often finds itself alienated from the Church.

Faith and Morals To Be Taught

Catholic faculty members, administrators and student bodies continue to ask: What is the role of the Catholic college? Has it anything special to offer? In reply the Church insists that there is a consistent teaching in faith and morals which should be the foundation of the Catholic college. This is its base of all teaching, research and community living. Certain ideas—though they are within the awareness of academic research and teaching—are not part of the living commitment of the Catholic college. Teachers, moreover, who are expositors of this alien philosophy of education are not admitted as part of the educational role of this college. In papal encyclicals, conciliar documents, and in the writings of such thinkers as Cardinal Newman, the Church finds that her schools' commitment must be to a *leading idea* that brings all other ideas into proper focus and expression.

For Cardinal Newman the leading idea in Christianity is the Incarnation. Christ is the one Mediator between God and men; as St. Thomas teaches, he performed the mediatory act as man and received them as God.[2] Because he is of our nature, his Incarnation transformed it and it is in this manner that we must conceive it. And so Christ dominates the order of intelligence.[3] His grace is not only for the will, but also for the intellect, so that we can reason with a nature enlightened by Revelation. We are invited "to live as Christians, to feel and think as Christians in a society that is not Christian"; and so we will ever be tempted to "diminish or adapt our truth, to render Christianity acceptable to the world." Resistance of this temptation is our Christian duty, and in the Church we will find our strength.

The Church is entrusted with Christ's Revelation: to proclaim, guard and interpret it. It is, in a sense, a divine sacrament which brings us into union with Christ; and without it we lack divine Life and cannot rightly preach the Word. As Etienne Gilson says, "to imitate the Church ought to be our rule, if we wish to put our intelligence at the service of Christ the King."[4] Essential to the Church is its structure which is protected in teaching Truth by the everpresence of the Holy Spirit. To attack the structure is to oppose the Holy Spirit who lives within it. This structure is presided over by those who constitute the hierarchy, those who are successors of the Apostles and in union with Peter's successor. They are the guardians of the deposit of faith, and the whole community of the Church must look to them as shepherds who teach with divine authority.

A serious evil in many Catholics today is a placing of their own rationalizations and action above the norms of the Church. They tend to look upon Christ's Mystical Body as a purely human society; and so, in preferring themselves and the world which they accept as teacher, they no longer are proud of their Faith. They have forgotten that reason must be guided by Faith; that human sciences need direction toward God, because he is the Lord of science and Faith. "Science and philosophy," says Gilson, "must regulate themselves under theology." They must recognize their limits, without transforming themselves into a theology.[5] Theologians must not engage in experiments which are sterile, when from the first hypothesis it is seen that they are in patent opposition to Revelation. Their special role is to study with the aid of prayer and reflection the revealed Word, and then strive to make it understood by the world. They are error-bound when they study the world in order to change Eternal Truths. Their study should be conditioned by the knowledge that Christ and his message will often be at odds with worldly teaching. He was prophesied to be "a sign of contradiction" to the world.

Employ Proper Focus

Today's secularism—with its emphasis on reality as a product of, by and for man—has made science the exclusive source of knowledge and reward for man. Such a belief begets a corruption of basic principles, what Newman calls "leading ideas," and leads to a relativity that is constantly changing its doctrines through subjective *experience*. This explains why the new catechetics—under the dominance of the physical and social sciences—is alienating itself from orthodox teaching and wedding itself to *life-experience*. Dogmas are rejected, and the magisterium is regarded as a mere help to individual experience, and not as clear and definitive teachings to be accepted by the individual. True development of the teachings of Christ, in contrast, always reveals a harmony with the Church's traditional teaching, a union with the leading principles and antecedent dogmas; and stands in stark contrast to the heresies which either break with the leading principles or deduce erroneous conclusions from them. To prevent error from corrupting the prophetic tradition, Divine Providence has given the care of the deposit of Faith into the hands of the Church. To gain the full experience of Revelation, the Catholic must accept its divine conditions; he must submit to the infallible Teacher, the Church, which is prevented from error by the Holy Spirit.

To counteract the naturalism of his time, Cardinal Newman insisted that "Revelation has introduced a new law of divine governance over and above those laws which appear in the natural course of the world." He says:

> As the existence of all religion is authority and obedience, so the distinction between natural religion and revealed lies in this, that the one has a subjective authority and the other an objective. Revelation consists in the manifestion of the Invisible Divine Power, or in the substitution of the voice of a Lawgiver for the voice of con-

science . . . What conscience is in the system of nature, such is the voice of Scripture, or of the Church, or of the Holy See . . . in the system of Revelation.[6]

As St. Philip aided the Ethiopian eunuch of good conscience to understand Isaiah,[7] so the Church teaches the reasoning conscience of the humble Christian. In a 1971 address, Pope Paul VI warned us of today's error of *naturalism* "which excludes all reference to God and to transcendence," and claims "man's absolute autonomy before his own destiny." From this has come "a secular version of Christianity" which by a strange absurdity and contradiction of terms, is called "Christian atheism."[8]

ENTRUSTED WITH CHRIST'S REVELATION

The true Catholic, as an individual, conforms his life to the teaching of the Incarnate Word who willed to speak to men through his Church which is both a Mystical union and a visible institution. Consequently, he is drawn into community-life with others who accept the full teaching of Christ, and is submissive to its structure, an hierarchical one, in which the successor of Peter has universal and plenary authority in teaching, discipline and sacramental life. As Newman says, "We must never murmur at that absolute role which the Sovereign Pontiff has over us, because it is given to him by Christ, and in obeying him we are obeying his Lord."[9] In the family, the Catholic considers the home as the domestic Church, and brings the teaching and devotions of the Church into this social and sacramental union. Another vital experience of the Catholic is his education which, when it is possible, he seeks in an environment that is Catholic.

Since the Catholic school is primarily oriented toward the full and harmonious development of the human faculties, under the guidance of Divine Grace and through the instrumentality of teachers who are in accord with that Divine Plan, it becomes necessary that the Catholic college have a clear commitment to that goal. The modern Catholic college has either wholly capitulated to the modernist dogma of "academic freedom" as the foundation of its educational experience; or it has so confusedly mixed its purpose that commitment to the Church and to absolute academic freedom stand side by side in a bad case of schizophrenia. There are few Catholic colleges today which fearlessly proclaim their allegiance to Catholic faith and morality. Most are dizzily whirling about in the vortex of modernism; and, without firm doctrinal principles in theology or a clear metaphysics in philosophy, engage in a keeping-up process of being relevant to the world. An example of this is one Catholic university president[10] who appeals to Gustavo Gutierrez's *Theology of Liberation* as one which leads the "committed Christian" to the "creation of a new world and a new man." The hidden meanings behind these words—a rationale of neo-Modernism and Marxism—seems to have escaped this busy president. To honor this pseudo-theology may give the image of an up-to-date university, but it can never be the theological basis of a true Catholic university. Another college president told the press that the *new* Catholic Church envisions "people believing and acting on their beliefs out of personal acceptance and not blind obedience." He also prophesied that "within five years, Catholicism will 'probably' also drop its prohibitions against divorce and remarriage."[11] The implications in such statements would need another article to expose and contest. But it is typical of people who—busy about this world—are left with little time to study and humbly accept what the Church teaches, or who have constructed a new Church that is momentarily acceptable to the modern world.

PROCLAIM, GUARD, INTERPRET

The greatest need of the Catholic college today is to have a great love of the Church which is its mother. Too many of our college administrators are so preoccupied with their secular tasks that they forget that their primary role is to bring the great Truth of Christ to fruition on the campus, instead of providing a bargain basement of mixed or no-value products. Unfortunately, there are Catholic teachers who are so infatuated with their own ideas that Divine Grace is rarely admitted into their autonomous teaching. The Catholic college, under such conditions, becomes a series of camps in which prima donna professors barter with fellow professors and students for a day in the campus limelight. The true Catholic institution is quite different; it is an agreement of both administrators and faculty to commit themselves to the Church in matters that concern Christian faith and morality.

The great Catholic thinker, Etienne Gilson, tells us that he found in the Church "an immense spiritual society which knows neither geographic barriers nor political boundaries and in which the Christian always feels that he is at home." He related his experience in the United States where he learned that "the Christian is not a stranger in any parish, for wherever there is a parish he stands on Christian soil." In speaking with love of Christendom, he calls it a temporal embodiment of the Church:

> This hierarchy that proceeds from the Pope down to the humblest believers; these churches, missions and parishes, with all their Christian members; these convents without number with their religious men and women; finally, all those *institutions,* whether corporal mercy or *instruction,* that form as it were the flowering and the growth of the Christian life of grace in the temporal order—all these manifestations are nothing other than the soul of the Church herself in her sensible incarnation and thereby rendered visible before all eyes.[12]

As an institution, with very special charisms and very demanding commitments, the Catholic college must accomplish "a public enduring and pervasive influence of the Christian mind in the furtherance of culture"; and so students in these institutions "are molded into men truly outstanding in their training, ready to undertake weighty responsibilities in society and witness to the faith in the world." While in the pursuit of scientific inquiry, their labors should be, "according to the example of the doctors of the Church and especially of St. Thomas Aquinas," directed to "a deeper realization of the harmony of faith and science."[13] From this commitment to Divine Revelation—interpreted by the Church of Christ—the Catholic college must never be inhibited by the secularist's absolutizing of academic freedom.

Holy Spirit Protects Teaching

Academic freedom, like all freedom, must only be conceived in relation to the individual's obligation to truth. No man has a right to unlimited freedom. In fact to possess true freedom, one must admit restraints upon one's thoughts, words and actions. God who is Supreme Truth and Goodness demands of every man a submission to his Law manifest in nature and Revelation. In man's social relation with others, no man may demand that all his impulses be satisfied, for to do so is to violate the freedom of others and bring society into disorder. In political society, the state's government—as representative of the common good of a people and with authority from God—is obliged to see that the willfulness of the individual does not destroy the rights of others or of the State which guards the commonweal. As Edmund Burke wisely said, "men are qualified for civil liberty in exact proportion to their disposition to put moral chains upon their own appetites. . . . It is ordained in the Eternal constitution of things, that men of intemperate minds cannot be free."[14]

Likewise, civil society must respect basic freedoms in man. As the Fathers of Vatican II teach, "religious freedom has to do with immunity from coercion in civil society." But, lest anyone imagine that either the individual or the State may disallow the teaching role of the Church, the Fathers added: "religious freedom leaves untouched traditional Catholic doctrine on the moral duty of men and societies toward the true religion and toward the one Church of Christ."[15] No State nor individual is superior to Revelation which comes from Divine Providence, nor may they supplant the Church which is divinely constituted to explain the Word of God. The Catholic conscience restricts itself before the teaching of the Church; obliges itself to give internal and external assent to what the Church proclaims in matters of Faith and morals; and so achieves the freedom of the sons of God.

In a Catholic college there must be a respect for and conformity with Catholic teaching. To do otherwise is to make the college superior or equal in validity of teaching to the Church established by Christ and protected from error by the Holy Spirit. When such autonomy is assumed, the college soon measures its philosophy by secular standards, rejecting the fact that Revelation—and the Church, its custodian—is one of the constituent elements of a Catholic college. As Russell Kirk well says: "The Medieval scholar was, and knew that he was the bearer of the . . . He enjoyed freedom, not in spite of, but because of, his dedication to Christian truth."[16] This, he says, is far distant from the "doctrinaire liberals" who confuse liberty and license by practically emancipating the professor from all restraints. The Church is necessary to the integrity of a Catholic college. In founding its university, says Cardinal Newman, the Church "is not cherishing talent, genius, or knowledge, for their own sake, but for the sake of her children, with a view to their spiritual welfare and their religious influence and usefulness." The Catholic university is "ministrative to the Catholic Church, first because truth of any kind can but minister to truth; and next, still more, because nature ever will pay homage to grace, and reason cannot but illustrate and defend Revelation; and thirdly, because the Church has a sovereign authority, and, when she speaks *ex cathedra,* must be obeyed."[17] Catholicism is of one whole and admits of no compromise or modification. The college may deepen through study the Church's teaching, but never deny its integral doctrine, nor pursue a line of reasoning that will result in its denial. There must be, Newman insists, "a direct and active jurisdiction of the Church over it (university) and in it . . . lest it should become the rival of the Church with the community at large in those theological matters which to the Church are exclusively committed."[18]

All elements in a college should be in harmony with its basic philosophy which is ancillary to theology which, in turn, as the science of God, has its inspiration and definiteness of teaching within the magisterium of the Church. Of special care, therefore, is the teaching of theology which expresses in doctrine Divine Revelation. And so Newman advises that absolutely novel doctrine is intolerable to the Catholic:

> All doctrinal knowledge flows from one fountainhead. If we are able to enlarge our view and multiply our propositions, it must be merely by the comparison and adjustment of the original truths; if we would solve new ques-

tions, it must be by consulting old answers . . . Revelation is all in all doctrine; the Apostles its sole depository, the inferential method its sole instrument, and ecclesiastical authority its sole sanction. The Divine Voice has spoken once for all, and the only question is about its meaning.

With brilliant awareness of the modern problem, Newman touched upon the heart of the error: "God Himself is the author as well as the subject of theology. When truth can change, its Revelation can change; when human reason can outreason the Omniscient, then may it supersede His work."[19] The Church has no concern to be the guardian of science; but she has been committed to a special trust, the care of theology. And, since theology is in the university—because it cannot fulfill its name without the recognition of revealed truth—the Church "must be there to see that it is a bona fide recognition, sincerely made and consistently acted on."[20] Well aware of the Catholic college's need to be committed to Catholic doctrine, the Sacred Congregation for Catholic Institutions, on April 6, 1973–with the approval of Pope Paul VI—insisted on the need for Catholic universities to commit themselves to a Catholic character and to keep in harmonious relation with the ecclesiastical hierarchy.

RATIONALIZATIONS SUPERSEDE CREED

Since the Church must have a guiding role in relation to all matters of Faith taught and practiced in Catholic colleges, the college has a right to require of its professors— in the areas where Faith is involved—a loyalty to the college's reason for existence. As Professor Dietrich Von Hildebrand has said, "It is unpardonable to teach under the cover of academic freedom things which are antithetical to the very basis and *raison d'etre* of the institution and which even aim at sapping it."[21] In fact, the Catholic college— since it must hold the Incarnation to be the great reality in the world—should be proud to proclaim the teachings of Christ, and alert to expose error, lest the innocent be deceived. To hold academic freedom in priority of right to Eternal Truth is to prefer the failing reason of man to the Word of God.

HUMAN FACULTIES GUIDED BY GRACE

In 1973, the Congregation on Catholic Education indicated serious lacunae in the document issued by the FIUC (International Federation of Catholic Universities) at the end of its Congress in 1972. It required an explicit statement on two matters: (1) "the necessity for each Catholic university to set out formally and without equivocation, either in its Statutes or in some other internal document, its character and commitment as 'Catholic' "; and (2) "the necessity for every Catholic university to create within itself appropriate and efficacious instruments so as to be able to put into effect proper self-regulation in the sectors of faith, morality and discipline." The Fathers of the Congregation also noted that the document was to be considered as a *whole,* and so prevent an extrapolation, out of context, that would allow for autonomy of teaching and research. It also remarked that, even in the cases where there are no statutory bonds between the Catholic university and ecclesiastical authority, such institutions are not removed from the ecclesiastical hierarchy "which must characterize all Catholic institutions."[22]

Needless to say, this instruction by the Congregation was widely rejected by most Catholic colleges. This became most apparent when the Bishop of Fort Wayne & South Bend, in 1973, protested Notre Dame's hosting a regional meeting of Planned Parenthood/World Population; and stated that "when religious and moral issues are involved in a given situation, it is the right and duty of the Bishop of the Diocese to refute publicly any public statement contrary to the teaching of the Church." The response of Father Hesburgh, President of Notre Dame, displayed no acceptance of the Church's teaching on the role of a Catholic university to be guided by Church teaching and to discipline itself accordingly. As he had consistently stood for academic freedom, above and beyond the teaching of the Church, in his interventions in the meetings of the FIUC, so he rejected the teaching of his bishop, Most

Reverend Leo A. Pursley.[23] In 1984, when Governor Cuomo made his defiant speech on the campus of Notre Dame, in respect to government funded abortions, and in opposition to Catholic teaching, President Hesburgh had no corrective word to say. Again he voiced his dogma of academic freedom, a dogma that would give an autonomy to any university, and free it from control by Church discipline. The Catholic university was to be above Church teaching in its commitment to truth and in its sanctioning of expression. Abortion and opposition to Church teaching were to have equal standing on the Catholic campus with Catholic doctrine, on the basis of the overlaw of academic freedom.

In 1983, the Holy Father, John Paul II, approved the new *Code of Canon Law* which, in a series of canons, set clearly the Church's law in relation to the nature of a Catholic institution of higher learning. It ruled that "information and education in a Catholic school must be based on the principles of Catholic doctrine, and the teachers must be outstanding in true doctrine and uprightness of life" (Canon 803). Besides, no school may bear the name Catholic, unless "by the consent of the competent ecclesiastical authority." In specific reference to Catholic universities, the Code stated that no university "may bear the title 'catholic university' except by the consent of the competent ecclesiastical authority" (C. 810).

CHURCH CANNOT BE SUPPLANTED

In the light of the consistent teaching of the Church, one wonders how many Catholic universities will return to their original commitment to the teaching of the Faith and morality of Christ. Many indications reveal little likelihood, as they permit wider aberrations in teachings and campus life, under the pressure of an ever-expanding secularism. The first step would have to be a change in the complexion of the boards of trustees: the replacement of secularists with Catholics who are clearly committed to the Faith and willing to reverse the trend. The next steps would have to be: the restoration of a university charter to its original character of full adherence to the Faith, a selection of faculty in accord with that philosophy of education, and a disciplining of students whose behavior on campus is immoral. Since the hue and cry would be immense, from within and without the university, the architects of restoration would have to be prepared for persecution. State and Federal funds would be denied or greatly restricted—a way of the government telling the Catholic institution that it must remain secularist—and the *new look* would require great retrenchment of finances and greater efforts of sacrifice. The battle would be joined and the goal would be worthy of those willing to risk martyrdom. It is possible that devoted alumni might then see the naked reality of what has happened to their Catholic image, teaching, and Catholic life.

In resume we observe that there are certain fundamental relationships in the Catholic vision of life and education. Reason is illuminated and guided by Revelation. Nature looks to Grace for its elevation, and for a more profound living in God's presence. The Catholic college must look humbly and often to the Church for correction and deepening in its special vocation of the Christian education of men. The Catholic institution must openly admit that it is different from its secular counterpart. It is not limited to worldly goals, but in all must look to God. It teaches in an environment of the Faith, and is committed to the Church, much less in contradiction. It is proud to proclaim its allegiance to Christ, to his Revelation of Faith and morality. While individual subjects are "pursued according to their own principles, method and liberty of scientific inquiry," at the same time new and current questions are investigated "according to the example of the doctors of the Church and especially of St. Thomas Aquinas," in order that "there may be a deeper realization of the harmony of faith and science."[24] In this way the Catholic College is corporately committed to the Church's teaching. To keep in harmonious relation with the ecclesiastical hierarchy is its need and means of fulfillment.

Notes

1. *Atlantic Monthly,* Oct., 1966. Also, for fuller treatment, cf. "The New Left," Memorandum, Subcommittee to Investigate the Administra-

tion of the Internal Security Act, Committee of the Judiciary, U.S. Senate, 90th Congr. 2nd sess., Oct. 9, 1968, pp.11ff.

2. *Summa Theologica*, III, qu. 26, a.1–2.

3. Etienne Gilson, "The Intelligence in Service of Christ," in *A Gilson Reader*, ed. Anton C. Pegis, N.Y., 1957, Image, 35.

4. *Ibid.*, 36–38.

5. *Ibid.*, 47.

6. J.H. Newman, *An Essay on the Development of Christian Doctrine*, N.Y., 1960, Image, 103–104.

7. Acts, 8/26–39.

8. *L'Osservatore Romano* (English edit.), Mar. 18, 1971.

9. J.H. Newman, *Sermons Preached on Various Occasions*, N.Y., 1900, Longmans, 281ff.

10. T.M. Hesburgh, *The Humane Imperative*, New Haven, 1974, Yale, 8–9.

11. E. Ryan, *Seattle Post Intelligencer*, July 26, 1975.

12. E. Gilson, "Where is Christendom?", in *A Gilson Reader*, 343–46.

13. *Declaration on Christian Education*, Vatican II, no. 10.

14. E. Burke, "Reflections on the Revolution in France," *Works*, IV, 319.

15. *Declaration on Religious Freedom*, Vat. II, no. 1.

16. Russell Kirk, *Academic Freedom*, Chicago, 1955.

17. J.H. Newman, *Idea of a University*, N.Y., 1959, Image, 7, 9, 416.

18. *Ibid.*, 222.

19. *Ibid.*, 229.

20. *Ibid.*, 232.

21. Dietrich Von Hildebrand, "Academic Freedom and the Catholic University," in *The Wanderer*, June 5, 1969.

22. Letter of the Sacred Congregation for Catholic Institutions, to the presidents of Catholic Universities and the Directors of Catholic Institutions of Higher Learning, Rome, April 25, 1973.

23. "Is Notre Dame Still Catholic?" by E. Michael Jones, in *Fidelity*, Sept., 1985.

24. *Declaration on Christian Education*, Document of Vatican Council II, no. 10.

On Defending Catholic Higher Education in America

Mark D. Jordan

This article originally appeared in *Communio* in 1986.

The Vatican's draft schema on Catholic universities, which was circulated confidentially in 1985, has found its way into print.[1] In what it says and what it does not say, the draft raises questions important for the intellectual life of the Church. Of course, it also proposes certain canonical norms for university administration. These have provoked wide press coverage and many spirited responses. One of the most substantial responses has been a summary of comments by members of the (American) Association of Catholic Colleges and Universities.[2] While this summary sharpens the issues between Rome and the Catholic schools, it skips over as many important topics as does the Roman draft. I would like to make up a few of those shared omissions in the hope that the debate can gain by being complicated—that is, by becoming more adequate to the untidy truth of things.

1. THE PRESENT DEBATE

The issues raised in the exchange so far are of very different kinds. The ACCU criticizes the language, the organization, and the internal consistency of the Vatican's draft. More important objections regard the timeliness of such a papal pronouncement and the practicability of its regulations. But the reiterated point of the ACCU respondents is that the proposed schema does not take into account the reality of Catholic higher education *in America*. For example, the document opens with an explanation of our system of accreditation. It then adds a statistical summary of the present state of Catholic colleges and universities in America; the point here is to show both size and variety. The most careful preliminary section explains the legal standing of Catholic schools, especially in regard to restrictions on government funding.

The American note is also struck many times in commenting on the draft Proemium. There are cautions against multiplying Catholic institutions in this country and emphases on the independent spirit of our institutional founders. But the tone is most insistent when discussing the Vatican's proposed norms. Here the American situation is invoked in the discussion of almost every topic: academic freedom, the use of 'Catholic' in university names, the juridical ways in which a university can become Catholic, the interpretation of canon law, and the use of religious criteria in faculty or administrative appointments. The character of the argument stands forth clearly in the response to regulations meant to insure episcopal control: "What is proposed here is contrary to the American values of both academic freedom and due process, both of which are written into most university statutes and protected by civil and constitutional law."[3] There is no plainer way to say that the Roman norms are un-American.

The ACCU reply deserves more attention than my bald paraphrase allows. Many of its points are well taken. The proposed norms are muddled in ways which would make them impracticable in any country.[4] More importantly, some parts of the draft are written in a tone of unreflective simplification. The remarks on "Church and University," for example, take a very complicated history and flatten it into fable. "From the beginning of her existence, the church has cultivated knowledge and has created numerous teaching centers."[5] It has also closed a number of them by edict, by violence, and by neglect. "When universities began to be formed, [the church] gave them all her support and interest." History, again, is both more complicated and more mixed. For example, it is famously true that the papacy interceded on behalf of the university masters at Paris in 1215 and 1231; it is equally true that the papacy broke its own principle of the masters' autonomy in the 1250's. But perhaps it is best to regard these opening remarks in the draft as an artifice of exhortation.

More difficult are the categories used in the draft section on the "Role of the Catholic University in Society." The ACCU response objects to the negative tone of the paragraphs on faith and science. Much more should have been objected against the general poverty of conception. The section assumes that intellectual life can be adequately described by the trichotomy faith/science, faith/culture, and promotion of values. Philosophy is not mentioned. Indeed, its place seems to be taken by faith, since it is faith that teaches to science "the mystery of existence, particularly the mystery of man."[6] Wisdom, which is mentioned once, is effectively reduced to ethics, that is, to values.[7] It is probably too late to erase that Nietzschean word, as it is too late to strike the arrogant word 'rights', but we might still be able hesitate over adopting 'culture' to cover everything that used to be meant by *scientia speculativa*. In short, the draft section on Catholic universities in the world succumbs almost entirely to the post-modern claim that all the teachable truth falls into three parts: the natural sciences, the socio-anthropological critique of culture, and the 'promotion' of values. No reference is made in this section to any piece of the admirable Catholic corpus of works on higher learning. Indeed, no document older than Vatican II's Declaration on Christian Education is cited, leaving one to draw some odd conclusions about the actual respect for tradition in the curia.

Of course on the other side, the ACCU might well have been more candid about the many good reasons for worry on Rome's part. It is one thing to insist upon the authority of the college trustees and something else to reflect on how they have exercised that authority. How many governing bodies have taken an active and intelligent role in overseeing the doctrinal integrity of teaching in Catholic institutions? How many would be capable of doing so? Yet the need for oversight is obvious to anyone with experience in Catholic schools during the last two decades. Theology departments have staged a number of disedifying spectacles: Curricula have been watered down or abolished. The balanced teaching of doctrinal development or of Church history has been scratched in favor of the polemical and the ephemeral; many students now never catch a glimpse of anything like an integral tradition. Whole libraries have been gutted by selling off or throwing out everything faintly 'Scholastic'. The study of scholarly languages has been deprecated. The ideologies of single issues have been allowed to dominate all discourse. Those holding orthodox views have been persecuted, sometimes to the point of dismissal, precisely for being orthodox. And so on. Other tales, less lurid perhaps, could be told about other departments. Not everything is gloomy, of course, and many of the worst outrages are now past. But enough has happened—and is happening—to cause alarm.

These are points which the ACCU response might have considered or confessed. It chose instead—and interestingly—to insist upon the legal questions and to do so by its emphasis on the American situation. There are farther and nearer echoes in this rhetorical strategy. Americans have been trying at least since our revolution to convince the Vatican that things are different here. Whether dealing with 'Republicanism' or 'Americanism', the Vatican has not been convinced. But the nearer echoes are the more interesting ones because they come from a debate that touched the most important of the missing points in the documents before us. The debate concerned American Catholic 'anti-intellectualism'[8] and the point was a question about *merit* in Catholic higher education.

2. The Debate of the 1950's

On May 14, 1955, John Tracy Ellis read a paper entitled "American Catholics and the Intellectual Life" before the CCICA, then meeting in St. Louis. The paper was first printed in *Thought* the following fall.[9] Reaction to it was quick and general: the paper was widely excerpted and reprinted; it provoked news accounts, editorials, formal replies, faculty meetings, symposia; and it brought Ellis both further occasions for speaking and a large correspondence.[10]

What did Ellis say in that famous paper? He began with the supposition that "the weakest aspect of the church in this country [lay] in its failure to produce national leaders and to exercise commanding influence in intellectual circles."[11] Ellis then went on to consider a number of explanations for this supposed state of affairs. Some were extrinsic, such as the historical prejudice against Catholicism, the immigrant character of American Catholics, the pastoral demands large-scale immigration placed on the Church, American materialism, and American anti-intellectualism. Other explanations were intrinsic and rather more painful: an overeagerness among Catholics for apologetics, a failure to appreciate the vocation of the intellectual, the mis-education of the clergy, a "betrayal of what is peculiarly [our] own" in favor of secular models, a "betrayal of one another" in unreasoning competition, and an overemphasis on schools as agencies for moral development. Ellis concluded with a dismal statistical survey in support of his original supposition.

This was not the first time that unflinching self-examination had been carried out by Catholic scholars. Ellis himself provides a historical pedigree reaching well back into the nineteenth century. George Shuster had written on the topic for several decades before Ellis, beginning in 1925 with "Have We Any Scholars?"[12] There was also an affecting conference volume published in 1938 under the title *Catholics and Scholarship*. The volume ends with a plea for action in aid of a generation of Catholic scholars yet to come.[13] But I think it safe to say that no one had made the indictment as forcefully, as succinctly, and with as much academic authority as Ellis.

The heat of the controversy died down after a few years, in part because of shifts in fashion, in part because some institutional steps were taken to remedy the situation, and in part because of the millennial fever spread by Vatican II. Moreover, the dialectic of the debate itself diffused the issues by generalizing them and by handing them over to sociological categories.[14] Indeed, by the mid-1960's, it could be argued that sociological evidence showed a marked change in Catholic educational patterns.[15] Thus Andrew Greeley, in his retrospective *The American Catholic*, summarizes the several NORC surveys and a later Carnegie report which showed that Catholics had for some years become productive scholars, even at "elite institutions," in just their proportion within the population at large.[16] If Catholics are still not fully represented at the very best institutions, Greeley urges, this must be attributable to a residue of anti-Catholic prejudice. John Noonan has concurred with this conclusion of changed circumstances, while adding several other replies to Ellis's.[17] Noonan refuses, for example, to distinguish immigrant from native-born in assessing contributions to Church life and wants to expand the very notion of 'Catholic' either by analogy to secularized Jews or by co-opting the intellectually sympathetic.[18] Still others have sought to explain the debate provoked by Ellis as an example of "reference group shift," in which American Catholics made anxieties for themselves by raising their sights.[19]

It may be true that Greeley and the sociologists have discovered a happy change in the academic fortunes of American Catholics. But this only touches a part of what was said in that earlier debate. Ellis was concerned with the under-representation of American Catholics in national academic institutions, but he was more especially concerned with the fate of Catholic universities and of the Church's mind. Indeed, Ellis would seem willing to sacrifice some worldly recognition in order to attain precisely the excellence of a *Catholic* intellect. As Greeley and the other sociologists freely admit, what has not happened in the last thirty years is a Catholic renaissance promoted by Catholic universities.[20] Philip Gleason noticed almost twenty years ago that the opposite seemed to be happening: Some disputants were taking a view of intellect that made Catholic intellect a contradiction in terms, even while the majority of Catholic professors were becoming intellectually indistinguishable from their non-Catholic peers.[21] Yet it was a Catholic renaissance that Ellis and the others wanted, and it was the lack of truly Catholic thought that moved them to both shame and anger.

Ellis wrote: "The chief blame, I firmly believe, lies with Catholics themselves. . . . It lies in their failure to have measured up to their responsibilities to the incomparable tradition of Catholic learning of which they are the direct heirs. . . ."[22] A year later, Annette Walters argued that the failure to produce Catholic intellectuals was due to "the absence of an intellectual tradition in our American Catholic population."[23] At another CCICA meeting, Gustave Weigel presented the same diagnosis and the same dream:

"The general Catholic community in America does not know what scholarship is. . . . There is no need to propose the good of secular contemplation as a merely natural good. Our long Christian tradition shows that it is a laudable Christian career. It is a true Christian vocation and an effective means of sanctification."[24] Exactly the same note is heard in the most perceptive retrospective view on the debate. John Whitney Evans writes, "We have yet to actualize our distinctly Catholic intellectual and cultural heritages into a prominent and influential pattern of American traditions, although we may yet do so."[25]

So the ACCU's response is right to insist upon the special character of the American situation. But that insistence risks becoming a spirited defense of mediocrity. To say that we want to defend the history of American colleges and universities only begs the question of how far that history is worth defending. Our present situation is filled with questions unanswered after thirty years: Does the Catholic community at large care about the intellectual quality of its institutions beyond wanting marketable degrees from them? How much will Catholics pay for such institutions? Is there any hope of distributing resources rationally—or will fluctuating enrollments decide survival? Have Catholic universities better understood the balance of vocational training, character formation, and the cultivation of intellectual virtues? Will Catholic scholars dwell in the Catholic tradition or will they chase after whatever scholarly banner whirls by?

There are so many questions still in need of answers—and so much anecdotal evidence that the answers being offered are the wrong ones. First, there is considerable internecine quarreling among Catholic 'intellectuals'. It is very hard to imagine fostering a renaissance when we are busy anathematizing one another. Second, there has been a wholesale substitution of orthopraxy for orthodoxy on both 'left' and 'right', so that the most identifiable Catholic issues are matters of morals, whether personal or political. Third, the gains made by many Catholic institutions have been due in large measure to the extraordinary pressures of the market in academic jobs. Some good teachers stay at Catholic schools because they cannot leave—and some schools survive because there are teachers willing to teach for unjustly low wages. Fourth, the crisis in vocations to the religious life and the priesthood continues to have uncalculated consequences, some good and some bad. The absence of religious has hastened the 'laicization' of the faculties, but it has also removed the longstanding intellectual witness of the more scholarly religious orders. At the same time, in an effort to secure vocations, many houses of formation have been tempted both to lower academic standards and to make programs more 'pastoral'. This has had the effect of debasing university curricula intended for the religious and candidates for orders. Whatever the defects of the Scholastic drill, and they were many, it is no comfort to see seminarians whose only philosophy is a bowdlerized Heidegger or four easy lessons in the logic of 'possible worlds'. The healthy growth of lay faculties ought not to be purchased by the speculative abdication of the clergy and religious.

Much more could be said, but my point is only to condense these anecdotal impressions into a single question: How could today's debate over the proposed schema help with the painful questions about American Catholic education already raised thirty years ago?

3. Some Dilemmas for Any Debate

The first answer to that question would be that any helpful debate must discuss with a steady and charitable candor some painful dilemmas of the American Catholic situation. Let me sketch four of these dilemmas, without pretending in any way to exhaust them, much less to resolve them. Their roots go much deeper than the American situation; they are our versions of more universal problems. But I will try to capture at least their American character.

The first dilemma concerns what I would call the prerequisites for responsible episcopal control by the American episcopacy. There is no question, of course, that the bishops can attempt to assert such control by main force—thus provoking costly litigation, bad press, and a further bleeding of already anemic faculties. There is also little question in my mind that the ideal of the episcopal office requires vigilance over the teaching of the faith. But responsible episcopal control will require a longer preparation on all sides, particularly in the episcopacy itself. It is true that the bishops must in fact offer more material support than they have. Excellent universities are both costly and vulnerable. The bishops must be willing to take hard choices in favor of supporting them, even at a cost to more immediate or more visible ministries. As it is, bishops too often compete with Catholic universities in the pursuit of philanthropists. But responsible episcopal supervision is much more than a matter of money. If the bishops will be *episkopoi* in regard to the universities, then they must give living testimony to the virtues of the mind. Intellectual authority can only be intellectual. This might seem a deliriously 'ideal' requirement had not the German episcopacy offered so strong a counter-case of a national church with many scholar-bishops. If every Ordinary must be a teacher so far as he is the pastor, if he must exercise specific authority over local teaching at all levels, then it would be consoling to see American bishops giving every evidence of profound theological formation—or, indeed, of genuinely liberal education.

But the first dilemma stands out here when one recognizes how far what Gleason calls 'Americanization' has become the sincere program of our bishops. To ask them to become exemplary Catholic scholars is to ask them to become something other than what the American church has demanded of them—has made of them. Americans have a complicated and paradoxical relation to liberal education.[26] This expresses itself in contradictory notions about university life—its governance by boards of non-academics, for example, and its evaluation in terms of useful production. Many of our bishops, who are most often products of the sedulously 'pragmatic' education in Catholic schools, have appropriated these paradoxes without quite recognizing them. So long as they grow in their insistence that they ought to think and act together as *American* bishops, they are hardly likely to do so. Responsible episcopal superintendence would require, then, not only responsibility for material concerns, but an overcoming in some crucial respects of the American education of the episcopacy.

The second dilemma concerns a false 'democracy' in the American Church. There is no problem with conceiving ourselves as the "people of God," with stressing community, with sharing ministries so far as possible. These are good things. But there is a dilemma when democracy comes almost naturally to be interpreted as enforced mediocrity. This misinterpretation is an old American habit, and the reception of Vatican II has only served to reinforce it within the American Church. Universities ought ideally to be aristocracies of spiritual and intellectual merit. Failing that ideal, as they must, universities fall back upon more accessible criteria for ranking, for assessing, for rejecting. Still, and however far the criteria are made routine, universities remain self-perpetuating communities requiring invidious intellectual discriminations. So much in recent American Catholicism has counted against discriminating judgment and for an all-embracing sentimentality—a tepid, windless lagoon of good feeling. Discrimination is the last thing wanted in our demotic liturgies, for example, which are pitched to the lowest common taste. The same attitude transposed into the intellectual life is just the counsel of mediocrity. Yet how are we to insist upon the necessity for intellectual discrimination without violating our deep distaste for aristocracies—and, in fact, our essentially egalitarian rendering of the supernatural virtue of charity?

A third dilemma lies in the 'professionalization' of American intellectual life, but particularly of theology. This will seem to be no dilemma, since professionalization might suggest itself as exactly what American Catholic thought has needed all along. But the dilemma arises when 'professionalization' means not the raising of standards or the increase of seriousness, but the progressive substitution of organizational means for intellectual ends. The ACCU report quotes Tocqueville on the American propensity for self-organization; the ACCU itself is a product of that propensity. This is a marvelous gift in many circumstances, but it can become in scholarly life a serious obstacle to thinking. We have national conferences thrice weekly, ardent new journals, books spitting from the presses, cumbrous 'procedures' of review and evaluation, study groups to review the methodology of the procedures—until one must wonder when there is any quiet time for meditating truths. The case of theology is particularly glaring, because theology can never be domesticated in the academic world. It depends too much on grace. The mandarinism of academic theology is now such that no theological question can be approached except by a licensed team—and preferably one prepared to project an encyclopedia, or at least a lexicon, with systematic bibliography. Here it becomes clear that this American dilemma is, in fact, our version of a universal tale. Rome itself has been the chief agent over a millennium in the spread of theological guild-mentality, and German scholarhip over the last two centuries has made an industry out of every theological sub-field. Yet so far as theology is an anticipation of the vision of the blessed—to use a Thomistic commonplace—it cannot be confined to departments of theology at all. It is the heartfelt end of every Christian thought. The professionalization of theology is, then, both a sign of intellectual seriousness and a symptom of reduction to the merely human.

A fourth and final dilemma is that of American 'Catholicity' in teaching or thinking, the central concern of the proposed Vatican schema. We must begin here by admitting that while Vatican II may have raised certain vital questions in *Gaudium et spes*, for example, it has by no means provided complete answers. That is perfectly understandable, given that the questions are of a fierce difficulty. What makes a thought Catholic or not Catholic in modern America? But there is no modern America; there are hundreds of competing worldviews. Each requires the most delicate analyses before its relations with Christian believing can be uncovered. The Christian might learn from each of them some new part of God's great providence. Alternately, the Christian might find faith distorted by taking on subtle lies. How do we discern, then, what it is to think as an American Catholic? We face many difficulties in addressing this question. There is our tendency to reduce intellectual positions to their effects on action. We are tolerant to a fault about opinions, but curiously and hypocritically intolerant of actions. So we tend at once to overestimate the possibilities for intellectual accommodations and then to stake all our faith on moral stipulations—not bothering to ask so much after the motives and reasons for action. Or we think that we have found an American Catholicism by being patriotic Catholics. Or we translate our Catholicism into a deliberate bad taste, because being American means being 'the common man' who hasn't much for what is 'artsy'. Or we make Catholicism into a sentimentality about the customs of the 'old country.'

What, then, makes a thought Catholic or not Catholic in modern America? So far as this question restates the dilemma of incarnation, the most perspicuous answers to it are negative, apophatic. To think as a Catholic is not only, I take it, to adhere to a set of moral standards, especially where the asserted moral standards have had numerous pagan adherents. Nor is it a matter of being sociologically Catholic—the parental home or the ethnic background. Nor can Catholicity of thought be defined only as obedience to institutional authority no matter what; this criterion forgets that the authority comes from God and that his authority is a pedagogy on the way to his truth. Catholicity in teaching or thinking is something more intrinsic, more embracing, more demanding, and more extraordinary than any of these proposed reductions.

The present debate could be an important one indeed if only it would help in bringing that 'something more' into view. To do that, however, the debate would have to turn from the claims of American privilege to the dilemmas of an American educational history that offers much and needs much. In those dilemmas, the ones mentioned here and the others, there still lies the possibility of very good schools given life by a truly American Catholic faith—and that possibility can be defended without apologies.

Notes

1. Congregation for Catholic Education, "Proposed Schema for a Pontifical Document on Catholic Universities" (dated April 15, 1985), *Origins* 15 (1986):706–711.

2. "Catholic College and University Presidents Respond to Proposed Vatican Schema," *Origins* 15 (1986):697–704. The document is a "synthesis" of 110 responses by members of the ACCU compiled by its executive director, Alice Gallin. The document is dated February 11, 1986.

3. *Origins* 15:703.

4. For example, there seems to be an inconsistency in regard to the review of non-Catholic faculty. On the one hand, the schema envisions non-Catholic teachers since they are enjoined to respect "the Catholic character of the universities" (Norms, 27.2). On the other hand, "*all* teachers who are to be chosen, nominated and promoted in accordance with the statutes are to be distinguished by academic and pedagogical ability as well as by *doctrinal integrity* and *uprightness of life.* . . ." (Norms, 26.1, emphases added). How can non-Catholic teachers, however respectful, be judged by Catholic standards of faith and morals?

5. "Proposed Schema," Proemium 4; *Origins* 15:706.

6. "Proposed Schema," Proemium 35; *Origins* 15:708. "Philosophical and theological" reflection is mentioned in 2.1(a) of the Norms, but only in connection with "evaluat[ing] the achievements of the various disciplines."

7. "Proposed Schema," Proemium 39; *Origins* 15:708.

8. Philip Gleason has shown at length the dangers in this term and its siblings; see his "Catholic Intellectualism Again," *America* 112 (January 22, 1965), pp. 112–119. I use it only when describing the debate and will use other language in the final section.

9. John Tracy Ellis, "American Catholics and the Intellectual Life," *Thought* 30 (1955):351–388. I follow the pagination of the book form, *American Catholics and the Intellectual Life*, pref. John J. Wright (Chicago: Heritage Foundation, 1956).

10. Ellis himself summarizes the first wave of reaction in his "No Complacency," *America* 95 (1956): 14–25. His conclusion: "On the whole therefore, the reactions summarized in the present report reveal a substantial agreement with the principal conclusions reached last fall in *Thought*" (p. 25).

11. Ellis, *American Catholics*, p. 16.

12. George N. Shuster, "Have We Any Scholars?", *America* 33 (1925):418–419. For Shuster's other writings, see Thomas E. Blantz, "George N. Shuster and American Catholic Intellectual Life," in *Studies in Catholic History in Honor of John Tracy Ellis*, edited by Nelson H. Minnich, Robert B. Eno, and Robert F. Trisco (Wilmington: Michael Glazier, 1985), 345–365.

13. John A. O'Brien, ed., *Catholics and Scholarship: A Symposium on the Development of Scholars* (Huntington, Ind.: Our Sunday Visitor, 1938).

14. Both the false generality and the optimistic sociology can be seen already in Thomas F. O'Dea, *American Catholic Dilemma: An Inquiry into the Intellectual Life* (New York: Sheed and Ward, 1958).

15. See the argument by Andrew Greeley and the counters by John D. Donvan and James W. Trent in the October 2, 1964 issue of *Commonweal*.

16. Andrew M. Greeley, *The American Catholic: A Social Portrait* (New York: Basic Books, 1977), chapter 4, pp. 69–89.

17. John T. Noonan, "American Catholics and the Intellectual Life," *Cross Currents* 31 (1981–82):433–46.

18. Noonan, pp. 440–441 and 442–446.

19. R. L. Schnell and Patricia T. Rooke, "Intellectualism, Educational Achievement, and American Catholicism: A Reconsideration of the Controversy, 1955–1975," *Canadian Review of American Studies* 7 (1977):66–76.

20. Greeley, "Why Catholic Higher Education is Lower," *National Catholic Reporter*, September 28, 1983, pp. 1–6; compare Schnell and Rooke, p. 68: "In brief, by the 1960's Catholic Americans (*if not their academic institutions*) had entered the mainstream of their society" [the whole is italicized in the original].

21. Philip Gleason, "The Crisis of Americanization," in *Contemporary Catholicism in the United States*, (Notre Dame: University of Notre Dame Press, 1969), 18–27, at pp. 24–26.

22. Ellis, *American Catholics*, p. 57.

23. Annette Walters, "Why is the American Catholic College Failing to Develop Catholic Intellectualism?", *Bulletin NCEA* 53 (1956):172–178, at 174.

24. Gustave Weigel, "American Catholic Intellectualism—A Theologian's Reflections," *Review of Politics* 19 (1957):275–307, at pp. 299 and 306.

25. John Whitney Evans, "American Catholics and the Intellectual Life: Thirty Years Later," in Minnich et al. eds., *Studies in Catholic History*, 366–393, at 391.

26. I mention something here which is profoundly and elegantly developed in Eva T. H. Brann's *Paradoxes of Education in a Republic* (Chicago: University of Chicago Press, 1979).

Part Four

MORAL THEOLOGY
IN PARTICULAR

The Drama of Morality

Joseph Ratzinger

This is a chapter from THE RATZINGER REPORT, by Joseph Cardinal Ratzinger with Vittorio Messori, 1985. Translated by Salvator Attanasio and Graham Harrison

---

FROM LIBERALISM TO PERMISSIVISM

So there is also a *crisis*—likewise grave—*of the morality* proposed by the Magisterium of the Church. A crisis, as we have already said, closely linked to that affecting Catholic dogma.

It is a crisis that for the moment affects the so-called "developed" world, particularly Europe and the United States. But, as we know, the models elaborated in these zones eventually end up in the rest of the world with the help of a well-known cultural imperialism.

At any rate, to quote the Cardinal, "In a world like the West, where money and wealth are the measure of all things, and where the model of the free market imposes its implacable laws on every aspect of life, authentic Catholic ethics now appears to many like an alien body from times long past, as a kind of meteorite which is in opposition, not only to the concrete habits of life, but also to the way of thinking underlying them. Economic *liberalism* creates its exact counterpart, *permissivism*, on the moral plane." Accordingly, "it becomes difficult, if not altogether impossible, to present Catholic morality as reasonable. It is too distant from what is considered to be obvious, as normal by the majority of persons, conditioned by the dominant culture with which not a few 'Catholic' moralists have aligned themselves as influential supporters."

In Bogota, at the meeting of the bishops who preside over the doctrinal commissions and episcopal conferences of Latin America, the Cardinal read a report—unpublished up to now—that tried to single out the deep motives of what was transpiring in contemporary theology, including moral theology, which was allotted a space corresponding to its importance in that report. Hence it will be necessary to follow Ratzinger in his analysis in order to understand his alarm in the face of certain paths upon which the West, and in its suite, certain theologies, have entered. He intends above all to draw attention to questions of family and sexuality.

"A Series of Ruptures"

Accordingly he observes: "In the culture of the 'developed' world it is above all the indissoluble bond between *sexuality* and *motherhood* that has been ruptured. Separated from motherhood, sex has remained without a locus and has lost its point of reference: it is a kind of drifting mine, a problem and at the same time an omnipresent power."

After this first rupture he sees another, as a consequence: "After the separation between sexuality and motherhood was effected, sexuality was also separated from procreation. The movement, however, ended up going in an opposite direction: procreation without sexuality. Out of this follow the increasingly shocking medical-technical experiments so prevalent in our day where, precisely, procreation is independent of sexuality. Biological manipulation is striving to uncouple man from nature (the very existence of which is being disputed). There is an attempt to transform man, to manipulate him as one does every other 'thing': he is nothing but a product planned according to one's pleasure."

If I am not mistaken, I observe, our cultures are the first in history in which such ruptures have come to pass.

"Yes, and at the end of this march to shatter fundamental, natural linkages (and not, as is said, only those that are cultural), there are unimaginable consequences which, however, derive from the very logic that lies at the base of a venture of this kind."

In his view we will atone already in our day for "the consequences of a sexuality which is no longer linked to motherhood and to procreation. It logically follows from this that every form of sexuality is equivalent and therefore of equal worth." "It is certainly not a matter," he specifies, "of establishing or recommending a retrograde moralism, but one of lucidly drawing the consequences from the premises: it is, in fact, logical that pleasure, the *libido* of the individual, become the only possible point of reference of sex. No longer having an objective reason to justify it, sex seeks the subjective reason in the gratification of the desire, in the most 'satisfying' answer for the individual, to the instincts no longer subject to rational restraints. Everyone is free to give his personal *libido* the content considered suitable for himself."

He continues: "Hence, it naturally follows that all forms of sexual gratification are transformed into the 'rights' of the individual. Thus, to cite an especially current example, homosexuality becomes an inalienable right. (Given the aforementioned premises, how can one deny it?) On the contrary, its full recognition appears to be an aspect of human liberation."

There are, however, other consequences of "this uprooting of the human person in the depth of his nature". He elaborates: "Fecundity separated from marriage based on a life-long fidelity turns from being a *blessing* (as it was understood in every culture) to its opposite: that is to say a *threat* to the free development of the 'individual's right to happiness'. Thus abortion, institutionalized, free and socially guaranteed, becomes another 'right', another form of 'liberation'."

"FAR FROM SOCIETY OR FAR FROM THE MAGISTERIUM?"

This, then, is how the dramatic ethical scenario of the liberal-radical "affluent" society presents itself to him. But how does Catholic moral theology react to all this?

"The now dominant mentality attacks the very foundations of the morality of the Church, which, as I have already said, if she remains true to herself, risks appearing like an anachronistic construct, a bothersome, alien body. Thus the moral theologians of the Western Hemisphere, in their efforts to still remain 'credible' in our society, find themselves facing a difficult alternative: it seems to them that they must choose between opposing modern society and opposing the Magisterium. The number of those who prefer the latter type of opposition is larger or smaller depending on how the question is posed: consequently they set out on a search for theories and systems that allow compromises between Catholicism and current conceptions. But this growing difference between the Magisterium and the 'new' moral theologies leads to unforeseeable consequences, also precisely for the reason that the Church with her schools and her hospitals still occupies an important social role (especially in America). Thus we stand before the difficult alternative: either the Church finds an understanding, a compromise with the values propounded by society which she wants to continue to serve, or she decides to remain faithful to her own values (and in the Church's view these are the values that protect man in his deepest needs) as the result of which she finds herself on the margin of society."

Thus the Cardinal believes he can observe that "today the sphere of moral theology has become the main locus of the tensions between Magisterium and theologians, especially because here the consequences are most immediately perceptible. I should like to cite some trends: at times premarital relations, at least under certain conditions, are justified. Masturbation is presented as a normal phenomenon of adolescence. Admission of remarried divorced couples to the sacraments is constantly demanded. Radical feminism—especially in some women's religious orders—also seems to be gaining ground noticeably in the Church (but we will speak about that later). Even as regards the question of homosexuality, attempts at its justification are in the making. Indeed, it has come to pass that bishops—on the basis of insufficient information or also because of a sense of guilt among Catholics toward an 'oppressed minority'—have placed churches at the disposal of '*gays*' for their gatherings. Then there is the case of *Humanae vitae*, the encyclical of Paul VI, which reaffirmed the 'no' to contraceptives and which has not been understood. Instead it has been more or less openly rejected in broad ecclesial circles."

But, I ask, is it not precisely the problem of birth control that finds traditional Catholic morality rather helpless? Doesn't one get the impression that here the Magisterium has exposed itself by its lack of solid, decisive arguments?

"It's true", he replies, "that at the beginning of the great debate following the appearance of the encyclical *Humanae vitae* in 1968, the demonstrative basis of the theology faithful to the Magisterium was still relatively slim. But, in the meantime, it has been broadened through new experiences and new reflections so that the situation is beginning to reverse itself. In order to understand the whole problem correctly, we are here obliged to take a look at the past. In the thirties or forties, some Catholic moral theologians had begun to criticize the onesidedness of the orientation of Catholic sexual morality toward procreation from the point of view of personalist philosophy. Above all they called attention to the fact that the classic treatment of marriage in Canon law, based on its 'ends', did not do full justice to the essence of marriage. The category 'end' is insufficient to explain this peculiarly human phenomenon. In no way did these theologians deny the importance of fecundity in the complex of values of human sexuality. But they assigned a new place to it within the framework of a more personalistic perspective in the way of considering marriage. These discussions were important and have produced a significant deepening of the Catholic doctrine on matrimony. The Council accepted and confirmed the best aspects of these reflections. But at this point in time a new line of development began to materialize. Whereas the reflections of the Council were based on the unity of person and nature in man, personalism began to be understood in opposition to 'naturalism' (as if the human person and its needs could enter into conflict with nature). Thus an exaggerated personalism led some theologians to reject the internal order, the language of nature (which instead is moral of itself, according to the constant teaching of the Catholic Church), leaving to sexuality, conjugal included, the sole point of reference in the will of the person. This indeed is one of the reasons that *Humanae vitae* was rejected and that it is impossible for many theologies to reject contraception."

In his view, "exaggerated personalism" is not the only ethical system being developed as an alternative to those of the Magisterium. Ratzinger—referring to the moral-theological discussions in the Western world—delineated to the bishops assembled in Bogota the lines of other systems that he considers unacceptable: "Immediately after the Council, discussions were begun as to whether specifically Christian moral norms, as such, existed. Some came to the conclusion that all the norms can also be found outside the Christian world and that, de facto, the greater part of Christian norms came from other cultures, particularly from ancient classic culture, especially the stoic. From this erroneous point of departure, they arrived unavoidably at the idea that morality was to be constructed solely on the basis of reason and that this autonomy of reason was also valid for believers. Hence no more Magisterium, no more God of Revelation with his Decalogue. In fact, many espoused the view that the Decalogue on which the Church has based her objective morality is nothing but a 'cultural product' linked to the ancient Semitic Middle East. Hence a relative norm dependent on an anthropology and on a history that is no longer ours. And so here we again find the denial of the unity of Scripture, the resurfacing of the old heresy which held that the Old Testament (the locus of the 'law') was surpassed and replaced by the New (kingdom of 'grace'). But for Catholics, the Bible is a unitary whole; the beatitudes of Jesus do not annul the Decalogue, which had been given by God to Moses and through him to men of all times. Instead, according to these new moral theologians, since we are 'now adult and liberated', we ought to seek other behavioral norms by ourselves."[1]

A search, I say, to be conducted on the basis of reason alone?

"As I have already indicated," he replied, "it is known that in the final analysis for genuine Catholic morality there are actions that reason will never be able to justify, since they contain in themselves rejection of the Creator God and therefore a denial of the authentic good of man, his creature. For the Magisterium there have always been fixed points of reference, landmarks which can neither be removed nor ignored without breaking the bond that Christian philosophy sees between *Being* and the *Good*. By proclaiming, instead, the autonomy of human reason alone, now detached from the Decalogue, one is forced to embark on a search for new fixed points: to what shall one adhere, how are moral duties to be justified if they are no longer rooted in divine Revelation, in the commandments of the Creator?"

What then?

"Well, one has arrived at the so-called 'morality of ends'—or, as it is preferred in the United States where it is particularly developed and diffused—of 'consequences', *'consequentialism'*: Nothing *in itself* is good or bad, the goodness of an act depends entirely upon its end and upon its foreseeable and calculated consequences. After becoming aware of the problematic character of such a system, some moralists have attempted to tone down 'consequentialism' to *'proportionalism'*: moral conduct depends upon the evaluation and weighing of the proportion of goods that are involved. Again it is a matter of individual evaluation, this time an evaluation of the 'proportion' between good and evil."

It seems to me, however, I observe, that the classical morality also made reference to calculations of such a kind: the evaluation of the consequences, the weighing of the goods involved.

"Of course", he replies. "The error lies in constructing a system on what was only an aspect of the traditional morality which certainly—in the final analysis—did not depend upon the personal evaluation of the individual, but upon the Revelation of God, upon the 'instructions for use' inscribed by him objectively and indelibly in his creation. Accordingly, nature, and with it precisely also man himself, so far as he is part of that created nature, contain that morality within themselves."

In the Prefect's view, the negation of all this leads to shattering consequences for the individual and for the entire society: "If we turn from the affluent societies of the West, where these systems cropped up for the first time, we find that in the moral convictions of many liberation theologies, a 'proportionalist' morality also often stands in the background. The 'absolute good' (and this means the building of a just socialist society) becomes the moral norm that justifies everything else, including—if necessary—violence, homicide, mendacity. It is one of the many aspects that show how mankind, when it loses its mooring in God, falls prey to the most arbitrary consequences. The 'reason' of the individual, in fact, can from case to case propose the most different, the most unforeseeable and the most dangerous ends. And what looks like 'liberation' turns into its opposite and shows its diabolic visage in deeds. Actually, all this has already been described with precision in the first pages of the Bible. The core of the temptation for man and of his fall is contained in this programmatic statement: 'You will be like God' (Gen 3:5). Like God: that means free of the law of the Creator, free of the laws of nature herself, absolute lord of one's own destiny. Man continually desires only one thing: to be his own creator and his own master. But what awaits us at the end of this road is certainly not Paradise."

Note

1. Unpublished address in Bogota.

On the Other Hand . . .

John Mahoney, S.J.

This article originally appeared in *New Blackfriars* in 1985.

On the opening day of the Second Vatican Council Pope John XXIII explained that the function of the Council was not just to preserve intact the treasures of Catholic doctrine. It was to be seen also as responding 'with enthusiasm and without fear' to the demands of society and the expectations of Christians by giving 'richer and deeper' expression to that doctrine. In so doing it would inspire and inform men's minds more fully and in a manner suited to a magisterium whose nature was primarily pastoral.[1] On the day before the Council closed Pope Paul VI began his reform of the Roman Curia by changing the name of the Sacred Congregation of the Holy Office to that of the Sacred Congregation for the Doctrine of the Faith with the commission 'to safeguard doctrine on faith and morals throughout the Catholic world'.[2] The purpose of drawing attention to these two events is not to make a cheap point about progress versus reaction. It is, rather, to highlight two indispensable characteristics of the Church, as of most societies in history, that of continuing fidelity to its inspiration and objective, and that of continual positive response to changing circumstances for the purpose of better achieving its objective. The Sacred Congregation for the Doctrine of the Faith exists in the Vatican to serve the former purpose. No permanent organ exists in the Church to serve the latter.

That is one reason why there is an inevitable onesidedness in the account of the Church presented by Cardinal Ratzinger. It could scarcely be otherwise from the Prefect of the CDF, who, whatever status is to be accorded his interview, is professionally charged with a cautious and conservationist role in the Church's life, and who is therefore committed to alerting the papacy and the Church to dangers and to the debit side in any theological auditing of the Church's books. In the nature of the case, the CDF is concerned more with debit than with credit, with delations more than with successful developments, with the anxiety and gloom more than with the joy and the hope contrasted in the opening phrases of the Council's Pastoral Constitution on the Church in Today's World. Indeed, if there were a Sacred Congregation for the doctrine of hope the account could be a markedly different one.

Even given such a partial perspective, however, and the need for a credit column in order to produce properly balanced accounts, it is important also to scrutinize individual entries in Cardinal Ratzinger's debit column, and to enquire whether they are not, rather, areas in which attempts were made at the Council and subsequently to provide Catholic doctrine with that richer and deeper expression which Pope John XXIII regarded as pastorally required of the Council and therefore also of the post-Conciliar Church. Three areas about which Cardinal Ratzinger expresses disquiet concern the salvation of non-Christians (5–7), developments in moral theology (20, 25–26) and episcopal activity within the Church (34–38). In considering these in turn our aim is not to refute the Cardinal, but to try to indicate how what some can view as crises inducing alarm and despondency can also be considered in more balanced and biblical terms as points of 'judgment' at which the Church is challenged to reflection in these days and which present evidence of positive growth in Catholic doctrine at least as much as of alarming decline.

Salvation in Christ

Study of the history of the Church's attitude to unbelievers makes it difficult to comprehend Cardinal Ratzinger's remarks on this subject. To describe as a long-standing 'traditional doctrine' and one 'taken for granted without any fuss', as he does (5), the idea that salvation is possible outside the visible Church to anyone who follows his conscience is a strange reading of the assiduity with which Councils and Popes for centuries wielded the grim verdict of Cyprian, third-century bishop of Carthage, that 'there is no salvation outside the Church'. Indeed, in his 1972 study *Das neue Volk Gottes*. *Entwürfe zur Ekklesiologie,* in a chapter on the history and possible interpretation of Cyprian's maxim, Joseph Ratzinger made no claim for such a 'traditional' Church doctrine, attempting only, with partial success, to mitigate the actual historical application of *extra ecclesiam nulla salus.*[3] It could scarcely be otherwise, given the teaching of the seventh-century Council of Toledo and the twelfth-century Creed prescribed for the Waldensians, which taught this doctrine without qualification, as did Pope Innocent III's Fourth Council of the Lateran in its declaration that 'there is one universal Church of the faithful, outside which absolutely no-one is saved'.[4] Boniface VIII's famous Bull *Unam Sanctam* and the Council of Florence were to follow suit.[5] Pope Gregory XVI described freedom of conscience as absurd, and condemned as depraved the view that salvation was obtainable by any profession of faith so long as it required a good moral life.[6]

The first official chink in the doctrine appears to be the acknowledgement by Pope Pius IX last century that invincible ignorance coupled with observance of the natural law and a readiness to obey God could lead to eternal life; although even this appears grudging alongside the 'error' rejected in his *Syllabus* that 'at least there is good hope for the eternal salvation of all those who are not included in the true Church of Christ'.[7] Almost a century later the Holy Office repeated the saving clause of invincible ignorance, but it now elaborated Pius IX's 'readiness to obey God' into an 'implicit wish or desire' to be incorporated into the visible Church. In this the Holy Office was taking its cue from Pope Pius XII's encyclical *Mystici Corporis,* which explained that such individuals were in fact related to the Body of Christ by 'an unconscious wish or desire'. Thus the way was prepared for Vatican II to repeat the teaching in the context of the salvation of non-Christians, as distinct from its much more positive breakthrough on the means to salvation actually present in other Christian Churches.[8]

Several points may be noted about this very recent development in Catholic doctrine, which Cardinal Ratzinger goes on to

describe as being onesidedly and improperly radicalised by catch-
phrases such as 'anonymous Christianity' (5). The last remark refers, of course, to the well-known thesis of his fellow-German Karl
Rahner, with whom Joseph Ratzinger did not always see eye to eye
and whom one may presume he had in mind in his broader treatment of 'anonymous Christians' elsewhere, in observing that 'the
Jansenists were not wrong in every respect when they accused the
Jesuits of leading the world to unbelief with their theories'.[9] What
is of more significance, however, is that in the course of only the
last thirty years the understanding of the traditional doctrine,
which the Holy Office had described as 'an infallible statement',[10]
of no salvation outside the visible Roman Catholic Church has
moved from viewing it as an absolute moral requirement calling for
compliance from all men on pain of damnation, with occasional
exceptions acknowledged only since Pius IX, to a positive theological explanation of how it is that salvation in Christ can possibly
come about in the case of all those who actually are saved 'outside
the Church'. It is not just a case of W.S. Gilbert's reluctant conces-
sion, 'What never? Well, hardly ever'. It denotes a radical shift in
our understanding of the means of salvation for the majority of
mankind and of the nature of the Church. There is a growing
appreciation of the generous extent of the saving grace of Christ in
history and in culture, and at the same time, as a result, a fresh
awareness of the nature and function of the Church as its most
visible realization. In other words, the former narrow focus of
Catholic theological concentration on the Church which Christ
founded has given way, through a deeper appreciation of history
and culture to a wide-angled consideration of the redemption of
mankind brought about in and by Christ, and to the place of his
Church within that cosmic panorama. The visible Church is no
longer seen in purely 'container' terms, the solitary Noah's ark of
salvation as the only possible refuge from a surrounding flood of
original and actual sins, as Cyprian and others after him were to
conceive it. It is more the tip of the iceberg of redeemed humanity;
or an outcropping on the surface of history of human beings' response to the grace of God in Christ which underlies the world in
every age and culture. As such it is to be discerned here and there
in varying degrees of human response, and it is most evidently and

most richly capable of expression in the visible communion of Christ's disciples. The visible Church is thus a disclosure to the world of the nature and destiny of mankind in God's providence for him, the reference point of humanity's self-understanding and self-acceptance in God's work of creation. All human beings are related to this Church, not as the narrow gate through which they must pass in order to achieve salvation, but as the sacrament of redeemed humanity.

To this deepened appreciation of the inherently sacramental function of the Church which was launched by the Council,[11] and which contains such immense pastoral riches, Cardinal Ratzinger makes only the slightest of references, and that in his concern to inculcate obedience to the hierarchy (16). His other concern is the resulting 'decline in missionary impetus' (5) to which he regards such a view of salvation as leading. It might be remarked, *ad hominem,* that a similar danger arises from his own appeal to a 'traditional doctrine' of the real possibility of salvation outside the visible Church, however this is to be explained theologically. Both approaches to the salvation of the non-Christian, in fact, call in question the motivation for missionary activity, but neither calls missionary activity itself in doubt. And it may be observed that much of the alarmist 'crisis' language in the Church appears to arise from a confusion between questioning and doubting received doctrine, as if seeking fresh and deeper understanding of the meaning and implications of a particular doctrine which will satisfy and inspire modern man, as Pope John hoped for from a pastoral Council, were tantamount to dismissing it as of no significance.

In his ignoring of other major faiths, to concentrate on animistic religions as 'of course' containing seeds of truth but as more productive of 'a world of fear' (7), by contrast with Christian 'oases of humanity' (6), the Cardinal's map is rather selectively drawn. The history of Christian Europe, to go no further afield, shows that the practice of Christianity cannot exempt it from Lucretius' verdict on the ills often attendant upon religion. And as regards more recent times it is perhaps salutary to recall Paul VI's observation on reforming the Holy Office, formerly the Roman and Universal Inquisition, that 'since charity casts out fear (1 Jn 4:18), the safeguarding of the faith is now better served by the office of promoting doctrine'.[12] There is still, moreover, a tendency to consider such promotion as exclusively a European export-drive rather than as also in large measure a programme in self-help and indigenous development. The balance between the two is, of course, a delicate one, but, if it is not to decline towards a cultural manichaeism, it is one which must not devalue the insight which the Council provided in its appreciation of 'the good and the true' to be found among non-Christians in whom grace is invisibly at work 'as a hidden presence of God'.[13] Nor can it ignore the Council's own Decree on Missionary Activity when it states that 'whatever good is found as sown in men's minds and hearts or in their particular rituals and cultures . . . is healed, enhanced and brought to completion' by such activity.[14] In thus espousing a view of God's continuing 'good' work of creation at the very roots of humanity the Council, and much post-conciliar theology, can be seen as making a bid to recover the patristic theology of God's Word sown and burgeoning throughout creation from the overlay of subsequent Augustinian anthropology which was for centuries to have melancholy consequences for Europe, and therefore for its missionary theology. A genuinely incarnational missionary activity should ever seek to disclose and reveal the God who is love as already tugging at men's hearts and minds, as Paul did at Athens (Acts 17:22–34), and should aim to bring those intimations to fuller voice and expression in the incarnate Word, thus in the process revealing man to himself. Not only is it thus more theologically satisfying, in recognizing the continuity between God's work of creation and salvation as culminating in Christ, but it is also more appreciative of humanity's inherent resources and dignity wherever these are to be encountered.

INDICTMENT OF MORAL THEOLOGIANS

Such positive acknowledgement of the 'human', with which Cardinal Ratzinger appears disenchanted, is of a piece with the Council's general programme of a 'new humanism' for the Church which it was trying to articulate in other areas of doctrine also, including its moral teaching.[15] So far as concerns moral theology itself, as it had existed between the Council and in the memories of the Council Fathers, there can be no gainsaying the bill of indictment brought in by the Council in singling moral theology out among all the theological disciplines as in need of 'special care' for improvement.[16] To describe the attempts of much subsequent moral theology, and of some of its best exponents in Europe and North America, to meet this conciliar mandate as 'liberation' from Christian ethics, especially from the traditional presentation of sexual ethics (20), is to beg a whole range of questions in a way which can only sound offensive to many, particularly when this charge is expanded in sweeping terms in the Cardinal's overview of the 'crisis' as it is to be encountered on the North American scene (26). Some appreciation is shown for the difficulties encountered in presenting the values of the Gospel in an educated modern society, although whether this is peculiar to the United States—or whether the description of American society is a fair one—is arguable. It is not clear what point is being made in the observation that moral issues are to the fore on the American theological scene and moral theology more active than in Europe, by contrast with exegetical and dogmatic studies, in which Europe has a clear lead. The comparison does scant justice to the distinguished moral theologians who are developing their subject on the European Continent (and who continue to have an important influence on moral theology in the United States), as well as to the important contributions of American and Canadian scholarship to biblical studies and the various branches of doctrinal studies. The introduction of theological league tables cannot be to disapprove of the attempt to renew moral theology in the United States, but it might be to imply that in the U.S. moral theology is biblically and dogmatically unbalanced or deficient. This could then help to explain the difficulty experienced there in presenting 'true' Catholic ethics, especially on contraception and other sexual matters, as having a genuine foundation. It might also explain why, when moral theology is then torn between confronting American society and confronting the Church's magisterium, 'many of the better-known moralists' choose to compromise with American society and its pseudo-liberating values.

However one attempts to understand it, and even as a personal view of the Prefect of the CDF, this is a remarkably sweeping description to present to first the Italian and then the German public of the condition of the Catholic Church in the United States and of moral theology within that Church, neither of them possessed of any redeeming features. To redress so pessimistic an imbalance two points may be briefly considered. One is, of course, the accuracy of recognizing that Catholic moral theology is today in need, and in search, of secure foundations. The question which this raises, however, is where those foundations are to be found upon which a moral theology honestly addressing the challenges of a new era to Christian discipleship can be constructed, and to what extent moral theology is to enlist the resources of the Bible, the Church (including its magisterium) and contemporary thought and society, none of which in itself is completely adequate for the purpose. In the Cardinal's strictures a confrontation is set up between the magisterium and society, with a theologically weak moral theology forced to choose between them. And it appears that the moral experience and reflection of the Church is taken to be co-terminous with its Magisterium in ways which the Council would not have recognized. Could it not be, however, that the role of moral theology within the Church is more positively an intermediary one between the Gospel values and modern culture? The Council chose a positive and collaborative role for the Church as a whole in relation to society, in observing that although the Church could draw general moral and religious principles from the Word of God which it safeguarded it does not always have a ready answer to particular questions as they arise, wishing to combine the light of revelation with humanity's own resources so that light could be thrown on the road on which mankind has recently embarked.[17] If some such role is considered appropriate to moral theologians in order to help the Church give richer and deeper expression to its moral doctrine in dialogue with society, the inevitable occupational hazard of such attempts to mediate is not only the danger of inclining too much to one side but the risk of being badly misunderstood by one or other side, depending to some extent on the preoccupations and presuppositions of the various parties.

The other confrontation which Cardinal Ratzinger sets up is, of course, that between 'many of the better-known moralists' in the United States and the Church's magisterium, and here one might have looked for a more sympathetic and theological approach from a contributor to the work of the International Theological Commission in such areas as the relationship between theologians and the magisterium and the increasingly urgent subject of pluralism. Could it not be that one function of moral theologians is to contribute to exploring the very doctrine of the Church's magisterium in moral matters, as many have done in the United States in the aftermath of *Humanae Vitae?* And, more generally, to exercise a mediating role between the hierarchical magisterium and the others of Christ's faithful? Such would appear to be the role envisaged by the Council in its recognition of the positive function of theologians within the whole Church as it assesses modern society and seeks a deeper understanding and more effective expression of revealed truth.[18]

BISHOPS IN THE CHURCH

Cardinal Ratzinger, however, appears to be of the view that not only many moral theologians but also some bishops have made too much of *rapprochement* with society and would have done better to choose a longer spoon, as is evident from the final section of his interview. What appears to emerge also here is an underlying lack of confidence in corporate activity within the Church. The Cardinal's comments (36) on the blandness and lack of evangelical "bite" which he considers inevitably characterise corporate, as contrasted with individual, statements are not such, presumably, as he would apply to the documents of the Council itself (at which he was a *peritus*) or, for that matter, to the publications of the Roman Curia, including his own Congregation. There is good scriptural evidence for Paul having taken counsel in formulating his preaching of the Gospel of Christ. And, of course, the slowly developing practice of episcopal collegiality as a context for papal teaching appears to be at variance with the sentiments here expressed. It appears that the equilibrium between community and individual on which he considers the Church relies must be firmly weighted in favour of strong individuals if one is to avoid 'well-intentioned human prudence' from episcopal bureaucrats.

But they must now be strong individuals of a certain kind, not like those bishops appointed in the years immediately following the Council according to the new criterion of 'openness to the world' (34) who have proved inadequate to later developments and to the 'crisis of 1968' (including, presumably, *Humanae Vitae*). Such sentiments inevitably raise a host of questions. How came it that the majority of the Council's bishops not apparently noted for their openness to the world could produce The Church in the Modern World? Who are the later unfortunates who have been found wanting (and by whom?) in evangelical 'salt' to combat a changed society? And how true is it that appeasement and weak compromise are characteristics of meetings of episcopal conferences (37)?

The Cardinal's championing of individual bishops against intimidation and faceless bureaucracy on the part of episcopal conferences raises perhaps the most important theological issue in his entire interview, notably in his insistence (35) that episcopal conferences 'are not based on theological foundations, as is the office of the individual bishop, but on practical functional considerations'. It is interesting, therefore, to contrast this categorical assertion with the article in *Concilium* written by Joseph Ratzinger in 1965, in which he explained:

> Let us dwell for a moment on the bishops' conferences for these seem to offer themselves today as the best means of concrete plurality in unity. They have their prototype in the synodal activity of the regionally different 'colleges' of the ancient Church. They are also a legitimate form of the collegiate structure of the Church. One not infrequently hears the opinion that the bishops' conferences lack all theological basis and could therefore not act in a way that would be binding on an individual bishop. The concept of collegiality, so it is said, could be applied only to the common action of the entire episcopate. Here again we have a case where a one-sided and unhistorical systematization breaks down.

The *suprema potestas in universam ecclesiam* which canon 228, 1 ascribes to the ecumenical council applies, of course, only to the college of bishops as a whole in union with the bishop of Rome. But is it always a question of the *suprema potestas* in the Church? Would this not be very sharply reminiscent of the disciples' quarrel about their rank?

We would rather say that the concept of collegiality, besides the office of unity which pertains to the pope, signifies an element of variety and adaptability that basically belongs to the structure of the Church, but may be actuated in many different ways. The collegiality of bishops signifies that there should be in the Church (under and in the unity guaranteed by the primacy) an ordered plurality. The bishops' conferences are, then, one of the possible forms of collegiality that is here partially realized but with a view to the totality.[19]

Now, however, Cardinal Ratzinger considers that the individual bishop is 'weaker rather than stronger' in discharging that responsibility for his diocese which is given to him alone and not to the local conference (35). But what is meant by 'weaker rather than stronger' here? It appears that what is at issue in any theological consideration of the topic is the interaction between power, jurisdiction and pastoral effectiveness. And light may be thrown on this by another work of Joseph Ratzinger, his Commentary on the *Prefatory Note* to the Council's Constitution on the Church. In this he observes of the relationship of the power of episcopal ordination to the power of jurisdiction that it is 'one of the thorniest legal and constitutional problems in all the history of the Church, one that is at the same time crucial in theology'.[20] He was writing in the immediate context of the relationship between the college of bishops and the Pope as explained in the Council's Constitution and the *Prefatory Note,* and he was addressing objections of a possible arbitrariness on the part of a Pope in acting 'according to his own discretion' and 'as he chooses'.[21] Ratzinger's counter-argument was that such juridical discretion was not absolute, but was limited by the phrases in the text: 'the requirements of his office' and 'considering the good of the Church'. He also observed that 'among the claims which his very office makes upon the Pope we must undoubtedly reckon a moral obligation to hear the voice of the Church universal. . . . Juridically speaking, there is no appeal from the Pope . . .; morally speaking, the pope may have an obligation to listen . . .'.[22] And in thus attempting to tease out the juridical tensions which arise from a consideration of collegiality in its entirety (i.e., including the papacy) within the Church, Ratzinger the conciliar theologian had occasion to add that collegiality is 'designed to recall the fact that the Church is essentially plural, is a *communio,* that centralization has its limits, and that ecclesiastical acts at a national or provincial or diocesan level have their importance—collegiate acts, that is, which do not qualify as *actus stricte collegiales.*'[23]

These observations on juridical autonomy and its limitations can cast light on the relationship of the individual bishop to his national or regional episcopal conference in three respects. First, there is the fact, as the earlier Ratzinger acknowledged, that such stages of intermediate collegiality, while falling short of *suprema potestas* in the Church, emerge as being vastly more than a useful sharing of episcopal experiences or than an overstructured bureaucracy, as Cardinal Ratzinger now alleges (35). Given that the Church is essentially *communio,* centralization certainly has its limits, as Ratzinger the theologian explained, but it is a mentality of diocesan centralization almost as much as Roman centralization which can impede truly collegial activity. And here Ratzinger's comment in his *Concilium* article is pertinent in explaining how the concept of collegiality refers to something which 'basically belongs to the structure of the Church' and which can be 'actuated in many different ways', including the way of episcopal conferences.

A second conclusion is that the individual bishop's exercise of episcopal jurisdiction in his diocese can be subject to moral considerations, as Ratzinger showed even of the papacy. But it may be that moral and juridical considerations should not be so sharply divided as this implies. For, thirdly, and perhaps most importantly for a deepened theology of jurisdiction in the Church, some 'moral' considerations may not be just extrinsic factors mitigating a too unilateral but nevertheless legitimate exercise of jurisdiction.

They may be actually intrinsic to the notion of jurisdiction itself. As Ratzinger observed, on the Prefatory Note, even papal jurisdiction is not unlimited, but is inherently qualified in its content by the 'requirements of the office' and by 'considering the good of the Church'. Thus in every case the good of the Church, which itself dictates the requirements of any office, appears actually to determine the content of the jurisdiction which is possessed, rather than simply morally qualifying its exercise.

The further crucial question which then arises is, the good of what Church? And it is here that the developing theology of the local Church is of such importance. The Council understood 'local' in terms of the diocese.[24] Many considerations today, however, call in serious question the pastoral efficacy of the diocese as a 'unit' in the Church, particularly when, as in England and Wales, it can lead to differing pastoral approaches to issues which are experienced as transcending diocesan boundaries by a Catholic community increasingly aware of its identity in the country as a whole and impatient of anything approaching ecclesiastical bailiwicks. No diocese today is an island; and the 'good of the Church' identifiable at regional or national level calls for an identifying and exercise of collegial jurisdiction at that level. Jurisdiction was made for the Church. *Salus populi Dei suprema lex;* the salvation of God's people is the highest law. Here is the ultimate 'theological foundation' for episcopal conferences, which Cardinal Ratzinger is at pains now to deny.

It is interesting to note how the three themes of the Cardinal's interview which have been considered here all turn out to centre on the Church, whether as viewing its function within God's will that all men be saved and come to know the truth (1 Tim 2:4), or in its moral teaching and the status of its *magisterium,* or in its localization in dioceses and nations as well as in Rome. It is interesting and perhaps revealing to note also how each of these themes can be expressed in alarmed tones as instances of those "centrifugal forces" within the Church which the Cardinal considers have come to the fore and are in large part responsible for 'the misfortunes that the Church has encountered in the last twenty years' (4). For it is at least equally possible to view such 'center-fleeing' forces as indicating a long-overdue expansion of the whole Church's awareness and of its concern to embrace mankind in all its universality and in its every particularity. Within such a perspective the Church's traditional doctrines are then to be seen not as something to be jealously, or even fearfully preserved intact but sterile against the return of a 'hard' Lord (cf. Mt 25:24). They are the patrimony which the Church is called upon in every age, and never more than today, to strive to express more richly and deeply, as Pope John hoped, in order to make the Church's magisterium a truly pastoral one.

Notes

1. *AAS* 54 (1962), pp. 791—92. This was Pope John's famous 'prophets of doom' speech.

2. 'cuius munus est doctrinam de fide et moribus in universo catholico orbe tutari', *AAS* 57 (1965), p. 954.

3. J. Ratzinger, *Das neue Volk Gottes. Entwürfe zur Ekklesiologie.* Dusseldorf, 1972, pp. 152–177.

4. 'Una vero est fidelium universalis Ecclesia, extra quam nullus omnino salvatur', *DS* 802. Cf. *DS* 575, 792. For Cyprian, cf. *PL* 3, 1123–24; 4, 503–504.

5. *DS* 870, 1351.

6. *DS* 2731.

7. *DS* 2866–67, 2917.

8. *DS* 3869–70, 3821; *Lumen Gentium* (= *LG*), 16.

9. In supra, n. 3, p. 168, n. 30.

10. *DS* 3866.

11. Cf. *LG* 9, 48; *Gaudium et Spes* (= *GS*), 45; etc.

12. In supra, n. 2, p. 953.

13. *LG* 16; *GS* 22; *Ad Gentes* (= *AG*), 9; *Optatam Totius* (= *OT*), 16.

14. *AG* 9.

15. Cf. *GS* 11, 40.

16. *OT* 16.

17. *GS* 33; cf. 62.

18. *GS* 44.

19. J. Ratzinger, 'The Pastoral Implications of Episcopal Collegiality', *Concilium: Dogma*, no. 1 (1965), p. 30. Repeated in the German n. 3 supra, p. 67.

20. J. Ratzinger, 'Announcements and Prefatory Notes of Explanation', in H. Vorgrimler (ed.), *Commentary on the Documents of Vatican II*, Herder, 1967, vol. 1, p. 300.

21. Ibid., pp. 303–304. Cf *LG* 22, and *Nota praevia*, nn. 3–4.

22. Vorgrimler, p. 304.

23. Ibid.

24. The outstanding conciliar statement on the local Church appears like a comet in *LG* 26. Rahner explains, in Vorgrimler (n. 20 supra, p. 216), that this was a late interpolation to meet complaints of a too one-sidedly "universal" treatment of the Church. Cf. also Rahner, *Theological Investigations*, vol. 10, London, 1973, pp. 9–11 and (on Ratzinger's charge that Rahner is extremely radical on the local Church) p. 101, n. 27.

Teaching Morality: The Tension Between Bishops and Theologians Within the Church

Joseph Fuchs, S.J.

This article originally appeared in *Christian Ethics in a Secular Arena*, 1984.

It is no secret that a certain tension exists between representatives of the Church's magisterium and representatives of scientific theology. This is indicated not only by occasional single incidents that attract notice, but also and much more by a rich theological literature on the specific theoretical and pastoral problematic. As was the case some decades ago with exegesis, it is moral theology that is today particularly affected. The fact that the American book series "Readings in Moral Theology" has seen fit to dedicate its third extensive yearly volume to the theme "The Magisterium and Morality" (1982), is eloquent.[1] Those who follow the copious "Notes on Moral Theology" which appear each year in the American Jesuit periodical *Theological Studies* will testify that this tension has been mentioned repeatedly in recent years. We are here referring not only to the magisterium of the Bishop of Rome and of his Vatican Congregations, but also to the teaching authority of the bishops in moral questions in general. This essay will deal particularly with the many bishops, scattered in various lands.

Ideally, the activity of bishops and moral theologians ought to display cooperation and a turning to each other for help; certainly, this does exist, yet it is impossible to overlook the tension that today is an extensive and worldwide fact. Bishops show skepticism; they believe that they ought basically to be suspicious about moral theologians—in general, because of the moral-theological method, and in special individual questions. Moral theologians feel that they are not taken seriously; their experience is that their research, endeavors, and results are met with reserve, and that indeed on occasion doubt arises and is expressed about the purity of their scholarly and ecclesiastical motives. Correspondingly, there is a certain suspicion on the part of moral theologians about the episcopal magisterium, in whose utterances the theological endeavors of moral theologians frequently are either not reflected at all or else, as we have said, are judged skeptically.

In the title of this essay, bishops and moral theologians are named intentionally without the article "the." For not all bishops are meant: there are also bishops who see and take very seriously the problematic of today's moral theology; there are some who say this openly, and some who occasionally admit it "tacitly." In the same way, not all moral theologians are meant: there are also some who are readily heard "above" because they take a skeptical stance before the problematic of today's moral theology and speak indeed from a position of defense, for they do not tackle the problems that arise today in the same way as their colleagues (as is their full right). These are able to give bishops the replies that some of them knew all the time anyway, and would be glad to see confirmed.

From what has been said so far, it follows that this essay speaks not only of bishops in their relationship to moral theologians, but also of a certain group of moral theologians, priests and laypeople, who for one reason or another do not accept their reflections, hypotheses and results of contemporary moral theology. But the primary subject here is the teaching authority of the bishops, which has a particular weight in the Church's moral teaching. Some of what is said here can be applied by analogy to other members of the Church in their relationship to today's moral theology or to certain of its representatives. The chief basic concern of this article, however, is not so much the correct relationship between episcopal magisterium and moral-theological scholarship, as rather concern about a correct Christian ethos and a genuine ethic of Christians' conduct in today's world, an ethic free or set free both from anxieties and from libertinism, i.e., an ethic that seeks to encounter and respond to the great and small problems of every

day with judicious objectivity, in the greatest possible independence of the presuppositions of one side or the other. The greatest
possible "objectivity"—that is our cue.

I.

CHRISTIAN MISSION AND CONCERN

The theologian who speaks on the theme of "bishops and
moral theologians" must necessarily begin by reflecting on the
mission and corresponding concern of the bishops. For their mission generates corresponding concerns; and these concerns will, or
can, easily determine the behavior of the bishops. The theologian
who cannot think himself into the situation of the bishops ought
not to express himself on this theme. Nevertheless, he cannot
avoid recalling his own mission and the concern that is generated
from it. We have here different missions and concerns, which,
however, serve the same end: that is, they are complementary and
supplement one another.

1. The Bishops' Function of Establishing Unity. The Christian
ecclesial body is a fellowship of those who follow Christ in freedom, as a fellowship of believers bound together in the Church—
hence, as a unity. The bishops are understood and respected as
those who maintain and care for unity as bearers of a corresponding mission. The bishops themselves must, and do, understand
themselves as bearers of this mission. This self-understanding is
the basis of their endeavor and of their care for the community of
Christians which understands itself as an ecclesial unity.

It is beyond doubt that the bishops have their particular "function" within the ecclesial community of the believers. They will see
their function as one of bearing concern and striving so that the
ecclesial community of Christians as such "functions." There exists,
however, the danger that they will identify the ideal with an attitude
in moral questions that is as free as possible from tension; an attitude that is uncritical, consciously "conformist," not pluralistic,
bound to tradition, and remaining aloof from the probing critical
questionings of "others"; and that they will encourage a life lived in

such an attitude. The use of the word "danger" here does intend to call into question the values of such an attitude; but it could be an attitude that contains an unnecessarily burdensome alignment of one's life, that fundamentally has little to recommend it.

The bishops' function of establishing unity is directed to the faith of the Christian community. The Second Vatican Council speaks explicitly of a faith that must be "applied" in Christian living.[2] Doubtless, Christian (moral) living has to do with faith; but there exists the danger that, for the sake of the unity and immutability of the Christian faith, one would wish to teach and proclaim a unity, uniformity, and immutability, grounded in this faith, of moral directives. Faith indeed has its importance for the establishment of moral modes of behavior, but by itself it does not make this establishing possible. This is what is meant by the teaching on natural law which is based in the Bible and in the Church's tradition. When the Second Vatican Council observes that in some cases even believing Christians with the same degree of conscientiousness can come to different solutions to significant human questions (hence, to moral questions),[3] this shows that the bishops' function of establishing unity in moral questions is not unlimited because of the one faith.

The bishops who are concerned and bear the heavy burden of their responsibility know that they are one part of a greater ecclesial community, and know that they are under obligation to this greater unity. For their teaching about Christian morality in accord with the Christian faith, they will seek the support of Christian tradition, of the teaching of other Christian communities and their bishops, and, in a special measure, of the direction of the Bishop of Rome as a basic foundation stone of Christian unity (and hence also of Christian moral teaching) and of his Vatican Congregations. And this is right, to avoid there being as many Christian communities with their own individual moral teaching as there are diocesan bishops. But even this self-insurance does not take the whole load off the bishops in their function of establishing unity, for these significant supports are not outside history, nor are they realities wholly raised above the process of evaluating and establishing.

If the bishops are concerned with the right functioning of their communities—in moral persuasion and perhaps also in the moral conduct of life—as indeed they must be so concerned, and as far as possible in fellowship with other Christian ecclesial communities scattered throughout the world, nevertheless functional unity must not be the chief aim of episcopal concern. If one grasps the difference between Christian faith and moral ordinance (even that of Christians), one will understand that a functioning unity in questions of faith is much more significant than a similarly functioning unity in moral questions. Church history also shows that the functioning unity in moral questions by no means implies the truth of the moral perspective taken up in this unity. In other words, the bishops must be more concerned with moral truth than with peaceful consensus in moral questions. For it can also be the case that moral statements, though widely accepted in a well functioning consensus, nevertheless permit freedoms or impose burdens that have no basis in Christian faith, and do not show themselves over a long period of time to be God's will.

2. *The Episcopal Service of Moral Truth.* The episcopal service aims, therefore, not so much at well-functioning unity as at unity in the truth—in the sphere of moral theology too. If more attention had been paid to this in the course of the centuries of the Christian Church, i.e., if *inter alia,* those who called for moral truth had been obeyed rather than the trend toward well-functioning unity, then certain events that we regret today would never have occurred (it is irrelevant whether we choose problems of freedom of conscience and religion, of the defense of unjustified use of force, of concepts in sexual ethics, etc.) This also means that, had one thought more about the question of the truth to be mediated in the case of moral behavioral norms for action in the world, rather than about the mediation of subjective security for the decision-making situations that necessarily arise, then many dramatic instances of conflict would have been avoided.

Naturally, the bishops themselves will feel the possible tension between the requirement that they mediate moral truth and the constantly repeated requirement that they preserve and mediate security for pressing moral decisions. The neo-Scholastic tendencies in theology and in the utterances of the Church's hierarchy—especially before the Second Vatican Council—often served a need for security more than they served the truth and the reasoned establishing of moral decisions. Today there is a frequent lament that this tendency led to an excessively static thinking about natural law, and also to a positivizing of "Christian" moral teaching through frequent interventions of the hierarchical magisterium.[4] If today's theologians—perhaps because they have become more open and more free for essential reflection on the basis of the common work of bishops and theologians at the Second Vatican Council—believe they must point to this factual situation, then the bishops cannot and must not close their eyes to this knowledge; and this allows them to experience the potential dilemma of security/truth in a new and different way.

To this extent, the role of the bishops in the sphere of moral questions is not wholly easy. Moral theologians have experienced a compassionate smile, or a smile that came from a security impervious to doubt, as their reward for being true to their tasks as theologians by pointing out genuine problems that were not seen elsewhere. Not infrequently, the theologian remains quiet, in order to escape such a smile or further consequences.

Nevertheless, no one should doubt that bishops wish to serve the truth in the sphere of morality. Is this not precisely why they ask the advice of moral theologians? But one must in turn ask, which moral theologians are consulted, or which advice of the various moral theologians is finally accepted? This often depends on the moral theology of the professor who taught the bishops (a few or many years ago) and whose views they now take (all too positivistically understood) as the "teaching of the Church," since they themselves have mostly been hindered from pursuing further studies in moral theology. This is, however, quite understandable; often there lies behind a concrete tension between bishops and moral theologians ultimately nothing other than the tension between different schools of moral theology. In any case, it is the bishop who bears the official service of the unity of the Church's fellowship; this service of the bishops is onerous, because the service of unity should be a service of unity in truth.

The Second Vatican Council draws the attention of all Christians, including bishops and moral theologians, to the fact that the Church is essentially a pilgrim Church, and therefore in constant need of renewal.[5] This is true also to a certain extent of the sphere of moral teaching. This has above all two consequences here: first, life in history, and especially the high speed of today's life, poses new moral problems, which have to be tackled not only by the moral theologians, but also—in relation to the theologians—by the bishops who are called to the service of unity; the solution of worldwide socioethical problems, the responsible use of atomic power, the position to be taken vis-à-vis bioethical problems of a completely new kind, the correct attitude to quite varied kinds of partnerships similar to marriage, etc. The required renewal in the sphere of moral theology implies, second, the recognition that new knowledge can also demand a rethinking of moral solutions of earlier periods, unless one wishes to take the risk of abdicating the effort of finding a greater objectivity than was possible at other periods, because of the wish for a definitive and "certified" possession of a body of knowledge; we shall return to this point. It is a matter of the episcopal service of unity in truth.

We must draw attention to yet another statement of the Second Vatican Council: namely, that we do not always have an immediate and valid solution ready-made in the Church when new ethical problems are posed.[6] Then the expert scholars must be allowed their say, and the (perhaps) disparate attempts at solutions by ethical philosophers and moral theologians must be taken into account, so that finally it may be possible to offer the service, not of an absolute edict or condemnation, but of a careful, very precisely formulated aid that is supported by well thought out reasons. Such statements, which clearly work toward moral truth, are surely a better service of unity than a definitive word that seeks to mediate a supposedly absolute certainty.

3. The Service of the Moral Theologians. In the first Christian centuries,[7] bishops were very often also the theologians of the Church; that is, they not only had the pastoral office of serving Christian unity in truth, but also undertook the theological work of reflection and of deeper understanding. They did this also in some moral questions. Even today, there are bishops who are theologians in the scholarly sense; but this is not normally the case. Theologians, including moral theologians, are today on the whole not bishops. There is no fundamental necessity for a commissioning by the Church in order to be a theologian. But where and when such a commission is given, it is not understood as a "delegation" of the specifically episcopal ministry or of the bishop's teaching authority; recently, Pope John Paul II, quoting Paul VI, explicitly pointed this out.[8]

Since the Council of Trent, but especially in the last century, a strongly juridical understanding of the magisterium as "demanding assent," has become central; this was not so earlier. According to this understanding, the moral theologian's task should be understood primarily and extensively as the scholarly reflection and confirmation of already existing magisterial directives in moral questions. This is how it is expressed above all in Pius XII's encyclical *Humani generis* (1950).[9] Even today, this understanding is widespread although the Second Vatican Council began to shift the emphasis by its reference to the whole People of God as bearer of the Holy Spirit. In other centuries, bishops and theologians mostly looked to the "teaching authority" (above all, the consensus) of the theologians and theological faculties,[10] but now reflection centers rather around the theme of the episcopal office. Moral theologians are aware of this situation, and work and behave accordingly, even though they often know the recognized limits of the authority of magisterial statements and instructions in moral theology. This situation certainly permits an harmonious and fruitful cooperation of the activity of bishops and moral theologians, as a common service of the People of God.

Experience teaches, however, that the situation just outlined contains dangers. One of these dangers is the tendency, already lamented, to a positivism of the magisterium, a tendency to which many believers and moral theologians, but also bishops, succumb. Such a positivism can hinder the research of moral theology, as well as the living process of the establishment of moral truth; this process is never definitely finished. (One should note that such a positivism can also lead to the one-sided granting of privileged status to one moral-theological school above the others). A second danger (easily verified today) is the encouragement of the belief that we encounter God's instructions, made known through positive revelation, in concrete moral directives (e.g., in concrete statements about social ethics, in concrete comments on questions of war and peace, in documents on sexual ethics, etc.). A third danger is that of cramping or narrowing moral-theological reflection. Finally, one should not overlook the fourth danger, that the situation sketched here is apt to promote a permanent "moral immaturity" in the establishment of moral truth (in L. Kohlberg's sense), or the formation of "superegos" (in Freud's sense)—as one may observe in laypeople, priests, moral theologians, and bishops.

Like other theologians, moral theologians too certainly have a particular authority of their own, whether they practice theology with an official commission (e.g., as professors) or not (even though it is true that the commission represents a certain sign of confidence on the part of the episcopal office). Moral theologians know that they are under obligation to the People of God, especially to the moral will of believing Christians. If publicly practiced theology is always implicitly proclamation, then so is publicly enacted reflection of moral theology. For it is the moral theologian's task in the Church to identify the relationships between ethos and moral ordinance with the faith, to undertake the hermeneutic reading of the Bible in the awareness of moral questions, to read hermeneutically the moral traditions (and their history) that have grown up in the course of time, to deepen and develop moral values, to establish moral principles and norms credibly and contextually, to clarify the significance for correct moral behavior of the findings of other sciences, to tackle newly arising moral problems, etc.

These tasks in the realm of moral theology are all the more important, in that the good, and especially the correct moral behavior of Christians to a great extent does not follow directly from the Christian faith, but must be established in a reasonable reflection and evaluation that is enlightened by faith.

Here we see too that the research of moral theologians serves not only the People of God in general, but in a particular way those who must undertake the episcopal service of unity in truth. The task of moral theologians is therefore not only to seek more deeply the reasons for the teaching that has already been laid down by the magisterium, but also to prepare such a teaching and to make it possible. Responsible episcopal directives cannot be drawn up without a serious listening to what serious moral theology has to say.

How often does one hear that the bishops are challenged to make a clear statement on particular significant moral questions. But do they always already possess the responsible answer that is demanded of them?

But what if some bishops do not trust "the moral theologians"? What if it seems to them that the moral theologians sow "confusion" in the People of God? Generalizations are a bad thing; but there is undeniably an imprudent and irresponsible speaking in public. But where moral theologians do not merely love *le dernier cri,* but work both competently and in awareness of their responsibility, one can ask whether the fear of "dangerous confusion" (which certainly can exist) does not sometimes appear rather as an anxiety that a smoothly functioning operation may be disturbed or, even more fundamentally, as a fear of having to speak and teach more responsibly and more credibly. Ought one not then seek a more intensive and more confident cooperation? The initiatives for this can ultimately proceed from both sides: as John Paul II has said, the theologians too should take initiatives.[11]

It will be seen, then, that tensions are not to be completely excluded. There is a fear of authority that can lead theologians to keep silent, even when they see that by their silence an important service is withheld from the People of God. Moral theologians, too, have a conscience that demands responsible action. Sometimes a still and careful reservation is more effective in the long term than a loud protest: often a careful and steady sowing of good seed by many hands among the People of God produces new insight and new life, even if only very slowly.

But another kind of behavior can suggest itself. In the notorious case of Savonarola, a cardinal publicly admonished the Master of the Sacred Palace, Pier Paolo Giannerini (a Dominican like Savonarola) not to defend Savonarola so energetically, but to defend the Holy See. He received the reply: "My commission is to fight for the truth, and in this way to safeguard the honor of the Holy See."[12] If all dissent in the Church were excluded, nothing could ever be corrected; one thinks, for example, of religious freedom.[13] Some time ago, H. Fries wrote (even though not specifically about moral theologians) that one must require of the theologian "the courage for criticism, for nonconformity" too, "especially when this is not conditioned by the need for prestige and vanity, but by responsibility for the task entrusted to theology."[14] (Must one point out specifically that, like moral theologians, bishops too who share the concerns of moral theologians can get into difficult situations with regard to official episcopal declarations or authoritative decrees?) Several years ago, the Canadian theologian F.E. Crowe, S.J., asked himself publicly whether the theologians' silence about the famous "Washington Case" had not made them guilty of failure to aid the priests and many laypersons affected by it.[15]

If a serious moral-theological attempt to stretch out a helping hand to the People of God runs the risk of creating the apparent impression of "confusion" among Christians who are unprepared or who are concerned about their inherited security, may not the present moment call for a common dialogue between bishops and moral theologians that works to establish insight and mediate understanding? In certain circumstances, however, it may be that what appears as "confusion" is in reality the long overdue beginning of a rethinking.

II.
TEACHING AUTHORITY AND MORAL-THEOLOGICAL PROBLEMATIC

A certain lack of cooperation and a corresponding tension between bishops and moral theologians are determined, *inter alia*, by pressing complexes of moral-theological problems; for neither scholarly moral theology nor ecclesiastical direction can be merely the repetition of what has already been said. It is indeed the case that what is true is always true; but one cannot deduce from this the existence of a block of definitive moral insights, once and for all "possessed" and so "to be handed on," for such a conception would make a mockery of the history of Christianity. In every age there are untruths (errors that are given out as truths), half-truths, attempts at reasoning which fall short, etc., and these challenge to renewed reflection. But, independently of this, man (mankind), and Christian man too, never ceases to reflect on what really exists, on how he leads his life, how he can give content to his life, and how he should make concrete decisions. This is so, simply in that he is a man and a

Christian, but also in that he realizes his humanity and Christianity always under the given circumstances, states of information, and valuations of particular periods and cultures.

The first consequence of this is that within moral theology there always is, and must be, a fresh insight, understanding, evaluation, and judgment. It is readily understandable that not all moral theologians in a particular cultural constellation will agree immediately about everything. Naturally, the situation of the "moral" magisterium in the Church too is affected by this—and is not made easier thereby. A second consequence of what has been said is that bishops who are not themselves active moral theologians can often acquaint themselves only to an insufficient degree with the complex new problems that arise. Thereby their episcopal service of unity in truth becomes harder. It will not be easy to meet this situation of need. In what follows, we shall attempt to expand what has already been said by tackling briefly three acute issues that generate problems in the realm of Catholic moral theology.

1. Moral Goodness and Correctness. The first set of problems which experience shows creates anxiety for many bishops (and other Christians) concerns the possibility (to use a simple formulation) of distinguishing between good and evil. The question that causes concern runs as follows: have not today's moral theologians made it very hard for the Church—the people of the Church and the bishops—to distinguish still, openly and clearly, between good and evil? If this were so, this situation would have to be regarded as very serious. But if it is fundamentally a matter of a different, less significant problem, then one would have to judge otherwise. In fact, not only many believers but also certain moral theologians and indeed many bishops, have not yet sufficiently realized a distinction that has been more clearly worked out in contemporary moral theology than it was in earlier epochs; hence many misunderstandings and anxieties arise.

Here it is the distinction between the concepts good and evil, and the concepts right and wrong, that is insufficiently differentiated and thus often confused; more precisely, it is the distinction between personal goodness and badness, on the one hand (the *person* is good or evil), and the moral rightness and wrongness of behavior in the world, on the other hand (the *behavior* of the personal human being is right or wrong). But since personal goodness or badness is much more oriented toward the act of Christian faith than the right or wrong realization of the world of man, and since the episcopal concern is correspondingly directed primarily to personal moral goodness and only secondarily to morally right behavior in the world, the insufficient distinction between the two spheres can lead to striking misunderstandings and predicaments.

A few years ago, the German translation of the Lord's Prayer (with a sympathetic knowledge of the bishops) altered the petition for deliverance from "evil/sin." The first concern of the Christian who pays heed to his salvation, and of the bishops who care for this salvation, is not freedom from all evil, even from the evil in the world that is caused by man through wrong behavior, but the freedom from *personal moral evil,* from *sin;* that is, to put it positively, a concern for personal moral *goodness.* Without personal moral goodness, i.e., the moral goodness of the person, faith would be without love and life, and hence dead. Relative certainty about right behavior vis-à-vis the goods or values of this world (a good thing—but not necessarily personal goodness) and its difference from humanly wrong conduct (an evil—but not necessarily personal evil), are therefore of great value. Such awareness, as the Christian understands it, is to be sought wherever possible; indeed it has repeatedly been sought in the Christian Church and, with varying success, has been found with sufficient certainty; but it does not determine personal moral goodness. It is not the rightness of our behavior in the world that belongs to the essence of personal moral goodness, but loyal adherence to what one is able to take for the right behavior. Uncertainties about personal moral goodness are essentially different from uncertainties about the rightness of behavior toward the goods of the world.

Believing Christians and their bishops should not allow themselves to be unnecessarily confused by misleading and often polemical laments or accusations; for with regard to the decisive distinction between good and evil—i.e., in the realm of personal morality—there are no uncertainties and divergences of opinion in contemporary moral theology. It is universally acknowledged that one may not act against a responsibly formed conscience; that one must always be morally good in one's decisions and may never be evil; that one should always respect and treat every human being as a person; that one must avoid, as far as possible, innerworldly evils in the realization of the world of man; that in the realization of the innerworldly reality one must proceed in justice, mercy, generosity, chastity, etc. (to the extent that one is able to recognize what justice, chastity, etc. concretely demand); that one may never employ something that is morally disallowed as a means to attain a good goal. It seems to be important to point out this final item, because the representatives of contemporary moral theology are often accused (falsely) of stating the opposite.[16]

As one may understand from the new formulation of the petition of the Lord's Prayer, a different kind of language is required for speaking of the distinction between right and wrong in the realization of the innerworldly reality than is required for speaking of the distinction between good and evil in personal morality. Because this is often overlooked, misunderstandings and "confusions" easily happen. This is all the more astonishing, in that a traditional formulation (even though an unhappy one) teaches the distinction and the possible non-coincidence of "formal" (personal) and "only material" sin. "Only material sin" is, however, a very bad formulation, for sin implies precisely the opposite of personal goodness. "Material sin" means what a better formulation calls, not "sin" at all, but "wrong behavior" in the realization of the innerworldly reality. It is only by analogy to personal moral evil that this wrongness is also called "moral" wrongness (because if one were aware of it—and one is obliged to strive for this awareness—its realization in freedom would represent moral evil, and hence personal sin).

If this is taken into account, if it is truly grasped that the question of "right or wrong" in the realization of the earthly reality of man-society-world is not the primary problematic of personal morality, but the secondary (though also very important) question of what kind of behavior in this earthly reality best corresponds to this human innerworldly reality, then it will perhaps be more easily seen that the solution to the problems of right or wrong behavior in the construction of the world—i.e., to the problem of norms of innerworldly behavior—will be neither easy nor uniform; nevertheless, it is not so urgent that it requires the "absolute," "universal," "*intrinsece malum*" character that applies to the realm of good/evil personal morality.

In concrete living, however, and for practical morality, the question of right/wrong in daily behavior is urgent, since moral goodness demands a striving for the best behavior possible. In the case of the problematic of right/wrong, unlike the more important problematic of good/evil, there are some statements of contemporary moral theology which could at first sight "confuse" one who knows only the moral theology of a particular period (without, however, knowing the variations in the history of moral theology). Where do the causes of such a "confusion" and of a corresponding reservation vis-à-vis today's moral theologians lie? To overcome such a reservation, should one not take the trouble to consider whether it may be possible to come to an understanding in some fundamental statements?

We may take as examples the following statements. 1. The pluriformity and mutability of earthly and historical realities have led in the past to judgments about the moral rightness of concrete behavior that were not the same in all periods. To take only one example in a field that oddly enough is repeatedly of prominent concern, sexual ethics: recent studies seem to establish that, on the one hand, intercourse within marriage, if practiced out of motives other than procreation, was for centuries held to be a sin, while the phenomenon of masturbation, unlike many other questions in sexual ethics, was not dealt with by moral theologians for about the first five centuries.

2. As Thomas Aquinas emphasized, it is a mistake to think that concrete actions can be completely resolved through the application of abstract norms (and not through the "*extensio*" that implies new insight).

3. The lack of sufficient explanations of the reasons for norms of behavior, i.e., the inability to make them comprehensible, can cause doubts about the rightness of such norms. This problem arose, for example, in the *propositiones* presented to the Pope at the 1980 Synod of Bishops in the case of two important problems

(contraception and the reception of the sacraments by divorced and remarried persons).

4. The well-known appeal to the "nature of the case" for particular norms can help bring about recognition of the structure of man (as personal, interpersonal, etc.) and the "laws of nature" (physiology, psychology, physics and chemistry, the finalities of nature, etc.). Yet the "nature" of particular realities cannot, as such, be the measure applied to discover right behavior. This measure is rather human reason, which examines the data of nature in the whole context of man's personal reality and thus can make a normative judgment about right human behavior. The false conclusion *ex natura rei* has long been denounced by many ethicists, and this has been more and more acknowledged even within Catholic moral theology, but it can still be found in statements in the Church's magisterium, and limits their credibility within and outside the Church's fellowship.

5. The problematic of the universal validity and applicability of humanly formulated norms of behavior should be recognized as a serious problematic. If one cannot go along with the "naturalistic fallacy" of the "*ex natura rei,*" one must argue teleologically through consideration of innerworldly (and thus not absolute) goods and ills of man's personal world. This does not totally exclude the possibility of coming to universal negative norms of behavior ("*intrinsece malum*"), but only on condition that one takes appropriate account of all the given, and even possible, morally relevant objectives, effects, and circumstances in them, for only thus is there a guarantee of full objectivity and universality. This presupposition is fulfilled only if further possible elements in a formulation are excluded (e.g., "do not kill, *only* because it pleases someone so," "do not pay an insufficient wage, *only* for the sake of one's own enrichment," the rightness of a particular act, e.g., the payment of a family wage, "in the given situation *at the present moment*", etc.). The many norms of behavior which are not formulated thus can give significant practical help, but scarcely exclude the theoretical possibility that further additional and morally relevant elements, if these have not already been sufficiently taken into consideration, may determine a

different judgment of moral rightness, and this can have effects *in praxi* too.

   2. Faith and Morals. A second set of problems is closely connected to the first. Christian faith has much to contribute to the question of the Christian's personal moral goodness, but questions of the rightness of innerworldly behavior do not have the same support from faith. This means that one who feels obliged to cast doubts upon certain concrete moral behavioral norms that are maintained in the Church does not thereby sin directly against his faith. Yet we constantly hear that Christians are bound by the fact of their being Christians to particular norms of behavior. This could be taken to mean that these norms in the whole of their content have their basis in Christian faith. Bishops must protect not only themselves, but their faithful, too, from such an error.

   In accordance with the tradition of moral theology, in point of fact, it is not the Christian faith, but the *recta ratio* (the right judgment of reason) that is the norm of behavior in the world. This "*recta*" *ratio* must be established through the human "*ratio*" (reason), and this reason, in order not to stray all too easily from the "*recta ratio*" (truth), receives help (according to Vatican II) through "the light of the gospel"; thus it is always still reason itself, "illuminated", it is true, "by the faith", and not simply the Christian faith itself that must establish what constitutes right behavior in this world. This is basically the traditional teaching of the natural moral law (even though this has not always been understood in the same sense). If there is discussion today among moral theologians about "ethics of faith" and "autonomous moral theology in the Christian context," the bishops should think not so much of Kant but of Christian teaching about natural law, when they hear the words "*autonomous* moral theology." It is rather the concept "ethics of *faith*" that should make the bishops concerned about the loss of the Christian teaching on natural law that tradition has maintained. This is not opposed to the fact that the establishment of what is morally right always takes place within the one act of Christian faith.[17]

   I am grateful to Hans Urs von Balthasar's *Theology of History* (published many years before his *Nine Theses on Christian Ethics* were published by Joseph Ratzinger in 1975) for the idea that the moral *ratio recta* of the moral natural law is based more deeply in Jesus Christ than in the *ratio* itself.[18] In this sense, a *recta ratio* exists for us finally within personal faith in Jesus Christ.

But because human reason (even that of Christians) can make judgments about moral behavior only under human and historical conditions and so only with "moral certainty," it frequently happens, for example, in episcopal statements, that the supposedly "more certain" appeal back to the Bible occurs, whether to the Ten Commandments, to the Sermon on the Mount, or to Paul. It is here that one hopes to find definitive certainty, or rather, security. But how justified is this?

When the ecclesial document, *Persona humana,* on certain questions of sexual ethics was published in 1975, certain German moral theologians lamented that its uncritical and hermeneutically unsatisfactory treatment of scriptural texts was no longer defensible by scholars today. When H. Schürmann made his contribution as an exegete, in the booklet of J. Ratzinger already mentioned, to the defense of an "ethics of faith,"[19] his final argument was that the words of the Lord and of scripture can demand only an "approximate carrying-out . . . in accordance with the situation."

When several episcopal directives appealed without further explanations to the fifth commandment in the discussion about abortion and the death penalty, certain questions inevitably arose, though the faithful and even some bishops seemed unaware of them: first of all, whether the word "kill" or only "murder" was germane to the Ten Commandments, and second, whether the condemnation of abortion and the death penalty were directly expressed in the commandment or only "along the lines of" the fifth commandment; and beyond this, whether an historical speaking or writing by God, or another theologically important event, accounted for the significance of the fifth commandment.[20]

When the American and German bishops had to give an answer recently to the pressing problems of peace and war, they had to face the question whether the Sermon on the Mount intended to introduce from above the absolutely new requirement of nonviolence into the history of mankind, or whether the Sermon intended only to admonish self-seeking mankind (in its varied manifestations: Jewish limitation of the full moral truth, Gentile misbehavior, tax collectors and sinners) to obey the requirement of love and mutual consideration already in force—though without spelling out clearly what this might mean in concrete cases. There is a danger in all these cases that one may take a one-sided attitude, deriving from the "ethics of faith," in a search for security about innerworldly behavior which this ethics cannot justify.

3. Competence and Authority. In order to be able to make valid statements about the various problems of morally defensible behavior (i.e., correct innerworldly behavior), it is obvious that a corresponding competence is required, in order to understand and judge the material problems which are always contained in such issues. A corresponding authority is also necessary, in order to make official statements about correct innerworldly behavior in the Christian community. Bishops and moral theologians both stand, in their different ways, before the double problem of competence and authority.

The competence required for corresponding statements is basically the same for bishops and for moral theologians (and other Christians). They can and must seek from appropriate sources the necessary information about the reality and implications of the use of nuclear weapons and of modern warfare in general, or about the scientific issues in modern genetics, or about the actualities of marriage in all its variety—to name only a few examples—if they intend to make a moral statement in each of these areas. They can and must master in the same way the knowledge of fundamental moral principles which is required to make such statements.

The question arises, however, whether a specifically episcopal authority is involved in such statements, that is, not only the question of a specific mission, but also of a specific "assistance" of the Holy Spirit corresponding to such a mission.[21] The answer must be affirmative but this does not necessarily mean the specific "assistance in questions of faith and morals," guaranteeing infallibility in certain circumstances, of which the First Vatican Council spoke. If the assistance of the Spirit is guaranteed to the Church as a whole, it is guaranteed also to the individual missions. But that includes the theologians as well, especially when they have received an official commission; they too have the authority that corresponds to their competence and to their mission in the Church.

The special mission and authority (not competence) of the bishops to establish the Church's unity in truth can fundamentally justify not only instruction, but also intervention against errors. This does not exclude moral theologians from the right and indeed obligation to take similar action; in principle, this could even include admonishing the bishops.

The question of what circumstances oblige bishops not merely to give positive instructions, but even to issue reprimands, is very delicate. They must be certain of the facts of the case; they must also bear in mind that concrete questions *de moribus* are usually not questions of faith, but questions of the natural law that must be established by reasoning, and that the two Vatican Councils did not speak in the same manner of all moral questions of the natural law when they used the formulation "in matters of faith and morals."

While the teaching of the two Councils does not exclude all dissent from officially ("authentically") but not "infallibly" presented teachings, the new Canon Law emphasizes the duty of the bishops to care for a corresponding unity in the Church's fellowship (including, therefore, the fellowship of moral theologians and bishops!) even in questions of (faith and) morals which are not presented infallibly. Canon 810 §2 vaguely requires the bishops to take care that "the principles of Catholic doctrine are faithfully maintained" in Catholic (and ecclesiastical: Canon 919) universities and faculties, but Canon 1371, 1 provides for the punishment of those who uphold a teaching condemned by the pope or by a council, or who reject a teaching taught by the authentic teaching authority of the pope or the college of bishops—even when no "infallible" statement is involved. According to Canon 753, the individual bishops, the episcopal conferences, and particular episcopal synods also exercise an "authentic magisterium," to which the faithful (including the moral theologians) must respond by a "religious readiness" (*obsequium religiosum*) to accept the teaching.

The authority and mission of the bishops to care for ecclesial unity seem to be clearly described here. What of care for the truth? Inasmuch as this care can be presumed in the case of the Church's statements, yes; but inasmuch as the viability of this presumption is not clearly established in every case (in noninfallible declarations), it is obvious that very precarious situations (according to the canonical situation we have set out) can arise.

The question has become freshly acute in the pastoral letters on peace and war which have been issued this year by the North American and the German bishops, and in the period of preparation of these documents.

1. In January 1983 (according to available reports) in the course of a meeting in the Vatican of representatives of several episcopal conferences which preceded the definitive publication, Cardinal J. Ratzinger, as leader of the discussion, warned that episcopal conferences as such have no *mandatum docendi*[22] (hence, only the individual participating bishops have this; but cf. also the new Codex, Canon 753, already quoted), and also that the bishops should apply their moral teaching concretely, but not in such a way that the magisterium would go beyond common moral principles to exercise pressure on the conscience in the case of individual political decisions.[23]

2. In their definitive letters, both episcopal conferences themselves drew attention to the various degrees of authority of various statements in their own documents. The statement of the Second Vatican Council mentioned above[24] is fundamental: despite their common faith and equal conscientiousness, Christians can come to different conclusions in many concrete questions about the construction of reality. Thus, the American bishops hold both tendencies that exist today in the Church, the more pacifist and the other "classical" tendency, to be justifiable.

Besides this, the American bishops distinguish a threefold authority of various statements in their pastoral letter: authority in general moral principles, in the Church's teachings, and in concrete applications. Precisely in the last case, they observe that they (the bishops) express their opinion (unlike the German bishops), but without wishing thereby to obligate the faithful; as an example, they adduce explicitly their stance on the much debated "first use" of atomic weapons.

The preparation of the American pastoral letter introduced yet another novelty: the preparation took place in the public eye for many months. Not only were specialists in various fields (including departments of the American government) and other episcopal conferences consulted, but reactions to the three successive preliminary drafts were accepted and taken into account. It took a long time for the episcopal conference to produce a text that was accepted by almost all the bishops.

This situation should not be without consequences for the future moral-theological teaching of bishops (and moral theologians).[25]

1. The process of the formation of opinion shows that the understanding of what is correct innerworldly behavior does not always lie at hand, nor is it obvious. It was always (or almost always) true that certain moral theologians were consulted in the preparation of episcopal statements on moral questions: it is obvious now that this consultation should have a broader scope (and include not only moral theologians). A question arises: how certain are the answers after such a long period of preliminary consideration?

2. It can be clearly seen that not all bishops have the same opinion in all questions. They are indeed not obliged to come to a consensus with other bishops. In the case of dissent among the bishops, which bishops should moral theologians and the rest of the faithful listen to? Some years ago, an American bishop insisted in this context that every Catholic must follow the magisterium of his local bishop; is this not a one-sidedly juridical concept of the magisterium?[26] It is right that an authentic magisterium of every bishop is accepted in the Church; but the *obsequium religiosum* which is expected clearly permits many different grades. What is the meaning for episcopal authority, when statements are made on questions of sexual ethics in a pastoral letter of the German bishops in 1973, in a decision of the German Synod in 1975, and likewise in 1975 in a document of the Roman Congregation for the Doctrine of the Faith—but in very different ways?[27]

3. It may not always be quite clear which episcopal statements belong to the first or to the second or to the third of the categories distinguished by the American bishops. The moral theologian will remain aware that episcopal statements may not be presented to an undifferentiated *obsequium religiosum* without distinguishing the various elements.

Tension between bishops and moral theologians is possible; it is not necessary in principle, but must be accepted as a fact of life. The distinct authority of bishops must be understood and seriously considered. Bishops too should acknowledge that not all the positions hitherto defended must be obvious and necessarily free of doubt. Moral theologians too are ready to accept the bishops as the officials responsible for safeguarding unity in truth, and to take them seriously—within the bounds of their official authority. Both sides must strive intensively for an understanding of the mission and situation of the other, and should seek mutual cooperation.

Notes

1. *Readings in Moral Theology, No. 3: The Magisterium and Morality*, ed. by C.E. Curran and R.A. McCormick, S.J., Paulist Press, New York (1982).

2. *Lumen gentium*, no. 25.

3. *Gaudium et spes*, no. 43.

4. Thus, for example, J. Ratzinger, "Theologie und Ethos," in: K. Ulmer, *Die Verantwortung der Wissenschaft*, Bonn (1975), pp. 45–61, on p. 56 criticizes the "mutation of the Christian ethos into an abstract system of natural law"; "more serious still is the ever greater positivism of the thinking of the magisterium, which takes this ethical system in hand and regulates it."

5. *Lumen gentium*, passim.

6. *Gaudium et spes*, nos. 33 and 43.

7. On this and what follows, cf. e.g., A. Dulles, "The Magisterium in History: A Theological Perspective," *Theol. Education* 19 (1983), pp. 7–26; Y. Congar, "Pour une histoire semantique du terme 'magisterium'," *Rev. de sc. phil. et théol.* 60 (1976), pp. 85–98; idem, "Bref historique des formes du 'magistère' et de ses relations avec les docteurs", ibid., pp. 99–112.

8. In: *L'Osservatore Romano*, 1 May 1983, p. 3.

9. Denzinger-Schönmetzer, *Enchiridion*, no. 3884.

10. Cf. Dulles and Congar (note 7).

11. Address to theologians at Altötting, 18 November 1980.

12. Quoted by J.W. O'Malley, "The Fourth Vow in Its Ignatian Context: A Historical Study," *Studies in the Spirituality of Jesuits* 15 (1983, no. 1), p. 17 (with no. 42).

13. One should recall the struggle in the Council about religious freedom before *Dignitatis humanae*.

14. H. Fries, "Die Verantwortung der Theologen für die Kirche," *Stimmen der Zeit* 200 (1982), pp. 245–58, at p. 258.

15. Thus, in W.C. Bier (ed), *Conscience. Its Freedom and Limitations*, New York (1971), 315 f.

16. For example, this complaint is found in a paper that the American moral theologian G. Grisez forwarded to the American bishops and also to the Vatican, against the second draft of the American Pastoral Letter on peace and war; at the January meeting of the bishops in the Vatican, the Vatican side drew attention to this accusation.

17. K. Demmer repeatedly draws attention in his writings to the unity between the act of faith and the establishment of moral judgments: cf., e.g., "Hermeneutische Probleme der Fundamentalmoral," in: D. Mieth and F. Compagnoni (eds.), *Ethik im Kontext des Glaubens*, Freiburg (1978), pp. 101–19.

18. In: J. Ratzinger (ed.), *Prinzipien christlicher Moral*, Einsiedeln, 2nd ed. (1975), pp. 67–93; idem, *Theologie der Geschichte*, Einsiedeln, 3rd ed. (1959).

19. H. Schürmann, "Die Frage nach der Verbindlichkeit der neutestamentlichen Wertungen und Weisungen," op. cit., pp. 9–39.

20. Cf., as a good synthesis, H. Schüngel-Straumann, *Der Dekalog—Gottes Gebote?*, Stuttgart (1973). Cf. also N. Lohfink, "Die Zehn Gebote ohne den Berg Sinai," in: *Bibelauslegung im Wandel*, Frankfurt (1967), pp. 129–57; F. Scholz, "Um die Verbindlichkeit des Dekalogs—Prinzipien oder Faustregeln?," *Theol. d. Gegenwart* 25 (1982), pp. 316–27; W. Molinski, "Die Zehn Gebote. Eine Grundlage für einen ethischen Konsens unter Glaubenden?" *Stimmen der Zeit* 201 (1983), pp. 53–60. Fundamental: F.L. Hossfeld, *Der Dekalog. Seine späten Fassungen, die originale Komposition und seine Vorstufen*, Göttingen (1982).

21. On what follows, see also my reflections "Sittliche Wahrheiten—Heilswahrheiten?", *Stimmen der Zeit* 200 (1982), pp. 662–76 (English translation, Chapter 4 of this book).

22. Cf. *The Tablet*, 30 April 1983. Cf. also the similar-sounding thesis of Archbishop J.F. Whealon, "Magisterium," *Homil. and Past. Rev.* 76 (July 1976), pp. 10–19; on this, R.A. McCormick, *Notes on Moral Theology 1965–1980*, Washington (1981), pp. 658–61.

23. *Herderkorrespondenz* (June 1983), p. 288.

24. *Gaudium et spes*, no. 43.

25. Cf. W. Seibel, "Hirtenbrief in neuem Stil," *Stimmen der Zeit* 201 (1983), pp. 145f.

26. Archbishop Whealon (note 22).

27. Cf. R. Bleistein, "Kirchliche Autorität im Widerspruch," *Stimmen der Zeit* 194 (1976), 145f.

Part Five

THE CURRAN CASE
AND ITS AFTERMATH

Letters to Curran

Joseph Ratzinger

These letters originally appeared in *Origins* in 1986.

SACRA CONGREGATIO
PRO DOCTRINA FIDEI
00193 Romae
Piazza del S. Uffizio, 11
Prot. N. 48/66

September 17, 1985

Dear Father Curran,

In your letter of August 24, 1984, you forwarded your response to this Congregation's critical "Observations" on your work which we had sent to you with our letter of May 10, 1983. We would like to assure you that your responses have been carefully studied and to say that we are now, after a multiple exchange of correspondence, in a position to bring this inquiry to a conclusion. The results of the Congregation's inquiry were presented to the Sovereign Pontiff in an audience granted to the undersigned Cardinal Prefect on June 28, 1985, and were confirmed by him.

The results of this study make it essential to refer here, however briefly, to some theological and juridical points which give definition to all theological teaching in the Catholic Church. Above all, we must recall the clear doctrine of the Vatican Council II regarding the principles for the assent of faith (*Lumen gentium* 25). This doctrine was incorporated in the revised Code of Canon

Law which in c. 752 sums up the thought of the Council on this point.

The Apostolic Constitution *Sapientia Christiana* makes specific application of these principles to the particular requirements of theological instruction and says that Catholic theologians, hence those teaching in ecclesiastical faculties, do not teach on their own authority but by virtue of the mission they have received from the Church. (*Sap. Chris.* 27 par. 1; cf. 26 par. 2). In order to guarantee this teaching, the Church claims the freedom to maintain her own academic institutions in which her doctrine is reflected upon, taught and interpreted in complete fidelity. This freedom of the Church to teach her doctrine is in full accord with the students' corresponding right to know what that teaching is and have it properly explained to them. This freedom of the Church likewise implies the right to choose for her theological faculties those and only those professors who, in complete intellectual honesty and integrity, recognize themselves to be capable of meeting these requirements.

In the correspondence exchanged between yourself and this Congregation, you have clearly affirmed that the positions you have maintained on various important elements of moral doctrine are in open contrast with the teaching of the Magisterium, about which the above-mentioned official documents speak. In what follows, we would like to list briefly the points on which this dissent has been verified.

The first area of dissent is with regard to the principle of the Church's teaching according to which every marital act must remain open to the transmission of life, and therefore artificial contraception and direct sterilization are forbidden as intrinsically wrong. This is in perfect agreement with the living tradition of the Church, made evident in the teaching of recent Popes, the documents of the Vatican Council II, and explicitly affirmed by Pope Paul VI in *Humanae vitae*. Since that time, it has been confirmed in *Familiaris consortio* by Pope John Paul II, and steadily repeated by him on several occasions.

Likewise, regarding the issues of abortion and euthanasia, the teaching of the Church, from which you dissent, has been unequivocal, and, despite pressure to the contrary, the Magisterium has recently reaffirmed the sacred and inviolable character of human life from the moment of conception. Every true Catholic must hold that abortion and euthanasia are unspeakable crimes, that is to say, actions that cannot be approved of for any motive or in any circumstance. No one can take the life of an innocent human being whether a fetus or an embryo, child or adult, elderly, incurably ill or near death, without opposing God's love for them, without violating a fundamental right, and therefore without committing a crime of the utmost gravity. (*Gaudium et spes* 51; *CDF Decree on Abortion* 14; *CDF Decree on Euthanasia,* II.).

With respect to the third area noted in the "Observations", i.e., masturbation, pre-marital intercourse and homosexual acts, all the faithful are bound to follow the Magisterium according to which these acts are intrinsically immoral. On this point, the 1975 *Declaration on Certain Questions Concerning Sexual Ethics* is clear. Whatever the motive may be, the deliberate use of the sexual faculty, outside normal and legitimate conjugal relations, essentially contradicts its finality, the purpose intended by the Creator.

Finally, as was again pointed out in the "Observations", the teaching of the Council of Trent on the indissolubility of sacramental and consummated marriage was clearly taught by the Vatican Council II, which described marriage as an indissoluble bond between two persons. A Catholic cannot affirm the contrary. (cf. *Gaudium et spes* 48–51). This truth has likewise been incorporated in the revised Code's c. 1056.

In light of the indispensable requirements for authentic theological instruction, described by the Council and by the public law of the Catholic Church (cf. supra), the Congregation now invites you to reconsider and to retract those positions which violate the conditions necessary for a professor to be called a Catholic theologian. It must be recognized that the authorities of the Church cannot allow the present situation to continue in which the inherent contradiction is prolonged that one who is to teach in the name of the Church in fact denies her teaching.

The consignment of this letter to you by the competent authorities is meant to assure a just resolution of this case for yourself and for all the parties involved.

We would ask that you forward your reply to this letter to the

Most Reverend Chancellor of the Catholic University as soon as possible in a time period not to exceed two months.

In your letter you indicated that you had not taken the positions you have, without "a great deal of prayer, study, consultation and discernment." This fact inspires us to hope that by further application of these means, you will come to that due adherence to the Church's doctrine which should characterize all the faithful.

Sincerely yours in Christ,
Joseph Cardinal Ratzinger

* * *

SACRA CONGREGATIO
PRO DOCTRINA FIDEI
00193 Romae
Piazza del S. Uffizio, 11
Prot. N. 48/66
July 25, 1986

Dear Father Curran:

This Congregation wishes to acknowledge receipt of your letter of April 1, 1986 with which you enclosed your definitive reply to its critical Observations on various positions you have taken in your published work. You note that you "remain convinced of the truthfulness of these positions at the present time. . . ." You reiterate as well a proposal which you have called a "compromise" according to which you would continue to teach moral theology but not in the field of sexual ethics.

The purpose of this letter is to inform you that the Congregation has confirmed its position that one who dissents from the Magisterium as you do is not suitable nor eligible to teach Catholic Theology. Consequently, it declines your compromise solution because of the organic unity of authentic Catholic Theology, a unity which in its contents and method is intimately bound to fidelity to the Church's Magisterium.

The several dissenting positions which this Congregation contested, namely, on a right to public dissent from the Ordinary Magisterium, the indissolubility of consummated sacramental marriage, abortion, euthanasia, masturbation, artificial contraception, pre-marital intercourse and homosexual acts, were listed carefully enough in the above-mentioned Observations in July of 1983 and have since been published. There is no point in entering into any detail concerning the fact that you do indeed dissent on these issues.

There is, however, one concern which must be brought out. Your basic assertion has been that since your positions are convincing to you and diverge only from the "non-infallible" teaching of the Church, they constitute "responsible" dissent and should therefore be allowed by the Church. In this regard, the following considerations seem to be in order.

First of all, one must remember the teaching of the Second Vatican Council which clearly does not confine the infallible Magisterium purely to matters of faith nor to solemn definitions. *Lumen gentium* 25 states: ". . . when, however, they (the Bishops) even though spread throughout the world, but still maintaining the bond of communion between themselves and with the successor of Peter, and authentically teaching on matters of faith or morals, are in agreement that a particular position ought to be held as definitive, then they are teaching the doctrine of Christ in an infallible manner." Besides this, the Church does not build its life upon its infallible magisterium alone but on the teaching of its authentic, ordinary magisterium as well.

In light of these considerations, it is clear that you have not taken into adequate account, for example, that the Church's position on the indissolubility of sacramental and consummated marriage, which you claim ought to be changed, was in fact defined at the Council of Trent and so belongs to the patrimony of the Faith. You likewise do not give sufficient weight to the teaching of the Second Vatican Council when in full continuity with the Tradition of the Church it condemned abortion, calling it an "unspeakable crime." In any case, the faithful must accept not only the infallible magisterium. They are to give the religious submission of intellect and will to the teaching which the Supreme Pontiff or the college of bishops enuntiate on faith or morals when they exercise the authentic magisterium, even if they do not intend to proclaim it with a definitive act. This you have continued to refuse to do.

There are, moreover, two related matters which have become widely misunderstood in the course of the Congregation's inquiry into your work, especially in the past few months, and which should be noted. First, you publicly claimed that you were never told who your "accusers" were. The Congregation based its inquiry exclusively on your published works and on your personal responses to its Observations. In effect, then, your own works have been your "accusers" and they alone.

You further claimed that you were never given the opportunity of counsel. Since the inquiry was conducted on a documentary basis, you had every opportunity to take any type of counsel you wished. Moreover, it is clear that you did so. When you replied to the Congregation's Observations with your letter of August 24, 1984, you stated that you had taken the positions you have "with a great deal . . . of consultation . . ."; and in the Congregation's letter of September 17, 1985, you were actually urged to continue the use of that very means so that an acceptable resolution of the differences between you and the teaching of the Church could be attained. Finally, at your own request, when you came for our meeting on March 8, 1986, you were accompanied by a theologian of your own choosing and confidence.

In conclusion, this Congregation calls attention to the fact that you have taken your dissenting positions as a Professor of Theology in an Ecclesiastical Faculty at a Pontifical University. In its letter of September 17, 1985 to you, it was noted that ". . . the authorities of the Church cannot allow the present situation to continue in which the inherent contradiction is prolonged that one who is to teach in the name of the Church in fact denies her teaching." In light of your repeated refusal to accept what the Church teaches and in light of its mandate to promote and safeguard the Church's teaching on faith and morals throughout the Catholic world, this Congregation, in agreement with the Congregation for Catholic Education, sees no alternative now but to advise the Most Reverend Chancellor that you will no longer be considered suitable nor eligible to exercise the function of a Professor of Catholic Theology.

This decision was presented to His Holiness, in an audience granted to the undersigned Prefect on the 10th of July of this year and he approved both its content and the procedure followed.

This Dicastery also wishes to inform you that this decision will be published as soon as it is communicated to you.

May I finally express the sincere hope that this regrettable, but necessary, outcome to the Congregation's study might move you to reconsider your dissenting positions and to accept in its fullness the teaching of the Catholic Church.

Sincerely yours in Christ,
Joseph Cardinal Ratzinger

Response of Charles E. Curran, August 20, 1986

Charles E. Curran

This response originally appeared in *Origins* in 1986.

From the very beginning of the public discussion of my dispute with the Vatican's Congregation for the Doctrine of the Faith I insisted on making this a teaching moment.

On Monday, August 18, at a 4:00 p.m. meeting, Archbishop James A. Hickey, the Chancellor of The Catholic University of America, handed me a letter addressed to me by Cardinal Joseph Ratzinger, the Prefect of the Congregation for the Doctrine of the Faith. Ratzinger informed me that I "will no longer be suitable nor eligible to exercise the function of a Professor of Catholic Theology." The Archbishop informed me that this letter had at that time been released to the press.

In addition Archbishop Hickey gave me his own letter in which as Chancellor of The Catholic University of America he initiated the withdrawal of the canonical mission which permits me to teach theology at this University. The letter also reminded me of my right to request the procedures found in the Canonical Statutes of the Ecclesiastical Faculties. If I do not exercise that right by September 1, he will notify the President of the University that the canonical mission has been withdrawn. In addition, he gave me his press release. He also said that he could give me no answer as to whether or not I would still be allowed to teach at the University in some faculty other than the faculty of theology. That answer according to Archbishop Hickey could only be given by the Board of Trustees.

In keeping with my aim of making this a teaching moment, I

want first to address the issues in Cardinal Ratzinger's July 25 letter to me and then to raise further issues not discussed in that letter. The issues involved in Cardinal Ratzinger's July 25 letter to me are basically three: the moral theological positions I have taken, the legitimacy of my theological dissent, and my criticisms of the process.

First, the letter of Cardinal Ratzinger gives the impression that on the specific moral issues involved in the dispute the official teaching is opposed to such actions and I am in favor of them. That is not the case. I have always developed my moral theology in the light of accepted Catholic principles. My positions on the particular issues involved are always carefully nuanced and often in fundamental agreement with the existing hierarchical teaching. Yes, occasionally I have dissented from the official teaching on some aspects of specific issues, but this is within a more general and prevailing context of assent.

Second, the issue of dissent. The July 25 letter refers to both the infallible and noninfallible magisterium. However, in all the correspondence before 1985 the Congregation for the Doctrine of the Faith recognized that the issue was public dissent from the noninfallible hierarchical magisterium as is spelled out in the very first sentence of the "Observations" sent to me in April 1983. In reality, the July 25 letter refers only to the indissolubility of marriage as defined at the Council of Trent and belonging to the patrimony of faith. However, all Catholic theologians recognize the teaching of the Council of Trent does not exclude as contrary to faith the practice of "*economia*" in the Greek church. I have maintained that the position I propose on the indissolubility of marriage is in keeping with this tradition.

Thus, we are dealing with the noninfallible hierarchical teaching. Here, too, in my writing and recent public statements I have not proposed the possibility and legitimacy of dissent from all noninfallible teaching. In moral matters, all Christians must recognize that the follower of Jesus should be loving, caring, just, and faithful. My disagreements are on the level of complex, specific actions which involve many conflicting circumstances and situations. By their very nature these specific concrete questions are far removed from the core of faith. Recall that official hierarchical teaching does not condemn all sterilization but recognizes that in some situations indirect sterilization is permitted. The 1968 statement of the Canadian bishops about Catholics who cannot accept the teaching of *Humanae vitae* absolutely condemning artificial contraception for spouses is most pertinent. "Since they are not denying any point of divine and Catholic faith, nor rejecting the teaching authority of the church, these Catholics should not be considered, or consider themselves, shut off from the body of the faithful."

In short, I have defended my dissent as being in accord with the norms laid down by the United States bishops in their 1968 pastoral letter "Human Life in Our Day." The Congregation still must answer the questions I have been asking for six years. Does the Congregation agree with the teaching proposed on dissent by the United States bishops or are they claiming that such teaching is wrong?

Third, the process. Most legal systems in the contemporary world recognize that the defendant has a right to the record of the trial including the right to know who are the accusers. No such record has ever been made available to me. The process itself does not allow the individual involved to have counsel in any official meeting with the Congregation or its officials. Cardinal Ratzinger himself maintained that my meeting with the officials of the Congregation was a nonofficial meeting. Ratzinger himself admitted in 1984 that the Congregation had decided to revise its present procedures but workload and time constraints have not allowed this to take place. In this context, I should also point out that I have been given a copy of a letter from a Cardinal member of the Congregation dated July 11, 1986, in which this Cardinal voting member says that he has never received any dossier on my case.

Now I want to raise three issues that are not found in the July 25, 1986 letter of Cardinal Ratzinger.

First, the right of the faithful to dissent in practice from some of the noninfallible teachings with which I disagree. Do the faithful have such a right? What is the ecclesial status of those who so dissent? What does their practice say about the present teaching of the church?

Second, the theological community. The evidence in the last

few months has clearly supported my contention that I am a theological moderate and that a strong majority of Catholic theologians support the legitimacy of my position. Over 750 theologians in North America have signed a theological statement of support for me.

This present support from the theological community is in continuity with the support shown for my theological endeavors over the last twenty-five years, most of which have been spent here at the Catholic University of America. The theological community has been in critical dialogue with my positions, but in the eyes of my peers I have been recognized as a significant Catholic moral theologian. My colleagues have elected me President of the Catholic Theological Society of America and of the Society of Christian Ethics. I was the first recipient of the John Courtney Murray Award of the Catholic Theological Society of America for outstanding achievement in theology.

What does this split between theologians and pastors say? This is a pressing problem for the Roman Catholic Church which has always given great weight and importance to the theological community. What action if any will be taken against people holding positions similar to mine? Are all those who maintain the possibility of legitimate theological dissent from some noninfallible teaching not suitable or eligible to exercise the function of a Professor of Catholic Theology?

Third, academic freedom in Catholic institutions. The vast majority of the leaders of Catholic higher education in the United States, including William J. Byron, the President of this University, have claimed that the ability of a church authority to intervene in the hiring, promotion, and terminating of faculty is a violation of academic freedom. Such procedures in Catholic institutions according to these educational leaders jeopardize the very nature of a university or college. Such interventionist procedures are now possible with the Statutes for the Ecclesiastical Faculties of The Catholic University. However, the present universal law of the church already enshrines the same legislation for all Catholic institutions of higher learning. In addition, proposed legislation for Catholic institutions of higher learning spells this out in greater detail.

Before concluding, some other issues must be addressed. My

colleagues have urged me to go through the process provided by the Statutes of the Ecclesiastical Faculties if I have the physical and spiritual strength to do so. I would like to honor their request, but there are some problems that must first be clarified. I have written that the existing canonical statutes are themselves a violation of academic freedom. Also in 1982 I wrote an official letter to the University asserting that these Statutes do not apply to me since my tenured contract with the University predates these Statutes and the University cannot unilaterally add anything to my contractual obligations. Only after receiving academic and legal counsel on these points can I make a final decision about the process.

In conclusion, I am conscious of my own limitations and my own failures. I am aware of the consequences of what is involved. But I can only repeat what I wrote Cardinal Ratzinger in my final response of April 1, 1986: "In conscience at the present time I cannot and do not change the theological positions I have taken." In my own judgment and in the judgment of the majority of my peers I have been and am suitable and eligible to exercise the function of a Professor of Catholic Theology.

I remain convinced that the hierarchical teaching office in the Roman Catholic Church must allow dissent on these issues and ultimately should change its teaching. My conviction in this matter is supported by a number of factors. First, the overwhelming support of my theological colleagues has buoyed me personally and strengthened my own hope for the ultimate acceptance of these convictions. Second, the best and the mainstream of the Catholic theological tradition support my basic approaches. According to Catholic theological tradition, the word and work of Jesus must always be made present and meaningful in the contemporary historical and cultural circumstances. The Catholic tradition also insists on the transcendence of faith and the principle that faith and reason can never contradict one another. In addition, Catholic ethics has insisted on an intrinsic morality. Something is commanded because it is good and not the other way around. Authority must conform to the truth.

Finally, some historical examples give me hope. Theologians who have been condemned have at later times been vindicated and their teachings have been accepted. The experience of the Second Vatican Council illustrates this fact.

From a personal perspective, I have been comforted and strengthened by the support of so many. I remain a loyal and committed Roman Catholic. I pray daily that I might continue to love and serve the Church without bitterness and anger.

I will continue to work for the legitimacy of some theological and practical dissent, the need to change some official hierarchical church teachings, the importance of academic freedom for Catholic theology, and the need for just structures to deal with the inevitable tensions that from time to time will exist between theologians and pastors. I believe these are all for the good of the Roman Catholic Church—my Church.

The Curran Case:
Conflict Between Rome
and a Moral Theologian

Bernard Häring

This article was first presented on West German radio in September 1986 and was translated from the German by Benedict Neenan, O.S.B.

Since July 1979, the Vatican has been conducting a formal investigation into the teachings of the well known North American theologian, Charles Curran. I have followed the case from its beginning up to the bitter end in August of this year. Curran, like other theologians who have recently been under investigation, has sent me copies of all the pertinent documents as the case has progressed. The public first became aware of this investigation in March of this year, after a "concluding conversation" took place with the three highest officials of the Congregation for the Doctrine of the Faith. As a result of its harsh verdict by which Curran is no longer able to teach at a Catholic university because of his dissent on some teachings, he has unwillingly found himself in the public limelight. Because of the publicity many are now asking: Who is this Professor Curran and what is the issue that has proved to be so controversial in the public discussion in the United States?

WHO IS CHARLES CURRAN?

The 52 year-old scholar is a priest of the diocese of Rochester, New York. Before the Council he received a licentiate degree in theology at the Gregorian University in Rome and later specialized in moral theology at the Academia Alfonsiana of the Lateran University, where I was one of his professors. Curran stood out not only because of his extraordinary talent but also because of his winning modesty. His doctoral dissertation concerned the role of conscience in the work of St. Alphonsus Liguori, a work which left a lasting impression on him. Curran was astonished to discover the deep reverence in which that Doctor of the Church held the majesty of conscience, even the erring conscience of the person honestly seeking the truth.

In 1961 Curran began to lecture in moral theology at the major seminary in his home diocese of Rochester and was received enthusiastically by the students as well as by the priests of the diocese. Beginning in 1962, together with other former students of mine, he arranged numerous conferences in which I have been able over many years to speak to thousands of American priests and laity. On those occasions I was able to witness anew the extraordinary popularity of this youthful priest.

When The Catholic University in Washington offered me a position as professor there in 1964 and I was unable to accept, I was asked to recommend someone else. Curran was my choice and he was, in fact, hired. There too, he quickly won the admiration of both colleagues and students because of his untiring availability and openness. Understandably he also encountered opposition from circles which were stamped by the pre-conciliar, strongly law-centered moral theology. As a result the Trustees of the University (composed primarily of conservative bishops) refused to grant him tenure. The spontaneous reaction was a strike of almost all the professors and students, who demanded that Curran not only be granted tenure but also be promoted. That is what then happened, though with great reluctance on the part of some of the bishops. It is important to keep this first conflict in mind in order to better understand subsequent conflicts.

Upon the publication of the encyclical of Paul VI, *Humanae vitae*, Curran, together with numerous other theologians, signed a statement seriously questioning the absoluteness of the norm prescribing total or partial abstinence from sexual intercourse as the only morally permissible method for the responsible regulation of conception. They argued that there were certainly cases of the conflict of values or of conscience in which artificial birth control was morally justifiable. The stir which this caused among conservative bishops, priests, and laity diminished somewhat as others, including entire bishops' conferences, came to similar conclusions, though in very carefully worded statements. Curran and his colleagues who had signed the document were later cleared of charges that they had violated their responsibility as theologians through their public dissent. A specially appointed committee concluded that not dissent as such, but only improperly expressed dissent with respect to a noninfallible teaching of the ecclesiastical magisterium, would constitute such a violation of the theologian's responsibility. This is precisely the question which lies behind the present long investigation and which must now be reexamined.

FUNDAMENTAL ACCEPTANCE OF THE TEACHING AUTHORITY OF THE CHURCH

Curran has never given the slightest cause to doubt that he fundamentally accepts the teaching authority of the Church, even in the area of noninfallible, reformable teachings. With the entire sound tradition, Curran also emphasizes of course that in the area of fallible teaching statements an assent of faith—an irrevocable "Yes"—cannot be demanded. To require a total assent to fallible teaching would contradict the once-and-for-all nature of the act of faith and stand in open contradiction to the teaching of the First Vatican Council. The draft concerning papal infallibility was adopted there only after the bounds of infallibility were clearly delineated. It is also a fact that at the time, curial and other circles were disappointed since they wanted papal teaching authority as such to be seen as unquestionable. Ever since the First Vatican Council there has been no lack of attempts to stretch the infallibility of the pope to such an extent that no dissent, even in the realm of fallible teaching, would be permitted. This is all the more astonishing in light of the fact that the minority of bishops who were able to advance this idea had been presenting as infallible a long list of papal teachings that were not only fallible, but in some cases actually incorrect.

The theology which we studied long before the Second Vatican Council provided the applicable qualifications for any authoritative teachings discussed so that any intelligent student could see where an act of faith was required and where a true faith assent was not possible.

Another question discussed again and again in the period before the Second Vatican Council concerned the safeguards which were built in or should be built in so that no false or unbalanced teaching of the Vatican could simply be promulgated. The most radical of those who emphasized authority solved the difficulty with the historically unverifiable position that at the proper time the Holy Spirit gives the person in authority the necessary insight to make the proper corrections. At the other extreme there were some, even well-known theologians, who taught that the proper corrective lay rather in the way of the non-acceptance of such untenable teachings by the faithful and theologians, thus keeping the way open to fuller insight into the truth.

Official magisterial texts do not require an assent of faith in the area of noninfallible Church teaching but rather a *religiosum obsequium* of intellect and will. The German translation of this phrase in the new Code of Canon Law is with "religious obedience of intellect and will" [*religiösum Verstandes- und Willensgehorsam*] (Canon 751). I consider this translation unfortunate. What does obedience of the intellect mean in regard to official teaching based on natural law when one can find no convincing foundation for the matter in nature? Sound theology understands the Latin expression *obsequium religiosum* as that religious loyalty which prepares the intellect and will of the faithful to receive such teachings honestly and sincerely, to endeavor with honest reasoning to understand them and to appropriate them. It should also prepare them, however, to examine the teachings critically and, should the situation arise, to assert those reservations which seem necessary without rebellion against authority. This, of course, must always be done in the spirit of shared responsibility with the Pilgrim Church which, in so many areas of newly emerging problems, is sometimes only able to give provisional answers and must continue to search for a more complete response.

Since *Humanae vitae,* Charles Curran has come to view dissent as an expression of honest loyalty to, and co-responsibility with, both the Church's magisterium and the entire People of God. He is genuinely concerned with that loyalty and honesty which alone can truly honor the Church and Church authority.

Thus when the press reports, as it did last spring, that "Curran refuses to submit to the magisterium," it is grossly misleading. The report should rather read, "Curran has declared that he, with all due respect to the ecclesiastical teaching office, cannot recant in certain question of sexual ethics as long as he is unable, after great effort, to see his own positions as false and the official teachings of the Church as undoubtedly correct." In this long process of investigation, Curran has continually asked the Congregation for the Doctrine of the Faith to clarify whether it considers dissent itself, whether from infallible or noninfallible teaching, to be a punishable offense in itself or if the Congregation considers as punishable only improperly expressed dissent.

THEOLOGIAN OF THE UNTIRING DIALOGUE AND OPENNESS TO REVISION

Curran is the author of at least 15 widely read books which in large part resemble those of Karl Rahner and consist of collected thematic essays on burning questions of the day. Typical titles of his books are *Catholic Moral Theology in Dialogue* and *Ongoing Revision in Moral Theology.* He deals primarily with fundamental questions of hermeneutics, methods of reappraising the tradition, evaluation of modern historical and social-scientific insights, and the resolution of conflict situations. He is impressed with Gandhi's view of the "open-ended compromise," which never abandons the possibility of fuller realization of truth in the future. He gives a certain priority, as I do, to the "goal commandments" grounded in the Bible and the human sciences rather than the more confining norms that forbid or require particular actions. The most important question for him is whether Christians and the Christian community are continuing to strive toward the goal commandments, living lives consistent with the Sermon on the Mount and the great commandment, "Love one another as I have loved you," thereby treating with an appropriate seriousness the "boundary-defining" norms which serve as mileposts along the way.

As a moral theologian with a great deal of pastoral sensitivity, Curran knows that an overabundance of these often poorly understood "boundary-defining" norms confuse the conscience. They can discourage the search for holiness, especially when they are all presented as absolutes despite the fact that in many cases they are very difficult to harmonize with one another.

His most vocal opponents and sharpest judges are to a large extent caught up in a purely normative ethic in which the goal commandments and the Beatitudes never appear and there is a predominance of only boundary-defining norms. They are missing the broader theological perspective of the theologian they attack. Not only by his words but also by his example of peaceful dialogue, his utter availability, and his lifestyle oriented to the Beatitudes, he points the way for his fellow Christians to the goal of a life oriented to the Gospel and to grace. Again and again he has made clear the foundation of his moral theology: as complete a vision as possible, though not without tension, of the doctrine of creation; the captivity of sin and solidarity with evil; redemption—which is the more decisive term in any discussion of sin; and the eschatological tension between the "already" of salvation's accomplishment and the "not-yet" of its final fulfillment and freedom.

If Curran's statements are taken out of the context of this broad overview and dynamic, and oversimplified in addition, then they certainly can become dangerous. But the opposite question presents itself immediately: Is not the purely static, norm-based teaching, a morality which is simply concerned with setting limits, even more dangerous—and theologically unacceptable as well?

THE SPECIAL NATURE OF CURRAN'S
DEVOTION TO THE CHURCH

Because of his image of the Church and because of his own character, Curran is deeply convinced that the first thing a theologian owes the Church is the complete honesty and uprightness of his thinking and speaking (and this includes writing). He will have nothing to do with the so-called "diplomatic" methods of those who through casuistic "watering-down" and hair-splitting interpretation of Church teaching in fact change the meaning of that teaching without the appearance of deviation. Curran is scrupulously honest in the presentation of what the Church's magisterium really says and means, even when it doesn't correspond to his own way of thinking. The primary thing for him is absolute loyalty in the presentation of the official position. If that teaching is based on arguments in the area of natural moral law, then he asks his reader what images of God and of humankind, what historical experiences are behind the arguments. Then comes the inevitable question: Are the arguments convincing? If they don't seem convincing to him, another question follows: Are there perhaps other convincing arguments that could be put forward that would support the official teaching? If, after all these considerations, he is of the opinion that the norm presented by the Church is in need of some refinement or in some cases a change, and he says so frankly, he then assumes the difficult burden of a partial dissent. Very seldom is there a total dissent. Curran is a straightforward, undiplomatic person, which is probably another reason why he has so many admirers. He has doubtless helped many to love the Church even though they have found themselves in situations in which they cannot accept certain norms of the Church's sexual ethic in its bare wording and strict interpretation of it. Such people find in Curran a priest and a fellow Christian who obviously loves the Church, works for it and, when necessary, also suffers for and in it.

DOES CURRAN GO TOO FAR IN ADAPTING TO THE AMERICAN CULTURE?

Curran is suspected and even openly accused by his opponents in Rome of wanting to adapt Catholic morality to the average North American "consumer." What can be said of this claim?

There is no question that Curran conducts theology in full consciousness of the North American scene. He knows that the reflective North American, the educated Protestants and, since the Council, at least the decisive Catholic elite, are not much moved, to put it mildly, by a claim to authority when patient dialogue has been refused. In a typically pluralistic society there is no progress without continuous, patient dialogue with the goal of convincing rather than demanding compliance. He lives in an environment in which new discoveries are constantly, or at least seemingly, being made not only in the areas of science and medicine but also in the social sciences and historical research. He wants to win a hearing in precisely this culture for the Church's morality—yes, even for the Church's magisterium—by arguing according to a principle which he himself has emphasized: "It is not true merely because authority says so; rather it can be asserted and taught authoritatively only to the extent that it can be proven to be true." In that area where strict faith is required, it is necessary to demonstrate that a teaching comes from divine revelation. But in the area of natural moral law it is necessary to present the teaching convincingly in the light of an accurate image of humankind. A Church which allows reexamination in an area where it has no explicit divine revelation in fact conducts that examination itself, gains trust, and is a respected partner in the continual search for the truth. This is true even when the Church has the courage to admit openly that some of its answers have only a provisional quality and that some answers which it gave in the past are no longer satisfactory.

This approach applies elsewhere, but it is especially urgent in North America. I fear that some of those in the Vatican as well as some American bishops who studied all of their theology before the Council and are very authority-conscious are not able to understand and value Curran's position sufficiently.

If one considers the living witness of the man himself and the totality of his writings in moral theology, then he would have to be very advanced indeed in the life of perfection and in the radical living out of the Gospel to entertain even a suspicion that Curran wants to conform morality to the American slogan, "Take it easy!" If one allows himself to be challenged by the goal commandments and the Christian virtues as Curran proposes, then he will quickly dismiss any temptation to accuse this man of permissiveness.

Is It Only a Question of Sexual Ethics?

Many ask this question, since all the complaints against Curran in the present investigation have to do with sexual ethics. In my opinion the central concern is not so much the particular positions the Church has taken in sexual ethics or even Curran's deviation from those individual positions; rather it is the unquestioning, integral acceptance of all of the Vatican's statements in this area. Yet it does remain also a question of the very difficult area of sexual ethics.

The decisive point in this regard, however, is this. Besides the understanding of authority which the Church officials bring to this question, there is also a great divergence in approaches to morality. This divergence exists between a classical approach, which emphasizes norms and tends to ignore historical development and the more contemporary approach, which is based primarily on historical consciousness. The Bible is not an abstract textbook, but dynamic and changing history, the report of a continuing event in which the householder brings forth from his treasury things both old and new. Revelation makes humankind aware that humanity is both formed by history and able to form it. One cannot speak of the "nature" of humankind without taking into consideration both of these dimensions: that it is both a product and a maker of history. Consequently, Curran and the spokespersons for contemporary Evangelical and Catholic moral theology have departed radically from the temptation to absolutize one particular culture or one particular moment in history. One must keep in mind when speaking of natural moral law that different cultures approach the truth differently.

The Church's social teaching as well as its sexual ethics—the statements of individual theologians, theological schools, and also the magisterium—require a hermeneutic. One must consciously and systematically inquire into the "Sitz im Leben" or life context "at that time" when the teachings were formulated, and into the life context of a Church which seeks to preach the Gospel to all cultures. Thus one cannot look for old answers in the archives of the Roman Inquisition and the Holy Office when one seeks to speak meaningfully today with the people of Rome or Europe, not to mention those of North America, Latin America, Africa, Asia, or Oceania.

A static insistence on formulations which were developed under very different historical conditions makes the proclamation of the Gospel to other cultures and times very difficult, if not impossible. If we proclaim these formulations as though they were constant and inflexible norms, although they previously meant something quite different and had a very different context, then we will not be listened to even when we proclaim the revealed truth in a timely fashion. Both the speaker and the listener become mired in a neuralgic impasse.

I would like to illustrate this with an example from one of the hottest points of this already hot conflict. In a couple of the documents pertinent to the investigation, the Congregation for the Doctrine of the Faith emphasized a well known formulation as a concrete point of difference between official teaching and Curran's position: namely, that "every conjugal act must be open to the transmission of life." I have no quarrel with the matter of concern behind this statement; the problem lies in its non-historical, "classical" formulation. What does it mean in the long-prevailing Augustinian sexual ethic? Clearly, it meant what the average person trained in a casuistic school would understand by it even today: Conjugal intercourse is not morally permitted unless one desires to beget new life here and now, so far as it depends on the couple and the type and time of the intercourse. In the Augustinian tradition, which has long been dominant, it is stated very concretely: In the marriage act the couple must have as their goal the begetting of children, for only this goal can fully justify the marriage act. Thus sexual intercourse would have to be strictly avoided in times when conception is obviously not possible, such as pregnancy, after menopause, etc.

If these matters had been presented to Curran and other moral theologians who are under investigation in a more understanding way—as, to use an analogy, in the practice of medicine one doesn't resort to an operation or dangerous medicines if the crisis can best be resolved through a healthy lifestyle and healthy human relationships—one would have undoubtedly encountered complete openness.

However, if one expects contemporary moral theologians who are historically conscious to use as their starting point formulations which are no longer understandable or communicable today, then he hinders their service to a Pilgrim Church which seeks to approach people of all times and places. If Curran had been asked, for example, whether he could accept the teaching of *Humanae vitae* as it is presented in the Königsteiner Statement of the West German bishops and the general synod of West German dioceses, I doubt if he would have had any problem giving it his full assent.

Another charge is that Curran is not true to the Church's teaching on the indissolubility of marriage. I admit that some of Curran's formulations are difficult for the Roman mind to understand; perhaps, too, they are too "unguarded." But basically Curran's position is no more and no less than that which was presented by the Roman Synod of Bishops on Marriage and the Family (1981) and approved by a large majority: that one should at least carefully study the possibility of the Roman Church's acceptance of the longstanding practice of *oikonomia* in the Orthodox Church, that is, the merciful application of the plan of salvation for someone whose first (canonically valid) marriage fails irreparably, though he or she has not been the cause. One cannot equate the malicious or irresponsible destruction of a valid marriage with the situation of spouses who, in spite of their good will, are abandoned.

In the newspaper, *Rheinischen Merkur,* a short, well-written essay about the Curran case carried the title, "When One Person Says What Many Are Thinking." What is there to say when one man says and writes what almost all respectable theologians are saying and what a majority of the members of a Roman bishops' synod has approved? Can he still be penalized because of dissent? Not at least on this point.

Is an Uncompromising Stance the Same as a Healing Adherence to Principles?

This question presents itself now in light of the final decision of the Congregation for the Doctrine of the Faith in Curran's case. How was this decision reached? The official process actually concluded around the end of last year with the notification that in light of his dissent, Curran could no longer be considered a "Catholic theologian." At that time it was suggested by the Congregation that it was open to holding a concluding conversation if Curran himself requested it. Before that time no meeting with Curran had taken place. Thus, there had never been a face-to-face encounter with the experts whose work, in my opinion, would have been much more careful and nuanced if a personal encounter with the accused had been a part of the process. Also, an open confrontation would have been able perhaps to throw some light on the obvious tension between a classical, static view of norm-based teaching and the pronounced historically conscious view of Charles Curran. One could say more about this, but let less suffice.

Curran took advantage of the offer, with the request that I be able to accompany him and eventually to defend him. The meeting took place on March 8th in the palace of the Holy Office. Besides myself, Curran was accompanied as far as the outer office by Msgr. George Higgins, a highly respected former official of the National Conference of Catholic Bishops, and by William Cenkner, the dean of the School of Religious Studies of The Catholic University of America, where Charles Curran is a professor. We used the time of waiting before the meeting for spontaneous prayer among ourselves, and just as Cardinal Ratzinger entered the outer office we were praying that God might help us to seek not our own victory but only the good of the Church, the furthering of the Kingdom of God. I told this to Cardinal Ratzinger and invited him to join us in our prayer. He nodded approval.

The meeting itself was difficult because we were reminded that it was not part of the official process, which had already been completed. However we agreed that both sides should be open to the possibility that the discussion could lead to new results. One of Curran's questions was, "Why am I being singled out when many have said the same things?" Cardinal Ratzinger challenged Curran to support with specific names his assertion that many moral theologians are saying similar things or going even further. Curran was bewildered at first and then said, "Surely I am not expected to report on my colleagues!" The subject was not pursued. Then together we presented again, this time more clearly, the "compromise" which Curran had already presented through the chancellor of the Catholic University, the Archbishop of Washington. The compromise was not accepted, though it was considered very seriously in our discussion, especially when Curran openly rejected as unjust and theologically very dangerous his disqualification as no longer being a "Catholic theologian" simply on the basis of dissent in the area of reformable teaching. Cardinal Ratzinger answered without long hesitation that this precise formulation was open to revision. Thus we inferred that the process might no longer be completely finished, and we had some hope that the compromise proposal might yet be considered.

What was the compromise proposed by Curran? Here I want to point out again that the phrase "open-ended compromise" plays a significant role in Curran's moral theology and that he feels obliged by deep conviction to accommodate the Congregation for the Doctrine of the Faith as far as his honesty and integrity would allow. Curran offered to continue his practice of not teaching sexual ethics at The Catholic University of America. In addition he promised to continue to examine these questions further. He asked that he not be required to recant, because fidelity to his conscience and the honesty he owes to God and the Church would not allow him to do so. I emphatically endorsed this compromise, especially in light of the fact that Curran had refrained on his own from teaching courses or seminars in the area of sexual ethics so that his partial dissent in this area would not cause difficulties for Catholic University. The meeting was conducted with full openness and without rancor on either side.

I had great hopes that the compromise would be accepted. Curran was asked to submit again a final position paper, which he did before the prescribed deadline. In that paper he emphasized that while he couldn't recant, he did not see his positions as apodictic; rather they were tentative and open to revision. In other words, he wanted fully and completely to be a responsible member of a Church on pilgrimage, seeking more light.

At this opportunity I expressed my own deep concern for the unfortunate pastoral consequences of a disciplinary action, particularly in light of the fact that Curran had submitted humbly as far as his conscience would allow him. With Curran, I pointed out the danger that an action which stripped him of his teaching position could lead to a lessening of respect for Catholic education and the Church's magisterium in the United States. Not least important, one should be very careful of the implications of such an action on the ecumenical dialogue and the ecumenical atmosphere.

I must say openly that when I learned of the "last word"— though I still hope that it is "next-to-the-last"—I was very disappointed and saddened. However, perhaps it is worthwhile not to be pessimistic now. And so I want to cautiously share with my listeners some optimistic considerations which have crystallized within me in recent days.

DANGERS AND RELEVANT OPPORTUNITIES AFTER THE CURRAN AFFAIR

First I want to mention a short-term and unpleasant danger. In some—though not many—organs of the press and other media Curran's dissenting views are presented in an oversimplified or crude manner. In light of the popularity that this man enjoys, one worries that some uncritical people will all too gladly take this simplistic version of his views as a justification for their own laxity. We must do all we can to limit such damage. I hope by my contribution here to serve this purpose.

I see a great opportunity in this for Curran, guided by his deepest convictions, to conduct himself in accordance with the Gospel value of nonviolence and the example of Gandhi. His faith and the strength he gets from his love for the Church have provided him with a great deal of inner peace and self-discipline. He has appealed to all of his supporters not to let anger or anti-Roman feelings take root in them because of the outcome of his case. He wants to give proof precisely in this situation of his love for the Church and for the cooperative search for a better understanding of the truth.

If we look more closely, we see that what is actually at stake here is not so much a "Curran Affair," but rather a field of conflict that has burdened the Church for two hundred years: a conflict between a majority of the leading moral theologians who are taken seriously by contemporary Christians and the representatives of the official magisterium. This conflict already became apparent last spring when the threatened sanction was first made public. Five former presidents of American theological societies (the College Theology Society and the Catholic Theological Society of America) and over seven hundred theologians and canonists declared their solidarity with Curran without concurring with each of his positions.

If Curran is able to persevere in the *Satyagraha*—that is, the strength-loving search for, and practice of, truth—and draw his many admirers into his example, then it is possible, though after some suffering, that a reconciliation of both sides might be the result. Besides, it is valuable in itself when a man of the stature of Curran sets a standard for nonviolent perseverance in a conflict.

I would be especially pleased if Rome concludes from this whole affair that the threat of punitive sanctions in the case of dissent—and because of dissent alone—in areas of reformable teaching should again be abandoned. At the end of this long and, for scholars, very aggravating process, the Congregation has applied canon 1371 par. 1 for the first time and to a particularly harsh degree. (It might be noted that this section of the new Canon Law did not come from the Committee for the Revision of the Code of Canon Law but was inserted just before promulgation by higher authorities.) The canon states: "The following are to be punished with a just penalty: . . . a person who pertinaciously rejects the doctrine mentioned in canon 752 and who does not make a retraction after having been admonished by the Apostolic See or by the ordinary." The referred-to canon 752 reads: "A religious obedience [the American translation of the Code reads "religious respect"—translator's note] of intellect and will, even if not the assent of faith, is to be paid to the teaching which the Supreme Pontiff or the college of bishops enunciate on faith or morals when they exercise the authentic magisterium even if they do not intend to proclaim it with a definitive act; therefore the Christian faithful are to take care to avoid whatever is not in harmony with that teaching." If the sanction of punishment were to be dropped again, one might translate the canon differently. Instead of "obedience of intellect and will," one could translate the Latin phrase something like "religiously grounded obedience." Its intent has to do with a sincere willingness to prepare the intellect and will to be open to the content of such teachings, and in case full agreement is not possible in spite of all good will, to exercise concern for the good of the Church in one's dissent. The final decision of the Congregation makes one wonder what is expected of educated theologians and laity when, in light of all the sad incidents in which the Roman Inquisition or the Holy Office missed the mark and brought unspeakable suffering on some good theologians, they are required to render an uncritical "obedience of intellect and will."

I would like to conclude with a wise word from Karl Rahner concerning this problem which has become so acute in our day:

> The representatives of the magisterium must explicitly say and practice, in the name of the magisterium, "We are human beings when we make our decisions; people who should not be rash or full of prejudices, yet this is unavoidable. Aside from the fact that the Spirit protects the Church from error through the ultimately binding decisions of the pope and a council, we can—and so can the pope—err in our decisions, and we have often done so in the past and up to our own day. This is a self-evident truth, which the legitimacy and function of a magisterium does not abolish. It is our duty to work under this risk because we still have a task and a function, even when the conditions and requirements of an ultimately binding decision are not present; just as a physician is not constrained from making diagnoses unless he has absolute certainty."

To us theologians, however, Karl Rahner lets the magisterium also speak:

> Neither do you theologians have the right to assume arrogantly from the very beginning that our decisions must be

false because they contradict the opinions which you, or at least a good number of you, have held.[1]

I believe that Curran can honestly agree with this appeal.

Note

1. Karl Rahner, "Theologie und Lehramt," in *Stimmen der Zeit* 198 (1980), 364–365.

Public Dissent in the Church

Charles E. Curran

This article originally appeared in *Origins* in 1986.

"The central issue involved in the controversy between the Congregation for the Doctrine of the Faith and
myself is the possibility of public theological dissent from
some non-infallible teaching which is quite remote from
the core of faith, heavily dependent on support from human reason and involved in such complexity and specificity that logically one cannot claim absolute certitude,"
Father Charles Curran told the annual convention of the
College Theology Society, held at the end of May in Cincinnati. Curran, a professor of moral theology at The
Catholic University of America in Washington, D.C., revealed in March that the doctrinal congregation has asked
him to retract positions he holds on contraception, sterilization, abortion, euthanasia, masturbation, premarital intercourse, homosexual acts and the indissolubility of marriage. He has since told the congregation that he cannot
retract. (See Origins, vol. 15, 665–680, 691–694 and 761–
771.) Curran said his case "raises questions of justice and
of the credibility of the teaching office in the church" and
affects not just the rights of theologians, but the "possibility and right of dissent by the Christian faithful." The text
of his address follows.

In the fall of 1985 I agreed to accept the kind invitation of our
convention program committee to give this plenary session on the

topic: "Authority and Structure in the Churches: Perspective of a Catholic Theologian." Since that time there has been some water over the dam. The Vatican Congregation for the Doctrine of the Faith has urged me to "reconsider and to retract those positions which violate the conditions for a professor to be called a Catholic theologian." According to Cardinal Ratzinger, the prefect of the congregation, there is an inherent contradiction if "one who is to teach in the name of the church in fact denies her teaching."

This paper will attempt to be faithful to the original topic by focusing on the pertinent issues and aspects involved in my present case. From the very beginning I am conscious of my own prejudices and biases. This paper is presented from my own perspective and therefore is bound to serve as an apologetic or defense of my position. However, at the same time I have the broader intention of using this case to raise up the important issues which the theological community, the hierarchical teaching office in the Roman Catholic Church and the total people of God need to address.

The subject of this paper will thus be specifically Roman Catholic, dealing with the role of the theologian in the Roman Catholic Church. However, the questions raised and the issues discussed have not only an indirect interest for other Christian churches and other Christian theologians, but they also deal directly with many of the same issues which arise for all Christian churches and all their theologians. Before pointing out and discussing the more specific issues involved in this case, it is important to recognize the context and presuppositions for the discussion.

CONTEXT AND PRESUPPOSITIONS

The general context for this paper and for the entire case is that of the Roman Catholic Church and Catholic theology. I have made it very clear that I am a believing Catholic and intend to do Catholic theology. Despite my intentions, I still might be wrong; but I maintain that my positions are totally acceptable for a Catholic theologian who is a believing Roman Catholic.

The mission of the entire church is to be faithful to the word and work of Jesus. God's revelation has been handed over and entrusted to the church, which faithfully hands this down from generation to generation through the assistance of the Holy Spirit. Roman Catholicism recognizes that revelation was closed at the end of apostolic times, but revelation itself develops and is understood in the light of the different historical and cultural circumstances of the hearers and doers of the Word.

Roman Catholic faith and theology have strongly disagreed with the emphasis on the Scripture alone. The Scripture must always be understood in light of the thought patterns of our own time. The Catholic insistence on the Scripture and tradition recognized the need to develop and understand God's revelation in Jesus Christ in the light of the contemporary circumstances. The early councils of the fourth, fifth and subsequent centuries illustrate how in matters touching the very heart of faith—the understanding of God and of Jesus Christ—the living church felt the need to go beyond the words of the Scripture, to understand better and more adequately the revelation of God. Thus, the Christian church taught there are three persons in God and two natures in Jesus. Fidelity to the tradition does not mean merely repeating the very words of the Scripture or of older church teaching. The Christian tradition is a living tradition, and fidelity involves a creative fidelity which seeks to preserve in its own time and place the incarnational principle. Creative fidelity is the task of the church in bearing witness to the word and work of Jesus.

In carrying out its call to creative fidelity to the word and work of Jesus, the church is helped by the papal and episcopal roles in the church. The existence of this pastoral teaching function of pope and bishops in the church must be recognized by all. However, there has been much development in the understanding of the exact nature of that teaching office, how it is exercised and what is its relationship to the other functions connected with the office of pope and bishops in the church. Much of the following discussion will center on what is often called today the ordinary magisterium of the papal office. This term *ordinary magisterium* understood in this present sense has only been in use since the 19th century. A Catholic must recognize the pastoral office of teaching given to the pope and bishops, but also to realize that this teaching function has been exercised in different ways over the years.

These aspects briefly mentioned in this opening section are very important and could be developed at much greater length and depth. However, in this paper they are being recalled as the necessary context and presuppositions for the discussion of the issues raised by the case involving the Congregation for the Doctrine of the Faith and myself. I understand myself to be a Catholic theologian and a Catholic believer who recognizes the call of the church to be faithful in a creative way to the word and work of Jesus and gratefully and loyally accepts the papal and episcopal functions in the church.

This paper will now focus on what in my judgment are the primary issues involved in my case. In the process I will state briefly my own position on these issues, but the primary purpose is to raise up for discussion the primary issues which are involved. Four issues will be considered: the role of the theologian, the possibility of public theological dissent from some non-infallible hierarchical church teachings, the possibility and right of dissent by the Christian faithful, the justice and fairness of the process. I have treated academic freedom in chapter 16 of this volume.

The Sept. 17 letter from Cardinal Ratzinger calls upon me to retract my positions in the following specific areas: contraception and sterilization; abortion and euthanasia; masturbation, premarital intercourse and homosexual acts; the indissolubility of marriage. However, as Richard McCormick perceptively points out, these issues and agreement with my positions on these issues do not constitute the major points of contention in the dispute between the congregation and myself. These are important topics, but they are primarily illustrative of the more fundamental issues involved. However, it is necessary to point out that in all these issues my position is quite nuanced.

ROLE OF THE THEOLOGIAN

There has been much written on the role of the theologian and the relationship between the function of bishops and theologians in the church. It is impossible to add to this discussion in this short space, but rather the purpose is to raise up the underlying issues involved in the present controversy. Many and probably the majority of Catholic theologians writing today see the role of the Catholic theologian as somewhat independent and cooperative in relationship to the hierarchical office and not delegated or derivative from the role of pope and bishops. The theologian is a scholar who studies critically, thematically and systematically Christian faith and action. Such a scholar must theologize within the Catholic faith context and must give due importance to all the *loci theologici,* including the teaching of the hierarchical magisterium. The Catholic theologian to be such must give the required assent to official church teaching, but the theologian does not derive his or her theological office from delegation by the hierarchical officeholders. Likewise the teaching function of pope and bishops uses an entirely different methodology from the teaching function of theologians. Note that I have described this understanding of the Catholic theologian as somewhat independent and cooperative with regard to the hierarchical role in the church. The above paragraph has tried to explain concisely in what the independence consists and how that independence is modified by the call of the theologian and all believers to give due assent to the pastoral teaching role of bishops and pope.

However, there is a very different understanding of the role of the theologian found in more recent church legislation. The new Code of Canon Law, which came into effect in the fall of 1983, and the apostolic constitution for ecclesiastical faculties and universities, *Sapientia Christiana,* understand the role of the theologian as primarily derived from the hierarchical teaching office and functioning by reason of delegation given by the hierarchical teaching office. A good illustration of this understanding of the theologian as delegate and representative of the hierarchical teaching office is found in Canon 812 of the new Code of Canon Law: "Those who teach theological subjects in any institution of higher studies must have a mandate from the competent ecclesiastical authority."

According to the code, this mandate is required for all those who teach theology in any Catholic institution of higher learning. Earlier versions of the code spoke of a "canonical mission" instead of a mandate. *Sapientia Christiana,* the apostolic constitution governing ecclesiastical faculties, requires a canonical mission from the chancellor for those teaching disciplines concerning faith or morals. The final version of the code uses the word *mandate* and not canonical mission because canonical mission appears to imply the assignment of a person to an ecclesiastical office. The implication of this new canon and of other recent legislation is that the Catholic theologian in a Catholic institution officially exercises the function of teaching in that school through a delegation from the bishop. The role of the Catholic theologian is thus derived from the hierarchical teaching function and juridically depends upon it.

It seems there has been an interesting, even contradictory, development in Catholic documents within the last few years. The more theoretical documents seem to indicate a recognition for a somewhat independent and cooperative role for theologians, whereas the legislative documents understand the theological role as derivative and delegated from the hierarchical teaching office.

There is no doubt that from the 19th century until recent times the role of the theologian was seen as subordinate to and derivative from the hierarchical teaching office. However, Vatican Council II in its general ecclesiology and in its understanding of theologians can be interpreted to adopt a more cooperative and somewhat independent understanding of the role of theologians vis-à-vis the hierarchical magisterium. The cooperative model does not deny the official role of the hierarchical office in protecting and proclaiming the faith, but theology is a scholarly discipline distinct from but related to the proclamation of the faith by the hierarchical teaching office.

However, canonists recognize that recent canonical legislation, including the new Code of Canon Law, understands the theological function as derivative from the hierarchical teaching function. Newer legislation and its interpretation by canonists indicate that the development has been moving very much in this direction. In the older Code of Canon Law there was no requirement for theologians in Catholic institutions to have a canonical mandate or mission to teach theology. The older code saw the role of the ordinary or diocesan bishop in terms of negative vigilance with regard to individual teachers of theology and not one of positive deputation.

There can be no doubt that present church legislation tends to see the theological function as derivative from the hierarchical teaching function. However, very many Catholic theologians today appeal to more recent developments in Catholic understanding to substantiate a somewhat cooperative and independent understanding of the theological role vis-à-vis the hierarchical role. History indicates that the derivative understanding really began only in the 19th century. In this section I have purposely and consciously used the expression hierarchical teaching office or function to indicate that the teaching function and role of the total church and of others in the church cannot be totally reduced to the hierarchical teaching office.

The correspondence between the Congregation for the Doctrine of the Faith and myself never explicitly goes into this question as such, but the congregation is operating out of a derivative understanding of the role of the theologian while I adopt the somewhat independent and cooperative understanding.

Public Theological Dissent from Some Non-Infallible Hierarchical Church Teachings

The correspondence from the congregation indicates that the problem is public dissent and not just private dissent. However, the meaning of public is never developed. The entire investigation centers on my theological writings, so the only logical conclusion is that *public* here refers to theological writings. Private dissent apparently means something that is not written and is not spoken publicly.

In 1979, after receiving the first set of observations from the congregation, I had the feeling that the investigation would soon focus clearly on the public aspect of dissent and on the manner and mode of dissent. Past experience was the basis for this judgment.

In 1968 I acted as the spokesperson for a group of theologians who ultimately numbered over 600 and issued a public statement at a press conference which concluded that Catholic spouses may responsibly decide according to their conscience that artificial contraception in some circumstances is permissible and even necessary to preserve and foster the values and sacredness of marriage. In response to this statement, the trustees of The Catholic University of America on Sept. 5, 1969, mandated an inquiry in accord with academic due process to determine if the Catholic University professors involved in this dissent had violated by their declarations and actions their responsibilities to the university.

A few months later the object of the inquiry had definitely changed. "Hence the focus of the present inquiry is on the style and method whereby some faculty members expressed personal dissent from papal teaching" and apparently helped organize additional public dissent to such teaching. The board of trustees did not question the right of a scholar to have or hold private dissent from non-infallible church teaching. In the context of the inquiry it became clear that public and organized dissent referred primarily to holding a press conference and to actively soliciting other theologians to sign the original statement. The primary question of public dissent thus was not regular theological publication but the use of the more popular media.

In response to this new focus of the inquiry, the subject professors at Catholic University, through their counsel, pointed out the changed focus but went on to show that such public and organized dissent in the popular media was a responsible action by Catholic theologians. The shift in the focus of the inquiry seemed to come from the fact that the trustees, including the bishops on the board of trustees, were willing to recognize the possibility of even public dissent in theological journals as being legitimate, but objected to the use of the popular media. The faculty inquiry committee fully agreed with the thrust of the argument proposed by the professors, and the professors were exonerated in this hearing.

However, to my surprise, the investigation from the congregation never moved explicitly into the direction of the manner and mode of dissent and even at times the use of popular media. The conclusion logically follows from the position taken by the congregation that the only acceptable form of dissent on these issues is that which is neither written nor spoken publicly. At most the theologian can think in a dissenting way, perhaps even discuss the matter in private and write private letters to the proper authorities explaining the reasons for one's dissent. It is safe to say that the vast majority of Catholic theologians writing today explicitly disagree with the position of the congregation. For this reason I have remained surprised even to the present day that the Congregation for the Doctrine of the Faith was proposing such a restricted notion of legitimate theological dissent from such non-infallible teaching. In principle, they seem to allow for no public theological dissent even in theological journals on non-infallible church teaching.

The central point at issue in the controversy is the possibility of public theological dissent from some non-infallible teaching. I have always pointed out in the correspondence that I have been dealing with the non-infallible hierarchical teaching office. This position was accepted by the congregation in all of the correspondence prior to the Sept. 17, 1985, letter to me from Cardinal Ratzinger. A very few Catholic theologians have maintained that the teaching on artificial contraception is infallible from the ordinary teaching of pope and bishops throughout the world. However, this position is not held by the vast majority of theologians and has not been proposed or defended by the congregation. One could also maintain that the Catholic teaching on divorce is infallible by reason of the teaching of the Council of Trent. However, the phrasing of the canons with regard to the indissolubility of marriage, the attempt not to condemn the practice of *economia* of the Greek church and the somewhat broad understanding of *anathema sit* at that time of Trent argue against the infallible nature of the Catholic Church's teaching on the indissolubility of marriage. Accepted standard textbooks, such as that of Adnès, recognize that the teaching on absolute intrinsic indissolubility is not infallible. Thus my position all along has been that I have never denied an infallible teaching of the church.

However, in the Sept. 17 letter Cardinal Ratzinger seems to claim that the assent of faith is somehow involved in my case. I have strenuously maintained that the assent of faith is not involved and we are dealing with the *obsequium religiosum* which is due in cases of non-infallible teaching. I assume as a result of my meeting with Cardinal Ratzinger in Rome on March 8 that we are in no way involved with the assent of faith. However, it is very clear that the congregation maintains that the *obsequium religiosum* due to non-infallible teaching does not allow the theologian to dissent publicly in these cases.

Cardinal Ratzinger himself has called the distinction between infallible and non-infallible teaching "legalistic." Only in this century have theologians made this distinction in such a sharp way. "When one affirms that non-infallible doctrines, even though they make up part of the teaching of the church, can be legitimately contested, one ends up by destroying the practice of the Christian life and reduces the faith to a collection of doctrines." Ratzinger de-emphasizes the distinction between infallible and non-infallible teaching to help support his position that a theologian cannot dissent publicly from non-infallible church teaching. What is to be said about Ratzinger's understanding?

It is true that the sharp distinction between infallible and non-infallible teaching is recent, for it became prevalent only at the time of the First Vatican Council (1870), which defended the infallibility of the pope. After that time, theologians quite rightly distinguished the two levels of teaching and the two different assents which are due to such teachings. All the faithful owe the assent of faith to infallible teaching and the *obsequium religiosum* of intellect and will to authoritative or authentic, non-infallible teaching.

The distinction became well entrenched in the theology manuals of the 20th century before Vatican II. Such a distinction helped to explain that official teaching on some issues had been wrong and had subsequently been corrected (e.g., the condemnation of interest taking, the need for the intention of procreation to justify conjugal relations). At the time of Vatican Council I and later it was also pointed out that Popes Liberius (d. 366), Vigilius (d. 555) and Honorius (d. 638) all proposed erroneous teachings which were subsequently rejected through theological dissent.

Vatican Council II changed many earlier teachings such as those on religious freedom and the relationship of the Roman Catholic Church to other Christian churches and to the true church of Jesus Christ. Scripture scholars for the last generation or so have publicly disagreed with the teachings that were proposed by the biblical commission in the first two decades of this century. The theologians thus recognized the distinction between infallible and non-infallible teaching and used it, among other purposes, to explain why certain earlier errors in church teaching did not refute the Vatican I teaching on papal infallibility. These theologians likewise recognized the possibility of dissent from such non-infallible teaching at times, but did not explicitly justify public dissent.

The theologians are not the only ones to use this distinction. *Lumen Gentium,* the Constitution on the Church of the Second Vatican Council, recognizes this distinction between infallible and non-infallible teaching and the two different types of assent which are due (No. 25). The new Code of Canon Law clearly distinguishes between the assent of faith and the *obsequium religiosum* of intellect and will which is due to the authoritative teaching of the pope and college of bishops even when they do not intend to proclaim that doctrine by a definitive act (Canon 752). This distinction is thus not only accepted by theologians but also by official documents and by the new Code of Canon Law.

Some theological manuals and many contemporary theologians understand the *obsequium religiosum* owed to authoritative, non-infallible teaching to justify at times the possibility of theological dissent and, at the present time, even public dissent. Some bishops conferences explicitly recognized the legitimacy of dissent from the papal encyclical *Humanae Vitae* issued in 1968. Also documents from bishops conferences have recognized the possibility of public theological dissent from some non-infallible church teaching. The U.S. bishops in their 1968 pastoral letter "Human Life in Our Day" pinpoint that in non-infallible teaching there is always a presumption in favor of the magisterium—a position held by most theologians. However, the pastoral letter also recognizes the legitimacy of public theological dissent from such teaching if the reasons are serious and well-founded, if the manner of the dissent does not question or impugn the teaching authority of the church and if the dissent is such as not to give scandal. Since I have developed at great length in my correspondence with the congregation both the arguments justifying the possibility of public dissent and the many theologians and others in the church who recognize such a possibility, there is no need to repeat this here.

One significant aspect of the question deserves mention here because of some recent developments—the understanding and translation of *obsequium religiosum. Obsequium* has often been translated as submission or obedience. Bishop Christopher Butler was, to my knowledge, the first to translate the word *obsequium* as respect. Francis Sullivan, in his book on magisterium, rejects the translation of "due respect," but still allows the possibility of legitimate public theological dissent from non-infallible church teaching. (Sullivan, a Jesuit professor at the Pontifical Gregorian University in Rome, in a recent interview strongly defends the distinction between infallible and non-infallible church teaching. Sullivan sees the position taken by the Vatican congregation in its correspondence with me as threatening the critical function of the theologian with regard to the non-definitive teaching of the magisterium. "The idea that Catholic theologians, at any level of education, can only teach the official church position and present only those positions in their writings, is new and disturbing." Sullivan, who considers his approach "rather moderate" and "standard," has been teaching the possibility of public theological dissent from some non-infallible teaching at the Pontifical Gregorian University in Rome. Sullivan adds that "no one has ever questioned what I teach.")

Sullivan claims that "submission" and not "due respect" is the proper translation of *obsequium*, but the Gregorian University professor still recognizes the possibility and legitimacy of public dissent from authoritative, non-infallible teaching.

The English text of the Code of Canon Law found in the commentary commissioned by the Canon Law Society of America and authorized by the executive committee of the National Conference of Catholic Bishops in the United States translates *obsequium* as respect. Ladislas Orsy, in a recent commentary on Canon 752, recognizes difficulties in translating *obsequium* but opts for respect. Orsy also recognizes the possibility of legitimate public dissent from some authoritative, non-infallible teaching. The discussion over the proper understanding and translation of *obsequium* has been an occasion for many to recognize the possibility of legitimate public dissent from some non-infallible church teaching.

There can be no doubt that church documents, the Code of Canon Law, theologians in general and canonists in general have accepted the importance of the distinction between infallible and non-infallible hierarchical teaching. Although I believe the distinction between infallible and non-infallible teaching is very important and necessary, there is a need to say more in dealing with the possibility of public dissent. I disagree with Cardinal Ratzinger's attempt to smooth over somewhat the clear distinction between fallible and non-infallible teaching, but his remarks show the need to say something in addition to the distinction between infallible and non-infallible teaching. What about the danger of reducing the Christian faith in practice to a small, abstract core?

In my own comments about this case, I have been careful not only to use the distinction between infallible and non-infallible teaching but also to talk about what is core and central to the faith as distinguished from those things that are more removed and peripheral. Also I have consistently spoken about the right to dissent publicly from *some* non-infallible church teaching. The distinction between infallible and non-infallible church teaching is absolutely necessary, but not sufficient. The older theology tries to deal with questions of the relationship of church teaching to the core of faith through the use of theological notes. These notes and their opposites, in terms of censures, attempted to recognize the complexity by categorizing many different types of non-infallible teaching. In a true sense there is a need today to redevelop the concept of theological notes in the light of the realities of the present time.

As important as the concept of infallible teaching is, there are some very significant limitations involved in it. Infallible teaching, especially of the extraordinary type by pope or council, has usually come in response to an attack on or a denial of something central to the faith. However, some points which have never been attacked, such as the existence of God, have never been defined by the extraordinary hierarchical teaching office. On the other hand, the limits and imperfections of any infallible teaching have been rightly recognized. Infallible teaching itself is always open to development, better understanding and even purification. Thus, one must be careful when speaking about infallible teaching both because some things might pertain to the core of faith which have at least not been infallibly taught by the extraordinary teaching function of the pope and bishops, and because even infallible teaching itself is open to development and further interpretation. However, in the present discussion the distinction between infallible and non-infallible is very important. It allows me to deal with a limited area—the area of non-infallible teaching. I am in no way questioning what is an essential matter of Catholic faith.

Within this large area of what is non-infallible and not central to the Christian faith, it is necessary to recognize various degrees and levels of relationship to faith. Here an updating of the older theological notes would be very useful. I have recognized this fact by consciously referring to dissent from *some* non-infallible teachings which are somewhat removed from the core and central faith realities. It is true that I have not attempted to develop all the distinctions involved in non-infallible teaching, but in the light of the purposes of the present discussion I have tried to show that the particular issues under discussion are removed from the central realities of Christian faith.

The Catholic tradition in moral theology has insisted that its moral teaching is based primarily on natural law and not primarily on faith or the Scripture. The natural law is understood to be human reason reflecting on human nature. Even those teachings which have some basis in Scripture (e.g., the indissolubility of marriage, homosexuality) were also said to be based on natural law. This insistence on the rational nature of Catholic moral teaching recognizes such teaching can and should be shared by all human beings of all faiths and of no faith. Such teachings are thus somewhat removed from the core of Catholic faith as such. The distance of these teachings from the core of faith and the central realities of faith grounds the possibility of legitimate dissent.

In addition, the issues under discussion are specific, concrete, universal moral norms existing in the midst of complex reality. Logic demands that the more specific and complex the reality, the less is the possibility of certitude. Moral norms, in my judgment, are not the primary, or the only, or the most important concern of moral teaching and of moral theology. Moral teaching deals with general perspectives, values, attitudes and dispositions as well as norms. Values, attitudes and dispositions are much more important and far-reaching for the moral life than are norms. These values and dispositions by their very nature are somewhat more general and can be more universally accepted as necessary for Christian and human life.

Within the church all can and should agree that the disciples of Jesus are called to be loving, faithful, hopeful, caring people who strive to live out the reality of the paschal mystery. Disrespect for persons, cheating, slavery, dishonesty and injustice are always wrong. However, the universal binding force of specific concrete material norms cannot enjoy the same degree or level of certitude. Norms exist to protect and promote values, but in practice conflicts often arise in the midst of the complexity and specificity involved. Thus the issues under consideration in this case are quite far removed from the core of faith and exist at such a level of complexity and specificity that one has to recognize some possibility of dissent.

It is also necessary to recognize the necessary distinction between the possibility of dissent and the legitimacy of dissent on particular questions. Reasons must be given which are convincing in order to justify the dissent in practice. The central issue involved in the controversy between the Congregation for the Doctrine of the Faith and myself is the possibility of public theological dissent from some non-infallible teaching which is quite remote from the core of faith, heavily dependent on support from human reason, and involved in such complexity and specificity that logically one cannot claim absolute certitude.

There is a further question which has not received much discussion from the Catholic theological community but which should at least be raised. We have generally talked about the responsibilities and rights of Catholic theologians in general. Are there any distinctions that must be made concerning theologians? Are the rights and responsibilities of Catholic theologians and the particular right to dissent in these areas the same for all Catholic theologians? Is there a difference between the theologian as teacher and as researcher and writer? Is there a difference if the theologian teaches in a seminary, a college or a university? In the particular cases under discussion, I would develop the thesis that these differences do not affect the possibility and legitimacy of public theological dissent. All of us can agree on the need to explore this question in much greater depth. In addition, more attention must be given to the limits of legitimate dissent.

The Christian Faithful and Dissent

There is a third aspect or issue which has not received the attention it needs—the possibility and legitimacy of dissent on the part of the members of the church. In a very true sense my present controversy involves more than just the role of theologians in the church.

There can be no doubt that much of the friction between theologians and the hierarchical magisterium has occurred on more practical questions, including moral issues touching on sexuality. The issues are not just abstract questions about which people speculate, but they involve concrete decisions about specific actions which are to be done. Problems arise in these areas precisely because they involve more than speculation. Here the position proposed by theologians might have some practical bearing on how people live. All must recognize that the distinction between the roles of bishops and theologians would be much clearer if the role of theologians were restricted to the realm of speculation, with no effect on what people do in practice. However, life is not so easily compartmentalized.

Elsewhere I have defended the fact that on some issues a loyal Catholic may disagree in theory and in practice with the church's non-infallible teaching and still consider oneself a loyal and good Roman Catholic. In a sense, under certain conditions one can speak of a right of the Catholic faithful to dissent from certain non-infallible teachings. In the aftermath of *Humanae Vitae* in 1968 some bishops' conferences recognized that dissent in practice from the encyclical's teaching condemning artificial contraception could be legitimate and did not cut one off from the body of the faithful. The congregation, in its correspondence with me, has not gone into this issue. Those who deny the legitimacy of such dissent in practice would seem to face a difficult ecclesiological problem when confronted with the fact that the vast majority of fertile Catholic spouses use artificial contraception. What is the relationship of these spouses to the Roman Catholic Church?

The importance of recognizing this possibility and even right on the part of the faithful greatly affects how the theologian functions. If there is such a possibility, then the individual members of the Catholic Church have a right to know about it. I hasten to add that the individual members also have a right to know what is the official teaching of the church and should be conscious of the dangers of finitude and sin that can skewer any human decision. Public dissent by a Catholic theologian would then be called for not only because theologians must discuss with one another in the attempt to understand better God's word and to arrive at truth, but also because the people of God need this information to make their own moral decisions. Thus, for example, in the light of the situation present at the time of the issuance of the encyclical *Humanae Vitae* in 1968, it was important for Roman Catholic spouses to know that they did not have to make a choice between using artificial contraception under some conditions and ceasing to be members of the Roman Catholic Church. The Catholic theologian, among others, had an obligation to tell this to Catholic spouses.

The possibility for legitimate dissent in practice by the faithful also affects the matter of scandal. The U.S. bishops in their 1968 letter proposed three conditions under which public theological dissent is in order. One of these conditions is that the dissent be such as not to give scandal. In my correspondence with the congregation I repeatedly asked them for criteria which should govern public dissent in the church. No developed criteria were ever forthcoming. However, in the April 1983 observations from the congregation, it was mentioned briefly that to dissent publicly and to encourage dissent in others runs the risk of causing scandal.

Scandal in the strict sense is an action or omission which provides another the occasion of sinning. In the broad sense, scandal is the wonderment and confusion which are caused by a certain action or omission. Richard McCormick has already discussed the issue of scandal understood in the strict sense. What about scandal as the wonderment and confusion caused among the faithful by public theological dissent?

There can be no doubt that in the past there has been a strong tendency on the part of the hierarchical leaders of the church to look upon the faithful as poor and ignorant sheep who had to be protected and helped. This same vision and understanding of the ordinary common people also lay behind an older Catholic justification of monarchy and government from above. Catholic social teaching itself has changed in the 20th century and accepted the need for and importance of democratic political institutions. No longer are the citizens the poor sheep or the "ignorant multitude," to use the phrase employed by Pope Leo XIII. So too the members of the church can no longer be considered as poor sheep; but greater importance must be given to their increased education and rights in all areas, including religion.

Perhaps at times theologians, who often associate with people who are well-educated, will fail to give enough importance to the danger of disturbing some of the faithful with their teachings. However, in this day and age it seems many more Catholic lay people would be scandalized if theologians were forbidden to discuss publicly important topics of the day such as contraception, divorce, abortion and homosexuality. These issues are being discussed at great length and in all places today, and theologians must be able to enter into the discussion even to the point of dissenting from some official Catholic teaching. In addition, if the faithful can at times dissent in practice and remain loyal Roman Catholics, then they have the right to know what theologians are discussing.

In this entire discussion it would ultimately be erroneous to confine the question just to the possibility and right of theologians to dissent publicly from some non-infallible teachings. This present discussion is complicated by the fact that the dissent is not just speculative but is also practical. There is need for further development and nuancing, but on all the moral issues under consideration I have carefully tried to indicate what the legitimate possibilities are for the faithful in practice. The right of the faithful in this matter definitely colors one's approach to public theological dissent and to the dangers of scandal brought about by such dissent or the lack of it.

JUSTICE AND FAIRNESS OF THE PROCESS

Catholic theology has always emphasized the incarnational principle with its emphasis on visible human structures. Catholic ecclesiology well illustrates this approach by insisting on the church as a visible human community—the people of God with a hierarchical office. The visible church strives to be a sacrament or sign of the presence of God in the world, in and through this visible community.

Within the community there are bound to be tensions involving the role of bishops and the role of theologians. Both strive to work for the good of the church, but there will always be tensions. To claim there is no tension would be illusionary and ultimately would deny that the church is a living, pilgrim community. The church is always striving to know and live better the word and work of Jesus in the particular historical and cultural circumstances of time and place.

The role of the theologian by definition will often be that of probing, pushing and tentatively pushing the boundaries forward. The hierarchical teaching office must promote such creative and faithful theological activity, while at the same time it must rightly wait until these newer developments emerge more clearly. The church, in justice, must find ways to deal with this tension in the relationship between theologians and the hierarchical teaching office. The good of the church, the credibility of its teaching office and the need to protect the rights of all concerned call for just ways of dealing with these inevitable tensions.

The present case raises questions of justice and of the credibility of the teaching office in the church. It is recognized by all that there are many Catholic theologians who publicly dissent from some non-infallible teachings. Likewise there are many Catholic theologians who hold similar positions and even more radical positions on the moral issues involved in the present case. However, the issues of justice and credibility go much deeper.

First, it is necessary for the congregation to state its position on public theological dissent from non-infallible teaching. Is such dissent ever allowed? If so, under what conditions or criteria? From the correspondence, it would seem that the congregation is claiming that all public theological dissent is wrong or at least public dissent on these particular issues is wrong. Does the congregation truly hold such a position?

As mentioned earlier, the U.S. bishops in 1968, in the light of the controversy engendered by *Humanae Vitae,* proposed three conditions for justifying public dissent from non-infallible teaching. The three conditions are: The reasons must be serious and well-founded; the manner of the dissent must not question or impugn the teaching authority of the church; and it must not give scandal. I have consistently maintained that my dissent has been in accord with these norms. The congregation was unwilling to accept these norms. Does the congregation disagree with the U.S. bishops and with the vast majority of Catholic theologians?

Archbishop John Quinn, then of Oklahoma City, at the Synod of Bishops in 1974 pointed out the real need to arrive at some consensus and understanding about dissent and urged discussion between representatives of the Holy See and representatives of theologians to arrive at acceptable guidelines governing theological dissent in the church (Origins 4, 1974–5, 319–320). Archbishop Quinn brought up the same problem again at the Synod of Bishops in 1980. For the good of the church there continues to be a "real need" to arrive at some guidelines in this area.

In addition, there is need for juridical structures which better safeguard justice and the rights of all concerned. Some of the problems with the present procedures of the congregation have already been pointed out in the correspondence. The congregation, in a letter to me, has defended its procedures because the *ratio agendi* is not a trial, but rather a procedure designed to generate a careful and accurate examination of the contents of published writings by the author. However, since the process can result in severe punishment for the person involved, it seems that such a process should incorporate the contemporary standards of justice found in other juridical proceedings.

One set of problems stems from the fact that the congregation is the prosecutor, the judge and jury. Some people have objected strongly to the fact that the cardinal-prefect has commented publicly on the present case and disagreed in the public media with my position while the case has been in progress. Problems have also been raised against the existing procedures from the viewpoints of the secrecy of the first part of the process, the failure to allow the one being investigated to have counsel, the failure to disclose the accusers and the total record to the accused, and the lack of any substantive appeal process (Granfield, 131f).

There have been many suggestions made for improvements in the procedures. The German bishops have adopted procedures for use in Germany. Cardinal Ratzinger in 1984 admitted that there has been a decree of the plenary session of the congregation in favor of a revision of the current procedures of the congregation. The proposals made by the German conference of bishops have been accepted in principle. However, because of the workload and time constraints, the decree has not been put into effect (National Catholic Register, Aug. 12, 1984, p. 6).

In 1980 a joint committee of the Catholic Theological Society of America and the Canon Law Society of America was formed to address the question of cooperation between theologians and the hierarchical magisterium in the United States, with a view toward developing norms that could be used in settling disputes. The committee prepared a detailed set of procedures in 1983, but they are still under study by the U.S. bishops.

In the meantime there has been one case involving the investigation of a theologian's writings by the doctrinal committee of the U.S. bishops. Little is known about the process itself, but the final statement from the committee indicates that the dialogue was fruitful and that the theologian in question, Richard McBrien, had the right to call other theologians to defend and explain his positions. Perhaps the process used in this case might prove helpful in other similar cases. A detailed discussion of proposed guidelines lies beyond the scope of this present paper.

The major points made here are that justice and the credibility of the church's teaching office call for a recognition of the norms or criteria governing public dissent in the church, the equitable application of these norms and the review of existing procedures to incorporate the safeguards of contemporary justice in the process of examining theologians. The call for these changes has been repeatedly made in the past. The need is even more urgent today.

In conclusion, this paper has examined what I think are the four most significant issues involved in my present dispute with the Congregation for the Doctrine of the Faith—the role of the Catholic theologian, the possibility of public theological dissent from some non-infallible hierarchical teaching, the possibility of dissent by the faithful in such cases, and some practical aspects. In discussing all these issues I have also indicated my approach to the questions under discussion. I welcome your reactions.

L'Affaire Curran

Richard A. McCormick, S.J.

This article originally appeared in *America* in 1986.

The March 12 issue of The New York Times headlined a front-page article "Vatican Orders a Theologian to Retract Teachings on Sex." Clearly the headline editor knew what she/he was doing. Every word is a grabber. "Vatican" and "Sex" jump at you. Then add to that "Orders" and "Retract" and the looming donnybrook takes even clearer shape. The scenario is given final touches with "Theologian" and "Teachings." It is not just anyone, but a theologian of the church, who is not just analyzing, examining, proffering opinions, but "teaching." Similar reports, without such telltale headlines, were read across the country, from Shreveport (where I was) to Toledo, from Sacramento to Boston.

What is going on here? The Rev. Charles E. Curran, revered and reviled professor of moral theology at The Catholic University of America, has been in correspondence with the Congregation for the Doctrine of the Faith (C.D.F.) since 1979 concerning certain of his writings. On March 8, there was a personal interview with Cardinal Joseph Ratzinger in Rome. The writings in question concern contraception, sterilization, indissolubility of marriage, abortion and euthanasia, homosexuality and masturbation. They could have concerned—but only by a vigorous stretch of the imagination—other issues, such as nuclear war, revolution, poverty, racial justice and economics. But, in a sense, the issues are not the issue. Beneath this bill of particulars is the tender nerve, dissent—and more precisely, as I shall make clear, public dissent.

What did Father Curran actually write about some of the subjects mentioned above? A few examples will suffice. In *Moral Theology: A Continuing Journey* (p. 144) he states: "Human beings do have the power and responsibility to interfere with the sexual faculty and act. The official Catholic teaching is often accused of a physicalism or biologism because the biological or physical structure of the act is made normative and cannot be interfered with. I take this dissenting position."

With regard to the indissolubility of marriage he writes: "In light of these and other reasons, I propose that indissolubility remains a goal and ideal for Christian marriage; but Christians, sometimes without any personal fault, are not always able to live up to that ideal. Thus the Roman Catholic Church should change its teaching on divorce" (*Issues in Sexual and Medical Ethics*, pp. 15–16).

Finally, with regard to homosexuality, he summarizes his position, expressed previously, in this way: "My position affirms that for an irreversible, constitutional or genuine homosexual, homosexual acts in the context of a loving relationship striving for permanency are objectively morally good" (*Critical Concerns in Moral Theology*, pp. 92–93).

Similar proposals could be adduced about sterilization, masturbation, abortion and premarital sexual relations. One thing should be absolutely clear: These conclusions do represent dissenting views. There should be no fudging on that.

But where do such views put Father Curran in the theological world? Is he the radical and notorious *enfant terrible* that The Wanderer describes and urges its readers to denounce to the Holy See? He has repeatedly argued that his positions, while departing from official formulations, fall within the mainstream of substantial Catholic concerns. He points to the fact that other theologians throughout the world have written similar things.

For instance, in his book *Medical Ethics*, Bernard Häring justifies direct sterilization in certain instances. Hundreds of theologians have dissented from the central thesis of *Humanae Vitae* (that every contraceptive act is intrinsically immoral). Any number of theologians have proposed "pastoral solutions" to the dilemma of homosexuality that do not always reflect the Congregation for the Doctrine of the Faith's 1975 "Declaration on Certain Questions Concerning Sexual Ethics." For instance, the conservative Roman theologian Jan Visser, one of the collaborators on this declaration, has admitted that it is sometimes the lesser of two evils for homosexuals to live in stable unions rather than in promiscuous relationships.

So far as the indissolubility of marriage is concerned, Catholic exegetes and theologians have been struggling for some years to read the implications of Jesus' words for our time. Thus the late George MacRae, S.J., once wrote: "We must discern the process by which the teaching of Jesus was remembered, communicated, interpreted, adapted and enshrined in the practice of the early Christian communities. That process, we have seen, is one of accommodation in circumstances that were not the context of the preaching of Jesus Himself."

Similarly, the distinguished exegete Joseph Fitzmyer, S.J., wrote in Theological Studies (1976): "If Matthew under inspiration could have been moved to add an exceptive phrase to the saying of Jesus about divorce that he found in an absolute form in either his Marcan source or in 'Q,' or if Paul likewise under inspiration could introduce into his writing an exception on his own authority, then why cannot the Spirit-guided institutional church of a later generation make a similar exception in view of problems confronting Christian married life of its day, or so-called broken marriages (not really envisaged in the New Testament), as it has done in some situations?"

None of these proposals—and many more could be adduced—is made in a spirit of defiance, with the authors claiming to be an official voice or competitive magisterium. Their intent as well as their tone is one of searching and questioning, of public theological wrestling proposed to scholars and the broader church community for careful consideration. The same can be said of Father Curran's writings, even though he proposes them under the rubrics of "position," "teaching," "dissent." He has a strong point, then, when he argues that in neither substance nor purpose do his writings constitute an extreme "left" position.

Why, then, is Charles Curran singled out for special scrutiny and threat? The answer to that question must remain speculative. Was it because he organized the public dissent against *Humanae Vitae* in 1968? It is no secret that some Roman institutions have elephantine memories. Was it because archconservative groups such as Catholics United for the Faith flooded the Congregation with mail against him? Was it because he is perceived as America's Hans Küng? Was it because Rome feels that now is the time to make an example of someone so that others will take note? As I say, "speculative."

When the Congregation for the Doctrine of the Faith first broached this matter with Father Curran, it listed some of the subjects of concern noted above. At first, he did not respond to the individual subjects of concern, but instead presented his view about the legitimacy of public dissent in the church. He stated that this was the key issue and that, before he could enter into dialogue with the Congregation, he would have to know its view on public dissent.

On June 21, 1982, he responded in detail to the Congregation's specific concerns with a 23-page letter. The Congregation was not satisfied with that reply and told him so in a letter dated Feb. 10, 1983.

On May 10, 1983, the Congregation again wrote Father Curran spelling out its problems. It listed issues where he was in clear dissent from the magisterium and some "issues that remain unclear," but stated that the "right to dissent publicly is at the basis of the C.D.F.'s difficulties with Father Curran." The Congregation implicitly admitted the right of *private* dissent but noted that "to further dissent publicly and to encourage dissent in others runs the risk of causing scandal to the faithful." It viewed such dissent as "setting up one's own theological opinion in contradiction to the position taken by the Church." Curran was asked to reply within a working month.

On Aug. 10, 1983, he wrote the Congregation, addressing only the first of its concerns (public dissent). He felt that the individual subjects of dissent could not be fruitfully addressed until the Congregation's view of dissent itself had been clarified. On Dec. 2, 1983, the Congregation wrote him again about the incompleteness of his reply ("We still await your complete reply").

Because the Congregation's letters were sent through Washington's Archbishop James A. Hickey, Father Curran wrote to Archbishop Hickey on Feb. 28, 1984, of his "growing frustration."

He stated: "My reaction is one of growing frustration. I mentioned this to you in earlier correspondence and have said the same in my most recent detailed response to the Congregation itself."

"From my very first response in Oct. 1979, I have tried to determine as exactly as possible the differences between the Congregation and myself on the question of dissent. I formulated five questions at that time, but the Congregation has been unwilling to respond to them. I ended my response of Aug. 1983, with the request that the Congregation state what are the norms that should govern dissent. . . . Why has the Congregation been unwilling to answer that question? Why are they stalling?" Curran was obviously referring to public, theological dissent, since private dissent is not the issue.

The Congregation wrote to Father Curran once more on April 13, 1984, asking for a reply by Sept. 1 on its specific points. On Aug. 22, he replied to those specific inquiries, but this reply was undoubtedly seen as unsatisfactory by the Congregation.

On Sept. 17, 1985, Father Curran received a letter from the Congregation stating that its inquiry had been completed and that the results "were presented to the Sovereign Pontiff in an audience granted to the undersigned Cardinal Prefect [Joseph Ratzinger] on June 28, 1985, and were confirmed by him." The letter called attention to the fact that "Catholic theologians, hence those teaching in ecclesiastical faculties, do not teach on their own authority but by virtue of the mission they have received from the church." The letter then continued with an explanation of this "mission":

"In order to guarantee this teaching, the church claims the freedom to maintain her own academic institutions in which her doctrine is reflected upon, taught and interpreted in complete fidelity. This freedom of the church to teach her doctrine is in full accord with the students' corresponding right to know what that teaching is and have it properly explained to them. This freedom of the church likewise implies the right to choose for her theological faculties those and only those professors who, in complete intellectual honesty and integrity, recognize themselves to be capable of meeting these requirements."

The letter then details the issues concerning which Father Curran dissents (contraception, abortion and euthanasia, masturbation, homosexuality, premarital intercourse and indissolubility of marriage). It concludes: "In light of the indispensable requirements for authentic theological instruction, described by the council and by the public law of the Catholic Church, the Congregation now invites you to reconsider and to retract those positions which violate the conditions necessary for a professor to be called a Catholic theologian. It must be recognized that the authorities of the church cannot allow the present situation to continue in which the inherent contradiction is prolonged that one who is to teach in the name of the church in fact denies her teaching."

The language in this letter is clear, and clearly ominous. "Indispensable requirements," "cannot allow the present situation to continue," leave little room for doubt or compromise. The inescapable message: Unless Father Curran retracts, he will be stripped of his mandate to teach as a "Catholic theologian." (That would mean practically that Father Curran could not teach theology at Catholic University, nor realistically at any Catholic university.) The only question now seems to be: When will the other shoe drop?

When I first saw the Congregation's letter, I wrote (Nov. 15, 1985) to Archbishop Hickey, noting that it would be tragic if the letter were made public. My letter continued: "I use the term 'tragic' deliberately and thoughtfully. The reason: The theology of the letter is, in my judgment, at variance with Catholic tradition and, as such, open to serious criticism. When such a letter becomes public, it will quite properly be read as the official Roman attitude toward theological inquiry. Such an attitude represents a self-inflicted blow on the credibility of the magisterium.

"Why? Because the letter explicitly states that agreement with the ordinary magisterium on every authoritatively proposed moral formulation is required if one is to be called a Catholic theologian. After detailing four areas where Curran's opinions are at variance with official formulations, Cardinal Ratzinger refers to 'those positions which violate the conditions necessary for a professor to be called a Catholic theologian.' This contention—which undergirds the entire letter—disallows dissent from noninfallibly proposed teaching in principle. Such a point of view cannot survive historical and theological scrutiny.

"If Cardinal Ratzinger's letter were to be applied to theologians throughout the world, it is clear that the vast majority would not qualify as Catholic theologians; for, as a matter of record, most theologians have found it impossible to agree with the central formulation of *Humanae Vitae* (see, for example, *Sittliche Normen,* ed. W. Kerber, Patmos, 1982, where this point is repeatedly made). Indeed, if Cardinal Ratzinger's letter represented an acceptable ecclesiology, we would not have the Decree on Religious Liberty as an official church document. Only because John Courtney Murray, S.J., conducted a long uphill battle, and a dissenting one, could Vatican II arrive at the Decree on Religious Liberty. Briefly, dissent in the church must be viewed much more realistically and positively—as the ordinary way to growth and development. Even quite traditional ecclesiologists now view the matter in this way (see *Magisterium: Teaching Authority in the Catholic Church* by Francis A. Sullivan, S.J.)."

When the Congregation will drop the other shoe and declare Father Curran no longer a Catholic theologian is not clear. *That* it will do so seems unavoidable from the logic of its approach. If so, it will be the first American instance of this and, as such, an important landmark in American Catholicism. For this reason, it is important to unpack some of the issues that surround this matter.

Nonissues. Before listing the issues, it would be useful to clarify things by explicitly eliminating nonissues. I see five.

Agreement with Father Curran. One need not agree with all or any of Curran's analyses and positions in rejecting the Congregation's threatened action. I have disagreed with Curran and he with me. Others have disagreed with both of us. That is neither here nor there, for discussion and disagreement are the very lifeblood of the academic and theological enterprise. We all learn and grow in the process, and it is a public process. Without such theological exchange and the implied freedom to make an honest mistake, the magisterium itself would be paralyzed by the sycophancy of theologians.

Dissent. Dissent as such is not the key issue. The Congregation admits as much when it states that personal dissent demands certainty that a teaching is erroneous—a statement whose rigor is open to serious challenge. The church does not and cannot expect assent to moral formulations that one judges to be erroneous. The mind can assent to what it perceives to be true in itself or it can assent because of trust in the teacher. Neither can occur when there are contrary reasons utterly persuasive to an individual. This is quite traditional teaching. The issue is rather *public* dissent.

Infallibility. There is no question here of dissent from infallible teaching. Infallibity is not the issue it was in the case of Father Hans Küng. It is generally admitted by theologians that the church's authentic teaching on concrete moral behavior does not, indeed cannot, fall into the category of definable doctrine. There is a recent tiny pocket of resistance to this, but even the Congregation for the Doctrine of the Faith makes no claim that Father Curran dissents from infallibly proposed teachings. In a press statement Bishop James W. Malone, president of the National Conference of Catholic Bishops, left the matter a bit murky. He referred to "the teaching of the church's magisterium on crucial points." What does "crucial" mean? Is everything taught authoritatively, especially if frequently repeated, crucial? Crucial to what? And are crucial teachings removed from the possibility of dissent? Why?

Authority of the church to teach. In dissenting from this or that authoritative formulation, one does not automatically deny the authority of the church to teach in the area of morals. Indeed, the very anguish, ardor and prayerfulness of one's dissent asserts the opposite. If one denied such authority, strenuous efforts, anguish and prayerfulness would be out of place. One simply would not care. Father Curran has repeatedly asserted the church's moral teaching authority. Such authority is a nonissue in this case.

The right and duty to safeguard teaching. All theologians would, I think, admit that the church has such a right and duty, and even that it could take the disciplinary form of removing one's mandate to teach as a Catholic theologian. That is not an issue. The issue is when and under what circumstances this form of safeguarding should be used. Only for outright heresy? For any dissent from any "crucial" teaching? I say "under what circumstances" because clearly Pope John XXIII acknowledged the church's "right and duty to safeguard teaching" (Bishop Malone's phrase), yet he rejected the punitive measures associated with Cardinal Alfredo Ottaviani's

Holy Office. "Nowadays," he said, "the Spouse of Christ prefers to make use of the medicine of mercy rather than that of severity. She considers that she meets the needs of the present day by demonstrating the validity of her teaching rather than by condemnations" ("Pope John's Opening Speech to the Council," *The Documents of Vatican II*, p. 716).

Issues. If the above are nonissues, what are the true issues we ought to think about? There is but a single issue, but one with many ramifications. That single issue is public dissent. If one judges a teaching authoritatively proposed to be one-sided, incomplete, partially inaccurate or even erroneous, what is one to do?

There are two possible answers to this question. One is the Congregation's. Simply put, it is: Keep silence. For if one writes of one's disagreement, the Congregation sees an "inherent contradiction." It states it as follows: "One who is to teach in the name of the church in fact denies her teaching." For the Congregation this is intolerable ("the authorities of the church cannot allow . . ."). It "runs the risk of causing scandal."

A second possible answer is presented by the late Karl Rahner, S.J. Writing in *Stimmen der Zeit* (1980), Father Rahner asked: "What are contemporary moral theologians to make of Roman declarations on sexual morality that they regard as too unnuanced? Are they to remain silent, or is it their task to dissent, to give a more nuanced interpretation?" Rahner was unhesitating in his response: "I believe that the theologian, after mature reflection, has the right, and many times the duty, to speak out against a teaching of the magisterium and support his dissent." In sum, where Rahner sees the right and duty to speak out, the Congregation sees scandal.

Most theologians would, I believe, share Father Rahner's view. A group of such theologians (all past presidents of the Catholic Theological Society of America and The College Theology Society) issued a statement on March 12 manifesting this and putting the following questions to the Congregation about the threat to Father Curran: "1) Which noninfallible teachings are serious enough to provoke such a result, and how are those teachings determined? 2) How many noninfallible teachings would one have to disagree with before this result would follow, and how is that number determined? 3) If disagreement with any noninfallible teaching of the Church is sufficient to provoke this result, on what theological, doctrinal or historical basis is that principle deduced?"

These are serious questions, and we as a community of believers deserve clear answers to them. If such answers are not forthcoming or are unsatisfactory, and if the threat against Father Curran is carried out, it will be hard to avoid the conclusion that we are dealing with an abuse of authority.

The letter of the theologians noted one more important point: "If Father Curran's views on the various issues mentioned in the letter [of the Congregation] are so incompatible with Catholic teaching that he must be declared no longer a Catholic theologian, justice and fairness would dictate that other Catholic theologians who hold similar views should be treated in exactly the same fashion. Indeed, the credibility of any action on the part of the Congregation would be seriously undermined by a failure to identify and act upon other such cases. The problem is, of course, that there are very many Catholic theologians who do dissent from noninfallible teachings."

The implications of the Congregation's approach should not be overlooked. The first is that, to be regarded as a Catholic theologian, one may not dissent from *any* authoritatively proposed teaching. The second is that "authentic theological instruction" means presenting church teaching, and never disagreeing with it, even with respect and reverence. Third, and correlatively, sound theological education means accepting, uncritically if necessary, official Catholic teaching. The impact of such assertions on the notion of a university, of Catholic higher education, of theology and of good teaching are mind-boggling. All too easily, answers replace questions and conformism replaces teaching as "theology" is reduced to Kohlberg's preconventional level of reasoning (obey or be punished).

One has to wonder about the notion of church that undergirds all of this, the notion of magisterium, the notion of teaching and learning, the notion of the autonomy of earthly realities proclaimed by Vatican II ("Church in the Modern World," no. 36), the notion of collegiality and the notion of lay competence. Vatican II discarded much of the cultural and theological baggage that produced *Roma locuta, causa finita* (Rome has spoken, the matter is closed). The Congregation's approach to theology and theological education reintroduces much of it. The invalidation of dissent discredits personal reflection and freezes the Church's learning process within the last available official formulation. There is simplicity and security in this—but also the stillness of the mausoleum.

Let teaching be an example here. Teaching means helping others to understand, to see what they did not see. It is the exhilarating experience of seeing eyes opened to dimensions of reality formerly hidden. In practical moral matters, the very last thing one arrives at is a moral norm. A moral norm is a generalization about the significance of our actions. It is a conclusion drafted from understanding that significance. When it is up front as the dominant preoccupation, it hinders teaching and learning by bypassing the struggles that lead to understanding. We call this moralism.

Yet I dare say, if many educated Catholics were asked, "What is the church's teaching on contraception, homosexual acts, masturbation?" the answer would be that they are intrinsically evil actions. One would not get an insightful view of the gift and challenge of sexuality as our capacity for human relatedness. One would get a conclusion, and a negative one. "Authentic church teaching" has come to mean a set of conclusions. In this perspective, "learning" degenerates into accepting such conclusions. Understanding the significance on which they are based is almost beside the point. This is a caricature of both teaching and learning, yet it is a caricature powerfully supported by the rejection of dissent *in principle* from Catholic theology. Dissent is not an endproduct; it is a way of getting at things, a part of the human process of growth in understanding. When it is viewed as having such enormous importance in itself (as it is when the title "Catholic theologian" is denied to one who dissents on noninfallibly proposed teaching), it is a sure sign that "authentic teaching" is being conceived in a highly moralistic way.

The Congregation's chief concern seems to be scandal. In its May 10, 1983, letter to Father Curran, it said of public dissent that it "runs the risk of causing scandal to the faithful." In the Curran dossier, that is the only peek we get at the Congregation's rationale. The introduction of the notion of scandal raises several interesting questions.

Scandal, it must be remembered, is not surprise or shock at the discovery of a skeleton in someone's closet. It has a technical theological sense, and the Congregation is using it in that sense. It refers to an action or omission that provides another or others with the occasion of sin. We must ask, therefore, what sin is occasioned by dissent from noninfallible teaching on sexual questions.

The first possible answer is that it occasions or facilitates those actions condemned by official teaching but approved by the dissenter. But that begs the whole question. It assumes that the actions condemned by official teaching are, indeed, morally wrong. Such an assumption would invalidate dissent, in principle, by elevating the teaching to the status of the unquestionably true. The church does not make such claims for her concrete moral teaching.

Another possible answer is that dissent is the occasion of others' neglect of, and disrespect for, the teaching office of the church. This seems to be the Congregation's view. For it uses the phrase "encourage dissent in others" and ties this to scandal. That will not work, either. Whether or not "encouraging dissent in others" is morally wrong depends on what the dissent is aimed at. If it is aimed at a teaching that is incomplete or inaccurate, it is quite appropriate, even obligatory. And that, of course, is precisely what the dissenter is saying. It is simply no response to object that dissent "encourages dissent in others," for if the teaching is inaccurate, that is what dissent should do.

But these are close arguments, and I would not expect everyone to appreciate them. There remain more general concerns stimulated by the term "scandal." Who are these "faithful" who are scandalized? Why are they scandalized? What is their notion of church, of theology? What is their notion of the magisterium? What is their notion of collegiality and the church's accountability to reason for its moral teachings? What is their attitude toward the commercialism of ideas in the university setting? What is their attitude toward tradition (learning from the past or embalming it)? Is tradition, to borrow from Jaroslav Pelikan, the dead faith of the living, or, as it should be, the living faith of the dead? Finally, and most tellingly, is not such intolerance of any dissent—in itself—a greater cause of scandal? Does it not lead many to believe that Rome is more interested in the authority of the teacher than in what is taught by the authority?

The Most Rev. Matthew H. Clark, Bishop of Rochester, N.Y. (Father Curran's bishop), issued a magnificent statement on March 12. After adverting to Curran's personal qualities as priest and scholar, he stated: "It is, I believe, commonly accepted in the Roman Catholic theological community that Father Curran is a moral theologian of notable competence whose work locates him very much at the center of that community and not at all on the fringe. I believe that perception is true. If Father Curran's status as a Roman Catholic theologian is brought into question, I fear a serious setback to Catholic education and pastoral life in this country. That could happen in two ways. Theologians may stop exploring the challenging questions of the day in a creative, healthy way because they fear actions which may prematurely end their teaching careers. Moreover, able theologians may abandon Catholic institutions altogether in order to avoid embarrassing confrontation with church authorities. Circumstances of this sort would seriously undermine the standing of Catholic scholarship in this nation, isolate our theological community and weaken our Catholic institutions of higher education."

In the same March 12 issue of The New York Times that reported the Curran affair, there appeared a report on the ethical aspects of certain sex-therapy techniques. The report cited the views of Moshe D. Tendler (Orthodox Jewish community) and Beverly Harrison (Protestant community). The article ended as follows: "Catholic tradition also forbids a practice like masturbation as violating the procreative purposes of sexuality. One Catholic ethicist, *who asked not to be identified* [my italics], said that an argument could be made for its use in therapy 'since it was designed to help people become sexually functioning and procreative.' "

Is such anonymity what we really want in the church of 1986?

The Search for Truth in the Catholic Context

Richard A. McCormick, S.J.

This article originally appeared in *America* in 1986.

The Sept. 27, 1986, issue of The New York Times headlined an article, "The Vatican and Dissent in America." The Chicago Sun Times of Sept. 28 featured a long report with the title "Catholics in Conflict: Papal Crackdown Exposes Bitter Split in the U.S. Church." The Sept. 28 Chicago Tribune carried an article on Archbishop Rembert G. Weakland of Milwaukee entitled "Archbishop Asks Rome to Ease Up." The Sept. 28 New York Times presented this headline: "Two Bishops Weighing Vatican Trip to Tell of Turmoil in Seattle Area."

And so it goes across the country. Because the ink has flowed so freely in recent weeks, it is safe to say that most people are at least passingly aware of the dramatis personae and the storyline. The actors are chiefly three: the Vatican, the Catholic University theologian Charles E. Curran and Seattle Archbishop Raymond G. Hunthausen. The bare facts of the storyline: Father Curran was stripped of his "canonical mission" (his juridical approval to teach as a Catholic theologian), and Archbishop Hunthausen's episcopal authority in five important areas (marriage tribunal, moral issues involving homosexuals and health care institutions, liturgy and worship, seminary and clergy formation, and the departure of priests) was transferred to recently appointed Auxiliary Bishop Donald W. Wuerl.

What is going on here? Are we dealing with two isolated and unrelated incidents? The situations are certainly different. One involves the perceived deficiencies of episcopal leadership, the other perceived aberrations in the academic world of theology. In that sense, one could make the case that they are unrelated, as Vatican spokesman Archbishop John P. Foley has tried to do. Similarly, one could mount arguments that they are isolated interventions affecting only Catholic University and the Seattle Archdiocese. Such incidents, it might be argued, are not likely to be repeated given the by-and-large negative furor they aroused. A symbol of this was the Rev. Andrew M. Greeley's bilious but basically on-target column (Chicago Sun Times, Sept. 14) headlined "Red Baron of Vatican at It Again."

To view these incidents as isolated and unrelated because they concern individuals in distinct places and areas of concern would be tempting but shortsighted. I am not referring to an orchestrated brush-up of the American church. I am referring to these interventions in terms of their implications and fallout. From this perspective they raise issues of the first magnitude for the American church. The basic question they pose is: "How is the search for truth to be conducted in the Catholic context?" By "truth" I mean especially moral truths, because they are the chief concerns. The fact that Archbishop Hunthausen acts largely at the pastoral level and Father Curran at the theological should not distract us from the coincidence of concerns raised by their distinct searches. As Roberto Suro worded it: "The concern most often raised by Vatican officials involves the leadership of the church in the United States, and both the Archbishop Hunthausen and Father Curran matters fall into this realm" (The New York Times, Sept. 27). The questioned leadership is heavily in the moral sphere.

Both Father Curran and Archbishop Hunthausen have provided their own answers to this question in their respective spheres. Father Curran has said that public theological dissent is essential to that search. The matter is less clear in Archbishop Hunthausen's case because the indictments remain fuzzy. But unless I am badly mistaken, Archbishop Hunthausen has been saying by his pastoral procedures that some of the following are essential to the search: compassionate understanding of human weakness and failure, patient and attentive listening, trusting proportionate responsibility to others, playing it loose as things work out and making bold, symbolic protest in some instances. The trouble is, or seems to be, that these responses are read by some as laxness on doctrine.

Most of us will have ready, even if unexamined, answers to the question raised above. Often enough such answers come packaged in aphoristic shorthand that displays a single dimension of the issue: local autonomy, authentic teachers, academic freedom, Roman centralization, confusion of the faithful, dual magisteria, personal responsibility, and so on. For instance, J.P. McFadden, editor of the ultra-right and muckraking Catholic Eye, summarizes the issue as follows: "The vast majority of Catholics are what they should be—sheep. The real intention of the church is to guide those sheep" (Chicago Sun Times, Sept. 28). End of analysis. Mr. McFadden did not describe his sheep as dumb because that would have been redundant.

Or again, Father Curran's dissenting writings have been likened to the disclaimers of a press officer who announces the policy of his company and immediately disagrees with it—as if such analogies accurately portray the notion of teaching and learning in the church.

In another attempt, Archbishop John R. Quinn of San Francisco summarized Father Curran's predicament in the light of obedience. "Through their [Congar, de Lubac, Murray, Gutiérrez, Boff] obedience to the church they grew in humility and holiness and ultimately had more influence in the church than they would have had otherwise." This implied exhortation to supineness suggests two reflections.

First, the subsequent influence and holiness of those who suffer repression is simply not an issue. What should concern us is the repression, why these things happen, whether and when they are justified, how they can be prevented if not justified and what their effect is on believers as well as nonbelievers. Cardinal Joseph Frings of Cologne, W. Ger., raised the proper issue when he told Cardinal Alfredo Ottaviani (former Secretary of the Holy Office) at Vatican II that the methods and behavior of the Holy Office "are a source of scandal to the world." He was, of course, referring to some of the very cases mentioned by Archbishop Quinn. Those creating scandal, however well intentioned, are doing something objectively morally wrong. And if this is the case, someone has to say so. I am not implying that this is the case in the Curran-Hunthausen affairs, but only that it is the issue.

Second, to talk about suppression of dissent in terms of obedience and subsequent holiness (this latter a judgment beyond our making) is perilously close to sanctifying evil means by a good end. There comes a time when calling a spade something other than a shovel disguises and transforms it.

One thing becomes clear in such "answers." Very little is enlightened. That is the legacy of one-dimensional reductionism. Theological preferences—and often psychological discomforts and the unexamined institutional loyalties from which they spring—are promulgated without benefit of analysis.

Let me say at the outset that I agree in principle with Father Curran and Archbishop Hunthausen—"in principle" because both not only tolerate but encourage debate about details and particulars as part of their search. Because the issues are of such gravity for the American church, and because they are dominantly theological, I want to list 10 points that structure my own agreement with Father Curran and Archbishop Hunthausen, as well as my profound disappointment in the silence of most bishops on these matters—notable exceptions are Archbishop Weakland, Bishop Matthew H. Clark of Rochester, N.Y., and Thomas J. Gumbleton, Auxiliary Bishop of Detroit. It would be highly imaginative to expect agreement on all of these points. But if they provoke more precise and enlightened disagreement, they will have served a useful purpose.

The search for truth does have a "Catholic context." This point might seem quaintly parochial. Truth is, after all, truth. There are well-accepted canons for its pursuit in the scientific community at all levels—historical, scientific, literary, philosophical, theological. Furthermore, earthly realities enjoy their own autonomy, as Vatican II expressly insisted. How, then, does the "Catholic context" make any difference in the search for truth?

The "Catholic context" makes a difference because theology is precisely theology. It is reflection on faith and its behavioral implications. In this sense, theology differs from other disciplines.

The facts (truths) that found and energize the believing community and influence its moral behavior are not like data from other disciplines. They concern God's nature, intentions and actions as experienced and interpreted by a historical religious community.

Catholics believe that Christ established His church with teaching authority as a protection against the opaqueness, weakness and other vulnerabilities of the human spirit. This authority roots in the conviction about the presence of the Spirit to the whole church, but it is thought to be enjoyed in a special way by its pastors. One classic way of stating the claims of the hierarchy's ordinary use of this authority (and by "ordinary" I mean without the claim of infallibility, which is the way of most church teaching, certainly moral teaching) is to say that it enjoys the presumption of the truth. This presumption in turn generates a particular response from Catholics. It is a type of respect that most often translates factually into assent or acceptance. To deny this presumption is evidently to deny the authority itself. This authoritative teaching dimension is the chief reason for speaking of the "Catholic context" in the search for moral truth. To reject such a context is to misunderstand either theology and/or its Catholic specification.

But there the consensus ends and the face-off begins. My following nine points will touch dimensions of these disagreements. It must suffice here to underline the term "presumption" in the phrase "presumption of truth." Presumptions are not carved in granite. Presumptions can be and have been undermined by further consideration, changed facts, the presence of human folly and other factors. In a word, so-called official teaching enjoys this presumption to the extent that the undermining factors have been avoided insofar as is humanly possible. This is especially the case in the moral realm, where human experience and reflection are so vital in discerning the morally right and wrong. More specifically, the pastors of the church enjoy this presumption only insofar as they have appropriately tapped the available sources of human understanding, as the late Karl Rahner, S.J., so often insisted. When they short-circuit these processes—whether by haste, hubris, pressure, political purpose or whatever—the presumption is correspondingly weakened. I say this for one simple reason: It is not often said. The terms "authentic" and "official" are often pressed on the noun "teaching" as if they were simply convertible with absolute certainty. When this happens we have corrupted a presumption of truth into presumptuousness.

There are limits to this teaching competence. This is a further specification of the point just made. The specification is necessary because, quite frankly, certain Catholic fundamentalists speak and act as if there were no distinctions or limits. This tendency was noted by the great French Dominican Yves Congar when he stated that the ordinary magisterium "has been almost assimilated, in current opinion, to the prerogatives of the extraordinary magisterium." Thus we have what is known as "creeping infallibilism."

Human hankerings after simplicity and certainty have conscripted two theological supports for this creeping. One is the sprawling usage (by the Councils of Trent, Vatican I and II) of "faith and morals," sprawling because it fails to distinguish the deposit of faith from matters outside of it or not essential to it.

The church's teaching competence is different when it deals with matters not of the deposit or not essential to it. Thus, traditional theology insists that the church's teaching competence is analogous. That is, it means different things and makes different claims depending on the subject matter. Briefly, it can be infallibly competent or noninfallibly competent (which is not to be equated with "certainly true" and "probably erroneous"). The response of the believer is remarkably different in the two cases. In the first case it is an act of faith. In the second it is not, although "creeping infallibilists" would have us think so as they divide the world simplistically into orthodox and unorthodox, loyalists and dissenters (note the assumptions in that asymmetry). "Faith and morals" is often the vehicle of this simplicism, as if everything authoritatively proposed in the moral sphere pertained to the deposit of faith and is therefore "almost infallibly" taught. There is virtual theological unanimity that concrete moral norms do not pertain to the church's infallible teaching competence.

The other support for "creeping infallibilism" is appeal to the "special assistance of the Holy Spirit" where ordinary moral teaching is involved. Pope Paul VI, in *Humanae vitae*, referred to this when he stated that "that respect [*obsequium*] . . . obliges not only because of the reasons adduced, but rather because of the light of the Holy Spirit which is given in a particular way to the pastors of the church in order that they may illustrate the truth" (No. 28).

The distinction of the church's teaching competence into infallible and noninfallible means, of course, that the assistance of the Holy Spirit is an analogous notion. That assistance can guarantee a teaching. If, however, the teaching is not presented in a final and definitive way, the assistance of the Spirit must be understood in a different (that is, analogous) way.

Further discussion of this point is unnecessary. The point I am making is that certain theological appeals ("faith and morals," "assistance of the Holy Spirit") can be and have been expanded uncritically in a way that removes any limits on the church's teaching competence and caricatures the search for truth in the Catholic context.

Theology has a necessary but limited contribution to make. When people reflect on their faith and its behavioral implications, theology begins. And clearly, such reflection occurs at different historical times, with different circumstances and needs, different problems and challenges, different cultures. In other words, the faith must be appropriated over and over again. We must wrestle to own it and deepen it for ourselves in our times, as others in the past did. The past is instructive. It is not imprisoning. This means that new symbols and new formulations must be discovered. Theology attempts to lead and coordinate this effort. Without such exploratory struggles, we will be dealing with faith-in-formaldehyde, what the ecclesiastical historian Jaroslav Pelikan called the "dead faith of the living." Almost everyone admits this creative and innovative role to be among theology's most important. Therefore, not much more need be said.

I say "almost" because a tiny but noisy minority still stumps for an orthodoxy that is defined in terms of mere repetition of the past. The Wanderer's A.J. Matt Jr. is the grand inquisitor of this movement. This minority is getting a hearing, a fact that fleshes out the Curran-Hunthausen story. As a senior Vatican official put it: "The conservatives in the United States organize letter-writing campaigns, and those letters get read even by the Pope" (The New York Times, Sept. 27). Who is protesting this nonsense?

But important as it is, theology's role is limited. Certain limitations are obvious. We all see darkly, make false starts, succumb to our enthusiasms, construct wobbly analyses and resist criticism. I do not refer to such limitations here. Rather, I refer to the fact that theology is a scientific discipline in the service of the faith. Whether this service is an aid to the continuing daily reappropriation and deepening of the faith in our times is a heavy charge laid upon the pastors of the church. In other words, theologians cannot speak for the whole church. Only the Pope and the bishops with the Pope can do that.

Thus within the believing community, the magisterium and theology have two different but closely related tasks that call for what the Most Rev. John S. Cummins, Bishop of Oakland, Calif., calls "respectful mutuality." Bishop Cummins rightly states that both theology and the episcopate "exist within that community of believers and are meaningful only in relation to it." To treat theologians—and their analyses and conclusions—as if they were bishops is to mistreat them.

It seems to me that this is at the heart of the nervous worry about public dissent. Dissent quickly gets popularized, trickles down and comes to be viewed by the unwary as equally valid pastorally as official teaching. If that is the case, theologians are threatened by being taken for what they are not. But the answer lies in education, not execution.

Theology is a public enterprise. This might seem to have the bite of a harmless truism. But in the present circumstances it is crucial to emphasize this concept. Theology is not a closed society of arcane theory-spinners. It is a reflection *on the faith of the church,* and therefore should flourish wherever that faith is found. Theological research examines, draws upon, challenges, deepens the faith of people—and therefore must interplay with, be available to, be tested by, make sense to those whose faith is involved. Briefly, since it is of the public, with the public and for the public, it must be done in public. Presumably Vatican II had something like this in mind when it stated that all the faithful possess "lawful freedom of inquiry and of thought, and the freedom to express their minds humbly and courageously about those matters in which they enjoy competence" ("Pastoral Constitution on the Church in the Modern World," No. 62).

Theology has an essential critical role. The church is a pilgrim church. It is *in via* (on the way). That means that its formulations of its moral convictions are also *in via,* never finished and always in need of improvement, updating and adjustment to changing circumstances. Not only are moral and doctrinal formulations the product of limited minds, with limited insight, concepts and language; they are historically conditioned by the circumstances in which they were drafted. The Congregation for the Doctrine of the Faith acknowledged a fourfold historical conditioning (*Mysterium ecclesiae,* 1973). Statements of the faith are affected by the presuppositions, the concerns ("the intention of solving certain questions"), the thought categories ("the changeable conceptions of a given epoch") and the available vocabulary of the times.

Vatican II expressly adverted to this conditioning when it distinguished between the substance of the faith and its formulation. It stated: "The deposit of faith or revealed truths are one thing; the manner in which they are formulated without violence to their meaning and significance is another" ("The Pastoral Constitution on the Church in the Modern World," No. 62).

This means that one of theology's most important roles is a critical one, a distancing from past formulations and the proposal of new ones more adequate to the circumstances and insights of the time. This distancing and reformation can be called critical evaluation or dissent. Without the fulfillment of this task—under whatever name—there is no doctrinal development. The church's teaching gets frozen into the last official formulation. Critical evaluation is, then, only common sense. Gov. Mario M. Cuomo (D., N.Y.) noted this in a recent address in Brooklyn at St. James Cathedral. After stating that dissent itself is not harmful to the church, Governor Cuomo asked: "How, after all, has the church changed and developed through the centuries except through discussion and argument?" (The New York Times, Oct. 3). How indeed?

The problem of the church, then, is not precisely dissent. That we have always had. Indeed it is essential to the health of a living community, as the present Holy Father himself has persuasively argued (*The Acting Person*). He called it "opposition." But whatever its name—whether opposition, dissent, disagreement, critical evaluation—a community without it is a community in comfortable stagnation. It is a community ripe for the picking by any ideologues—fascists. Communists, left-wingers, right-wingers, nationalists and, let it be said softly, curialists.

The problem of the church, then, is not dissent, but how to use it constructively, how to learn from it, how to profit by it. Every magazine editor knows this. Every public servant in a democracy knows it, too. Yes, yes, of course the church is not a democracy. Left unsaid in that sweeping put-down is that the nondemocratic church would have inflicted far fewer self-wounds had it made use of some democratic procedures in its teaching-learning processes. Americans know this down to their pulses. Vatican II learned it and asserted it in principle over and over again. The only remaining problem is to convince some Catholics that dissent is not a threat—unless they conceive the church as an isolated fortress—but an invigorating contribution to continued life and growth. Dissent is an anathema only or especially to those who claim to have captured—really imprisoned—God and God's purposes in their own conceptual fortress.

In summary, since theology is both public and critical, public critical evaluation, or dissent, is part of its task. I am astonished at—and at some point deeply afraid of—those who question this or are threatened by it. Their agenda is showing.

To acknowledge the public and critical role of theology is not to espouse two magisteria. This statement is meant to meet head-on those who reject any public dissent as equivalent to espousing a second magisterium. That is, with all due respect, a red herring. Two different competences do not two magisteria make. Both competences—scholars and the magisterium—must relate healthily, even if not without tension, if the church's teaching office is to be credible and effective.

So there is no question of the Pope vs. theologians, or bishops vs. theologians. Theologians will never be able to speak for the church as the Pope can. That juridical point is not the issue. The issue is: What must the church do to insure that its teaching is the soundest reflection of the Gospel at a particular time? Does the "certain charism of truth" traditionally and rightly attributed to the Pope and hierarchy exempt them from listening to the voice of experience and theological reflection? If the church is intolerant of dissent, is it not excluding a possible source of correction and improvement, as well as of error? Is not public exchange the risk it must run if it is to be open to all sources of knowledge? What notion of church and church teaching is implied in the silencing of dissent? These are the true issues. To state them in terms of two competitive magisteria is utterly to juridicize such issues. If scholars present their views as if they were the last word ("authentic teaching"), then they are wrong, and that should be clearly pointed out. If, however, that "pointing out" takes the form of negating theology's essential critical role, then that error, too, must be identified for what it is—overkill.

The point can be made—how persuasively I leave to others—that the "confusion of the faithful" is not rooted exclusively or even primarily in theological dissent at all, but in the failure of authorities to listen in any meaningful way to the "sense of the faithful" and theological analyses that draw upon it. When traditional formulations are simply repeated in the face of competent challenges to them, teaching is reduced to ecclesiastical muscle-flexing. That *is* confusing, and it ought to be.

Dissent has its limits. Such limits are both pastoral and doctrinal. At the pastoral level, a prudent (I did not say pusillanimous) scholar will always view the value of his own opinions in the light of a larger whole—the good of the church. This is but Christian realism. Sometimes the time is just not ripe for saying or doing what one thinks ought to be said or done. To act as if it were is to waft theology into an unreal world and exempt it from any accountability based in the messiness of reality.

As for doctrinal limits, Father Curran has argued that he dissents from no infallibly proposed teachings and follows the criteria for dissent established by the American bishops and therefore is within the limits of legitimate dissent. This has been rejected from two sources.

Cardinal Joseph Ratzinger's is the first rejection. "The church," he said in a letter to Father Curran, dated July 25, 1986, "does not build its life upon the infallible magisterium alone but on the teaching of its authentic, ordinary magisterium as well" (see *Origins*, Aug. 28, 1986). True enough. But the implications of this statement are startling. The equivalent argument is that those teachings upon which the church builds its life are removed from critical evaluation, or dissent. Even recent history would be harsh on that statement. Was not the rejection of common worship with other Christians a part of the church's life prior to Vatican II? The same for rejection of religious liberty? The same for tolerance of slavery for so many centuries? Was not procreation as the primary end of marriage part of the church's thought and life prior to Vatican II? And so on.

The second rejection is that of The Most Rev. James A. Hickey, Archbishop of Washington, D.C. He states that the norms for dissent established by the American bishops "are simply not workable." What does "not workable" mean? What are the criteria for workability? Who is to blame and why if any public dissent is "not workable"? And who decides these things? It may be comfortably left to the American bishops to decide whether a single member of the hierarchy can abrogate policies they have established for the entire U.S. church.

Finally, it has been urged (by both Cardinal Ratzinger and Archbishop Hickey) that the church has the right to have its doctrine taught faithfully and clearly, and to certify only those professors who will do so. That is certainly true, but it is certainly not all of the truth. Does it mean that after the official teaching is presented, no critical evaluation of it is ever called for, is ever permissible? Does that not imply that no criticism is *possible?* And if no criticism is possible, what has happened to the historically conditioned character of church utterances clearly admitted by the Congregation for the Doctrine of the Faith? What has happened to doctrinal development? Indeed, what has happened to the distinction between infallible and noninfallible? And what has happened to our historical memories? The person who excludes dissent in principle from the role of the Catholic teacher, especially at the level of higher education, has confused teaching with indoctrination.

There are reasonable criteria for public dissent. This statement flows from the previous one. If there are limits to *what* may be the object of dissent, these limits themselves clearly act as criteria. Here I am underlining the quality of respect that ought to accompany dissent. This is one of three conditions (the others being absence of scandal and serious reasons) proposed by the American bishops for the legitimate expression of dissent. Such respect is not an assumed public politesse. It flows spontaneously from the conviction that the pastors of the church have a unique, if not the only, voice in our moral guidance. Such respect will translate effortlessly into 1) respect for the office of the teacher; 2) critical reassessment of one's own conclusions; 3) a reluctance (and only that) to conclude to error because one knows that the wisdom of the entire church (see above on the notion of presumption) has gone into the teaching in question, and 4) conduct in the public forum that fosters respect for the teaching office of the church.

I would be dishonest if I omitted a gloss on No. 3 above. It is my unavoidable impression that much dissent in the church is related to the suspicion that the wisdom resident in the entire church has *not* gone into some teachings. More directly, bishops, theologians, priests and other competent Catholics have told me repeatedly that *in certain areas* Rome will say only what Rome has said. Why sexuality and authority are indissolubly wed in this way I shall leave to others.

To suppress dissent is counterproductive. One good reason for saying this is that disciplinary suppression is unnecessary. If Rome disagrees with the theology of Father Curran or the pastoral procedures of Archbishop Hunthausen, it could easily say so—*urbi et orbi.* But why remove a bishop's jurisdiction or a theologian's canonical mission to teach as a Catholic theologian? Why intimidate all bishops and all theologians in the process? Why undermine the very credibility of the magisterium in the process?

Another good reason for the counterproductivity of dissent-suppression is historical. Archbishop Weakland, in a refreshingly courageous analysis, reminded his diocese, and really all of us, that suppression of dissent leads to the comfort—and vitality—of the tomb. Roman interventions at the beginning of this century led to 50 years of theological ossification in the United States. Is that what we want when the world is being challenged as never before by scientific, technological and cultural sea-changes?

The solution lies in education of Catholics. Education to what? A host of things: history (yes, we need you desperately now, John Tracy Ellis, Gerald Fogarty, John O'Malley, James Hennesey, *et al.*); the role of bishops and theologians in the church; the fact that God writes with crooked lines, and among those crooked lines are all of us; the real meaning of Catholic education, and so forth. The task is huge and the shortcuts tempting. But in the long haul there are no shortcuts.

How is the search for truth to be conducted in the Catholic context? The American bishops have provided us with a powerful example in the open and revisionary process used in the development of their recent pastoral letters on peace and on the economy. They have welcomed all points of view, even dissenting ones. A similar example can be provided by Catholic colleges and universities. The word "campus" is really the Latin word (*campus*) meaning field. It designates the arena where armies settled disputes with lance and sword. College campuses exist in part to render such incivility obsolete. The vigorous exchange of ideas by the open-minded in the university setting is the way to reconcile our differences. That is why colleges have campuses, open forums for the discussion and clash of ideas. The word "campus" should stand as a reminder that the clash of swords, the targeting of missiles and any use of force represent human failure, that vigorous but civil exchange is a form of loyalty to and protection of our humanity.

Suppression of dissent is a use of force. Can the Catholic Church learn a small lesson from the American bishops and its own universities on how the search for truth is to be conducted in the Catholic context? The question is far larger than the issues of Father Curran and Archbishop Hunthausen.

Curran and Dissent:
The Case for the Holy See

David Fitch, S.J.

This article originally appeared in *America* in 1987.

The Curran "affair" has surely become a "cause célèbre" with wide implications for the American church. As all are aware, the Congregation for the Doctrine of the Faith, in a letter signed by Cardinal Joseph Ratzinger dated July 25, 1986, has judged the Rev. Charles E. Curran, popular teacher of theology at The Catholic University, Washington, D.C., to be neither "suitable nor eligible to teach Catholic theology." Father Curran has in turn replied that current Vatican trends are a form of "creeping infallibilism" and has determined to fight to retain his teaching position. It is clear that this is not merely a dispute between Father Curran and the Holy See. It has vast implications for the teaching of theology and pastoral practice for the church in this country and throughout the world.

In the April 5, 1986, issue of AMERICA, Richard A. McCormick, S.J., distinguished American moralist and professor of Christian ethics at the University of Notre Dame, shared his reflections on this controversy in an article entitled "L'Affaire Curran." Since Father McCormick has enjoyed immense prestige in the American theological community during the past 15 or 20 years and has served as president of the Catholic Theological Society of America, it seems safe to say that he has articulated the thinking of a great many American theologians in his support of Father Curran and his opposition to Vatican policy in this matter. The case for the dissenters has thus been competently and respectfully presented.

It is now time, it seems to me, to state as well as possible the case for the Holy See as represented by Cardinal Ratzinger, the Congregation for the Doctrine of the Faith and, ultimately, Pope John Paul II, who explicitly approved the action of the Congregation in the Curran case. I am aware that this is an unpopular stance in the light of AMERICA's editorial policy and the thinking of many of AMERICA's readers. It will seem to some as a voice from the Dark Ages. However, I ask for a fair and open hearing.

First of all, taking a leaf from Father McCormick's article, which begins by disposing of "nonissues," let us dispose of some of Father McCormick's "nonissues."

Theological dissent is widespread. Father McCormick points out that other theologians throughout the world have written things similar to Father Curran. Granted. But this begs the question, which remains: Is this wide-spread public dissent in the contemporary church legitimate or unwarranted? Prominent names in the dissenting column are no substitute for persuasive arguments any more than the common retort "Everybody is doing it" justifies misbehavior in everyday living. Surely "half the world" followed Arius, the 3d-century heresiarch, in denying the divinity of Christ; and the entire English hierarchy, with one notable exception, deserted Thomas More and supported Henry VIII when he proclaimed himself head of the Church of England. If it is further urged, "Why pick on Father Curran?" the answer undoubtedly lies in the fact that he has been something of a leader and a catalyst of dissent in this country since he secured the signatures of over 650 American theologians in opposition to *Humanae Vitae* in 1968.

The policy of the Holy See in this case is against the spirit of Vatican II. Father McCormick alleges that "Vatican II discarded much of the cultural and theological baggage that produced *Roma locuta est, causa finita est (Rome has spoken, the matter is closed)*." This is a sweeping statement, which tends to ignore the oft-quoted No. 25 of the "Dogmatic Constitution on the Church": "This religious submission of will and of mind must be shown in a special way to the authentic teaching authority of the Roman Pontiff, even when he is not speaking ex cathedra (infallibly) . . . according to his manifest mind and will."

John Courtney Murray was a leader of dissent opposing the Holy See in a similar case. This is a final nonissue, a questionable argument at best. Father Murray never considered himself in dissent from church teaching on religious liberty. He believed the church had never dealt with the issue as he proposed it, as he explicitly stated in an article published in AMERICA ("This Matter of Religious Freedom," Jan. 9, 1965). Further, when silenced temporarily, he responded with admirable obedience.

Having briefly treated these peripheral nonissues, let us now examine what Father McCormick rightly considers the basic issue in this dispute: Is it legitimate to engage in public dissent vis-à-vis noninfallible but authentic church teaching, particularly in the crucial areas of abortion, premarital relations, homosexuality, artificial contraception and the indissolubility of sacramental marriage? Father Curran, Father McCormick and probably the majority of American theologians approve of such dissent. The Holy See does not because it causes "scandal."

In examining the problem, it must be borne in mind that noninfallible, in this case, does not mean uncertain. On the contrary, the teaching of the church on all the issues of the Curran case is presented by the Vatican as *certain,* requiring a certain religious assent on the part of the faithful in accordance with No. 25 of the "Dogmatic Constitution on the Church." If these teachings on homosexuality, artificial contraception, and so on, were presented by the church as merely probable opinions, these teachings would not be morally binding in conscience. *Lex dubia non obligat (A doubtful law does not oblige).* The teaching on contraception has not only been taught as certain from the very early days of the church, but it has been emphatically reiterated by recent popes.

On the other hand, noninfallible teachings, by definition, are not taught with absolute certainty excluding even the possibility of error. They are rather taught as morally certain—that is, excluding all reasonable doubt. This can be likened to a jury verdict based on evidence that excludes reasonable doubt. It could possibly be wrong, but this is most unlikely. So with the noninfallible moral teaching of the church.

A second point to be remembered is that though we are dealing here with norms for public dissent, the norms for licit private dissent are closely related to the norms for licit public dissent. After all, that which is illicit private dissent will be illicit public dissent. So we ask what is legitimate private dissent, according to the Holy See? In this dispute, the congregation has not opposed private dissent in all cases but has strictly limited it to questions where the dissenter is "certain" of his or her dissenting position. Karl Rahner takes the same approach in commenting on the encyclical *Humanae Vitae*: ". . .as a Catholic, one must have *precisely proven* and *self-critically* reflective arguments in order to be able to dissent conscientiously from a declaration of the church magisterium" (italics mine). And Cardinal John Henry Newman takes a similarly strong position in his letter to the Duke of Norfolk, as quoted by the American hierarchy in their collective pastoral "Human Life in Our Day" (1968): "When it [conscience] has the right of opposing the supreme, though not infallible authority of the pope . . . it . . . must follow upon serious thought, prayer and all available means of arriving at a right judgment on the matter in question. And further, obedience to the pope is what is called in possession; that is, the *onus probandi* [burden of proof] of establishing a case against him lies, as in all cases of exception, on the side of the conscience. Unless a man is able to say to himself, as in the Presence of God, that he must not, and dare not, act upon the papal injunction, he is bound to obey it and would commit a great sin in disobeying it." In other words, when dealing with the authentic but noninfallible teaching of the pope, the presumption is always in favor of the pope. The burden of proof is on the dissenter. In case of doubt, the pope is presumed to be right and guided by the Spirit.

In the light of this theology of dissent, albeit private dissent, it would seem to be quite exceptional when a member of the church would feel legitimately qualified to dissent from papal doctrine on an issue of importance. For in the case of most of us, it would be most difficult, if not impossible, to marshal "precisely proven and self-critically reflective arguments" against papal doctrine. This, in my opinion, is the crucial point of the present controversy. If this principle of private dissent is accepted, a position of Cardinal Newman, Father Rahner, Cardinal Ratzinger and the congregation and presumably of Pope John Paul II, it seems to me that the position of the Holy See regarding public dissent in "L'Affaire Curran" holds together and makes good sense.

Let me explain by posing several questions: How many members of the American Catholic laity who are in de facto private dissent from *Humanae Vitae* can present "precisely proven" theological, unemotional arguments against the papal position? Further, how many members of the American theological community can *prove* with sound theological argument that Pope Paul VI and Pope John Paul II are in error on the issue of contraception? (I choose contraception for the purpose of my argument because it is an issue in the Curran case and is a doctrine that has inspired the widest dissent from any papal teaching in recent years).

Artificial contraception is a complex moral issue. To deal with it competently requires no little theological expertise, and this in the field of moral theology. Therefore it appears to me that those in the church who can *prove* its legitimacy by valid theological argument are few indeed.

If the above argument is granted, then the American church is in wide and deplorable disarray, at least on the issue of contraception. Can it honestly be said that the wide publicity given to dissenting American theologians has not contributed to this situation where the American Catholic in the majority of cases feels free "to follow his own conscience" and to ignore the authentic teaching of the Holy See?

This is what Cardinal Ratzinger means by saying that public dissent from moral teachings causes "scandal." "Scandal" is used here, as Father McCormick points out, in a technical sense: "It refers to an action or omission that provides another or others with the occasion of sin."

Father McCormick asks incredulously, "What sin?" I reply with Cardinal Newman that to dissent from the noninfallible teaching of the pope without first assuming the *onus probandi* "is a great sin." If one replies that neither the American Catholic clergy nor laity in dissent see this as a sin, I can only reply that it is objectively sinful nonetheless and such dissenters are only saved from guilt because the waters have been muddied by the strident voices of dissenting theologians. Probably one cannot blame most of these dissenters if they conclude from the public dissent of prominent theologians, which up to now has been permitted, that contraception is a matter of dispute in the church and thus they "can follow their own conscience."

One final matter needs to be treated: How will the science of theology progress if public dissent is suppressed on noninfallible teaching? Father McCormick feels that "discussion and disagreement are the very life-blood of the theological enterprise. We all learn and grow in the process and it is a public process. . . . Without such theological exchanges . . . the magisterium itself would be paralyzed by the sycophancy of theologians." (Note the loaded words "paralyzed" and "sycophancy.") In other words, public dissent, according to Father McCormick, is not only permissible but required if the theological enterprise is to move forward and not stop "dead in the water." Noninfallible teaching, by definition, could be wrong, however unlikely in most cases. How can it be corrected if not by public dissent and discussion?

I would hazard that, since the *possibility* of error exists, even where reasonable doubt has been excluded, some public "probing" of noninfallible teaching might be allowed in exceptional cases. An example of such "probing" might be the work of the commission on birth control established by Pope Paul VI prior to his encyclical *Humanae Vitae*. During that period, the doctrine banning contraception continued to remain in force and was "not in doubt" as the Pope explicitly said. (The Pope, at least, was not in doubt but was merely reexamining the evidence to see if his position of "no reasonable doubt" was in need of some modification.) The result was, as all are aware, that the Pope remained unconvinced by the majority report, and the teaching of the church on contraception was reaffirmed. The probing, according to the mind of the Pope, was to be done in private by the commission, though both the majority and minority reports were later leaked to the press.

If such probing is to be done on occasion in public, I would suggest the following cautions. First, care must be taken that these articles or books remain "probes" purely and simply and that church teaching is not publicly contradicted, as in the present case with Father Curran. To avoid misunderstanding and scandal, an introductory statement could be appended to such articles stating that the author does not consider this position "solidly probable," at this time in the light of church teaching to the contrary, since, as Cardinal Newman would say, it is not "in possession." He might further state that he does not wish to imply that the People of God are not bound to follow the teaching of the magisterium on this issue. So much for a sincere effort to avoid scandal. Second, I would suggest that such probing, not dissenting, articles be confined to scholarly and theological journals and learned meetings of theologians, granting that in our day even these restricted communications are readily reported to the press. Finally, I would propose that such articles only be published at times and in circumstances that are relatively free of danger of scandal, with church authorities being the final judge of what is appropriate.

To summarize: Private dissent from noninfallible teaching is only legitimate when the dissenting opinion is *objectively proven* to the satisfaction of the dissenter. Public dissent from noninfallible teaching causes scandal because it encourages unjustified private and public dissent. Hence public dissent cannot be permitted. Public probes of noninfallible teaching may sometimes be permitted, provided the danger of scandal is minimal. Church authorities should make decisions in these matters according to times and circumstances.

Christ's contemporaries found His teaching extraordinary because He taught "with authority and not like the scribes." The church has received the commission from Christ to teach with authority, both on the infallible and noninfallible level. The latter calls for a "religious submission of mind and will" as taught by Vatican II. The question remains: Is it possible for the church to teach with authority on the noninfallible level, with large numbers of theologians in public dissent?

How To Deal with Theological Dissent

Germain Grisez

These articles originally appeared in *Homiletic and Pastoral Review* in 1986.

THE RECENT ASSEMBLY OF THE SYNOD AND THE CRISIS OF FAITH

The recent extraordinary assembly of the Synod of Bishops was called to celebrate, confirm and promote Vatican II. The final report shows that these purposes were fulfilled. By way of celebration, the Synod Fathers say that Vatican II was the greatest grace of this century and that it remains the Church's magna carta for the future (II, D, 7).

But my reflections begin from their confirmation of Vatican II. As John Paul II said in his address on December 7, the assembly had seemed necessary so that the Synod Fathers could "express their judgment on Vatican II in order to avoid divergent interpretations." Divergent interpretations arose because many people considered the Council not as the magna carta for the future, but as the first—and, in their view, much too hesitant—step in a revolution, which they hoped would conform the Catholic Church to the contemporary world.

The Synod Fathers firmly reject such divergent interpretations. They attribute difficulties which have arisen since Vatican II to a "partial and selective reading of the Council" and to the "failure to distinguish correctly between a legitimate openness of the Council to the world and the acceptance of a secularized world's mentality and order of values" (I, 4). To correct these mistakes, the final report not only reaffirms Vatican II but lays down conservative principles for its interpretation: "It is not legitimate to separate the spirit and the letter of the Council. Moreover, the Council must be understood in continuity with the great tradition of the Church" (I, 5).

The Synod Fathers are less optimistic than were the Fathers of Vatican II. The signs of the times have changed (II, A, 1; II, D, 2). So the final document calls for renewed emphasis on "the value, the importance, and the centrality of the cross of Jesus Christ" (II, D, 2). *Aggiornamento* does not mean "an easy accommodation that could lead to the secularization of the Church"; rather, it means "a missionary openness for the integral salvation of the world" (II, D, 3). And pluralism is rejected (II, C, 2).

Every faithful Catholic should thank God for this assembly of the Synod. Personally, I am happy with its outcome and with one small exception agree with the good things the Synod Fathers say about Vatican II. The exception: I am not sure whether the Council was the greatest grace of this century.

DISSENT PROVOKED CRISIS OF FAITH

No doubt, it was a great grace, but the century is not yet over. Since Vatican II, there has been a crisis of faith in the Church, brought on by widespread theological dissent from many Catholic teachings. The happy resolution of this crisis perhaps would be an even greater grace than the Council itself.

The Synod Fathers hint at the ongoing crisis of faith, when they express "regret that the theological discussions of our day have sometimes occasioned confusion among the faithful. Thus, communication and reciprocal dialogue between the bishops and theologians are necessary for the building up of the faith and its deeper comprehension" (II, B, a, 3).

Frankly, that sounds like Pollyanna, the heroine of a now unread novel whose name has nevertheless come into the English language as a synonym for blind optimism. Indeed, the documents of this assembly of the Synod sometimes remind one of the conversation of a gathering of family and friends around the bed of a person whom everyone fears to be afflicted with a fatal disease.

They attentively note every sign of health, mention some problems which can be remedied—"This room needs light; let's open the shutters."—but carefully avoid talking about what is at the very front of everyone's mind.

The first assembly of the Synod, in 1967, was franker about the crisis of faith, which had already erupted. Its final report said:

> In a special way the Fathers deplored the fact that some actually call into doubt some truths of the faith, among others those concerning the knowledge we have of God, the person of Christ and his resurrection, the Eucharist, the mystery of original sin, the enduring objectivity of the moral law, and perpetual virginity of the Blessed Virgin Mary.
>
> For this reason, there is noted a state of unrest and anxiety in the Church, both among the faithful and among pastors, and therefore the spiritual life of the People of God suffers no little harm.

Among the causes of the crisis of faith, the 1967 report noted failure to distinguish "between those matters which belong to Catholic doctrine and those which are left to the free and legitimate discussion of theologians" and the spreading of questionable opinions "by priests, religious, theologians, educators, and others, without sufficient regard for the way in which the faith is taught."

Among remedies, the 1967 report proposed: "Those who are rash or imprudent should be warned in all charity; those who are pertinacious should be removed from office." By comparison, the 1985 report's call for increased dialogue between theologians and bishops seems quite weak and deficient.

Even so, the 1985 report includes suggestions which reveal the Synod Fathers' awareness of the crisis. For just as the 1967 assembly called for a declaration concerning questions of faith—Pope Paul VI responded with the Credo of the People of God—so the 1985 assembly calls for the composition of "a catechism or compendium of all Catholic doctrine regarding both faith and morals" and urges that textbooks used in seminaries, "besides offering an exposition of sound theology in a scientific and pedagogical manner, be permeated by a true sense of the Church" (II, B, a, 5).

Moreover, anyone who reads both the final report of the 1985 assembly of the Synod and *The Ratzinger Report* can see how much the Synod Fathers' thinking was influenced by the Cardinal's diagnosis of the Church's present state. Cardinal Ratzinger is no Pollyanna; indeed, his realism led some to accuse him unjustly of being a reactionary and prophet of doom. *The Ratzinger Report* leaves no doubt that the Catholic Church is experiencing a crisis, in which theological dissent is a factor. But the Cardinal mentions several other causal factors, both outside and inside the Church.

While Cardinal Ratzinger's more inclusive diagnosis proved useful, it also will be useful to summarize the range and modes of theological dissent, as a basis for considering how the Church could deal with it more effectively.

II:
THE RANGE OF MODES OF THEOLOGICAL DISSENT

Theological dissent from Catholic teaching on the inerrancy of Scripture, the permanent truth of dogmas, and the magisterium's authority has made the content of Catholic faith seem unclear and unsure. Thus, such dissent has weakened catechesis, both by making catechists' work more difficult, and by depriving catechetical programs of clear content and confident presentation.

Theological dissent from Catholic teaching on the Trinity and the Incarnation attacks the very heart of the faith. This dissent contributes to movements which transform the substance of Catholic faith and life into some sort of secular humanism, dressed in the clothing left behind by a departed faith.

Theological dissent from Catholic teaching on the resurrection of the body, heaven, and hell has tended to make this world seem to be the only reality. Thus, this dissent has contributed to an overemphasis on this-worldly concerns and a loss of the sense of mystery. Many Catholics live without thought—and thus without real hope—of life everlasting, and so understandably ignore their vocation to holiness in this life. This situation underlies both the general decline in prayer and devout reception of the sacraments, and the specific decline in the number of those entering and remaining faithful in the priesthood and religious life.

Theological dissent from Catholic teaching on original sin, Jesus' uniqueness as mediator, and the importance of Church membership for salvation undermines evangelization and tends to make baptism seem unnecessary. Thus, such dissent has been a factor in lessened interest in missionary activity, the decline in adult converts, and the neglect of baptism by some Catholic parents.

Dissent Destroys Evangelization.

Theological dissent from Catholic teaching on Jesus' bodily presence in the Eucharist, his redemptive sacrifice, and its sacramental renewal in the Mass has made the Mass and the Blessed Sacrament seem less sacred and less important. Thus, this dissent is a factor in liturgical abuses, reduced Sunday Mass participation, and lessened reverence for the devotion to the Eucharist.

Theological dissent from Catholic teaching on God's omniscience and omnipotence has tended to weaken consciousness of divine providence and desire to live in response to it. Thus, such dissent is one reason why Catholics pray less, ignore providential signs such as those of one's vocation, and often respond to problems and adversity with either disheartened stodginess or crafty manipulativeness rather than with confidence in God's help together with creative and faithful perseverance in fulfilling responsibilities.

Theological dissent from Catholic teaching on Mary's perpetual virginity and special graces detracts from her nobility, and so tends to lessen Marian devotion. Since that devotion used to be so large a part of Catholic spirituality, its decline has weakened the spiritual lives of many Catholics.

Theological dissent from Catholic teaching on the freedom normal people have to commit mortal sins, the duty to struggle against venial sin, the need for confession, and the reality of purgatory and hell has tended to make the sacrament of penance seem unnecessary. Thus, its use has declined drastically. Moreover, general absolution without individual confession often is used as if it were an ordinary rite. Yet for many who participate in that rite, the sacrament is invalid, since they have no real purpose of amendment and no intention of ever making a specific confession of their mortal sins.

Theological dissent from Catholic teaching on sex, marriage and innocent life tends to undermine Christian marriage, responsible and generous parenthood, and the struggle for chastity. Hence this dissent has contributed to an increase in extramarital sexual activity, divorce and remarriage, and the practice of contraception and abortion by Catholic couples, married and unmarried. It has ruined the spiritual lives of many seminarians, priests, and religious.

Theologians initiate dissent in different ways. Sometimes many in a certain field openly reject a whole body of doctrine—for example, many theologians first dissented from Catholic teaching on contraception and then went on to deny all the specific absolute norms of Christian morality. Sometimes theologians deny doctrines indirectly by proposing theories which are incompatible with them—for example, some theologians explain revelation and dogma in ways which cannot be reconciled with Vatican I's solemn teaching in *Dei filius*. Sometimes a principle is explicitly rejected with important implications—for example, a few Scripture scholars maintain that Scripture contains erroneous assertions. This implies that Scripture is not divinely inspired, and this in turn has further implications. Sometimes theologians ambiguously treat a central doctrine of faith—for example, some seem to deny Jesus' resurrection, yet what they say might admit an orthodox interpretation. Sometimes important doctrines were denied in the past by scholars no longer considered Catholic theologians. Sometimes dissent from Catholic teachings originates in the works of non-Catholic theologians and Scripture scholars, whose opinions some Catholic theologians treat as authoritative.

Dissent Takes Subtle Forms.

Dissenting opinions are expressed in different ways. Sometimes Catholic teachings are simply rejected as erroneous. Sometimes an opinion incompatible with Catholic teaching is presented as a better "theology" or as a "reformulation." Often, especially in respect to defined doctrines or central truths of faith, dissent takes a subtle form. Neither the Catholic teaching nor its contrary is asserted, but the contrary position is insinuated. The Catholic teaching is ignored or treated perfunctorily. The contrary position is presented favorably and at length; minor objections to it are answered carefully, and major objections ignored.

No matter how theological dissent begins or is expressed, it often becomes blunter and less qualified as it passes from professional theologians to seminarians, priests, teachers, and journalists. Sometimes dissenting theologians themselves start this process by expressing their views more boldly in their teaching than in their publications.

Even sound and carefully presented theology is often distorted in transmission. But errors rooted in dissenting theology are not mere confusions. They are a sickness of faith which is inevitable when the firm anchor of the magisterium is discarded and the faithful are cast adrift on the heaving sea of dissent.

Finally, in homilies and the catechesis of children, where most instruction of the faithful occurs, Catholic teaching is not usually denied outright. Yet even here theological dissent has pernicious effects, for it leads to confused, hesitant, diffident, and incomplete instruction. For example, catechists seldom deny Catholic teaching on mortal sin but often explain it in such a way that children become sure that one cannot sin mortally without aiming to offend God. Many preachers and teachers who believe in heaven never talk about it. Homilists do not tell people that repentance and good works are unnecessary, but many preach sermon after sermon on God's mercy, without ever mentioning amendment of life, the sacrament of penance, or the availability of God's grace to overcome temptation. Many priests who believe that Catholic moral teachings are correct have given up trying to teach and help the faithful to live up to them.

III:
How Can So Many Have Gone So Far Wrong?

Clearheadedness and courage are required to continue to consider theological dissent unacceptable. If a mere handful of theologians dissented, the flimsiness of their arguments would be easy to see. But when one considers the magnitude of the crisis, one naturally hesitates, not only because of practical considerations, but also because one feels a shadow of a doubt. Surely, many dissenting theologians are good Catholics and capable scholars. How can so many have gone so far wrong?

To answer this question, one must recall the state of Catholic theology before Vatican II.

As everyone agrees, the seventeenth and eighteenth centuries were not a golden age for Catholic theology. Theologians ignored much of the Christian tradition; the theological disciplines suffered from mutual isolation; theological method followed inappropriate models from law and rationalistic philosophy; the virtual exclusion of the laity from theological studies limited the pool of talent available; the direction of most theological work to the formation of seminarians meant that every treatise had to be reduced to its essentials; defensiveness stifled creativity; and a ghetto mentality made the problems posed by modern thought seem unimportant.

Like any other intellectual discipline, theology flourishes only when theologians face difficult questions, enthusiastically develop ideas, freely express themselves to one another, constantly criticize one another's views, and continuously refine both their methods and their theories. But the magisterium and religious superiors generally required theologians to follow safe paths. Censorship guaranteed that the body of published theological writings could serve as a kind of appendix to Church teaching. The magisterium itself taught by referring to "approved authors."

During a century and more preceding Vatican II, both the magisterium and Catholic scholars worked for renewal in theology. These efforts bore fruit, but also had serious limitations.

Catholic Scripture scholars regarded the magisterium as an extrinsic norm or curb on their scholarship; they seemed unable to interiorize this norm and develop a specifically Catholic historical-critical method. Other scholars mined the Fathers and Doctors of the Church; their work revealed the deficiencies of textbook theology. Few, however, had the speculative power to use the riches they discovered to improve textbook theology. St. Thomas had many brilliant disciples, but most Thomists treated his works as a kind of deutero-canon rather than as a model for a return to the realities themselves studied by theology. Transcendental Thomism and various non-Thomistic attempts at theological synthesis used modern philosophies, but often too uncritically, as if Kant, Hegel, Heidegger, and so on were fresh theological sources to be received with trusting faith.

While efforts to renew theology proceeded, various attempts also were made—in France and elsewhere—to exploit Catholic teaching and Church authority for secular political purposes, especially those of the right. Such a political approach cares little about doctrine's truth, but cares greatly about its utility. Thus, well before Vatican II, these political pressures introduced an irrelevant model into almost everyone's thinking about theology and its relationship with the magisterium. The use of this model would lead to the reduction of complex theological issues to the opposition between "integrists" and "progressives," and to attempts to resolve theological issues by political methods, such as counting votes and issuing manifestos, rather than by careful study and clear thinking.

Politics Introduces Irrelevancy

In this situation, also Church officials since the time of Pius XI, especially those engaged in ecclesiastical diplomacy, understandably formed the habit of preferring moderate policies. Appropriate enough for political problems, such a habit easily causes paralysis when one is confronted with a pair of contradictory propositions and looks for a safe middle way between them. Even worse, if those in authority think of the magisterium in political terms, they will try to defend doctrines with the same methods they use to defend choices of changeable policies: by delay, diplomacy, and discipline rather than by study, reflection, and judgment.

The Modernist crisis at the beginning of the twentieth century accentuated the defects in modern Catholic theology's relationship with the magisterium. Modernism was not so much overcome as suppressed. In its aftermath, the heavy use of discipline to defend Church teaching both reflected and strengthened the tendency to think of the magisterium as if its task were to legislate and enforce rather than to discern and proclaim the truth. Theologians who did creative work had to be very circumspect and even so were likely to be disciplined.

Theologians who worked secretively for years stored up ideas and unpublished manuscripts. They circulated this material among trusted colleagues. It never benefited from unfriendly criticism. Such theologians reinforced one another and became very sure of their work's soundness and importance. Moreover, many of them were bonded together in resentment and antagonism toward the Church authority which exacted the obedience which inhibited their work.

Under these difficult conditions, renewal in Catholic theology made slow progress. When John XXIII was elected Pope, no contemporary theologian's work approached the quality of the best theology in the Christian tradition—for example, that of St. Thomas. The general level of Catholic theology was more like that of the twelfth century than like that of the thirteenth. Given another century, the renewal might have matured and its results been consolidated. But theological renewal was not yet mature, and the bishops of the world had no theology in common to work with beyond that of their seminary textbooks.

With Catholic theology in this state, Pope John announced the Council. Of course, neither he nor anyone else was clearly aware of the weaknesses of Catholic theology and the restlessness in the theological community. Thus, what happened was largely unpredictable.

Still, the first thing which occurred was necessary and expected: Differing theological views began to be expressed and their expression tolerated. But then, unexpectedly, ideas long nurtured underground, some of them quite strange, began to be brought out into the open. Safe theologians had nothing new to say. The media ignored them or treated them as troglodytes. Over night, theologians saying new things became stars.

As Vatican II approached and began, Pope John exhorted the Church to prayer and penance. But many Catholics—priests, religious, and laity alike—rather than doing as he asked, suddenly began neglecting prayer and relaxing self-discipline. This unexpected response to the Pope's exhortations was an early sign that all was not well with the Church. No doubt, theologians too, especially those traveling a good deal, with money in their pockets, exhilarated by their success, and deprived of the customary framework of their priestly and religious lives, were tempted to follow the trend of the time.

Safe Theologians Suffered Defeat

Safe theologians prepared the schemata for the Council. But their ecclesiastical superiors could not protect them from critics, especially from bishops whose theological advisors they had once helped to suppress. And so the safe theologians suffered a stunning defeat. Some, by no means all, who helped administer that defeat almost immediately started the revolution of theological dissent. Why did they trigger it?

I recall personally observing an early stage of the theological revolution around the end of 1964, just after the conclusion of Vatican II's third session. It was during a long evening's reception, dinner, and conversation, at which several of the Council's leading *periti* were guests of honor. As the evening passed and inhibitions relaxed, they became increasingly open and vehement. As I had expected, they were gratified by their successes. But, surprisingly to me, their dominant attitudes were hostility toward their opponents and anger about everything in the emerging results of the Council's work that was not entirely to their liking. For them, Vatican II had no real authority. To the extent that it embodied their views, they would use it. But to the extent that its outcome did not please them, they already rejected it. For Vatican II had committed an unforgivable sin by not giving their work the sort of respect the Council of Trent gave the *Summa theologiae* of St. Thomas. I was amazed at their arrogance and contempt for the Council's authority.

In the 1960s, every group which felt that it had not been fairly treated was ready to overturn established structures. Thus, for the theological revolution to reach its full intensity, only a few prominent theologians had to begin publicly expressing their rejection of the magisterium. For in the academic world, desire for recognition is a dominant motive. Theologians who became well known before and during the Council received due honor from their peers, who in turn, were eager to emulate the prominent. So, once began, dissent spread very rapidly.

Thus we see how so many have gone so far wrong.

IV:
DISSENT BECOMES CHRONIC

The preceding explanation of how so many Catholic theologians came to reject the magisterium's authority and teaching, and to look elsewhere for their principles of judgment, has been cast in psychological, sociological, and political terms, rather than in terms of intellectual challenges to faith and conflicting theological proposals about how to respond to them. The terms of explanation are demanded by the facts, which show that what has been happening has not been some mere quarrel between different schools of theology. Indeed, properly theological questions, ideas, and arguments have been quite secondary in the dissent of the past twenty-five years.

As dissenting opinions spread, the Holy See and the bishops around the world were busy. Besides their normal work loads, they had to deal with the Council and the beginnings of its implementation. Moreover, the theological staff available to the Pope was the battered remnant of a defeated battalion, which never had been trained and equipped to deal with the assault it now faced. It would take time to find fresh troops and to develop a suitable strategy to meet the challenge. Meanwhile, there could be no return to the use of discipline to suppress dissent.

Paul VI began by steering a moderate course. Perhaps the dissent was only a passing phase. In any case, integrism had to be avoided, and schism had to be prevented at all costs. Most other bishops waited for the Pope to act; they had no experience in dealing with theological dissent and were not equipped to deal with it. They also excused themselves from acting because the problem extended beyond and, for most, originated outside, their own dioceses.

By 1967, the theological revolution was far advanced. Thus, although that year's assembly of the Synod of Bishops acknowledged the crisis of faith and recommended measures for dealing with it, those suggestions were only partly carried out and their effectiveness was limited. The Credo of the People of God and the establishment of the International Theological Commission were positive steps. Without them, the crisis probably would have become worse. But the controversies over the Dutch Catechism and *Humanae vitae* deepened the crisis and established a pattern of conflict, which has been repeated in other controversies—for example, those over *Persona humana* and liberation theology.

Although there are variations, this pattern typically has several moments. First, some Catholic teaching is called into question, and the Holy See reaffirms and insists on it. Second, a significant group of theologians openly criticizes the Holy See's action and rejects the reaffirmed teaching. Third, some bishops support the dissenting theologians, at least by making it clear that they find some part of their view acceptable or worth entertaining. Fourth, some theologians defend the teaching reaffirmed by the Holy See, and show that the principles underlying dissent will have further serious consequences. Fifth, the Holy See avoids entering into theological controversy and tries instead to resolve the situation by a combination of negotiation and disciplinary measures. Sixth, the dissenting theologians draw out the more radical implications of their views; the bishops who support them either overlook or tacitly approve these radical implications. Seventh, many come to regard the Catholic teaching and the dissenting opinion as acceptable alternative theologies.

Various factors can make it seem that theological dissent is not as bad today as formerly. Despite dissent, sound efforts at renewal often are well received. Thus, today one can easily focus on Vatican II's good fruit and overlook dissent's bad fruit. Again, dissent often is less strident now and no longer has shock value. Thus, dissenting opinions are less likely to be noticed by the media. Further, some dissenting theologians have left the Church.

At the same time, many who once called attention to the intolerability of dissent have grown silent through discouragement, old age, or death. In 1967, Paul VI, plainly anguished by the outbreak of dissent, repeatedly expressed his concern. Today, dissent has become commonplace, and the Church has learned to live with it as a nation enslaved by a totalitarian regime learns to live with its arbitrariness and intimidation.

But despite appearances, the crisis of faith which afflicts the Church is not improving. Few theologians who have taken dissenting positions have retracted them. Indeed, a principle which initially underlies dissent on one issue often is later extended to others. Attempts to justify dissent have led some theologians to take positions in fundamental theology and ecclesiology irreconcilable with Vatican I's definitive teaching.

Thus, the magisterium's efforts to teach without straightforwardly confronting dissent have not led dissenting theologians to reconsider their positions. Indeed, they increasingly argue that the magisterium's toleration amounts to approval in practice of dissenting opinions. They say that the "official teaching" is a mere facade, which the magisterium realizes is no longer relevant, but is too embarrassed to abandon openly.

Of course, this view is countered when the Holy See backs up teaching with disciplinary action. However, as a general approach to the problem of dissent, discipline remains quite unpromising. On occasion, it is necessary, but discipline itself neither overcomes erroneous opinions nor leads anyone to better understand and accept the truth of Catholic teaching. Authority's use of discipline also provokes greater solidarity among dissenting theologians, and even gains them the support of those who dislike dissenting opinions but dislike discipline even more.

Discipline Provokes Solidarity

Then too, on some matters—for example, on the moral norms concerning marriage, sex, and innocent life—dissenting opinions are very widely held. Using cumbersome disciplinary processes against such a tide of dissent is like a Mrs. Noah trying to stop the deluge with mop and pail, slopping up water as it flows into her doorway and throwing it out a nearby window.

Moreover, dissent is now institutionalized in the Church. Dissenting theologians hold many academic and ecclesiastical positions, control many journals and scholarly associations, and enjoy many opportunities to influence bishops. Dissenting theologians' works often are translated and effectively promoted. Much of the Catholic press publicizes them and popularizes their contents.

At the same time, many who reject dissenting positions are afraid to say so openly; dissent has become a new and oppressive orthodoxy. Many faithful theologians make little use of their professional training; they engage in other activities or limit themselves to noncontroversial matters. Thus, there is little serious debate and mutual criticism in Catholic theology.

Consequently, it is quite unlikely that, left to itself, Catholic theology will ever recover its equilibrium. If the magisterium waits for the theological community to heal itself, it might wait until the Parousia.

Nevertheless, the present crisis cannot be allowed to continue indefinitely. Dissenting opinions are corrupting Christian lives and destroying faith. The widespread acceptance of dissenting opinions also is generating a false pluralism or syncretism in the Church, which prevents unified and effective evangelization, catechesis, and the witness of Christian fellowship in charity. Moreover, the magisterium itself is divided and is simultaneously saying "yes" and "no" on essential points of Catholic teaching. This division is plain insofar as some bishops openly support dissenting theologians. But it also, though less plainly, exists when bishops who personally reject dissent appoint or continue in office people who hold dissenting views and openly teach or apply them.

Considered together, the preceding facts about the condition which afflicts the Church make it clear that theological dissent is like a cancer, growing in the Church's organs, and interfering with her vital functions.

V:
THE RIGHT RELATIONSHIP OF THEOLOGIANS TO THE MAGISTERIUM

Despite its gravity, I believe that the present crisis can be overcome. To overcome it, those who make up the collegial magisterium must begin to work more effectively together, and Catholic theologians must be brought into a new and more appropriate relationship with the magisterium. But what is the appropriate relationship of theologians to the magisterium?

It is neither the relationship which existed before Vatican II nor the one which now exists between the magisterium and dissenting theologians.

Before Vatican II, too much conformity was demanded of

Catholic theologians. Their work was so closely integrated with the magisterium's work that there was virtually no room for them to propose views which the magisterium could not at once accept and approve.

Since Vatican II, dissenting theologians have adopted a stance similar to that of Protestant theologians toward their churches' pastoral leaders. Protestant pastoral leaders are not authoritative teachers. In Protestant theory, every Christian has equal access to revealed truth and must interpret it personally. In practice, Protestant theologians enjoy the authority of scholarship to interpret Scripture, analyze and reason about issues, and formulate judgments. Protestant pastoral leaders speak for their churches, but their statements carry weight only insofar as the leaders follow good theological advice and reflect the faith consensus of their followers.

Similarly, dissenting Catholic theologians treat the magisterium as a nonauthoritative leadership function. It is not clear whether they believe that the magisterium ever speaks with divinely given authority; various dissenting theologians probably would take different positions on that question. But in practice, they all ignore magisterial statements or treat them only as more or less impressive witnesses to the Church's faith, not as norms to which theological opinions must conform. Still, since the magisterium does have a leadership function, dissenting theologians very much desire that it give official voice to their good theological advice or, at least, that it not give official voice to their opponents' bad theological advice.

To see how Catholic theology should be related to the magisterium, one must begin by noticing that divine revelation is located somewhere in the world. If it were not, God would not have succeeded in communicating his truth and life to humankind; divine truth and life would remain entirely in heaven. But where in the world is divine revelation to be found? Both Catholics and Protestants agree that it is not to be found in monuments and documents, not even in the Bible insofar as it is a mere book. Rather, divine revelation is located and must be found where it is received, accepted, and held fast: in the faith of believers. And so, divine revelation, as God's successful communication to humankind, is located in this world in believers. It is the content of Christian faith, worship, and life.

But Protestants and Catholics disagree about how revelation is present in believers. For Protestants, it is present primarily in the faith of individual believers, and only secondarily in the Christian community. For Catholics, faith belongs first to the Church as a communion, then to each believer as a participant in this communion. Of course, insofar as the Church is a human society, she has no collective interiority; the Holy Spirit is, as it were, her soul. Therefore, as a communication received from God and available to us, revelation present in the Church's faith can be located primarily in certain official acts—that is, in certain papal and episcopal acts which count not only as their personal acts but as the Church's own acts.

Thus, the Catholic Church believes something only if the pope and bishops acting as such assent to it; the Church worships only if the pope and bishops (or priests ordained to assist them) act liturgically in the person of Jesus; the Church teaches only if the pope and bishops propose something as Catholic teaching. All members of the Church, including popes and bishops themselves, personally share in these elements of the Church's life by participating in the official acts and conforming to their essential requirements. The continuity of these official acts over time is the tradition by which, as *Dei verbum,* 8, says, the Church hands on all that she herself is, all that she believes.

When it is necessary for the Church to rearticulate her faith, to develop it in response to new questions, and to defend it against alternatives, only the pope and bishops can act. No matter what professional theologians say or do, their saying and doing does not mean that the Church herself has said or done anything.

This leadership office of the pope and other bishops exercised in teaching—their sacred magisterium—enjoys a unique and supernatural authority. Its uniqueness is not in its being given for service; all authority is given for service. Rather, the uniqueness of the magisterium's authority is that it is both similar to and different from two natural kinds of human authority.

One kind of human authority is that of experts and scholars.

Because of their experience and training, experts and scholars have special access to a subject matter, and so have an ability to discern truth which less competent people ought to respect. In making judgments, authorities of this sort try to conform to reality; their judgments, if sound, usually can be verified by others.

Human Authorities Judge

Another kind of human authority is that of leaders—parents in a family, officials of a government, and so on. Because of their special position and responsibility, leaders have the task of making decisions and giving directions, which other members of the community should obey. Authorities of this sort try to determine what is most appropriate for their community to do. Such judgments involve choices and cannot be verified by others.

The pope and other bishops do have governing authority in the Church, which they use, for example, in making laws, managing Church property, and so on. But that authority must not be confused with their teaching authority. For although the teaching office belongs to the leaders of the Church as such, its exercise is not a matter of choosing among possible courses of action and giving directions. On the contrary, their authority is like that of experts and scholars, insofar as the magisterium's judgments seek to conform to the reality received in faith.

Yet the pope and other bishops are not more competent than Christians generally by virtue of some special experience and training; they do not have that sort of special access to the subject matter. Rather, their special power is sacramental. It is like the authority of a proxy or agent appointed to act on someone's behalf. Popes and other bishops speak with authority because they are messengers from God. God's own authority is like that of an honest eye-witness; it is based on his truthfulness and his unique and perfect access to the reality about which he testifies.

When they are about to make fresh judgments in the exercise of their sacramental teaching office, popes and bishops must look to the normative faith of the Church in the same place every believer finds it—in the Church's official acts. But since they themselves are engaged in such acts—of worship, teaching, governing the community—members of the magisterium can find essentially what they are looking for by immediate reflection. However, present official acts are not isolated; their whole meaning and import can be unfolded only by considering them in the unity of the tradition to which they belong. The rest of tradition can be made present only by examining witnesses, beginning with sacred Scripture. Thus, popes and bishops need access to Scripture and to other witnesses of faith, and the better their access is, the more perfect their judgments will be.

Theologians Can't Judge

While theologians can contribute in other ways to the Church's life and mission, their proper relationship to the magisterium is settled precisely at this point. Their special competence is to elicit the testimony of witnesses of faith on matters about which the magisterium must judge. Here theologians have scholarly authority, which the magisterium should respect.

However, judgment belongs not to theologians but to the magisterium. Hence, even if there is no theological disagreement, the magisterium must decide whether and when to make a judgment. Obviously, when theologians or groups of theologians disagree among themselves, the magisterium also must decide which body of theological opinion is more acceptable. In making this decision, the magisterium will first exclude theological views incompatible with faith itself and then evaluate the competence of the proponents of theological views compatible with faith but incompatible with one another.

Theologians often assist the magisterium in another way: by proposing the material or conceptual content for possible judgments by which the faith will be freshly articulated and developed, or challenges to it answered. However, in many cases, those without theological training can speak with greater authority than theologians about the content of possible magisterial judgments. For the faithful at large can propose material from their experience; Christian philosophers can propose material from their understanding of theories and clarification of natural moral knowledge. Christians in the human and social sciences can point out the opportunities and challenges the world presents at a given moment—that is, they can read the so-called signs of the times.

In assisting the magisterium by proposing content, however, the authority of all these groups, including theologians, even more plainly is subordinate to the magisterium's judgment than is the special assistance of theologians when they elicit the testimony of witnesses of faith on matters about which the magisterium must judge. For in proposing content, theologians and others only help the magisterium to formulate propositions; they do not help it to discern whether any proposition should be asserted or denied. But in doing their unique theological work, theologians help the pope and other bishops to appreciate the whole meaning and import of the formal principle of their magisterial judgment.

VI:
THE BIRTH CONTROL COMMISSION AS MODEL AND CAUTIONARY TALE

Is there any promising fresh approach the magisterium might take in dealing with dissent? To begin to answer this question, it will be useful to reflect upon Paul VI's attempt to deal with the contraception controversy, and to evaluate that attempt in the light of the preceding clarification of the appropriate relationship between the magisterium and theology.

In setting up a commission of theologians and others, Paul VI showed respect for their authority and sought to make use of their scholarship and expertise. In judging between the theological opinions which emerged, he fulfilled the magisterium's duty to judge—in this case, to judge how to answer the challenge which had been posed to Catholic teaching. So far, so good; what Pope Paul did was an experiment with the process the magisterium should use. However, with the advantage of hindsight, we can see that this experiment can be improved upon in three ways.

First, Paul VI involved other bishops in his judgment, but did not make the judgment collegially. He involved other bishops at three stages. In November 1965, he tried to negotiate some relevant amendments to Vatican II's treatment of marriage. In the spring of 1966, he asked sixteen cardinals and other bishops to review the commission's work. After publishing *Humanae vitae* in

1968, he invited the bishops around the world to explain the encyclical to their people.

But all three times Paul VI failed to form a consensus with other bishops or to persuade them to accept and support his judgment. Bishops who wanted contraception approved got Vatican II to leave the door open. Nine of the sixteen cardinals and bishops who reviewed the commission's work approved contraception. And some bishops explained *Humanae vitae* by telling their people they could dissent from it.

Second, Paul VI responded only imperfectly to the challenge to Catholic teaching on contraception. It involved three claims: that the arguments against contraception were not convincing, that couples need contraception to have good marriages, and that society needs it to solve socioeconomic problems related to population growth. *Humanae vitae* says something to each of these claims, but does not respond to any of them straightforwardly. Thus, Pope Paul sounded like a teacher who, lacking the direct answer to a difficult question, answers it only obliquely.

Pope Paul VI Pondered The Pill

Third—and most important for the relationship between the magisterium and theology—the commission was not well organized and properly directed in its work.

In June 1964, Paul VI, speaking about the emerging controversy over the pill and birth control, and intending to forestall precipitate abandonment in practice of the received teaching, unfortunately implied that he might eventually feel bound in conscience to change the principles laid down by Pius XII. Pope Paul did not say which principles he had in mind, but obviously meant those concerning the pill, not the Church's teaching on contraception as such. Nevertheless, this statement suggested that the Church's position on contraception was a matter of changeable policy. By the time he published *Humanae vitae*, Pope Paul was well aware that the issue was one about which he had no choice. However, his earlier, somewhat confused view had led the commission to focus more on what the Pope should do about contraception, than on what is *true* about it.

Moreover, Paul VI never made clear to the various segments

of the commission what sort of help he expected of them—for example, he did not ask the theologians to elicit the testimony of witnesses of faith, the married couples to explain the challenge which pertained to them and to propose possible responses to it, and so forth. Rather, by seeking consensus from the whole study group, as if he wished the theologians and others to be direct partners in the magisterium's judgment, Pope Paul created the impression that the commission was a panel of judges rather than a body of witnesses called to help him make a judgment.

These defects in the organization and instruction of the commission contributed to the expectation on the part of many theologians and others that its opinion—or that of its majority—would determine the magisterium's judgment. This false impression would have been avoided if the Pope had responded differently to the irreconcilable opposition between theological positions which emerged in the commission. He could have directed the leading theological proponents of the opposed positions to divide the group into two teams, expand each team as seemed useful to them, and submit complete and thorough cases for both views. Instead he allowed the commission to become politicized, with the bad result that its so-called majority report was craftily transformed, even before *Humanae vitae* was ready for publication, into the most important statement of dissent from the church's constant and very firm teaching on contraception, which Pope Paul reconfirmed, at the end of his meticulous and courageous work of study and clarification.

VII:
HOW THE SYNOD COULD BE USED
TO OVERCOME THEOLOGICAL DISSENT

What can be learned about how to deal with theological dissent from the preceding reflections on Paul VI's handling of the contraception controversy? Some, who consider the situation virtually hopeless, will say: Nothing. For, they will point out, the theological revolution has made steady gains and consolidated them. Indeed, at present, on some important issues, dissenting theologians claim the support of quite a few bishops.

In reply, one must acknowledge these reasons for pessimism. But there also are factors in the situation, often overlooked, which could be turned to advantage. To see how to do so, one must consider what these favorable factors are, and then think out a new, magisterial process. This process should involve the bishops of the world more fully than the papal magisterium now does, and it should use theologians more effectively than hitherto, according to their true relationship to the magisterium.

Dissenting vs. Faithful Bishops

One of the favorable factors which could be turned to advantage is that even where the Holy See is confronted with theological dissent supported by some bishops, many other bishops agree with the Holy See. But these bishops feel isolated, and see no opportune way to turn their agreement into effective witness to the truth as they see it. A more collegial process would overcome their sense of isolation and provide them with a way to fulfill their responsibility.

Another favorable factor is that wherever the magisterium is confronted with some dissenting theologians, many other theologians support its teaching. But these theologians cannot compel their dissenting opponents to engage in scholarly debate, and often cannot gain a hearing from bishops who support the dissenting opinion. A better process would ensure that the theological case for the teaching reaffirmed by the magisterium would be taken more seriously.

Dissenters Avoid Mutual Criticism

A third factor which might be turned to advantage is that dissenting theologians disagree with one another on many substantive issues, but, at present, tend to avoid mutual criticism. This reflects their solidarity in the common cause of rationalizing their present inappropriate stance towards the magisterium. A better process would encourage all theologians, and especially dissenting theologians, to pay more attention to substantive issues and their disagreements on them, and so to engage in fruitful mutual criticism.

The fourth, and most important, favorable factor in the situation is the papal office itself. The pope can work towards judgment by collegial consensus or can seek collegial acceptance for a judgment he makes. Much as a scholar does when he leads a seminar with a group of colleagues, the pope can take an active role as leader of the collegial dialogue. He need neither reserve controversial matters to himself, nor sit by silently while the other bishops discuss issues among themselves.

These considerations suggest the main lines of a better magisterial process, centered in the pope, closely involving the bishops, and properly using the theologians. The process should have three features.

First, the pope and other bishops should first listen together to theological debate, then dismiss the theologians and engage in their own reflection. Organizing the work of the theologians and the magisterium in this way, as two separate stages of one unified process, would itself distinguish the role of the magisterium from that of theologians, clarify both roles, and help relate them properly to one another. The very structure of this process would make clear to everyone the quite limited and relative value of all theological arguments, much as the very structure of a high court's process makes it clear that the arguments of the advocates for each side of a case settle nothing, and that decisions are made only by the judges when they meet in their own conference and dispose of cases.

Second, theologians and others invited to make their appropriate contributions to the theological debate should be instructed clearly regarding what is expected of them. Where opposed views have significant support of theological or other authority, both sides should be given equal and adequate opportunities to present their cases and debate them.

Third, to assure collegial solidarity in magisterial judgments, those which concern disputed questions ordinarily should be made in a collegial manner as the outcome of such a process. The pope should engage actively in the collegial dialogue with his brother bishops, just as Peter did in the Council at Jerusalem.

A process with these three features could be carried on in various ways, either by a general council or by a new and special kind of assembly of the Synod. Since the Synod is a continuing institution which will meet regularly in any case, the possibilities it offers are more immediately interesting.

My proposal is that at least some assemblies of the Synod, organized in this new and appropriate way, be devoted to the study, discussion, and resolution of particular, very important issues of faith and morals, where there is significant theological dissent.

Such an assembly could begin with a well-prepared theological debate, which could include sessions in which the bishops, in preparation for their own role, could ask questions and make objections in order to compel both groups of theologians to clarify and defend their views. Then the theologians could be dismissed, and the bishops, as a panel of judges conferring among themselves could discuss how to resolve the issue. Initially, their discussion might best be carried on in the small discussion groups, with regular reports to the pope how all the discussions were going, and he could visit and take part in the discussions of some of the groups, if that seemed to him likely to help bring about consensus. But if no consensus among the bishops began to emerge, the pope could convene a plenary session, present his own tentative judgment and reasons for it, and lead all the Synod Fathers together in the work of reaching one judgment in discerning the truth.

Imagine if Paul VI Had Done This

Imagine what it would have been like if Paul VI had organized this kind of assembly of the Synod in the spring of 1966 to deal with the contraception issue. Fair and equal time would have been devoted to both theological cases, so there would have been no majority or minority presentation. The Synod Fathers would then have discussed the matter in small groups. Although there is good reason to think that most of the bishops participating would have considered the received teaching true, there would not have been complete consensus. But Pope Paul himself could have conducted a dialogue, which he might have initiated by asking several questions. Why are some of the theologians so sure that contraception is morally acceptable? Because they feel it is? Because many people think it is? Because of philosophical arguments, which, however, prove too much if they prove anything? What sort of reasons are these, and what have they to do with faith? Let us see now: What does faith tell us about marriage, the bodily person, parenthood? What, then, does it tell us about contraception?

Various new arrangements would facilitate this new use of the Synod.

One plainly would be provision of a suitable place for meetings in conclave, so that the pope and bishops trying to reach consensus on delicate issues could work and live together for some days or weeks, with at least temporary secrecy and so without outside pressures on their reflections.

Another desideratum would be a new method of electing bishop participants to ensure that they included those bishops most interested in and well informed on the particular issue to be settled, but otherwise representative of the entire collegium. Perhaps all the bishop participants could be elected by their fellow bishops, using some procedure which would guarantee good representation. For example, all the bishops of the world, regardless of their nationality, present office, and age, might be divided into several large groups, whose members' places of residence and language skills would make it reasonably easy for them to meet and communicate. Then all those in each such group could be divided randomly into small groups of about thirty. Between the sending out of preparatory materials and the opening of the assembly of the Synod, these groups of thirty could meet, pray together, share their thoughts, and elect someone to participate in the assembly.

VIII:
THE PRACTICABILITY OF THE PROPOSAL

Some will point out that the fatal flaw in the process Pope Paul undertook in dealing with contraception was that in announcing the commission's work, he signaled that the teaching might change, with the result that many Catholics began to think and act as if it had already changed. This observation will lead to the objection that the proposed process would suffer from the same fatal flaw. By initiating the process, the pope, and now the Synod too, would suggest that the magisterium itself was open-minded on the issue to be settled, and that the dissenting position might be correct. This suggestion, the objector will argue, leads to a dilemma: Either the issue really is open or it is not. If it is, the dynamic of the process, carried on over many months in the full glare of publicity, would further undercut the teaching and nullify the force of any reaffirmation of it, long before the process could be completed. Thus, dissent would be reinforced. But if the issue is not really open, the process would amount to little more than a fraudulent attempt to embarrass and outmaneuver dissenting theologians, who would quickly recognize and reject it as such. Thus, the process would do nothing to bring them into submission to the magisterium. Consequently, the objector's dilemma concludes, whether the magisterium really is open-minded on the issue or not, the proposed process would do nothing to overcome theological dissent.

The Pope and Synod Can Compel

But this dilemma, impressive as it is, can be rebutted.

For, on the one hand, if the magisterium is really open-minded on an issue, but dissenting theologians refuse an invitation to participate in this process for settling it, their rejection of their responsibility as Catholic theologians will be clear to everyone, and they will lose their influence in the Church. If, however, they take part in the process, they will by that very fact publicly commit themselves to accepting the magisterial judgment to which it will lead. If they subsequently dissent from that judgment, their bad faith will be evident. Thus, if the magisterium is really open-minded on an issue, by this process the pope and Synod can compel dissenting theologians to change their stance toward the magisterium.

And, on the other hand, if the magisterium is not really open-minded on an issue, then even if dissenting theologians refuse to take part in the process, it will enable the collegium itself to become fully aware of its own solidarity, and so enable the magisterium to reaffirm with one powerful voice the truth from which there is dissent. The pope can then settle the issue once for all, with the collegial consensus behind him, by solemnly proclaiming the teaching. All faithful Catholics would accept such a definition, especially if it proclaimed a collegial consensus reached after as careful as possible a theological debate—one from which dissenting theologians were absent only because they refused to participate.

Thus, the rebuttal concludes, whether the magisterium really is open-minded about a particular issue or not, the proposed process is a sure way to overcome theological dissent.

This rebuttal is helpful, because it reveals the potentialities of the proposed process if put to work on issues which are extremely open or extremely closed. However, like the original dilemma, this rebuttal, while neat and illuminating, is not entirely in touch with the real situation. And so it is appropriate to escape between the horns of both dilemmas.

For the truth is that many issues are neither entirely open nor entirely closed, either for the church at large or for the magisterium itself.

For, on the one hand, wherever there is significant theological dissent from Catholic teaching, to that extent an issue already has been opened up. If there were no sympathy for the dissenting view within the collegium, it would pose little challenge, but to the extent that there is sympathy, the magisterium itself is open-minded. For it is not necessary that the pope or many other bishops have doubts about an essential matter of faith or morals before the collegial magisterium itself has a problem to whose authentic solution it must be open. Moreover, those who reject dissenting theological opinions can admit that there could be some overlooked truth in their vicinity, and that there is always room for clarification and development of doctrine, so that a collegial effort to settle an issue is likely to have some results unpredictable in advance, to which the work of dissenting theologians might at least make some positive contribution.

And, on the other hand, dissenting theologians claim to be holding to the substance of received teaching, and only rejecting excessively rigid theological interpretations of it. Hence, they cannot take the position that any issue which would be dealt with by the proposed process is open as to its essentials. Rather, they must take the position that nothing more is at stake than optional details of the teaching and the most appropriate way of expressing its substantial truth. Therefore, in initiating the process, the pope and Synod need not concede that anything essential is open, but only that there is a need to clarify the line between essentials and nonessentials.

Four Considerations Tell

It also is important to note that the process proposed here would not aggravate the bad effects of dissent nearly as much as the first horn of the original dilemma suggests. Four considerations tell against that argument.

First, Paul VI signaled that the teaching on contraception might change, not simply by his effort to settle the controversy which was emerging, but by a particular statement he made. To try to resolve an issue on which there is significant theological dissent, the pope and Synod hardly need say they might feel bound in conscience to change received teaching.

Second, open dissent on contraception was not widespread until after Pope Paul announced the study, but it swelled continuously during the four years which passed before *Humanae vitae* was published. But theological dissent on the issues which must be resolved now has been going on for years and has already done its damage. Moreover, the pope and Synod could settle an issue within a year or so after the calling of an assembly to deal with it.

Third, much of the sort of damage which occurred in connection with the birth control commission would be precluded by a process which allowed no opportunity for the official development of theological majorities and minorities, and for the leaking of supposedly secret documents.

Fourth, since *Humanae vitae* lacked unified collegial support, it failed to resolve the contraception controversy, and so very great damage was and is still being caused by the theological dissent which the encyclical occasioned. But an adequate process should result in the moral unanimity of the collegium itself on any essential question of faith or morals. If that were not sufficient to elicit dissenting theologians' submission to the magisterium, the pope could always take the final step of formulating the collegial consensus as a proposed solemn definition, perfecting the formulation with the appropriate help of the bishops of the world, and then promulgating the magisterium's judgment ex cathedra.

Having replied to the objection, it remains necessary to say that the pope and other bishops should face up to and resolve the important doctrinal and moral issues which today divide the Church. In the face of dissent, it is good to teach Catholic truth serenely, over and over, with clarity and firmness. But since that has been done and theological dissent is still advancing rather than retreating, its challenge needs to be countered frontally. One need only recall Matthew's Gospel and the Epistle to the Galatians to know how Jesus and St. Paul answered theological objections to their teaching. Is there any good reason to think that either of them would proceed any differently today?

Moreover, as explained above, theological dissent is a cancer in the Body of Christ. This cancer is interfering with the Church's vital functions, and no treatment attempted thus far has had more than palliative effects. Therefore, new and more effective means to resolve the issues which divide the Church must be found and used, whatever the consequences of using them, to deal with theological dissent.

Nor should anyone fear that a collegial effort to settle essential doctrinal and moral issues will lead to deadlock in the collegial magisterium itself. If the pope and bishops set to work, one can be sure they will succeed, because Jesus promised to stay with his Church, and he is her faithful Lord. With the pope's leadership, collegial discussion can be expected to lead to consensus, because Jesus prayed for Peter, and so assured him of the power to confirm the faith of his brother bishops.

Besides, the magisterium's task is to make judgments, not on matters about which many views could be well grounded, but on matters of God's truth. That truth is real, present in the faith of the Church, and available to the pope and other bishops in their own official acts. Only one view of it is well grounded. And so, one can be confident that with the Holy Spirit's charism of certain truth, the pope and bishops will meet in this one view, discern God's truth, and so be able to announce: It is the Holy Spirit's judgment and ours too. . . .

If Pope and Bishops Fail

Someone might say: Since the Church is assured of divine help and protection, it matters little what the pope and bishops do about theological dissent. The answer is that while the Church's survival is guaranteed, the Lord's promises were given to encourage his followers to carry out their proper missions, not to lessen their drive and diligence. Being fruitful branches, doing Jesus' works and ones greater still, living one's life of providentially prepared good deeds—these ennoble Jesus' friends. Thus, if the pope and bishops were to fail to treat the Church's present crisis of faith as the disaster it truly is, if they were to fail to seek and try new ways of dealing more effectively with theological dissent, they would fall short of the glory to which they themselves are called, for they would fail to fulfill their own great responsibility. True, the Church's survival is assured whatever the pope and bishops do or fail to do. But if they were to fail to do their very best, they would miss a splendid opportunity to be forever honored among the greatest of the pastors and doctors of the Church.

The preceding reflections on the recent assembly of the Synod have taken us a long way. Admittedly, my analysis of the present crisis and its causes is drawn with a broad brush, and my suggestion for dealing with it is novel. However, I hope that everyone who agrees that there is a crisis of faith will resist the temptation to brush these reflections aside. Even insofar as the present theological essay is inadequate, perhaps it will encourage others to think about the great matter with which these reflections have been concerned. If so, may their effort help to alleviate the condition of the patient around whose sickbed we have been gathered. For she is our holy mother Church, and though she cannot die, she can suffer, and she is terribly afflicted.

Comments on the Curran Case: PRO

The Learning Church

Kevin Kelly

This article originally appeared in *The Tablet* in 1986.

The heart of the dispute between the Congregation for the Doctrine of the Faith and Fr Charles Curran lies in a question of fundamental importance for Catholic theology. It is the issue of dissent, especially public dissent, from authoritative church teaching. The congregation's observations of April 1983 leave us in no doubt on that point: "The issue of whether a person who privately dissents from the ordinary magisterium of the Church has the consequent right to dissent publicly is at the basis of the Sacred Congregation for the Doctrine of the Faith's difficulties with Fr Curran."

There is no disagreement about the possibility of private dissent. The crucial question is—what about *public* dissent? Is this legitimate? Has a Catholic the right to voice his or her dissent publicly?

The case for public dissent can be argued from the very theology which provided the vision of renewal in Vatican II itself. Vatican II enabled the Church to grow out of the restrictive theology which had made theologians limit dissent to respectful silence or, at most, to non-public expressions of dissent in the rarified atmosphere of professional theological debate. The pre-Vatican II model divided the Church into the teachers—the Pope and the bishops—and the learners—the rest of us. The teacher was presumed to possess the truth and his basic role was to pass on that teaching to the learners, whose principal task was to receive it docilely. Learning was interpreted virtually as an exercise of obedience. The emphasis was on acceptance of what was taught. That was why public dissent from the Church's teaching authority, the magisterium, was seen as open rejection of it, and was thus unthinkable. This is far removed from the earlier understanding of a more shared magisterium which is found in the Church's tradition.

When the bishops met for Vatican II, almost the first thing they did was to reject this juridical and hierarchical model of the Church as determinative. Instead they chose to see the Church primarily as the whole people of God. Within this community, the Pope and the bishops fulfil a God-given service. They do not stand over against the Church and they are not above the Church. According to this model the whole Church is a learning Church and shares a teaching mission. And learning comes before teaching. Evangelisation begins with the Church itself. In each age the Church has to receive and make its own the revelation given in and through Jesus and entrusted to it. This revelation is not a lifeless body of religious information that is passed on from age to age. It is not a timeless deposit. It is a living tradition which is only truly received when it becomes incarnate in the minds and hearts of Christians belonging to a particular age and culture and trying to grapple with contemporary life in the light of the Gospel. Revelation does not truly occur in each age and culture without this process of reception. Before it can be a teaching Church, the Church must first be a learning Church; and to be a learning Church, it must necessarily be a listening Church.

This model of the Church was not thought up out of nothing by the bishops at Vatican II. It had a sound basis in Scripture and tradition. It also corresponded to the "signs of the times" as interpreted by the council. The greater appreciation of the dignity of each individual person and the corresponding values of personal freedom and participation as well as communal responsibility and solidarity were seen as movements in the world which clearly came from the promptings of the Holy Spirit. These "signs of the times" obviously had implications for how the Church should understand itself and live its life in this present day and age.

SHARING

It is in the light of this deeper self-understanding of the Church that the issue of public dissent needs to be reexamined. Fr Curran is clearly aware of this when he argues, in his response of 10 August 1983, that the question of public dissent needs to be treated "in the light of the Church's contemporary teaching on the right to know, the duty to inform, the right to free self-expression, the role of public opinion in the Church and the use of modern means of communication". The Congregation for the Doctrine of the Faith, however, seems unwilling to move beyond the limits imposed on dissent by theologians before Vatican II. Yet the situation now is radically different.

If learning is a primary focus within the Church's life, then the dynamism of the learning process has to be properly respected. That dynamism demands that all the riches of genuine experience, interpretation and understanding available within the Church are shared as widely as possible. Within the learning model a good teacher is one who tries to make sure that all the riches of the individual members of the learning group are shared with the whole group. The teacher's role is one of enabling individuals to share, empowering the whole group to grow in collective understanding and occasionally checking out that collective understanding by trying to articulate it in a way that does justice to the level of learning the group feels it has achieved. As a member of the group the teacher will, of course, have his or her own personal contribution to make, but that will be incidental to his or her other main teaching role as outlined above. And in a group with great riches to be shared, the teacher's personal contribution might be quite minimal.

This is not to deny that within the Church the Pope, as supreme teacher, does not need the permission of the Church before he articulates its faith. However, it does mean that his articulation is binding because it is the faith of the Church that it articulates. His own personal viewpoint, as personal to him and not as an expression of the faith of the Church, will be listened to with respect, but individuals may disagree.

I would suggest that one of the greatest examples of teaching in the Church in recent centuries was John XXIII's calling of the Second Vatican Council. Although John XXIII may have contributed little to the council himself, he enabled the tremendous riches with which the Spirit had blessed so many individuals and movements in the Church to be made available to and shared by the Church as a whole. In this way John XXIII was a most powerful teacher; he empowered the Church to grow.

Against this kind of background public dissent is seen in an altogether different light. Obviously it will still need to be honest and responsible dissent. By that I mean that the teaching being dissented from has been examined seriously and a real effort made to grasp its truth. Also, grounds for dissent must not be trivial but based either on special expertise, personal experience or general understanding arrived at either through one's own reflection or through dialogue with others whose wisdom and integrity one respects. Granted this kind of dissent, to share this with others and, when appropriate, to voice it publicly would seem to be a form of positive and responsible participation in the learning process in the Church.

NEED FOR DIALOGUE

In fact, unless one has already sufficiently aired one's dissent and one's reasons for it, keeping a respectful silence could be seen as a form of disloyalty to the Church and an evasion of personal responsibility. Karl Rahner states this very clearly in his *Theological Investigations:* "In the concrete conditions prevailing today in the Church and in public life in the world, the respect which the moral theologian has to pay in his teaching to an authentic but not defined pronouncement of the Church's magisterium can no longer imply that the moral theologian concerned must either defend a doctrinal pronouncement of this kind through thick and thin as absolutely the only opinion which is certain and admissible for all ages or else he must simply be silent. In conformity with what has been said up to now he cannot in honesty adopt the first position, and if he adopted the second he would both be failing in his task as a moral theologian and at the same time doing no service to the

Church, to the moral standards of the faithful, and to the Church's teaching authority" (vol. XI, pp. 283–284). As Fr Curran pointed out in his press statement of 11 March, other world-acclaimed Roman Catholic theologians such as Yves Congar and Bernard Häring propose the same position. So have many American Catholic theologians, such as Avery Dulles, Richard McBrien, Richard McCormick, and David Tracy.

Avoidance of scandal is one of the accepted criteria for discerning whether a particular exercise of dissent is legitimate. Scandal means harming others by leading them astray. If we see ourselves as a learning Church and if we see morality as based on truth rather than on authority or law, we might well be guilty of scandal if we remain silent when we believe that the guidance given to people is either not true or else does not do full justice to the truth. Curran puts this very succinctly in his letter of 10 August 1983: "One can rightly conclude that at times it would be a scandal if theologians did not dissent publicly."

It seems clear that the congregation are working on entirely different principles. For them public dissent constitutes a challenge and a threat to teaching authority in the Church. "Suspension of [private] assent does not provide grounds for a so-called right to public dissent, for such public dissent would in effect constitute an alternative magisterium," they say in their Observations of April 1983. This is a long way from the process of dialogue appropriate to the learning model.

Serving the Truth

Kevin Kelly

This article originally appeared in *The Tablet* in 1986.

In their dispute, neither Cardinal Ratzinger nor Fr Curran have done full justice to themselves and to what is really at stake. For they have made dissent the main issue. This is unfortunate.

Dissent is a negative word. It belongs to the same stable as terms like deny, oppose, contradict. There is nothing positive or affirmative about it. Focusing on the issue of dissent, therefore, has two unfortunate consequences. It creates a climate of confrontation and it makes true dialogue virtually impossible. Moreover, it deflects attention from the fundamental question which underlies the whole dispute: the respective roles of the teaching authority, theologians and all believers in the Church's mission of serving and proclaiming the truth.

The Church has to penetrate the truth more deeply and understand its implications for contemporary life. It must discern how humanity can become increasingly true to itself as made in the image of God and bearing responsibility for the stewardship of God's creation. This is a task which is shared by all the members of the Church. It is shared also, as we are more aware since Vatican II, by all Christians and, in their own way, by non-Christian religions and even non-believers. It is a common search.

In this task, Christianity has a specific and essential contribution to give; but this does not make the contributions of the other participants any less important. The common search remains a shared human venture. As *Gaudium et Spes* put it (33): "The Church guards the heritage of God's Word and draws from it religious and moral principles without always having at hand the

478

solution to particular problems. She desires thereby to add the light of revealed truth to mankind's stores of experience." Seeing the Church as a servant of the truth in this way, it is not surprising that Vatican II laid such a strong emphasis on dialogue as the method most in keeping with this mission (see *Gaudium et Spes*, 43–44, 58, 62, 92; cf Paul VI, *Ecclesiam Suam*).

Dialogue, according to Vatican II, is not simply the appropriate way for the Church and Christians to engage themselves with society at large. Dialogue is also to be fostered and respected within the Church itself (*Gaudium et Spes*, 92). It is acknowledged that true dialogue demands freedom of inquiry and thought within the area of one's own field of competence and experience. Thus *Gaudium et Spes* recognises that "All the faithful, clerical and laity, possess a lawful freedom of inquiry and of thought, and the freedom to express their minds humbly and courageously about those matters in which they enjoy competence," (62). Real dialogue also implies mutual respect in the face of honest disagreement: "Solutions proposed on one side or another may be easily confused by many people with the Gospel message. Hence it is necessary for people to remember that no one is allowed in the aforementioned situations to appropriate the Church's authority for his opinion. They should always try to enlighten one another through honest discussion, preserving mutual charity and caring above all for the common good" (43).

Necessary Tension

Dissent does not fit easily into the context of dialogue. It is too much of a conversation-stopper. That is why Fr Curran is not doing himself justice when he describes his stance as one of dissent. The heart of his position is not captured by the statement "I dissent from the Church's teaching." More accurate would be something like: "Drawing on the riches of the Church's tradition and in the light of the Church's deeper knowledge of this aspect of human life gained through its dialogue with the human sciences today, I believe that what I and many Christians are saying is a more adequate expression of the richness of our present Christian understanding than is found in the current statement of the Church's teaching." The term "dissent" has no feel for all that is positive in such a position—respect for tradition, concern for the truth, love of the Church, shared responsibility for the Church's mission in the world. It does not express the respect for teaching authority in the Church which motivates someone adopting this kind of stance.

Teaching authority, when properly exercised, empowers. It helps people to have a better understanding of the truth. The critical stance described above does the same. It seeks to make sure that the truth in all its richness is not sold short by the teaching authority. Understandably this often gives rise to tension, as the International Theological Commission has recognised. In its *Theses on the Relationship between the Church's Magisterium and Theology* (6 June, 1976), the commission acknowledged that the role of theologians in interpreting the teaching of the magisterium "entails a function which is to some extent critical, while being positive and not destructive" (8, 3). It went on: "It is not uncommon to find tension in the exercise of the tasks of the magisterium and of theologians. Nor is it surprising. And there is no ground for hoping that this tension will be fully resolved on earth. Wherever there is real life there is tension. And it is not enmity nor opposition but a living force and a stimulus to exercising together by means of dialogue the tasks proper to each."

The purpose of such dialogue, the International Theological Commission maintained, was "to serve the truth." To be faithful to this purpose, the Congregation for the Doctrine of the Faith should spend more time exploring why responsible theologians like Fr Curran are dissatisfied with some of the Church's authoritative teaching. Whether such teaching adequately expresses the richest understanding within the Church should, after all, particularly concern a congregation commissioned to serve "the doctrine of the faith".

The International Theological Commission stated that "the whole field of truth" was "suitable matter for dialogue" between the teaching authority and theologians. But, it warned, "this truth is not something continually to be sought as if it were uncertain and unknown. It has been truly revealed and given to the Church to be faithfully guarded. Thus the limits of the dialogue are the limits of the truth of the faith," (thesis 11). That there is no question of Fr Curran's intending to go beyond these limits by denying any "truth of the faith" is clear from the statement in his 11 March press release: "Note clearly that I do not disagee with any dogmas or defined truths of the Catholic faith."

On a few occasions in the long exchange between the congregation and Fr Curran, I get the impression that real dialogue is beginning to occur. Thus the congregation in its April 1983 Observations asked him a series of penetrating questions designed to draw into clearer focus precisely what he meant by some of his positions: his view that the magisterium's general teaching does not bind absolutely in every case; his theory of "compromise decisions" which acknowledge personal and situational limitations; his referring to New Testament "ideals" rather than moral norms; whether he considered that the actual number of Christians dissenting had any theological significance for moral teaching; what part the physical dimension of our make-up plays in determining human morality; and so on. These questions elicited from Curran some excellent moral theological writing which many will find extremely helpful. However, the dialogue stopped there. After empowering Curran to express himself even more clearly, the congregation failed to continue the process. The rest of us are the poorer. It could have been a very fruitful exchange and a positive learning experience for all involved.

Cardinal Ratzinger's final letter to Fr Curran invited him to "reconsider and to retract these positions which violate the conditions necessary for a professor to be called a Catholic theologian". The cardinal said that church teaching had to be "reflected upon" and also "interpreted" but "in complete fidelity". Indeed; this fidelity, however, is first of all to the truth. That is why the critical interpretation mentioned by the International Theological Commission must surely qualify as interpretation "in complete fidelity."

Cardinal Ratzinger said also that students had a "right to know what the Church's teaching is and have it properly explained to them". That, again, is true. But the "right" of the students in question is not really being respected if the Church's teaching is presented to them uncritically. When some of it is being questioned responsibly by theologians or by the faithful in general, that suggests at least the possibility that it is not presenting adequately or satisfactorily what the Church (the People of God) believes. A "proper explanation" of the Church's teaching has to take this "theological fact" fully into account. It would be the death of true theology to insist that budding theologians and prospective pastors should be denied knowledge of such divergent views. That applies also to adult Christian education. Christian adults have a right to know what are the riches of current Christian understanding that responsible theologians believe are lacking in authoritative church statements. In matters of morality this can have profound implications for their lives.

If the Congregation for the Doctrine of the Faith considers Fr Curran's teaching unacceptable, it will want to declare this publicly as part of its role of service in the Church. To express its disagreement publicly, giving all its reasons why it considers his teaching to be unacceptable, would be a helpful contribution to the process of dialogue. Moral theologians and others of a like mind to Fr Curran would then be given the opportunity to evaluate how well-grounded are the congregation's reasons for disagreement. If they found them convincing, it would provide a stimulus for them to rethink their own positions. However, this does not seem to be the procedure the congregation has chosen to follow.

A BETTER WAY

Very understandably the congregation wants to safeguard teaching authority within the Church. And no Catholic would deny the teaching authority of the Pope and the bishops within the Church. Yet how precisely should that teaching authority function within the dialogue model? It is not immediately evident. Vatican II's strong emphasis on dialogue as the correct method means that the complementary roles, within the Church's teaching mission, of the teaching authority, theologians and Christians in general need to be reexamined very carefully. Such a reexamination would also need to look at how these roles are affected by Vatican II's teaching that other Christian Churches are partners in this dialogue. The congregation would be performing the empowering function of teaching if it were to promote dialogue on these questions among theologians and in the Church at large. If so, the tension between it and Fr Curran could yet turn out to be a growth point for theology. At present, however, the signs are not hopeful.

At present one particular school of moral theology—essentialist, a-historical, deductive, aiming at certain and unchanging knowledge—seems to be dominating the thinkinng of the congregation. This is a matter of considerable concern, especially when this school does not represent the mainstream of contemporary Roman Catholic moral theology. In fact, the action threatened against Curran will be seen by many as a condemnation of that mainstream. That in itself is serious. Even more serious, however, are some of the consequences that might follow. If the congregation takes action against Fr Curran, his own bishop, Matthew Clark of Rochester, fears that "theologians may stop exploring the challenging questions of the day in a creative, healthy way because they fear actions which may prematurely end their teaching careers." Furthermore, the kind of action being threatened against Curran will almost certainly be a serious scandal in the ecumenical field.

Theologians Under Fire

Richard P. McBrien

This article originally appeared in *The Tablet* in 1986.

The case of Fr Charles Curran, professor of moral theology at the Catholic University of America, reminds one of a Second World War film in which the commander of a crippled submarine orders his men to place clothing, equipment, and even a corpse into the torpedo tubes, and then to propel them to the ocean's surface in the hope of convincing the captain of the enemy destroyer that his depth-charges had hit their mark.

Although Fr Curran and the Congregation for the Doctrine of the Faith had been in correspondence since 1979, and although Cardinal Ratzinger had notified Fr Curran of the Vatican's decision on his case in late September 1985, and although Fr Curran had met Cardinal Ratzinger and others in the Vatican on 8 March, the public had heard nothing but rumours. The waters remained calm and clear, but the silence was eerie. Then on 12 March the debris suddenly appeared all around.

At a press conference in Washington, Fr Curran disclosed what had been taking place. He had been informed that his mandate to teach theology in a Catholic institution would be revoked unless he retracted certain of his views concerning sexual ethics. Since he did not intend to retract them the Vatican would have the next move. Unless some compromise were accepted, he would lose his position in the Catholic University theology department.

The Curran case is reminiscent of the second World War film scene for another, more important, reason. Judgments are being made about the case on the basis of a diverse assortment of secondary and even tertiary issues (the floating debris) while the immediately primary issue (the submarine on the ocean floor) remains obscured.

Everyone seems to have an opinion: from left-wing Catholics who see this as one more example of the male-dominated hierarchy's intellectual and moral bankruptcy, its "hang-up" on sex and power, and its determination to crush freedom of speech in the Church, to right-wing Catholics who seem to reduce it all to a matter of obedience to the teaching authority of the hierarchy, binding theologians and "simple faithful" alike to toe whatever doctrinal or moral lines are drawn for them.

In fact, however, neither Fr Curran nor his theological supporters question the need for, or the authority of, the hierarchical teaching authority. Neither do they contend that theologians constitute a parallel teaching authority to which the faithful owe the same "religious submission of mind and will" that is due to the pope or the episcopal college in the exercise of their authoritative teaching office. Neither Fr Curran nor his fellow theologians, with the obvious exception of Hans Küng, have challenged the first Vatican Council's definition of papal infallibility. And whatever the outcome of this case, Fr Curran will continue to enjoy the full protection of American law to teach, to write, and to lecture—everywhere, that is, except in a theology department of a Catholic seminary, college, or university.

The primary issue at stake here is none of the above. It is the nature of theology and the role of the theologian in the Church.

Listen attentively to what Fr Curran's detractors (or Cardinal Ratzinger's supporters, call them what you will) say in the heat of argument about the case. Read carefully what they write and publish, whether in formal articles or in correspondence columns. Note their answers to questions in press interviews. Then ask yourself if their remarks would have to be modified in any way whatever if Fr Curran were not a theologian, but rather a catechist, a bishop, a preacher, or a diocesan director of communications.

What tacit notion of theology is operative in their thinking, and how specifically does such a notion differentiate a theologian from other ministers and officers of the Church? If a "definition" of a theologian does not differentiate the theologian from other ministers and officers in the Church, then it is no definition at all and the question is begged. Who or what *is* a theologian?

Does a theologian exist to "hand on the faith", to teach authentic Catholic doctrine, and to defend the teachings of the Church? Of course, but so especially do catechists and bishops. And so does every member of the Church.

Does a theologian exist to proclaim the Word and to bring people to open themselves to the Spirit? Of course, but so especially do preachers. And so does every member of the Church.

Does a theologian have any responsibility of loyalty towards the institutional Church, for example by trying to persuade the general public of the wisdom of some church teaching or disciplinary policy? Of course, but so especially do bishops and official diocesan representatives. And so does every member of the Church.

What is it, then, that a theologian does, in addition to all of the above, that sets him or her apart? What is it that *defines* the theologian's role in the Church?

Although rooted in faith and in the life of the Church, theology is, unlike catechesis, preaching, and pastoral instruction, a scientific discipline. It is not charged primarily with the "echoing" of the faith (which is the literal meaning of catechesis), nor the proclamation of the Gospel, nor the official transmission of the faith to the general membership of the Church. The theologian's distinctive task is one of understanding: "faith seeking understanding," as St. Anselm expressed it.

CREEPING INFALLIBILITY

From this perspective, a recent comment by Francis A. Sullivan SJ, in an interview for the American press, has force. "The idea that Catholic theologians, at any level of education, can only teach the official church position, and present only those positions in their writings, is new and disturbing," said Fr Sullivan. He has been teaching ecclesiology at the Pontifical Gregorian University in Rome for 30 years, where his reputation has always been that of a reasonably conservative theologian.

In his carefully balanced book, *Magisterium: Teaching Author-*

ity in the Catholic Church (New York: Paulist Press, 1983), he is critical, for example, of the so-called double magisterium proposal and of Hans Küng's views on papal infallibility. He continued: "I don't know of any previous case that has raised the issue of dissent in a way that tends to threaten the critical function of theologians, with regard to the non-definitive teaching of the magisterium. I find this quite extraordinary, if what is meant is that infallible and non-infallible church teachings are equally beyond criticism. This is new."

And yet that is precisely the position taken by Cardinal Ratzinger. In an April interview with the Italian magazine *30 Giorni*, he declared: "Only in this century have theologians posed the problem of distinguishing between infallible teachings and non-infallible teachings in such a sharp way."

But although infallibility was not defined until 1870, even medieval theologians (Thomas Aquinas, Bishop Guido Terreni, and others) used equivalent terms to distinguish between ordinary teaching and a "final judgment" by the Church. The second Vatican Council itself honoured this distinction when it modified traditional "official teaching" in several areas, especially in the matter of religious liberty. Indeed, had there been no Vatican II and no Declaration on Religious Freedom, and were John Courtney Murray SJ, still alive today, *his* theological mandate would be as much under question as Fr Curran's, and for exactly the same reasons. No one familiar with the record of Fr Murray's difficulties with the Holy Office in the 1950s and 1960s could regard that possibility as remote.

Moreover, if there were no practical difference between infallible and non-infallible teaching, all non-infallible teaching would have to be taken *as if* it were infallible (the problem of "creeping infallibility"). In that case, all church teaching would be unchangeable. But, in fact, church teachings *do* change. And therein lies the problem.

How and why do church teachings change? Primarily through the critical probings of theologians and other scholars who raise questions not only about the wording of official teachings, but about their conceptual underpinnings as well. The Congregation for the Doctrine of the Faith implied as much in its 1973 declaration, *Mysterium ecclesiae:* "Even though the truths which the Church intends to teach through her dogmatic formulas are distinct from the changeable conceptions of a given epoch and can be expressed without them, nevertheless it can sometimes happen that these truths may be enunciated by the sacred magisterium in terms that bear traces of such conceptions."

Cardinal Ratzinger, however, seems to leave little or no room at all for such developments. "When one affirms that non-infallible doctrines, even though they make up part of the teaching of the Church, can be legitimately contested," he has said, "one ends up by destroying the practices of the Christian life and reducing the faith to a collection of doctrines." The statement is remarkable. He is saying that no church teaching, infallible or non-infallible, can ever be "legitimately contested." Accordingly, the theologian has no distinctive role in the Church other than that of a high-level catechist or a kind of institutional ideologue.

I am not proposing, over against Cardinal Ratzinger's view, that theologians should function without any pastoral restraints whatever. The theologian cannot treat official teachings as if they were the private speculations of fellow scholars, subject to the same kind of intellectual scrutiny and public criticism. Theology is indeed "*faith* seeking understanding", and theologians are men and women of the Church. Nor, in turn, is the Church an academic community. It is a community of disciples, of learners, of people on the way to sanctity.

The nature of the theologian's *audience,* therefore, is also crucial to the discussion. When the theologian is speaking or writing for a general audience, the theologian has to be careful to present the Church's official teaching accurately and fairly, and to distinguish that teaching carefully from his or her own theological views. A university classroom or lecture hall, however, is a different situation. There the theologian has an academic responsibility to identify and explain all positions, including dissenting views, and to analyse them on their own merits. The teaching of theology at this level is neither catechesis nor pastoral instruction, and so is not subject to the criteria which govern these two ministerial activities. Nevertheless, Fr Curran's own colleagues in the theology department of The Catholic University of America have attested in a public statement that even in the university classroom he is "thorough and respectful in his presentation of official teaching and of the Catholic moral tradition."

The same pastoral principle applies to publications. If theologians are writing for a general readership, they are bound by one set of restraints. But if they are writing for their peers, or even for educated nonspecialists, in books and professional journals, theologians are held to different standards from catechists, preachers, pastors, and those who speak officially for a diocesan or national church. Otherwise, the theological enterprise itself breaks down.

THE REAL ISSUE

But Cardinal Ratzinger seems to allow for no diversity of audience. It is as if everyone—university students, seminarians, theologically sophisticated parishioners, uneducated parishioners, and young children alike—is to be regarded as part of the "simple faithful". In his very lengthy paper, "The Church and the Theologian," given on 15 April at St Michael's College, Toronto, the cardinal put it straightforwardly: "The Church's main job is the care of the faith of the simple. A truly reverential awe should arise from this which becomes an internal rule of thumb for every theologian." Once more, the role of the theologian is collapsed into that of the catechist.

"Believers have confidence in the Church's word," Cardinal Ratzinger continued, "and so naturally transfer that confidence to those who teach in her name." Here again Fr Sullivan's comment is pertinent: "The idea that Catholic theologians, at any level of education, can only teach the official church position, and present only those positions in their writing, is new and disturbing."

We find ourselves, therefore, in a *cul de sac*. Theology becomes "Denzinger theology," as Karl Rahner once called it. Theologians can only deal with questions already addressed by the hierarchy, and their answers can never deviate from those already "on the books". There can be no real development of doctrine. *A fortiori,* there can be no change in doctrine.

But there is development and change, and there always has

been. How account for it? In the course of formulating an answer, one will have begun to describe the distinctive (and necessary) role of the theologian in the Church.

In the debate over Fr Curran, the nature of theology and the role of the theologian is the immediate primary issue. It is the submarine on the ocean floor. In the meantime, however, we continue to poke at floating debris.

The Case of Charles Curran

Christine Gudorf

This article originally appeared in *Christianity and Crisis* in 1986.

On April 10 the *New York Times* reported that, in a meeting with conservative moral theologians, Pope John Paul II had severely rebuked Catholic theologians who dissent from the church's traditional teachings on sexuality. It was the pope's first, and surely not his last, major statement on sexual issues since the Rev. Charles E. Curran announced at a March 11 press conference that he was being censured by the Vatican's Congregation for the Doctrine of the Faith.

Curran, a theologian at the Catholic University of America in Washington, D.C., revealed at his press conference that a September 17 letter from Cardinal Joseph Ratzinger, prefect of the Congregation, stated that some of his moral stances "violate the conditions necessary for a professor to be called a Catholic theologian." The letter explicitly mentioned Curran's positions on contraception, direct sterilization, abortion, euthanasia, masturbation, premarital intercourse, homosexual acts, and sacramental and consummated marriage, but did not specify how Curran's positions on these vary from official teachings. Nevertheless, if Curran fails to retract those positions, he will not be permitted to continue teaching as a Catholic theologian.

A letter to elicit support for Curran is being circulated by a group of past presidents of the Catholic Theological Society of America (CTSA) and the College Theology Society (CTS), including Walter Burghardt, Vera Chester, Bernard Cooke, Richard McBrien, Richard McCormick, Luke Salm, Gerard Sloyan, David Tracy, and Rodger Van Allen. It attacks Ratzinger's assumption that dissent from noninfallible teaching effectively places one outside the body of Catholic theologians, and asks four questions: (1) Which noninfallible teachings are serious enough to provoke such consequences? (2) How many noninfallible teachings must one disagree with before incurring this penalty, and how is this number determined? (3) If disagreement with any noninfallible teaching is sufficient to incur this penalty, from where is this principle deduced? And (4) if one is no longer a "Catholic theologian," is one's relationship to the church modified, and if so, how? The letter also calls for consistency in the application of sanctions (since there are many other Catholic theologians besides Curran who also dissent from these same official teachings), points out the dangers to the academic integrity of Catholic universities posed by the Congregation's threatened action, and ends with a collective testimonial to Curran's character and integrity.

The threatened action does not come as a surprise to observers of the Vatican scene. Curran has been out of favor with Rome since he became the focal point for much of the theological resistance to the papal ban on artificial contraception in the late 1960s. At the same time Curran is a careful scholar, theologically moderate, whose dissent from official teachings tends to be partial and limited to certain restricted sets of circumstances. He is no despoiler of tradition.

Both Hans Küng and Leonardo Boff, in different ways, have been disciplined recently for taking positions critical of the institutional church. It was only to be expected, then, that the Congregation would not ignore theologians in the U.S. who dissent from the moral conclusions in official teaching. In its action against Curran the Congregation for the Doctrine of the Faith is following the lead of the Congregation for Religious, which last year threatened 27 religious with expulsion from their orders if they did not retract the views expressed in their September 1984 *New York Times* ad calling for Catholic dialogue on the morality of abortion.

Understandably, the letter from the CTSA and CTS in support of Curran focuses on the issues of legitimate dissent, due process, and equal treatment. These are important issues, and the Catholic church has neither a long nor a consistent record of valuing any of them. Also, support for an individual faced with disciplinary action by authority is usually easier to gain by focusing on the issues of process, since it is difficult to be against individual rights and equal treatment, easier to disagree on specific issues. It is also safer to press process issues. Those who do are seldom placed in jeopardy along with the accused, as they would be if they had explicitly supported the views of the accused.

In this case, it is important that supporters of Curran speak out on the substantive theological issues as well as issues of process. The area of sexual ethics is a wasteland in the Catholic church. Teachers of Catholic sexual ethics have the choice of either addressing real life with useful critical moral reflection, or being faithful to the *magisterium* (the official teaching authority of the Catholic church located in the pope and the bishops). It is impossible to do both. More bluntly put, one can either be Christian, or one can be faithful to the magisterium. The church insists that artificial contraception and direct sterilization are *never* morally permissible, that masturbation is *always* serious objective evil, that direct abortion is *always* murder, that homosexual acts are *always* serious moral disorders even by those with involuntary homosexual orientation, and that once a consummated sacramental marriage exists *no* other morally acceptable marital union is possible for the spouses. Holding these convictions, the church eliminates the possibility of dialogue with contemporary society. It also denies the claim of innumerable Christians that they can and do discern the movement of the Spirit in their lives. Furthermore, this insistence disregards the priority given by Jesus himself to the needs and the religious hopes of his followers and the contempt he expressed for priests, scribes, and Pharisees who interpreted the Law in absolute terms, and used it as a yoke on the neck of the people.

A CALL TO COURAGE AND SOLIDARITY

In this time of crisis in the Catholic church courage and solidarity are demanded of both theologians and bishops to insure the fulfillment of the promise of Vatican II. For example, collegiality can only happen if the bishops continue to demand and expect it.

Theologians can protect their historic authority as teachers in the church only by defending those who are attacked when responsibly exercising that authority.

But courage and solidarity are most necessary for theologians and bishops because only through them can the voices from below penetrate the isolated realms where Vatican inhabitants seem to dwell. If bishops and theologians do not elucidate the experience of the laity to Rome, Rome will never have the possibility of speaking with authority to the people of God concerning those issues which are at the heart of most people's experience—issues of sexual identity and behavior, issues of fertility and birth, issues around the end of life or the end of marital love. An institution which fails to understand a people's experience of life's beginning and end, of love and sex, cannot ever hope to authoritatively articulate for that people norms for the socio-politico-economic structuring of human society.

Since the 19th century religion has been understood as primarily, if not exclusively, relevant to domestic life and personal relationships. In modern industrial society increasing worker alienation and loss of autonomy in production gradually led to an increased emphasis on marriage and family as the area of life in which *real* fulfillment could be expected. Because much of our society still understands marriage and family as the center of real life, credibility in this area is more crucial for the magisterium than other areas.

Theologians must continue to insist not only on faithfulness to Vatican II, but that faithfulness to Vatican II does *not* consist in repeating ad infinitum Vatican II texts. Instead, certain basic assumptions and conclusions require assimilation:

1. Human knowledge of God is always mediated by human persons, whether it comes to us through Scripture, church tradition, magisterial teaching, or our own experience. Therefore, no knowledge is above question.

2. God communicates with human beings through experience; no area of human experience, including sexuality, is closed to God's self-revelation.

3. God's love for human persons is for the whole person, for all aspects of human life, material as well as physical. God intends

our total welfare, and made both law and authority to serve human needs.

4. Human experience is complex. Options are rarely purely good or evil, but varied mixtures of both. Moral choice is opting for the better among less-than-optimal choices.

5. Because the welfare of human beings is God's first priority, it must be the priority of Christians, too. Human welfare is affected by consequences of our actions, so consequences must figure prominently in our choice of moral options.

6. The calculation of consequences must include not only the effect of the action on the person of the agent (both material and moral effects), but the effect on all the actors and witnesses, including future generations, insofar as that can be calculated. The call to be stewards of the earth requires the extension of love of neighbor to include future neighbors.

7. Suffering and sacrifice are not moral goods; pleasure and convenience are not moral evils. Moral evil is harm done to human beings; moral good is that which contributes to human welfare. Sexuality is not flawed because it is pleasurable; the appropriateness of traditional prohibitions (on artificial contraception, divorce, masturbation, sterilization, homosexual acts, and abortion) is confirmed neither by their difficulty nor by their ability to cause pain and suffering. In fact, new criteria are needed to judge these acts. Sacrifice and suffering are means, not ends, in the following of Jesus. They are good only when voluntarily undertaken in the service of the inbreaking of God's reign—a reign in which suffering is abolished and sacrifice no longer necessary.

8. Women are ends, not means; agents not objects. Women are *moral* agents and must be treated as such in reproduction as well as in nonreproductive areas of life.

9. The Jesus of the Gospels surrounded himself with the sinners of his day, called his disciples to be servants and not judges, urged on them forgiveness of one another, condemned legalism and self-righteousness in the Pharisees, identified sin in terms of injustice and victimization, and presented God as endlessly compassionate. No system of absolute moral laws complete with penalties which entail exclusion from the community can be legitimated on the basis of the life and teachings of Jesus.

10. Conscience must not be coerced. Persons who have devoted decades of their lives to the responsible construction of a moral stance must be presumed to stand on conscience, not on whim. When supported by threat of reprisal, demands for retraction of a stance of conscience are attempts to coerce conscience. A person of conscience would not retract, upon threat of reprisal, positions constructed as the work of a lifetime; persons who would so retract would not be fit to instruct others in morality.

We must continue to articulate such points not only in defense of Charles Curran, but in defense of the future of the Catholic church. If we hope to be able to retain our children in the faith tradition we inherited, we must not accustom them to the spectacle of Catholics being forced to choose between responsible conscience and membership in good standing.

Curran is unlikely to be the last theologian under attack. Thus far theologians selected to be censured have been priests (Küng, Boff, Schillebeeckx, Gutierrez, Curran), but even lay theologians may come under attack. When the May 1985 Vatican schema on Catholic universities was circulated (which in turn was based on the more general regulations in the new code of canon law), those who pointed out the potential for Vatican repression of dissent in faculties of theology and philosophy were shunned as alarmists. "Don't worry," they were told, "the bishops don't want to press those issues, and even if they did, the civil laws and the court system will uphold tenure, academic freedom, and nondiscrimination." Vatican documents are powerless against the U.S. courts, they said.

The February 12 dismissal of *Maguire v. Marquette* in U.S. district court demonstrated the limitations of and should undermine confidence in the courts as the defender of the right to religious dissent. Dr. Marjorie Maguire's discrimination case against Marquette for refusing to accept her applications for open positions in the theology department, a department in which there were no women, was dismissed on the grounds that Marquette was a religious institution and was therefore "protected from judicial review." Discrimination in religious institutions is evidently protected, even if, as in the case of Marquette, the institution is not owned by a church or a religious order, and receives large amounts of government funding. If this ruling stands, and it is similar to some recent National Labor Relations Board decisions on religious institutions, nothing protects theology and possibly philosophy faculties in Catholic universities from being purged of critical thought, except the resolution of the local bishop faced with orders from Rome.

The Vatican is correct about one thing: The authority of the church's teaching is at stake. The question is whether that authority resides in the magisterial articulation of a communal consensus based in reflection on the Spirit at work within the community, or whether it proceeds from ecclesial office which commands a privileged experience of the Spirit. The Second Vatican Council did not deal specifically with sexual ethics, but it did teach many Catholics that they are the people of God, the church, who hear the Spirit. It remains to be seen whether the dove can be recaptured and caged again in the Vatican. Rumor in the U.S. has it that the bird has discovered that it enjoys flying free.

Comments on the Curran Case: CON

These comments originally appeared in *Catholicism in Crisis* in 1986.

JAMES HITCHCOCK

Among its many dimensions, the Curran case focuses attention on the social role of the theologian in our time. Father Curran and his supporters argue that theologians have the right to pursue their researches (more precisely, their speculations) freely, unmolested by threats from outside the academy. Only in such a serene, tolerant environment, it is argued, can truth germinate. Yet Father Curran is, and has been for many years, much more than an academic theologian, and were his writings mainly aimed at other scholars they would probably not have drawn the Holy See's attention. Father Curran has constantly sought, and attained, the widest possible public forum for his opinions. Like many dissenting theologians, he has become something of a media star.

The circumstances under which he achieved academic tenure, in 1967, were hardly in keeping with the usual procedures of the academy. On that occasion organized protests and public demonstrations were used to bring pressure to bear on the university board to reverse its earlier decision against him. His position at Catholic University was attained through extra-academic means common on American campuses at that time but deeply destructive of the peace and integrity of the universities.

The next year Father Curran orchestrated the public attack on *Humanae Vitae* (describing his role in that affair with remarkable candor in the volume *Journeys,* edited by Gregory Baum). There Father Curran admitted that his main concern was publicity and expressed pride that "American Catholics could read in their morning papers about their right to dissent. . . ."

The Jesuit theologian Donald Keefe has pointed out (in *Com-*

498

munio, Summer, 1977) the way in which Father Curran's stand on abortions is intertwined with a rather garbled understanding of church-state relations, the nature of a pluralistic society, and the Second Vatican Council, causing him to defer to the state in moral matters in a way which hardly does justice to the seriousness of the issues. Once again, what seems to govern Father Curran's thought are not purely intellectual and academic considerations but a certain sense of the social role of the theologian, defined in part by "outside" agencies like the government.

Over the past two decades some American Catholics have had the experience of objecting to certain ambiguous (or worse) teachings about sex found in catechisms and other Catholic books, only to be met with the reply that such theories are in harmony with the work of Father Curran, a professor at the bishops' own university and a man whose orthodoxy must therefore be assumed. There is, and continues to be, a "catch 22" at work here—if the Church repudiates Father Curran's theories, it is accused of tyranny; if it does not, those theories are treated as presumptively orthodox.

The question of academic freedom is scarcely adequate to encompass the far-reaching issues which are ultimately at stake here.

PHILIP F. LAWLER

I am a journalist, not a theologian; my academic specialty was politics. So perhaps I should have no comment on the Curran affair. But wait. When he returned from his meetings at the Vatican, Father Curran called a press conference. Is this the world of theology, or of journalism? Soon groups of Curran's supporters were collecting signatures on petitions. Is this a theological disputation, or a staged political event?

Late in March, the National Catholic News Service printed excerpts from Father Curran's correspondence with the Vatican. That correspondence was "obtained by NC News Service"—in other words, leaked. As any political journalist knows, "leaks" do not occur by accident; they happen when someone believes that the publicity will help him. Selective leaking has become a standard political device. Only recently has it entered into the theologian's repertoire.

The mass media, with their usual incapacity for understanding Catholic affairs, have depicted a sudden Vatican crackdown on Curran. The reality could not be more different. The Vatican began correspondence with Curran six years ago. And while Curran told the assembled press, "My posture is neither defiant nor disrespectful," his letters to Rome were certainly not obsequious. In August 1983, he opened a missive with the announcement: "In the course of our correspondence I have constantly reiterated that the quality of dialogue is poor." His letters consistently lecture the Vatican; they rarely provide direct responses to direct questions.

Perhaps the most intriguing aspect of the correspondence, however, is the distinction Father Curran attempts to draw between the Vatican and the American bishops. The American bishops, he claims, "recognize the possibility of public dissent" in a way that the Vatican does not. Is he willing, then, to subject himself to the authority of the American bishops, but not to the bishop of Rome? That is a theological question, beyond doubt. But it is question with powerful political overtones.

Consider, too, the strategy Curran employed in responding to the Vatican's complaints. After his last meeting in Rome, he rushed back to Washington. "Since I am a member of a university faculty and belong to the community of theologians," he announced, "I have felt it imperative to communicate all these matters with my faculty colleagues and other theologians." So he called a press conference. The people who attended that press conference—carrying television cameras and notepads—were not primarily professors, let alone theologians. Most of them had only a vague notion of the issue at stake. But they did supply plenty of publicity. Which, obviously, is what Curran had intended.

Why does a theologian crave publicity? By all accounts, Father Curran is an honest and sincere man. But evidently he believes that his confrontation with the Vatican is an inherent part of his theological work. To the *Washington Post,* he explained that a theologian "should always be in dialogue with the world . . . should always be in tension with the Church." That's not a misprint: *dialogue* with the world, *tension* with the Church. Stand that sentence on its head, and you have a reasonably accurate description of the Catholic theologian's proper role.

In Curran's view many activities which were once universally condemned (such as masturbation, fornication, homosexual acts, abortion, and contraception) may be morally justifiable. Many people agree with him. The official Catholic Church—and here Curran has been commendably forthright—does not. That Rome should overthrow two millennia of constant teaching on the strength of Curran's theological dissent is, to say the least, unlikely.

But suppose, just for the sake of the argument, that some future synod could decide to accept Curran's views. Suppose that the Church *could,* then, condone abortion and fornication. (The strain on the imagination illustrates just how foreign Curran's ideas are to Catholicism, but leave that aside.) Why isn't Father Curran content to work quietly toward that goal? Other theologians—John Courtney Murray and Henri de Lubac come immediately to mind—have continued their controversial work unobtrusively, avoiding public confrontations, and finally seen their ideas adopted by the universal Church. Why is it so vital that the whole world know—right away— what Curran thinks?

If the Church were to adopt Curran's views, that decision would be made by bishops, not by theologians, and certainly not by the general public. Yet that, precisely, is Curran's complaint. He readily admits that the institutional Church rejects his views. But he hopes, using the leverage of public opinion, to force a change in the Vatican's posture. (Or perhaps, more ominously, to promote divisions within the hierarchy—notably between the American bishops and Rome.) In dialogue with the world, in tension with the Church. Charles Curran is true to his ideas.

THOMAS P. MELADY

The current discussion on the proposed Vatican action to void the right of Father Charles E. Curran to teach Roman Catholic doctrine has aroused a variety of comments and responses. All are interesting, but only several focus on the central issue. Let us say in the beginning that all parties would be well served to refrain from extraneous issues and to engage in the discussion in a calm, cool, and collected fashion.

Father Curran is a popular professor at my alma mater, The Catholic University of America. His erudition is well known. He is respected by his academic peers. It is also apparent that a good number of Catholic clergy and laypersons concur with his opinions on sexual issues. Some even hold that a majority of American Catholics accept some of Father Curran's views.

The central issue is whether an official spokesman or representative should teach the official doctrine of an organization. Father Curran has a canonical mission to teach at the Catholic University of America.

There are some organizations where there is no official doctrine. In some churches each believer can accept or reject any teaching, but still remain a member in good standing. In other organizations, there are official positions which must be publicly held by anyone having an official capacity within that group.

I have held two positions where my position required me to reflect the official capacity. As an Ambassador of the United States, I had a clear duty to communicate the official position of my government. I was selected for that reason and, when taking the oath of office and acquiring the authoritative title of Ambassador, agreed to do so as long as I held that title. As a University President, I am the official representative and report to the Board of Trustees. This organization, too, has official positions. There is freedom in styles, timing, and circumstances, but *none in what the official position is*. As President, I cannot, on official matters, speak differently. As an Ambassador, I could not publicly disagree with the official position of my government.

In both these capacities, there has not been an honorable alternative to representing—to teaching—the official position. If, in either case, I could not do so, I had the other honorable alternative—to resign my official position.

Father Curran's position of influence springs from his being a member of the theology faculty at the Catholic University of America. This is one of the three departments at the Catholic University chartered by the Vatican. He speaks from an influential position because of his official role.

Consequently, the issue is Father Curran's continued authorization to teach in the name of the Catholic Church. No one has ever claimed that the Catholic Church decides doctrine based on what people do or want. The Catholic Church is the Church where certain teachings are "given." There is no question that many Catholics do not follow some Church teachings on sexual ethics. Human weakness has existed since the beginning of the human race. However, on this important policy matter—whether an official spokesman can disagree with an official position—the Church has no choice but to clear up the confusion. The authoritative nature of the Catholic Church requires that official teachers of the Church must teach what the Church teaches.

It would be quite a different matter if Father Curran's teaching appointment did not carry the official imprimatur of the Church. If I did not accept the official position of the United States government, I would not expect to retain the title of the official spokesman for my government. If I could not follow the policies of the university trustees, I would not expect to remain as president and as their official spokesman.

Father Curran has an excellent reputation as a teacher. He is popular with many of his students and respected by his peers. He has been clear and candid in the areas where he disagrees. The issue is clear: he does not accept some of the official Vatican views on sexual ethics. Consequently, he should not be authorized to teach in the name of the Catholic Church. There are various subjects that he could teach, but not as the authoritative teacher for the Catholic Church.

CHRISTOPHER WOLFE

The Vatican Congregation for the Doctrine of the Faith has asked Father Charles Curran of Catholic University to "reconsider and to retract those positions which violate the conditions necessary for a professor to be called a Catholic theologian." Unless he does so, he will be unable to continue teaching theology at C.U., in accordance with norms laid down a number of years ago for "pontifical universities," which have a special juridical relation with the Church.

But the impact of any action with regard to Father Curran will go far beyond pontifical universities. Many American academics and university administrators are scurrying fearfully to mobilize opposition in an attempt to head off the action, because they see it as the first step in a broader process. The draft of a schema on Catholic higher education is currently being circulated for comment around the world, and it would provide similar norms, in this regard, for any educational institution which puts itself forward as Catholic.

The academics are right to be fearful. There is considerable truth in at least the last part of Father Curran's statement that "it is unjust to single me out when so many other Catholic theologians hold the same basic position," namely, that they are free to dissent from what they call these authoritative but noninfallible teachings. Let me first deal with the issue of Father Curran, and then the broader issue.

Father Curran's main line of defense has been that he has a right to dissent from noninfallible Church teaching. For the record, I think that it is not correct to characterize those teachings as noninfallible. The teaching on divorce is defined, for example. The other issues, I think, fall into the category of teachings that are irreformable though as yet not formally defined. But putting that to the side, and assuming for the sake of argument that they were noninfallible, there is still no right of dissent such as he and his supporters assert. The Church's authority is not simply coterminous with its infallibility, but extends well beyond it.

Parents have authority in the family, though none of them makes any claim to infallibility. The pope and the bishops should not be treated as "individuals with merely private opinions, *unless* they invoke the power to define infallible teachings." Vatican II, for example, is very strong on the authority of "noninfallible" teaching. *The Dogmatic Constitution on the Church* says that "loyal submission of the will and intellect must be given, in a special way, to the authentic teaching authority of the Roman Pontiff, even when he does not speak *ex cathedra* in such wise, indeed, that his supreme teaching authority be acknowledged with respect, and that one sincerely adhere to decisions made by him."

Nor would it make any sense to create such an artificial gap between "the teachings that are binding" and "the teachings that are not binding." That would suggest that if the Church really wanted to be obeyed in any matter, it would have to invoke its power to define infallibly. Is that what the dissenters want? Or, knowing that the Church explicitly uses that power only rarely and cautiously, do they use this argument as an excuse to evade the Church's authority?

Are all noninfallible teachings binding in such a way that dissent from them is illegitimate? The above citation from Vatican II indicates how "ordinary" teachings are to be adhered to: "conformably with his [the Roman Pontiff's] manifest mind and intention, which is made known principally either by the character of the documents in question, or by the frequency with which a certain doctrine is proposed, or by the manner in which the doctrine is formulated." Does anybody have any doubt as to the pope's "manifest mind and intention" in regard to the matters at issue in Father Curran's case? In all candor, it must be said that one would have to be willfully obtuse to find grounds for dissent on these issues in the voluminous writings and allocutions of John Paul II and in documents approved by him; on the contrary, traditional Church teachings are stated clearly and in very strong terms, with every indication one could expect that they are not open to debate among theologians.

It is difficult to see much substance in Father Curran's case, then. Nor is it a requirement of justice that the Vatican move at the same time against each and every theologian who shares those views. As a matter of fact, dealing with Father Curran as an individual is one way for the Vatican to make its "manifest mind and intention" known in a less draconian way.

But—moving from Father Curran to the broader question of the alleged threats to the legitimate freedom of American Catholic universities—does this truly portend an era of "Vatican repression" in Catholic universities (assuming that they would rather bow to the Church than drop their identification as Catholic—a very uncertain assumption)? Some people interpret the action in Father Curran's case, together with the new schema on Catholic higher education, as a basis for "search and destroy missions," with authoritarian Church officials seeking out and discharging people they disagree with. A more accurate characterization is that the Church is merely acting in self-defense against an extraordinarily dangerous and powerful attack.

One of the distinctive features of Catholicism—what makes it different from other Christian churches—is that it claims that Christ gave authority to Peter and the apostles, and that this authority was handed down to subsequent popes and the bishops in communion with them. This authority is of such great importance because it is the guarantor of the Church's unity, which is one of the marks of the true Church: Christ prayed "that all may be one, even as Thou, Father, are in Me, and I in Thee; that they also may be one in us, *that the world may believe that Thou hast sent me.*" Moreover, it provides a clear, readily identifiable source of guidance as to what God asks of Christians, thus sparing them the paralyzing incertitude that would inevitably flow from making themselves the arbiters of what God had revealed.

Today this authority is under sharp attack. Unlike earlier attacks, however, which led people to leave and set up other churches, today there is a concerted effort to reject authority and to claim that this reflection is perfectly compatible with Catholicism. Theologians who attack the Church's teaching, with the support of many in the media, claim that one can remain faithfully Catholic not only while privately rejecting, but also while publicly agitating against, the Church on moral and dogmatic issues.

What is at stake for the Church, then, is its very identity. Does Catholicism demand adherence to the teaching of the pope and bishops, or can Catholics turn to some other source of authority: private theologians, "public opinion" in the Church, or their own isolated consciences?

Now in this context, what is taught as Catholic theology in Catholic universities is of profound importance. If leading Catholic universities provide a platform for the teaching of "Catholic" theology by theologians who dissent from and agitate against the

Church's teachings, they are—whether intentionally or not—throwing their weight into the battle on the side of the dissenters. They provide them with their "credentials" as Catholic theologians, without which they would have a much more difficult time getting people to take them seriously.

As a matter of simply defending its own identity, therefore, the Church cannot permit theologians and universities to employ the name "Catholic" and then serve as a sounding board for those who undermine official Catholic teaching.

None of this means that teachers and students are to be muzzled and prevented from studying any teaching that is contrary to the Church's. Part of education is studying views with which the ideals of the educating institution may be at odds, and there will certainly be times when it is appropriate to study ethical views at odds with the Church's. Nor is there anything objectionable about non-Catholics teaching in a Catholic university, since there are perfectly reasonable grounds to study non-Catholic teaching and to foster a dialogue between Catholic and non-Catholic scholars. What is objectionable is that non- or anti-Catholic teaching be taught as if it were perfectly consistent with Catholicism.

That is what the debate on Father Curran—and, in the background, the new schema on Catholic higher education—is all about. If teachers and universities want to call themselves Catholic, then they must be willing to let those who have the authority to say what is or is not Catholic teaching, exercise that authority to prevent the teaching of "Catholic" theology by those who actually oppose it.

Perhaps under those conditions, as I suggested above, American Catholic universities will simply choose to stop calling themselves Catholic, preferring to have leeway to let their people teach whatever they want. (Whether they can prosper or even survive without being Catholic is a question which may cause some of them to hesitate, however). That would be unfortunate, I think—much better that they renew themselves within the Church's fold—but it would have the virtue of clarifying the situation. They would no longer be in the position of obscuring for many people an essential part of what it means to be a Catholic.

Ecumenical Dimensions of the Curran Case: The Vatican Moves To Repress Dissent

John C. Bennett

This editorial originally appeared in *Christianity and Crisis* in 1986.

The action of the Vatican against Father Charles Curran, deny-ing him the right to teach Catholic theology, may prove to be a major event in the beginning of a repressive process in the Catholic church which will be a calamity for all churches and for our coun-try. It may be the end of a very creative period in Catholic theologi-cal and ethical thinking from which we have all benefitted. The church in this country, however, has so much intellectual initiative and courage one can hope that ways will be found to break through these repressive barriers.

On the surface this appears to be a special case. Father Curran was in one of only three departments in the Catholic University under the control of the Vatican. Most other Catholic institutions are free from such direct control. But pressure can be placed on Catholics who formally have more institutional freedom to encour-age silence on some issues and self-censorship. This will make very difficult fresh, creative thought in relating the tradition to modern problems.

The Catholic church and other churches have a right to see their official teachers represent their essential faith. The central issue in this case is that the Vatican has rigorously limited the area in which dissent from any aspects of its teaching is permitted. For many years Curran has fought for the right to dissent on matters not covered by the infallible teaching of the church. Cardinal Ratzinger in his letter to Curran said that the "infallible Magisterium" is not limited "purely to matters of faith nor to solemn definitions." Any particular position emphasized by the magisterium is binding. The contrast between infallible and noninfallible teaching as a basis for dissent is rejected. This means that Catholic minds are subject to an external authority that can determine essential teachings at any time, even required interpretations of these teachings. This leaves very little margin for freedom, and any margin that one may believe to exist can be taken away by this external authority. Such a situation is stifling for the mind.

Father Curran began an intense struggle for freedom to dissent on noninfallible teachings in 1968. For many years he was victorious. He had led the opposition in this country to the section of the encyclical by Paul VI, *Humanae Vitae,* which forbade the use of artificial contraceptives. Twenty-one members of his own theological faculty joined him in this. He was able to secure over 600 signatures by recognized Catholic teachers of theology or moral theology who opposed the pope's position on artificial contraceptives in an extremely clear and forthright statement.

The most immediate effect of this was an enquiry by the university about whether Curran and his colleagues had acted wrongly in the academic context. Out of it came two volumes: One of them had the fine title *Dissent In and For the Church.* Much emphasis was placed on the importance of this right to dissent for the health of the church. Curran and his colleagues won in this academic context; the academic authorities did not overrule this result (Paul VI, who shared many of the ideas of John Paul II, was more permissive).

In 1968 the American Catholic bishops in a pastoral letter, "Human Life in Our Day," affirmed this right to dissent from noninfallible teaching with several safeguards: Sufficient reason must exist; deference must be given to authority; scandal must not be created. This pastoral letter gave support to this victory for freedom to dissent.

Charles Curran moved on to other issues. He wrote almost a

book a year for 16 years in which he struggled to adjust the absolutes of Catholic moral theology to concrete human experience.
The title of one of these books is revealing: *Ongoing Revision.* He
was involved in a long process of revision of the legalistic moral
theology of the manuals and he was one of very many Catholic
thinkers involved in this process. The more complex issue of abortion received his scrutiny: He sought to secure permission for some
abortions in the first weeks of pregnancy, and also in the case of a
few kinds of moral conflict in which abortion may be considered
the lesser evil. (Those are my words and not his.) He also was clear
on the limits of law as related to abortion, emphasizing the principle that prudentially it may be consistent with Catholic teaching to
affirm that to seek to prevent almost all abortions by law may do
more harm than good. Whether a law can be fairly enforced is one
prudential consideration.

Curran diverges from the present teaching and practice of the
church in emphasizing the need, for pastoral reasons, to include in
the sacramental life of the church many of the millions of remarried divorced Catholics instead of forcing them to remain second-
class members of the church for their whole lives. In this Curran
has strong support among Catholic thinkers, including some bishops in this country. This also allied him with his mentor, probably
the greatest moral theologian in the church, Bernard Häring,
whom he quotes with approval.

He has more trouble in dealing with homosexuality because
he is so strongly convinced that "the ideal meaning of human
sexual relationships is in terms of male and female." But he has
come to recognize that a small minority of persons are what he
calls "irreversable" homosexuals. In their case he concludes that
"homosexual acts in the context of a loving relationship striving for
permanency are objectively good." That judgment separates him
from all who would discriminate against homosexuals in the church
or in society.

Curran is in no way an aggressive rebel. He is deeply loyal to
his church and he comes to his conclusions involving dissent after
the most careful and fair exposition of the alternatives in his many
books. The need for the church to accept the right to dissent and
his advocacy of the particular positions that I have mentioned that

are the content of his dissents are matters of deep conviction; they give him a sense of mission in the interests of truth and because of his pastoral concern for people. He has very strong support in the church. The dean of his theological faculty supports him. The president of his university has announced his willingness to have him serve in other departments not under papal control. His own bishop in Rochester, N.Y. supported him in principle but came to accept the action of the Vatican. More than 750 Catholic theologians from the United States and Canada have signed statements supporting him. Rome is in for trouble in its attempts to overcome the progressive dynamism and the broad ecumenical spirit which characterize so large a part of the American church, but it can create great anguish of mind and conscience and it can greatly hinder for a long time the expression of fresh and creative thought.

Since the action against Charles Curran was announced, we learned of the steps taken against Archbishop Raymond Hunthausen of Seattle stripping him of his powers in key areas, transferring them to an auxiliary bishop appointed with the purpose of counteracting his influence. This is a new dimension of repression: the undercutting of bishops who have shown some independence. Appointments of conservative and obedient bishops during this pontificate have already modified trends in the hierarchy.

As one who has welcomed the leadership of all Christians by the American Catholic bishops through their pastoral letters about peace and nuclear war and about the economy, I hope that this leadership will continue. For the American churches and for the country as a whole it would be an enormous loss if this witness of the American bishops were silenced or if they should lose credibility because they would be viewed as part of a system of repression. May many of them show signs of independence of the system!

The Ecumenical Impact of the Curran Case

J. Philip Wogaman

This article originally appeared in *The Christian Century* in 1986.

Not surprisingly, the Vatican's crackdown on Catholic theologian Charles E. Curran has received extraordinary attention in both the secular and religious press. For the Vatican to reach across the ocean to repudiate one of the church's best-known thinkers is, to say the least, unusual, and the controversy seems loaded with portents for the future of Roman Catholicism.

Despite the wide discussion of the controversy, however, the ecumenical impact of Father Curran's disciplining has been neglected. Though the Vatican's move has generated great concern among Protestant leaders and theologians, they have been reticent to express this concern as an issue affecting ecumenical relationships. A few months prior to the action, the American Theological Society and most of the past presidents of the Society of Christian Ethics publicly voiced their support for Curran as a highly respected colleague and theologian, but their statements centered on the issue of academic freedom and their high regard for Curran's work rather than on the implications of the Vatican's actions for the ecumenical church. Similarly, articles and editorials in the ecumenical journals have mostly emphasized the effects on the Roman Catholic Church and American society.

This response is understandable. Apart from the broader cultural symbolism of the Curran affair, it might appear to be a purely internal matter for the Roman Catholic Church. Non-Catholics might oppose the action and even be alarmed by it, but is it really any of their business? No doubt the Vatican itself would consider any public protests by non-Catholics to be a bit of an intrusion. The issue, after all, hinges on whether the church can designate its own spokespersons. If Curran is no longer acceptable to the church as a teacher of doctrine, doesn't the church have every right to say so? Isn't an objection from an outsider a bit like, say, an American objecting to whom the British or the Japanese choose as their ambassador. Whatever we might think of a certain ambassador, we can hardly complain if the British or Japanese withdraw the ambassador because they no longer find him or her a suitable representative of their views and interests.

But is the Curran affair entirely an internal matter? It may be the exclusive right of a faith community to determine what its message is and who its messengers should be, but the message is not directed exclusively to the people within the church. It is also directed to people outside the church and, particularly in the post-Vatican II era, to other Christian communions (and even to other religions). All those engaged in ecumenical dialogue with the Roman Catholic Church are bound to pay close attention to the designation or repudiation of an official theologian. Such an action is an important way for a church to communicate to other churches as well as to its own members.

It is a particularly important communication when the theologian repudiated takes positions acceptable to other religious bodies. In Curran's case, the offending views are fairly moderate expressions of opinions that are held much more strongly by most mainline Protestant denominations. For example, Curran accepts the legitimacy of contraception, using language that most Protestants would consider very mild. By repudiating him on that point, the Vatican emphasizes its disagreement with most Protestants. Similarly, in rejecting Curran's understanding of the relationship between infallible dogma and the more flexible expressions of church doctrine, the Vatican repudiates the theologian at a point where his understanding is still rather conservative by Protestant or, I think, even Eastern Orthodox standards. The result is to deepen the disagreements between the Vatican and most ecumenical Christians on the proper teaching role and authority of the church—reversing a post-Vatican II Council trend toward greater mutual understanding of perennially divisive issues of ecclesiology.

One Catholic theologian, Romanus Cessario, who supports the Vatican's action against Curran, made this difference painfully clear in an October 19 *Washington Post* article titled "Get This Straight: America's a Democracy; the Church Isn't." Protestants cannot deny the right of the Catholic Church to communicate such points. But it would be naïve to expect Protestants not to regard these actions as a message to them about the unacceptability of views they consider acceptable.

There is another ecumenical problem. By emphasizing that, in the words of Washington, D.C., Archbishop James A. Hickey, "there is no right to public dissent," the church has called into question whether Catholic theologians are real theologians or only official advocates of positions taken by church authorities. When a Catholic theologian takes a position, can ecumenical counterparts consider this to be truly the result of reflection? When one interacts with a Catholic colleague, is it useless to try to persuade him of what I consider to be the better case for a different theological interpretation? There may be some irony lurking here, for by insisting that Catholic theologians never voice public reservations about official positions, the church invites doubts about the authenticity of the statements that support those positions.

Is the church to be understood as a community in which people march in lockstep to official doctrine, defined with some rigidity by a relatively small hierarchy? Or is it a community of faith in which personal integrity is deeply valued and cultivated? The hierarchy is entitled under its own canon law to run things as it wishes; but it needs to know that it is defining the church in ways that may make it singularly unattractive to those who view the faith in a more open way.

I recognize that no church body can tolerate the total repudiation of concepts and methods absolutely fundamental to its faith. The struggle over what is fundamental and what is peripheral is central to the Curran case. But here again, the ecumenical community gets a distinct message: the Catholic Church regards a handful of issues, mostly related to sexual ethics (which Curran has addressed moderately and infrequently), as of truly fundamental importance; apparently outweighing in significance the broad sweep of Curran's work on the Bible, natural law and Christ. Moreover, those who have interacted with Curran through the years in scholarly theological circles know him to be deeply Christian in personal character and commitment. Those qualities are not, by themselves, a substitute for intellectual trustworthiness. But the personal spiritual qualities of this man, combined with his intellectual gifts, lead ecumenical colleagues to wonder what it means when a church repudiates one who best embodies the spirit of the Second Vatican Council.

There is a still deeper question—one that Curran himself may have to face in a new way: How are we to identify the presence of the church in the world? Most of our church loyalties and sense of religious identity are tied up in our relationship to particular church communions. We identify with specific institutions and a visible community of fellow believers. That is largely as it should be, for the church is nothing at all if it is not a visible presence. But the full meaning of the church can never be enclosed by the walls of particular institutions, even those of a world church with many millions of members.

In the earlier years of the modern ecumenical movement, Theodore O. Wedel, canon of Washington Cathedral, wrote of the "coming great church," meaning the universal church that is beyond our particular church loyalties. He had in mind not a monolithic institution but a fellowship of faith transcending institutional boundaries. The reality of the "great church" has been affirmed by those within other denominations (such as the Southern Baptist Convention and the Lutheran Church—Missouri Synod) who have had to come to terms with their deeper loyalties in the face of denominational hardening of the arteries.

I have been deeply impressed by Charles Curran's loyalty to the Catholic Church in the face of its repudiation of his work. The question is whether there must be a higher loyalty even than that. The ecumenical perspective summons Christians to be loyal to the "great church" that is beyond our particular churches. And in the case of theologians, it calls them to be first of all theologians of and for the "great church."

That is why those of us committed to an ecumenical expression of Christian faith continue to participate in dialogue and cooperation, in spite of setbacks. We are relating to one another in the "great church," not confronting one another as simple adversaries; that day is past. Thus, as we affirm the splendid examples of Catholic witness in the contemporary world—such as the recently adopted Bishops' Pastoral on the U.S. Economy—we also make bold to register our deep dissent in those instances, such as the Curran case, where we believe a particular church authority has broken faith with the truly universal church. That dissent must be filed unapologetically in the ecumenical sphere, not as a return to old hostilities, but as an affirmation of the unity we must not lose.

Dissent in Moral Theology and Its Implications: Some Notes on the Literature

Richard A. McCormick, S.J.

This article originally appeared in *Theological Studies* in 1987.

<hr>

The May issue of *Catholicism in Crisis* referred to the case of Charles E. Curran as "the most crucial intellectual issue now facing the Catholic church in America."[1] It was no secret then how that journal wanted the issue resolved. Be that as it may, the matter was concluded by the July 25 letter (delivered to Curran August 18) of Joseph Cardinal Ratzinger informing Curran that he is no longer "suitable nor eligible to exercise the function of a professor of Catholic theology."[2]

I say "the matter was concluded." That the "most crucial intellectual issue now facing the Catholic church in America" was not truly *resolved* seems clear from the remarkable journalistic response to be briefly chronicled here. The chronicle begins with the statement of Archbishop James Hickey: "I fully support this judgment of the Holy See."[3] Archbishop Theodore E. McCarrick (Newark) also praised the decision. "We who are teachers in the church have an obligation to teach what the church teaches." "It is," he said, "a case of truth in packaging. If the box is labeled salt and contains pepper, it can't be left on the shelf to confuse the shoppers."[4] Spelled out, McCarrick's truth-in-packaging metaphor would read: "If a person is labeled a 'Catholic theologian,' and presents anything but the official line, that person cannot be left in place to confuse the faithful." In other and starker words, the task of the theologian is to repeat uncritically what the magisterium has said.

But the pundits have far outworded the prelates. Norman Podhoretz, of all people, saw in the decision a sign that "the Vatican has demonstrated that it still has a definable identity whose integrity it will defend."⁵ In this way it "puts to shame all other institutions in our day, most notably the universities." Podhoretz is not unhappy about this because he wants "barriers in contemporary society against the spread of sexual permissiveness." Yet he wants someone else to build those barriers and take the flak. One is tempted to pursue the barrier metaphor with some questions. Is it not possible, for instance, to construct barriers from the wrong material or to place them in the wrong spot? Is it possible for barriers to rust?

Joseph Sobran, a senior editor of the *National Review,* argued that a "priest in the employ of a pontifical institution . . . may just have to take orders from Rome now and then."⁶ Of course. Ergo? Msgr. Charles O. Rice insists that "Catholic truth . . . is determined not by counting noses or consulting opinion polls but by the magisterium."⁷ Once again, a question: Is this an exhaustive listing of the alternatives? Michael Novak believes that "the judgment of the church is correct in this instance."⁸ He urges Curran to follow the example of John Courtney Murray, S.J., by keeping silent and allowing history to decide—an interesting and soothing counsel of passivity from one who dissented from *Humanae vitae* and organized the dissent against the pastoral on the economy.

John Catoir is not hesitant. Curran should be fired because he is "not merely a theologian; he is a teacher of theological opinions which undermine church teachings. Some things are right and some things are wrong. Nothing is both right and wrong at the same time."⁹ Foreign to Catoir's conceptual categories are notions such as "inadequately formulated," "in need of improvement," "doctrinal development," etc. Michael McManus concludes that Curran used his "theological breathing room with reckless abandon."¹⁰ William F. Buckley, Jr., notes that the Vatican's decision "has brought on a goodly amount of loose lip."¹¹ Regretfully, Buckley adds to this lip-load by denying that the church "has persecuted its prophets whose teachings it has gone on, in later years, to incorporate as its own." Murray, Congar, deLubac, et al. would choke on that one.

By far the majority of commentary has been critical of the Vatican decision. William J. Gould, Jr., asserts: "Rome is threatening to do grave damage to the richest and most powerful Catholic church in the world just at the time it is about to make a major and distinctive imprint on American life."[12] Jonathan Yardley sees the decision as the source of big trouble for Catholic higher education, trouble "that the old men in Rome have cooked up for it."[13] William Newell argues that Curran was condemned "for being modern in thought and American in the way he does things."[14] The *Syracuse Post Standard* editorialized that just when Catholics have the impression that they are beginning to be listened to, "they get slapped down again for raising questions."[15] Kenneth Vaux attributes the whole sad happening to "Curran's latitude and openness to new convictions."[16] Warren Hinckle predicts that "the Curran case is fated to become the church's new Galileo case, with the same unfortunate consequences for all involved."[17] Leonard Swidler observes that by removing Curran, "the Vatican wants to send the message that no dissent—no matter how reasonable, responsible and moderate—from the dictated position will be tolerated: 'Obey!' " His conclusion: "In face of this scandalous Vatican suppression of dialogue and dissent, all good Catholics should dissent."[18]

William V. Shannon is no less straightforward. He sees Curran's predicament as "an occasion for immense sadness."[19] The pope, he says, is unwise in "attacking the wrong man on the wrong issues." Curran is only doing his critical job as a theologian. "What is alienating is his [pope's] determination to crush disagreement and impose his own version of orthodoxy on all topics." Similarly George Armstrong, an American correspondent in Rome, concludes that "Curran and the other inquisitive theologians have been told that they should consider themselves to be enthroned catechism teachers, or mere repeaters, not researchers seeking new truths in old scriptures."[20]

Jim Fain believes the decision represents "backward-looking orthodoxy" and is a tragedy "for a church that is digging itself into irrelevancy. If it continues, the gulf between U.S. Catholics and Rome will be unbridgeable."[21] Daniel Maguire interprets the Vatican intervention as symbolic of a power grab.[22] After Vatican II, laypersons entered theology on college campuses where academic freedom is sacred. "The Vatican has taken poorly to this loss of power and is struggling to regain it." Rodger Van Allen refers to Rome's "clumsiness in dealing with Catholic universities" and attributes it to lack of experience (Italy has but one Catholic university, and that without a theology faculty).[23] He concludes: "The posting of 'no dissent' signs may suit the Kremlin. It does not suit the Catholic University of America." *The Journal-Gazette* is convinced that officials in Rome "have only ensured that Father Curran's views will be more widely disseminated."[24] In a similar vein the *Louisville Courier Journal* concluded its editorial: "An institution so large and so deeply rooted in Western Civilization need not fear either dissent or gradual change and, in fact, like any organization, will be healthier if it accepts some of both. That is the message Pope John Paul II can expect to hear back from his American flock."[25]

Both *America* and *Commonweal* carried splendid editorials. The latter highlighted the *sotto voce* style of theologizing that the Vatican intervention invites. It just will not work and will be damaging.[26] *America* laments the passivity of the American hierarchy and the pastoral confusion the disciplining of Curran will introduce.[27] Finally Roy Meachum argues that the cost of this Vatican victory "will be higher than understood by anyone behind Vatican walls, which still shut out the changing world."[28]

This is literally but a small sample. I record it for two not unrelated reasons. First, much of it shows the depth of anger at what was perceived to be a foolish and tyrannical intervention. Second, it throws a quite unforgiving glare on a major source of demoralization in the American church: the conviction that authority is being used ideologically to neutralize or abrogate important dimensions of Vatican II. During thirty years in the field of moral theology I have never seen so many priests—and many laypersons—so deeply angry and utterly alienated. The overview of much of the public response to the Curran affair is but a testament to that.

The heart of the immediate issue is public dissent, a point this compositor attempted to highlight in an earlier essay.[29] Is public dissent permissible within the "Catholic idea"? Under what conditions? How much? With what cautions or reservations? With what purpose? Since the answers to questions like these are at the heart of the theological enterprise, I want to review several recent contributions—both by bishops and by theologians—that discuss this issue.

BISHOPS

Archbishop Rembert Weakland, O.S.B., authored two columns that are the equivalent of a pastoral letter to his people.[30] He first recalls that the Catholic church has been willing, even if hesitantly at times, to accept truth wherever it comes from and to integrate it with revelation. But often enough that has involved struggle. These struggles brought with them two characteristics: excessive cruelty to human beings and fear. "In such an atmosphere, amateurs—turned theologians—easily became headhunters and leaders were picked, not by their ability to work toward a synthesis of the new knowledge and the tradition, but by the rigidity of their orthodoxy." Weakland uses the first decade of this century as an example. The suppressions associated with the Modernist crisis "resulted in a total lack of theological creativity in the U.S.A. for half a century." The struggle for purity of doctrine, Weakland urges, "must avoid the fanaticism and small-mindedness" of past years of church history. He concludes by citing Pope John XXIII: "Nowadays, however, the spouse of Christ prefers to make use of the medicine of mercy rather than that of severity. She considers that she meets the needs of the present day by demonstrating the validity of her teaching rather than by condemnations."

There can be no doubt that Weakland was referring to the Curran and Hunthausen cases for he explicitly states that the integrative challenges of today come from psychology and the human sciences and "thus the troubled territory today is sexuality."

Weakland's message is pellucidly clear: We should have learned from history that suppression—the type that the Vatican is now pursuing—is no way to deal with the pursuit of truth. Needless to say, this author not only agrees with Weakland's analysis[31] but also applauds his courage.

The second statement on dissent is a speech delivered April 2,

1986, at a meeting of the National Catholic Educational Association by Archbishop William Levada.[32] Noting that the distinction between infallible and noninfallible teaching "is at the heart of current discussions about dissent from church teaching," Levada proposes his understanding of both. Dissent from teaching that is infallibly proposed, he correctly notes, "excludes one from the communion of the faith." Refusal to accept a noninfallibly proposed teaching "also implies a separation from full communion with the church teaching, believing and practicing its faith, although such separation does not necessarily exclude one from the church."

Why such a separation? Levada says that the reason lies in the type of guarantee that stands behind noninfallible teaching. While the guarantee is not absolute, still

> we are given the assurance that the Holy Spirit is guiding the authorized teachers in the church to enable them to propose what we must know and do for the sake of our salvation as Christians.
>
> What would allow us to separate ourselves from this church teaching given with the promised assistance of the Holy Spirit? Nothing trivial, to be sure. For we can rightly presume that such teaching is correct.[33]

Here a question or two is in order. First, with regard to the "separation from full communion *with the church*"[34] that Levada sees in dissent from noninfallible teaching, what is the source and evidence for this idea? What if great numbers in the church share the dissent? Who is separating from whom and what does "separation" mean? Was John Courtney Murray, S.J., in "separation from full communion with the church" because he disagreed with the Syllabus of Errors? Is it not rather that the Syllabus was separated away from the "church teaching, believing and practicing its faith"? I am afraid that Levada's notion of separation reveals a far too static concept of the church's magisterial process.

And that raises the second point. If we are given, with noninfallible teaching, "assurance that the Holy Spirit is guiding the authorized teachers," then *nothing* (not simply Levada's "nothing trivial") would "allow us to separate ourselves from this church teaching." Missing in Levada's presentation is the analogous notion of the assistance of the Holy Spirit. That assistance is necessarily different when it guarantees a teaching and when it does not. Failure to take this into account leads to the "almost infallible syndrome."

Levada next discusses the case of a person who is "truly expert" in the area treated in noninfallible teaching. Dissent would be justifiable if the person had "truly convincing reasons," although how this is conceivable I fail to see if the assistance of the Spirit is "assured." Levada continues:

> Such withholding of assent or "personal dissent" is by its very definition an exceptional and rare event in regard to the authoritative, noninfallible magisterium, which enjoys the presumption of truth—all the more so because it not only involves a personal judgment about some teaching which is connected intimately to the deposit of faith, but it also implicitly contains a judgment that such teaching has not enjoyed the presumed assistance of the Holy Spirit.[35]

Once again several points. Much of the church's noninfallible teaching in the moral sphere is not "connected intimately with the deposit of faith." If an intimate connection with the deposit of faith is Levada's chief reason for holding that dissent is "an exceptional and rare event," then that reason does not lead to his conclusions. Certainly it is difficult to understand how "by its very definition" withholding of assent is "exceptional and rare." Here we see the "almost infallible syndrome" at work.

My second point returns to the 'presumed assistance of the Holy Spirit." This is Levada's second reason for saying that dissent must be rare. However, when the analogous notion of that assistance is admitted and analyzed more carefully, it may not support the conclusions he draws.[36]

Finally Levada treats public dissent. He notes that personal or private dissent "remains open to achieving a fuller understanding of the issue in such a way that will allow one to remain in harmony with the church's teaching authority." Public dissent is different. Here is Levada's analysis.

> Public dissent, in which one proposes a personal opinion or conclusion which directly contradicts some teaching of the church's noninfallible magisterium, is no longer a step on the path of dialogue toward a growth in understanding of church teaching. Rather it contains a decision to place one's own judgment on a par with that of the magisterium and implicitly suggests that the question or doubt which has led one to withhold assent or dissent has now become an answer which one offers to others to accept and imitate as a legitimate position for a Catholic believer.[37]

With all due respect, I believe that paragraph is simply false, and for several reasons. First, Archbishop Levada, earlier in his essay, had referred to the need of "submitting them [dissenting opinions] to the judgment of my peers." How is one to do this except publicly in scholarly journals? Why is this "no longer a step on the path of dialogue"? Furthermore, if the questions at issue touch the lives of people in very concrete ways, they presumably will want to know about these discussions, indeed to contribute to them.

Second, and most crucially, public dissent need not at all involve one in placing "one's own judgment on a par with that of the magisterium" and in implying that "the question . . . has now become an answer." All one need imply or say through public dissent is that one is offering an opinion to the judgment of one's peers and other interested and competent persons. To present public dissent as necessarily involving a competitive magisterium, as Levada has done ("equivalently an alternative, personal magisterium") is to negate the public and critical character of theology, and to caricature the free flow of ideas in the church against the express wishes of Vatican II.[38]

On June 6, 1986, Archbishop Daniel Pilarczyk (Cincinnati) issued a pastoral letter on dissent.[39] Pilarczyk first distinguishes three levels of church teaching: formally and specifically defined, infallibly taught though not defined, true though not infallibly taught and not necessarily unchangeable. At whatever level the church teaches, it is saying two distinct things: 1. "This is true and is in accord with divine revelation." 2. To teachers (whether catechists, preachers, writers, theologians) the church says: "We want you who teach under the auspices of the church to present this teaching to your public as true and as binding in accord with the level of authority with which it is presented." This is what Pilarczyk calls the "public church order" aspect of church teaching.

He next focuses on dissent by one who has a teaching responsibility in the church. If such a person cannot accept a particular teaching, that person can 1) submerge his/her doubts; 2) keep quiet about one's doubts but also about church teaching; 3) openly oppose the teaching. Those who choose either of the latter two courses "are not in compliance with the church's 'public order decision.' " As Pilarczyk words it: "Public dissent always involves deliberate refusal, even if for conscientious reasons, to carry out an order from church teaching authority."

What should church authorities do when confronted with public dissent? Pilarczyk lists several possibilities: keep quiet and wait to see what happens; invite the dissenter to change his/her mind; demand public retraction; deny the person the right to be called a Catholic theologian.

Finally, the pastoral letter treats the specific critical role of theologians ("to investigate, to refine it, [church teaching] to probe it, to push back its horizons"). He acknowledges the theologian's responsibility to address conscientiously those teachings thought to be inaccurate. But rather than a "right to dissent," Pilarczyk states that "we might better ask how much dissent church authorities should tolerate, how much is permissible?" He notes that "what is at stake here is a refusal . . . to accept the directives of church leadership about what is to be taught in the name of the church." So, finally, theologians may dissent "but when they do so they do so at their own risk."

What is unavoidable in the Pilarczyk letter is the dominance of the juridical as if the major concern is public order, not precisely truth. The question of church teaching is elaborated within an intense, almost nervous concern for superior-subject relationships. Thus church teaching always includes a command to present it as true and binding. Dissent is a refusal to carry out this order—really disobedience. It is only to be tolerated, etc. Church authority resembles a policeman keeping order rather than a participant in the search for truth. Nowhere is there the notion that perhaps the dissenter should be listened to, his/her reasons carefully discussed and weighed, his/her person supported. The presumptions are all against any dissent. The dissenter is marginalized before the issue is faced. Almost regardless of its inherent value dissent involves that "refusal . . . to accept the directives of church leadership about what is to be taught in the name of the church."

But a closer scrutiny of Pilarczyk's idea of the command that accompanies church teaching is called for. Pilarczyk's understanding of this command—directed to preachers, catechists, writers, and theologians—is that they are to present church teaching "as true and binding." But Pilarczyk seems to sense the indiscriminate character of this lumping of preachers, catechists, writers, and theologians; for at another point he refers to the "demand that the teaching be presented in the church as church teaching." There is a remarkable difference between presenting something "as true and binding" and "as church teaching."[40] This latter category allows amply for critical evaluation and even dissent. If Pilarczyk understands the implied church directive accompanying noninfallible teaching to mean always "present this teaching as true and binding" without any critical evaluation, he has, I believe, gone too far. Specifically he has confused the roles of preacher, catechist, and theologian. I know of no theological sources that would validate such an understanding. Indeed, it would, besides flying in the face of history, cripple theological education, trivialize the role of the theologian, and paralyze doctrinal development. But unless I am mistaken, this is the understanding in Pilarczyk's pastoral letter.

In summary, then, while the letter acknowledges the different ecclesial roles of preachers, catechists, and theologians, eventually the dominance of the juridical perspective smothers these differences (cf. below sub McBrien).

A remarkably different presentation is that of Bishop Michael Pfeifer, O.M.I. (San Angelo, Texas).[41] Pfeifer uses the disciplining of Charles Curran to reflect on some basic Christian and Catholic moral themes. After noting that it is God who has created us free and called us to faithfulness, Pfeifer turns to the formation of conscience, "that place where we finally choose to activate the implications of our Christian call."

The formation of conscience involves us in a "constant dialogue" with God's scriptural revelation, with tradition and official teaching as well as "with our experience and understanding of the daily demands which face us as individuals and as a community." Pfeifer then has a brief but realistic word about the place of bishops, the pope, and theologians in this dialogue. For instance, he acknowledges that "theologians are also teachers in the church." As he puts it: "Their writings and teaching also form a part of the teaching of the church, and they participate in the assistance that is given to all in the formation of our Christian conscience."[42] This is a far cry from the attitude of those who view theological reflection in the church as "merely speculative," and "non-official."

Pfeiffer then turns explicitly to official teaching. He deserves full citation here.

> Official teaching cannot replace the responsibility of Catholics to seek the truth in those teachings and to give their assent to that truth. And no one of us can simply sit back and wait for church authorities or theologians to figure things out or to make up our minds for us. This responsibility and freedom is nowhere more evident than in the areas where no final assurance can be given that God's own truth has been found.[43]

In cases like this, the church offers guidance "according to the best available resources at its disposal." Of this guidance Pfeifer states that we can "rely on this official teaching *at least* not to lead us astray."[44] It is this assurance that leads us to be open to what is taught, ready to give assent. But we cannot, Pfeifer notes, stop there. Because the teaching is not final, "both church authorities and Catholics in general must be open to ongoing exploration and even revision when greater clarity emerges. This ongoing exploration is carried out especially by theologians."

In the process of this exploration, church teaching may achieve greater refinement. At other times it may be impossible to reconcile official teaching with emerging qualifications, and church authorities may ask a theologian to cease to publish his/her views on a certain point. But "in no way is this a final judgment on the *question* at issue, but only a warning that a certain point of view seems irreconcilable with what has been taught so far."

Pfeifer concludes by noting that since official teaching must be addressed to the whole Catholic world, it "cannot take into account the specific circumstances of each person who seeks sincerely to hear the church's guiding word." Prayer, study, reflection, and consultation are required "before one would make an exception for oneself." Pfeifer insists that moral questions be approached not as "simple legal demands," but in the far broader context of our faithfulness and generosity.

In these important matters tone is crucial, and I believe Bishop Pfeifer, in contrast to Levada and Pilarczyk, has hit exactly the right tone. For example, he views official church teaching as an ongoing process often capable of improvement and revision, an assertion of modesty not often found in official statements. Our openness to such teaching must include openness to its growth (attention Catholics United for the Faith, *Wanderer* et al.). Our assimilation of that teaching is a personal responsibility rooted in our freedom and fidelity. It is an assimilation that must deal prayerfully but realistically with the provisional character of some teaching as well as with the fact that it cannot exhaustively state individual circumstances in its articulation. These are themes that theologians have been urging for some years and it is refreshing to see them appear in an episcopal pastoral letter. What Pfeifer has achieved is a relative rarity in our time. He has managed to make the notion of "official teaching" look inviting and attractive. That is an enormous achievement at a time when powerful forces are acting, unwittingly I am sure, to reduce the teaching of the magisterium to an imposed ideology.

THEOLOGIANS

Charles Curran, in discussing his own case before the College Theology Society, identifies five key issues in his dispute with the Vatican: the role of the theologian; the possibility of public theological dissent from some noninfallible teachings; the possibility and right of dissent by the Christian faithful; the justice and fairness of the process; academic freedom for theology, and Catholic institutions of higher learning.[45]

As for the theologian, Curran sees the role as "somewhat independent and cooperative with the hierarchical role." By this wording he is contesting the view that theologians derive their office from delegation by the hierarchy, a view found in canon 812 of the new Code of Canon Law as well as in Cardinal Ratzinger's correspondence with Curran. Curran argues, successfully I believe, that the ecclesiological perspectives of Vatican II will not support recent legislative attempts to make of the theological role an entirely derivative one.

Curran next turns to public dissent by the theologian. He acknowledges that *obsequium religiosum* is due to noninfallible teaching but that this does not not exclude dissent. Cardinal Ratzinger denied this in his Sept. 15 letter to Curran. "It must be recognized that the authorities of the church cannot allow the present situation to continue in which the inherent contradiction is prolonged that one who is to teach in the name of the church in fact denies her teaching."[46]

Curran then states in exact detail his bases for claiming that dissent is appropriate at times. Within the realm of noninfallible teaching, *some* (Curran himself insists on this qualifier) teachings are at a distance from the core and central realities of the faith. "This distance . . . grounds the possibility of legitimate dissent." Furthermore the moral issues in question involve a level of specificity and complexity that makes certitude more elusive. As Curran summarizes it:

> The central issue involved in the controversy between the CDF and myself is the possibility of public theological dissent from some noninfallible teaching which is quite remote from the core of faith, heavily dependent on support from human reason, and involved in such complexity and specificity that logically one cannot claim absolute certitude.[47]

Ratzinger denies this by deflating the distinction between infallible and noninfallible teaching. "The church," he says, "does not build its life upon its infallible magisterium alone but on the teaching of its authentic, ordinary magisterium as well."[48] The implication of this statement is, as I have noted elsewhere,[49] that whatever the Church builds its life upon is not a proper matter for public dissent. That contention is, I believe, unsupportable. Briefly, Ratzinger disallows public dissent in principle, a sweeping negation that led ecclesiologist Francis Sullivan, S.J., to remark: "The idea that Catholic theologians, at any level of education, can only teach the official church position and present only those positions in their writings, is new and disturbing."[50]

Curran next treats the possibility and legitimacy of dissent on the part of members of the church. This possibility was recognized by some episcopal conferences in the wake of *Humanae vitae*. And since that is the case, this "greatly affects how the theologian functions." Theologians present their analyses and views publicly not simply to exchange views with their peers, but also because the people of God have a stake in these discussions. To approach such public discussions dominantly in terms of scandal (in the nontechnical sense of wonderment and confusion) is to perpetuate Leo XIII's description "the ignorant multitude"—as well as the now obsolete sociological assumptions behind that phrase.

Curran's essay ends with some edifying things to say about justice and fairness.[51] I cannot detail them here.

Richard McBrien argues that the primary issue at stake in the Curran affair is the nature of theology and the role of the theologian in the church.[52] Unlike catechesis, preaching, and pastoral instruction, theology is not charged primarily with "echoing" the faith. Obviously the theologian must present the church's teaching clearly. But theology is above all "faith seeking understanding." Cardinal Ratzinger's statements disallow *any* disagreement with noninfallibly proposed teachings. McBrien rightly rejects this. It denies theology's critical role and reduces the theologian to a high-level catechist. Church teachings do change and they change primarily through the critical probings of theologians and other scholars. He cites Francis Sullivan on the Curran case:

I don't know of any previous case that has raised the issue of dissent in a way that tends to threaten the critical function of theologians, with regard to the non-definitive teaching of the magisterium. I find this quite extraordinary, if what is meant is that infallible and noninfallible church teachings are equally beyond criticism. This is new.

McBrien argues that in forfeiting theology's critical role, Ratzinger allows for no diversity of audience. Everyone is to be regarded as part of the "simple faithful." That is just unreal in our time.

The third study of dissent in the church is that of Avery Dulles, S.J.[53] Dulles first notes several differences between political and educational institutions and the church. The church has a deposit of faith and cannot accommodate the same kind of ideological pluralism acceptable in the secular state or university. Second, the church was established by the action of God in Jesus Christ and its members are not free to alter its beliefs and structures in a substantive way. Third, the church uses different means than secular societies and has special aids at its disposal ("Behold, I am with you all days, even to the close of the age" [Mt 28:20]). Dulles then lists the various authorities in the church (scripture, tradition, popes, bishops, consensus of the faithful, theologians) and notes that sometimes conflict of opinions can arise. In the face of such conflicts two mistakes are possible: excessive permissiveness and excessive rigidity.

At this point Dulles treats the matter of dissent. The difficulty arises in the sphere of noninfallible teaching. Where such teaching is concerned the church asks for *obsequium animi religiosum*. Of this term Dulles, following the excellent study of Ladislas Orsy, S.J.,[54] notes:

> This term actually includes a whole range of responses that vary according to the context of the teaching, its relationship to the gospel, the kind of biblical and traditional support behind it, the degree of assent to it in the

church at large, the person or office from which the teaching comes, the kind of document in which it appears, the constancy of the teaching, and the emphasis given to the teaching in the text or texts.[55]

This is of capital importance. There are still very many, even theologians, who refer to *Lumen gentium* (n.25, *obsequium religiosum*) as if it were a simple univocal concept. Dulles puts this to rest. "Because the matter is so complex, one cannot make any general statement about what precisely amounts to 'religious submission of mind.' "

While Vatican II did not teach the legitimacy of dissent by its words, Dulles argues, "it did so implicitly by its actions." The German bishops did so explicitly in their pastoral letter of 1967 (Sept. 22). A year later (Nov. 15, 1968) the American bishops in *Human Life in Our Day* agreed with the German letter but went beyond it in treating the *expression* of dissent. Such public dissent, the Americans said, is acceptable under three conditions: 1) The reasons must be serious and well founded. 2) The manner of dissent must not impugn the teaching authority of the church. 3) The dissent must not be such as to give scandal. Dulles mischeivously notes that "anyone who wants to reject the teaching of these documents on dissent is thereby dissenting from the noninfallible magisterium, and thus confirming that very teaching." That "anyone" is an unmistakable reference to the archbishop of Washington who declared that the conditions stated by the American bishops are "not workable."

Dulles concludes his balanced and respectful study by noting the harm that comes from the effort to stamp out dissent. "It inhibits good theology from performing its critical task, and it is detrimental to the atmosphere of freedom in the church."

This represents but a brief overview of some recent literature on church teaching, especially in the moral sphere and dissent from it. I want to conclude with an attempt at a synthetic theological reflection. The Curran affair, and with it the case of Archbishop Raymond Hunthausen was cover-storied by *U.S. News and World Report* as follows: "The Pope Cracks Down: Taking on American Catholics."[56] That may appear to be a bit epochal and tumultuous, but it underlines a key ingredient with profound theological implications: coercion. Dulles has noted that this "inhibits good theology" and harms "the atmosphere of freedom in the church." This inhibition and harming can easily have the following impacts.

1. *The weakening of the episcopal magisterium.* Here we should recall the theological force of episcopal agreement described in *Lumen gentium,* n. 25. If the bishops around the world are united with the pope in their teaching, then that teaching can achieve a greater level of stability and certainty, and indeed achieve infallible status if the teaching is a proper object of infallibility and is presented as something to be held definitively. But the unity must be genuine and clear.

In a coercive atmosphere both the genuinity and clarity are put in serious doubt. First, the genuinity. Here we should recall one of the arguments made during the deliberations of the so-called Birth Control Commission. It was contended that the church could not modify its teaching on birth regulation because that teaching had been proposed unanimously as certain by the bishops around the world with the pope over a long period of time. To this point Cardinal Suenens replied:

> We have heard arguments based on 'what the bishops all taught for decades.' Well, the bishops did defend the classical position. But it was one imposed on them by authority. The bishops didn't study the pros and cons. They received directives, they bowed to them, and they tried to explain them to their congregations.[57]

In a coercive atmosphere people will repeat things because they are told to and threatened with punishment if they say anything else. Episcopal unity is revealed as enforced, not genuine.

As for clarity, the more likely scenario in a coercive atmosphere is that the bishops (some at least) will say nothing if they disagree. In such circumstances, to read episcopal silence as unanimity is self-deceptive. That is the importance of the Terrance Sweeney incident. It gave us a peek at genuine episcopal disagreement in matters where official insistence would lead us to believe that there was unanimity. Many of us have known this, of course.

Some years ago I authored with Corrine Bayley, C.S.J., an article[58] proposing that certain sterilizations could be justified. A bishop friend remarked to me: "I can name a hundred bishops who agree with you, but not one who will say so publicly." What seemed clear unanimity (if only in silence) clearly was not.

When the genuinity and clarity of episcopal agreement have been cast into grave doubt by a coercive atmosphere, the episcopal magisterium itself has been undermined. The meaning of consensus has been eviscerated. The bishops should be the first ones to protest this diminishment of their magisterium, and the atmosphere that grounds it.

2. *The weakening of the papal magisterium.* This follows from the first point. If bishops are not speaking their true sentiments, then clearly the pope is not able to draw on the wisdom and reflection of the bishops in the exercise of his ordinary magisterium. When this happens, the presumption of truth in papal teaching is weakened because such a presumption assumes that the ordinary sources of human understanding have been consulted, as the late Karl Rahner so repeatedly argued. That is why what is called the "enforcement of doctrine" is literally counterproductive. It weakens the very vehicle (papal magisterium) that proposes to be the agent of strength and certainty.

3. *The marginalization of theologians.* Coercive measures will almost certainly have the effect of quieting theologians, at least on certain issues. This further erodes both the episcopal and papal magisterium by silencing yet another source of understanding and growth. Archbishop Weakland, as noted above, underlined this. Many bishops, most recently James Malone, have noted the absolute necessity of theology for their work. These are Malone's words: "As a bishop in an episcopal conference which has devoted substantial time and energy to the place of the church in the world, I can testify to the irreplaceable role of the theological enterprise."[59] If reputable theologians are marginalized, the magisterium is proportionately weakened. And it is no response to exclude from the "reputable" category those with whom one disagrees. That begs the or any question.

4. *The demoralization of priests.* When juridical coercion (which is not altogether out of place) too easily dominates the

church's teaching-learning process, priests (and other ministers) become demoralized because they are expected to be the official spokespersons for positions they cannot always and in every detail support. Thus they become torn by their official loyalties and their better judgment and compassion. *Commonweal,* in the editorial cited above, referred to this as "occupational schizophrenia." Archbishop John Quinn adverted to this in the Synod of 1980.[60]

5. *The reduction of the laity.* Coercive insistence on official formulations tells the laity in no uncertain terms that their experience and reflection make little difference, this in spite of Vatican II's contrary assertion: "Let it be recognized that all of the faithful—clerical and lay —possess a lawful freedom of enquiry and of thought, and the freedom to express their minds humbly and courageously about those matters in which they enjoy competence."[61] If such humble and courageous expression counts for nothing, we experience yet another wound to the authority of the ordinary magisterium. The search for truth falls victim to ideology.

6. *The compromise of future ministry.* When a rigid orthodoxy is imposed on seminarians in the name of unity and order, the very ability of these future priests to minister to post-Vatican II Catholics is seriously jeopardized. I have seen this happen. Many thousands of Catholics have studied and struggled to assimilate the council's perspectives. They do not understand and will not accept a new paternalism in moral pedagogy. This means frustration and crisis for the minister trained to practice such a pedagogy.

7. *The loss of the Catholic leaven.* Coercive insistence that the term "official teaching" is simply synonymous with right, certain, sound, and unchangeable (an identification powerfully supported by the suppression of any public dissent) will lead to the public perception that the role of Catholic scholars is an "intellectual form of 'public relations,' " to borrow from Clifford Longley.[62] That means the serious loss of theological credibility in precisely those areas of modern development (e.g., science and technology) where the church should desire to exercise a formative influence. The present pontiff wants both to unite the church and shape the world, both utterly laudable apostolic objectives. The means to the former could doom the latter.

In conclusion then, I cannot but agree with *Commonweal's*

excellent editorial conclusion: "In the end, the move to exclude the possibility of responsible, public theological questioning of established but noninfallible church teaching will provoke the very fragmentation and loss of authority it is meant to prevent."[63] It will also deprive the people of God of the fruits of open and honest reflection on the behavioral implications of their faith. They have a right to this. Therefore, I exhort my theological colleagues to stay the course and to embrace, with both humility and courage, their public critical function.

Notes

1. "Curran, Dissent and Rome," *Catholicism in Crisis* 4 (n.5, May, 1986) 6.
2. *Origins* 16 (1986) 203.
3. *Origins* 16 (1986) 204.
4. *Star-Ledger,* Aug. 20, 1986.
5. *Washington Post,* Aug. 29, 1986.
6. *Washington Times,* Aug. 28, 1986.
7. *Pittsburgh Catholic,* Sept. 5, 1986. Whether the printers revolted or Rice dozed is not clear in the following entry in Rice's text: "Following what I believe to be the lead of Paul V in *Humani generis* . . ."
8. *Washington Post,* Aug. 28, 1986.
9. *Catholic New York,* Aug. 28, 1986.
10. *Miami News,* Aug. 30, 1986.
11. *Washington Post,* Aug. 23, 1986.
12. *Washington Post,* Oct. 19, 1986.
13. *New Haven Register,* Aug. 27, 1986.
14. *Hartford Courant,* Sept. 7, 1986.
15. *Syracuse Post Standard,* Aug. 25, 1986.
16. *Chicago Tribune,* Sept. 8, 1986.
17. *Newsday,* Sept. 8, 1986.
18. *Miami Herald,* Aug. 24, 1986.
19. *Boston Globe,* Aug. 27, 1986.
20. *Los Angeles Times,* Aug. 25, 1986.
21. *Atlanta Journal Constitution* , Aug. 24, 1986.

22. *Los Angeles Times,* Aug. 24, 1986.

23. *Philadelphia Inquirer,* Aug. 27, 1986.

24. *Journal-Gazette,* Aug. 24, 1986.

25. *Louisville Courier Journal,* Aug. 25, 1986.

26. "The Curran Effect," *Commonweal* 113 (1986):451–454.

27. "Charles Curran: 'Silencio,' " *America* 155 (1986):81–82.

28. *New York Times,* Aug. 29, 1986.

29. Richard A. McCormick, S.J., "L'Affaire Curran," *America* 154 (1986):261–267.

30. Rembert Weakland, O.S.B., "The Price of Orthodoxy," *Catholic Herald,* Sept. 11 and 18, 1986.

31. Not everyone did. Archbishop Philip M. Hannan (New Orleans) accused Weakland of "wildly exaggerating" and of treating the pope "unfairly" (*National Catholic Register,* Nov. 16, 1986). He asked: "Is the good archbishop himself not wildly exaggerating in comparing the decisions of the Holy See toward Father Curran and Archbishop Hunthausen with the Inquisition and witch hunts?" He went on to say that the Vatican decisions "were needed." This is a rather oddly provocative conclusion from one who is known as the major dissenter from the episcopal magisterium in the United States on matters of peace and war.

32. William Levada, "Dissent and the Catholic Religion Teacher," *Origins* 16 (1986):195–200.

33. *Ibid.,* 198.

34. Emphasis added.

35. *Ibid.,* 198.

36. Cf. my "Bishops as Teachers and Jesuits as Listeners," *Studies in the Spirituality of Jesuits* 18 (n.3, May, 1986).

37. Levada, 199.

38. "The Church in the Modern World," in *Documents of Vatican II,* edited by Walter M. Abbott, S.J., (New York: America, 1966) n.62, p.270.

39. Daniel Pilarczyk, "Dissent in the Church," *Origins* 16 (1986):175–178.

40. This point was raised in an interesting little sideshow that played itself out in London. John Mahoney, S.J., published in 1984 his *Bioethics and Belief.* It contained an *imprimatur.* In a joint statement Mahoney and Rt. Rev. Ralph Brown, Vicar General of the Archdiocese of Westminster, explained why the *imprimatur* was withdrawn. At one point they state that the *imprimatur* is no more than a "declaration that a book or a pamphlet is considered to be free from doctrinal or moral error." They then state very interestingly: "However, the question can arise, particu-

larly in light of the passages of the Second Vatican Council quoted above, as to whether a work which contains passages which are at variance with the church's current official teaching on a particular moral matter is to be considered by that fact as containing moral error." The question can arise, indeed. If history is our guide, the answer to that question is a clear "no." Being "at variance with the church's current official teaching" is not tantamount to being wrong. That is why Ratzinger's rejection of any public dissent is devoid of historical and theological warrants. Cf. *"Bioethics and Belief:* a Joint Statement," *Briefing 86* 16 (July, 1986):186–187.

41. Michael Pfeifer, O.M.I., "Thoughts on Freedom, Conscience and Obedience," *Origins* 16 (1986):391–392.

42. *Ibid.,* 392.

43. *Ibid.,* 392.

44. Emphasis his.

45. Charles Curran, "Public Dissent in the Church," *Origins* 16 (1986):178–184. Cf. also *Commonweal* 113 (1986):461–472, as well as *Faithful Dissent* (Kansas City: Sheed and Ward, 1986). This latter includes all the documents in Curran's dealing with the Holy See.

46. *Origins* 15 (1986):668.

47. *Origins* 16 (1986):181–182.

48. *Origins* 16 (1986):203. Archbishop Roger Mahony (Los Angeles) dissents from Ratzinger on this point (*Origins* 16 [1986]:372–375). He grants the legitimacy of theological dissent on certain issues but rejects the idea that theologians may present their opinions as the basis for pastoral practice. Mahony's paper is on the whole a very balanced presentation. Thus he distinguishes carefully between catechists and theologians. He also acknowledges theology's "critical and creative role" and admits that it may be difficult to distinguish a development of doctrine from a deviation. The essay suggests two closely related questions that have received only incomplete treatment. First, what characteristics determine whether an analysis is presented as a personal opinion only or as the basis of pastoral practice? Second, when and through what mechanisms does authentic teaching cease to be authentic, that is, give way to a new formulation in the church? And then more specifically, what is the position of the individual Catholic conscience during this transitional period? For instance, John Courtney Murray was right about religious liberty before Vatican II authenticated his view. Indeed, only because he was seen as right could the Council adopt his view. If Catholics realize this rightness in advance of official recognition (before it is "authenticated")—for instance because it is supported by many trustworthy theologians—could they not form their consciences accordingly even before the teaching is publicly authenti-

cated? Mahony's remarks do not answer these questions. I believe that they are at the core of some contemporary disputes.

49. Richard A. McCormick, S.J., "The Search for Truth in the Catholic Context," *America* 155 (1986):276–281.

50. NC news release.

51. The notion of fairness raises a chilly little side issue. One is embarrassed to report that a center devoted to ethics (Pope John XXIII Center, Braintree, Mass.) would publish an *anonymous* four-page attack (*Ethics and Medics* 11 [June, 1986]:i–iv) on a modest little effort entitled *Health and Medicine in the Catholic Tradition* (New York: Crossroad, 1984) by this author. One's embarrassment is compounded when he learns that the anonymous attack was submitted as a paid advertisement to a national monthly, *Health Progress,* but was flatly rejected. Embarrassment turns to mystification when this anonymous review is reported by Thomas O'Donnell, S.J. (*Medical-Moral Newsletter* [Sept., 1986]:27–28), as being authored by Albert S. Moraczewski, O.P. O'Donnell kindly describes the book as "a deceptive tangle of truths sometimes inadequately expressed and errors half concealed." He also has other warm and supportive comments.

52. Richard McBrien, "Theologians Under Fire," *Tablet* 240 (1986):675–677.

53. Avery Dulles, S.J., "Authority and Conscience," *Church* Fall 1986:8–15.

54. Ladislas Orsy, S.J., "Reflections on the Text of a Canon," *America* 154 (1986):396–399.

55. Dulles, 12.

56. *U.S. News and World Report,* Nov., 1986.

57. Robert Blair Kaiser, *The Politics of Sex and Religion* (Kansas City: Leaven Press, 1985), 170.

58. Corrine Bayley, C.S.J., and Richard A. McCormick, S.J., "Sterilization: the Dilemma of Catholic Hospitals," *America* 143 (1980):222–225.

59. James Malone, "How Bishops and Theologians Relate," *Origins* 16 (1986):169–174.

60. John R. Quinn, " 'New Context' for Contraception Teaching," *Origins* 10 (1980):263–267.

61. Cf. note 38.

62. Clifford Longley, "Cynicism and Sexual Morality," *The Times* (London), Aug. 4, 1986.

63. As in note 26.

List of Contributors

John C. Bennett is Professor Emeritus and former President of Union Theological Seminary, New York.

Edward J. Berbusse, S.J., frequently contributes to theological journals from his residence with the Jesuit Community at Georgetown University.

John P. Boyle is Associate Professor and Chair of the School of Religion at the University of Iowa.

Charles E. Curran is Professor of Moral Theology at the Catholic University of America and served as Kaneb Visiting Professor of Catholic Studies at Cornell University in the 1987–88 academic year.

Avery Dulles, S.J., is Professor of Systematic Theology at the Catholic University of America.

David Fitch, S.J., frequently contributes to pastoral and theological journals from his residence in Santa Clara.

Joseph Fuchs, S.J., is Professor of Moral Theology at the Gregorian University in Rome.

Germain Grisez is the Rev. Harry J. Flynn Professor of Christian Ethics at Mount St. Mary's College, Emmitsburg, Maryland.

Christine Gudorf is Associate Professor of Theological Ethics at Xavier University in Cincinnati.

Bernard Häring, C.SS.R., is Professor of Moral Theology at the Accademia Alfonsiana in Rome.

James Hitchcock is Professor of History at St. Louis University.

Mark D. Jordan teaches in the Department of Liberal Studies at the University of Notre Dame.

Kevin Kelly is a Lecturer in Moral Theology at Heythrop College in London.

Philip Lawler is Editor of the Boston *Pilot*.

William Levada is Archbishop of Portland in Oregon.

Richard McBrien is Crowley-O'Brien-Walter Professor and Chair of the Department of Theology at University of Notre Dame.

Richard A. McCormick, S.J., is John A. O'Brien Professor of Christian Ethics at the University of Notre Dame.

John Mahoney, S.J., holds the Chair of Moral Theology at Kings College in London.

Roger Mahony is Archbishop of Los Angeles.

Thomas P. Melady is President of Sacred Heart University, Fairfield, Connecticut.

Jon Nilson is Associate Professor and Chair of the Department of Theology at Loyola University in Chicago.

Michael Novak holds the George Frederick Jewett Chair in Religion and Public Policy at the American Enterprise Institute.

Ladislas Orsy, S.J., is Professor of Canon Law at the Catholic University of America.

Michael Pfeifer, O.M.I., is Bishop of San Angelo, Texas.

Daniel Pilarczyk is Archbishop of Cincinnati.

The late Karl Rahner was the author of *Theological Investigations* and *Foundations of Christian Faith*.

Joseph Ratzinger is Cardinal Prefect of the Congregation for the Doctrine of the Faith.

Francis A. Sullivan, S.J., is Professor of Ecclesiology at the Gregorian University in Rome.

John Strynkowski is Professor of Canon Law and Rector of Immaculate Conception Seminary in Huntington, Long Island.

Rembert G. Weakland, O.S.B. is Archbishop of Milwaukee.

J. Philip Wogaman is Professor of Christian Ethics at Wesley Theological Seminary in Washington.

Christopher Wolfe teaches Political Science at Marquette University.

READINGS IN
MORAL THEOLOGY NO.5
Official Catholic Social Teaching

CONTENTS

READINGS IN
MORAL THEOLOGY NO. 4
The Use of Scripture
in Moral Theology

CONTENTS

Foreword *Charles E. Curran and Richard A. McCormick, S.J.* • Jesus, Ethics and the Present Situation *Richard H. Hiers* • Biblical Revelation and Social Existence *James H. Cone* • The Question of the Relevance of Jesus for Ethics Today *Jack T. Sanders* • Commands for Grown-Ups *Richard J. Mouw* • The Actual Impact of Moral Norms of the New Testament: Report from the International Theological Commission *Text by Hans Schürmann, Introduction and Commentary by Philippe Delhaye* • Scripture: The Soul of Moral Theology? *Edouard Hamel* • The Changing Use of the Bible in Christian Ethics *James M. Gustafson* • The Place of Scripture in Christian Ethics: A Methodological Study *James M. Gustafson* • The Role and Function of the Scriptures in Moral Theology *Charles E. Curran* • The Use of Scripture in Ethics *Allen Verhey* • The Moral Authority of Scripture: The Politics and Ethics of Remembering *Stanley Hauerwas* • Scripture and Christian Ethics *James F. Childress* • Scripture, Liturgy, Character and Morality *Richard A. McCormick, S.J.* • The Biblical Hermeneutics of Juan Luis Segundo *Alfred T. Hennelly* • A Critical Appraisal of Segundo's Biblical Hermeneutics *Anthony J. Tambasco* • Exodus and Exile: The Two Faces of Liberation *John Howard Yoder* • Toward a Feminist Biblical Hemeneutics: Biblical Interpretation and Liberation Theology *Elisabeth Schüssler Fiorenza*

READINGS IN
MORAL THEOLOGY NO. 1
MORAL NORMS AND CATHOLIC TRADITION
CONTENTS

READINGS IN
MORAL THEOLOGY NO. 2
THE DISTINCTIVENESS OF CHRISTIAN ETHICS
CONTENTS